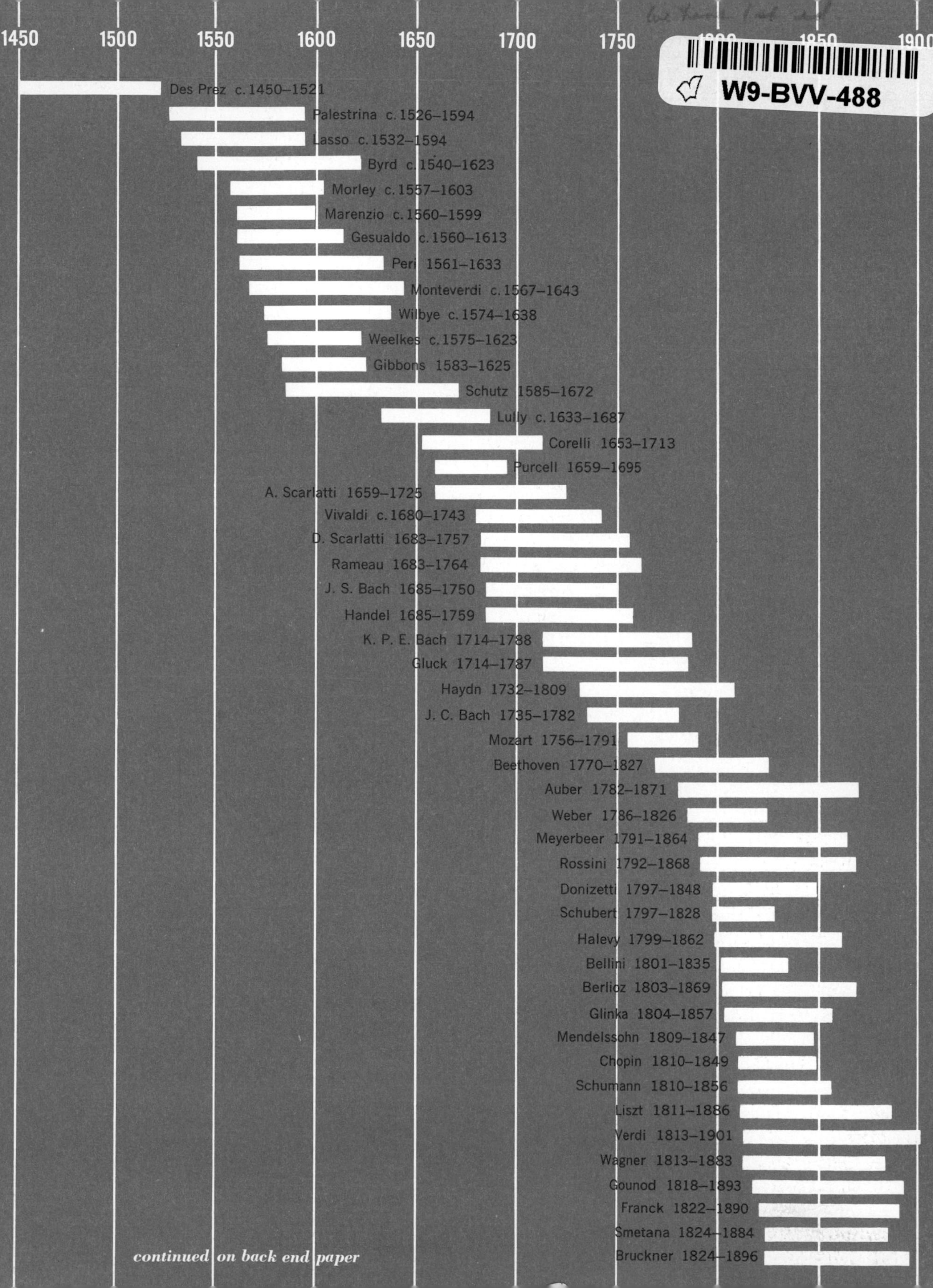
1450
1500
1550
1600
1650
1700
1750
1800
1850
1900
Des Prez c. 1450–1521
Palestrina c. 1526–1594
Lasso c. 1532–1594
Byrd c. 1540–1623
Morley c. 1557–1603
Marenzio c. 1560–1599
Gesualdo c. 1560–1613
Peri 1561–1633
Monteverdi c. 1567–1643
Wilbye c. 1574–1638
Weelkes c. 1575–1623
Gibbons 1583–1625
Schutz 1585–1672
Lully c. 1633–1687
Corelli 1653–1713
Purcell 1659–1695
A. Scarlatti 1659–1725
Vivaldi c. 1680–1743
D. Scarlatti 1683–1757
Rameau 1683–1764
J. S. Bach 1685–1750
Handel 1685–1759
K. P. E. Bach 1714–1788
Gluck 1714–1787
Haydn 1732–1809
J. C. Bach 1735–1782
Mozart 1756–1791
Beethoven 1770–1827
Auber 1782–1871
Weber 1786–1826
Meyerbeer 1791–1864
Rossini 1792–1868
Donizetti 1797–1848
Schubert 1797–1828
Halevy 1799–1862
Bellini 1801–1835
Berlioz 1803–1869
Glinka 1804–1857
Mendelssohn 1809–1847
Chopin 1810–1849
Schumann 1810–1856
Liszt 1811–1886
Verdi 1813–1901
Wagner 1813–1883
Gounod 1818–1893
Franck 1822–1890
Smetana 1824–1884
Bruckner 1824–1896
continued on back end paper

MUSIC: A DESIGN FOR LISTENING
Third Edition

MUSIC: A DESIGN

FOR LISTENING

THIRD EDITION

HOMER ULRICH

THE UNIVERSITY OF MARYLAND

HARCOURT, BRACE & WORLD, INC.

NEW YORK CHICAGO SAN FRANCISCO ATLANTA

To Charles Manning,
for his understanding and support
of all the arts.

Library of Congress Catalog Card Number: 74-97861

Printed in the United States of America

ACKNOWLEDGMENTS FOR ILLUSTRATIONS:

Courtesy of the Ashmolean Museum, Oxford: 337
Courtesy of Milton Babbitt: 433
The Bettmann Archive, Inc.: 130, 135, 137, 186, 197, 204, 206, 219, 256, 260, 267, 275, 276, 281, 287, 290, 293, 297, 320, 338, 380, 385, 391, 396, 398
Bibliothèque Nationale: 387
Brown Brothers: 226, 250, 357
Cleveland Orchestra: 55
CBS-TV: 419, 439
Columbia Records: 10, 96–97, 99, 386, 436
Culver Pictures, Inc.: 108, 190, 214, 342, 345, 424
Martin J. Dain: 401, 427, 430, 434
Éditions Rencontre: 157, 216, 237, 257, 354, 369
M. Grimoldi: 327
Hans Hell from *Patrocium Musices* by Orlando di Lasso (1573–76): 312
S. Hurok: 72, 92
From *An Illustrated History of Music,* published by Reynal & Company, New York: 305
Indiana University School of Music: 252
Ulrich H. Kerth: 183, 244, 340
Laurentian Library, Florence: 304
Dennis Stock from Magnum Photos, Inc.: 417
Louis Melançon: 248
The Metropolitan Museum of Art; The Crosby Brown Collection of Musical Instruments, 1889: 70; Gift of Harry G. Friedman, 1956: 110–11; Whittelsey Fund, 1949: 316
Mozart Museum, Salzburg, Austria: 143
From *Musica Getutscht* by Sebastien Virdung, Basle, 1511: 71
National Ballet of Canada: 231
Reproduced by courtesy of the Trustees, The National Gallery, London: 310
New York Philharmonic: 58, 64
New York Public Library, Prints Division—Astor, Lenox & Tilden Foundation: 67
Philadelphia Museum of Art: 295
Photo Files: top 416
From *A Pictorial History of Jazz* by Orrin Keepnews and Bill Grauer, Jr., © 1955. Used by permission of Crown Publishers, Inc.: bottom 416
RCA Records: 54, 56, 117, 118
Fred Sher: 8, 69, 255
Georges Sirot: 223, 247
Louis Spohr Memorial and Research Institute: 201
Staatsbibliothek Berlin Bildarchiv (Handke): 167, 350

Martha Swope: 233, 395, 431
Universal Edition, reprinted by permission of the Theodore Presser Company: 438
University of Maryland, photo by Bill Clark: 105
University of Michigan School of Music: 152
N. X. Willemin from *Monuments Français Inedits Pour Servir à l'Histoire des Arts,* by A. Pottier, Paris, 1839: 53

Drawing by Ben Shahn, courtesy Kennedy Galleries: ii
Woodcut by Pierre de Teghi, 1547: v
"Group of Musicians Listening to a Flute Player." Pen and wash by Rembrandt van Rijn, 1635. Donnington Priory, courtesy G. M. Gathorne-Hardy: xii
"The Music Lesson." Drawing by Thomas Gainsborough, copyright by the Trustees of the British Museum. Photo by Freeman: 122
"Le triomphe." Woodcut by Hans Burgkmair. New York Public Library Prints Division: 300
"Stravinsky rehearsing le Sacre du Printemps." Drawing by Jean Cocteau. Dance Index, Vol. VI, 1947: 376

Endpapers: Drawing by Raoul Dufy, authorization S.P.A.D.E.M. 1969 by French Reproduction Rights.

PREFACE TO THE THIRD EDITION

Past users of this book will find that the new edition reflects major changes in organization and content. In the dozen years since the book first appeared, it has been widely used in all parts of the country, and the present edition incorporates improvements its users have suggested and experience has shown to be desirable. Yet its purpose remains unchanged: to guide the listener in his search for musical enjoyment and understanding.

The music that comes to performance today represents a wide variety of styles, but the overwhelming majority of it still reflects similar fundamental principles. A listener profits from knowing about the elements that all music has in common as well as the elements that differentiate one composition from another. He can then become conscious of what he is hearing, and consciousness is the beginning of musical enjoyment. The revisions in the present edition were designed to speed that process.

The material in Part One, dealing with Elements and Forms, has been rearranged for the sake of greater clarity and more logical presentation. Large sections have been rewritten, and many details of chord structure and manipulation have been eliminated. The material on musical notation has been removed to an appendix, where it is still available for the reader who wishes to improve his music-reading skills. Further, material on musical forms has been reduced by moving the discussions of larger forms to later sections of the book, where they are taken up in conjunction with the periods in which those forms flourished.

The portion of the book dealing with the literature of music itself has also been completely rearranged. Many listeners find Renaissance and Baroque music more accessible after they have gained some familiarity with the Classical and Romantic repertoires. Part Two therefore begins with the Classical period, covers the whole of the nineteenth century, and ends with the transitional styles of the twentieth century. Part Three takes up the earlier music from the fifteenth through the early eighteenth centuries. Finally, Part Four deals with the new music of the twentieth century. It devotes considerable attention to the American scene, including a chapter on jazz, and it has been expanded and brought up to date.

The thematic outlines of representative compositions, which were introduced in the Second Edition, have proved to be a useful and well-liked feature, and they have been augmented by the addition of an outline of Brahms' *German Requiem.*

The author has profited from many comments and suggestions from users of the book and acknowledges their help with gratitude. It is his hope that this new edition will serve even more successfully than its predecessors in helping students to find their way into the satisfying world of music.

Homer Ulrich

CONTENTS

Part One: Elements and Forms

Part Two: The Traditional Repertoire

Part Three: The Older Music

PART ONE Elements and Forms

Chapter 1

SELECTIVE LISTENING AND THE MUSICAL EXPERIENCE

When a composer writes a piece of music, he is expressing in musical symbols certain ideas, feelings, or states of mind. What he writes is determined by what he has to communicate and by his ability to do so. The specific emotional response he hopes to arouse, the form and size of the music, and many other factors are parts of that communication. When the composition is completed, we may assume that the composer has expressed his thoughts and feelings within a given context. But for whom are they intended? To whom has he communicated his musical ideas? To one or a thousand listeners, present or potential. To everyone who takes the trouble to listen. And unless the composer has a listener, the music fails to reach its goal.

The listener is an essential part of the musical process. True, performers are necessary to bring the music to life; but the composer and the listener are the terminals between which the music flows. Both are necessary in the art of making music; we must not underrate the importance of the listener in this area. At the moment of listening, he is sharing what another human being has seen fit to express.

The significant moments in life often come out of such sharing, for that act satisfies one of the deepest human needs, communication. Whether it is a secret, an emotion, or an idea, the thing shared is a means of bridging the gap that separates each individual from the rest of humanity. And in music we deal with individuals who have worthwhile things to share with us. The composers we shall meet in the following pages were outstanding human beings. They were men who penetrated deeply and keenly into rich areas of mind, imagination, and feeling, and who have communicated their insights in notation so that we may share them.

Listening to music is actually sharing the composer's insights. The result of this may be called a musical experience; and the aim of this book, quite simply, is to help the reader gain such experiences.

How can musical experiences be recognized? The question deserves to be asked, for many listeners unwittingly pass such experiences by. These listeners, fearful that they "do not understand music," may fall under music's spell without realizing that it has worked its magic in spite of their imagined shortcomings. Perhaps a better form of the question is: What can music do to you?

A musical experience is first of all an adventure in emotion; but it is also an intellectual adventure. It is a source of both pleasure and insight. Has a merry, lilting tune ever brought a smile to your lips? Has hearing a stirring march exalted your spirits? Has a brilliant piece of music left you feeling momentarily breathless, then relaxed? Have you looked forward eagerly to familiar parts of a well-remembered composition? Then you have had musical experiences. You have been lifted out of the rut of everyday experience, have shared a joyous or spirited or profound insight with the composer, and have been returned, a richer person, to yourself.

Some music may impel you to leave a concert quietly, walk slowly, and avoid conversation on the way home. Other music may fill you with the resolve to approach your daily tasks more courageously. Still another composition may arouse a feeling of humility or sheer joy. Musical experiences are manifold in their effects.

But if we accept such experiences passively and simply permit them to happen to us, we close off the pleasure of becoming involved—of allowing ourselves to become wrapped up in music. And involvement presupposes knowledge. To know how a musical effect is made, to know why a composer writes as he does, to know what to expect in an unfamiliar composition—that knowledge is an essential part of the musical experience. Further, that knowledge helps us to recognize subtle musical nuances that might otherwise pass us by unnoticed. In fact, every encounter with music calls upon the mind to a greater or lesser degree.

For example, think of any piece of music you know well. Can you avoid coming to some conclusion about what it is or how it is constructed? You know that it is a waltz or a symphony, an example of blues or rock, that it contains a text or is based on a legend, or similar facts about it. When next you listen to it, notice that you follow its principal melody attentively, recognize it when it returns, and take note of any changes it undergoes—and you do this even while you are enjoying the whole. You may become aware of details of rhythm as you listen, or the characteristic use of an instrument, or the significant setting of a word of the text. You may observe that the composer has repeated one musical idea without change, or has balanced one short section against another, or that he has employed certain proportions in the various parts. You will find yourself doing some or all of these things—perhaps only in part consciously—as the music is played. Such an experience is both emotional and intellectual, and one aspect of the experience enhances the other.

Unfortunately, some hearers prevent themselves from experiencing music as fully as they might. They stand in the way of their own complete musical enjoyment by believing that knowledge interferes with pleasure, that it is good not to know anything of a technical nature, that if they become familiar with the "rules" of music they will be barred from enjoying it.

That attitude is probably one of the last survivors of the sentimental aspects of Victorianism, of a period in which "feeling" was everything and things of the mind were looked at suspiciously. Luckily, that viewpoint is dying out, but it still has enough spurious vitality to be dangerous. Imagine a person's being convinced that he can enjoy a baseball game better if he knows none of the rules, or believing he can make sense out of another's conversation if he is ignorant of sentence structure and the very meanings of the words he hears!

A moment's reflection should convince the reader that this old-fashioned attitude need not be taken seriously. For a person who listens only from the sensory point of view can make contact only with the tonal material itself. The composer's artistry, which is shown in the planned manipulation of that material according to well-defined principles, must remain closed to the listener if the principles are unknown. Thus, an essential part of musical experience will pass him by.

It may be helpful at this point to describe a few of the kinds of musical experiences that lie ahead for readers of this book. The passages that provide those experiences are taken more or less at random; similar great moments abound elsewhere in the literature. They may occur in unexpected places and in the works of both famous and obscure composers.

The "Hallelujah" Chorus from George Frideric Handel's *Messiah* provides one example. The observant listener has thrilled to the power and majesty of the music and has been carried along by the sweep and momentum of its first section. The contrasting second part, on the text "The kingdom of this world," and the brilliant third part "And He shall reign" prepare him for the overwhelming weight of the closing section. The endlessly reiterated "hallelujahs," heard singly, together, and in overlapping fashion, bring the music to an enormous climax of sound and movement. The last half-dozen rhythmic shouts are almost unbearable in their intensity when the inexorable drive is suddenly broken off (see Example 1). There comes a moment of silence during which the sonorities and solid harmonies quickly melt away. And out of this vast and eloquent silence comes the final slow, massive, and triumphant "Hallelujah!" like a gigantic amen. No one who has been thoroughly responsive to the power and compulsion of this chorus will fail to be moved by this dramatic pause.

Later composers, notably Beethoven and Brahms, have used eloquent silence in similar fashion. At the hands of a sensitive conductor, such moments are emotionally effective to a high degree. In works that contain this device, the element of extreme contrast is at work. From fullest sonority to complete silence, from relentless drive to dead stop—these contrasts remain with the listener long after the music has ended.

The element of surprise can also give rise to a memorable experience. A new harmony, a phrase heard out of context, or a shift of tonality may be among the rewards of intensive listening.

The "Crucifixus" from the B minor Mass of Johann Sebastian Bach employs this device. The entire movement is based on a four-measure phrase (a *basso ostinato,* literally an "obstinate bass") in E minor, heard in the lower instruments. The text, in Latin, is from the Nicene creed: "He was also crucified for us, suffered under Pontius Pilate, and was buried." Bach chose to set the text in an involved, intense, and sustained style. Tight overlapping of text phrases, restrained dissonances, and a gentle motion toward the final measures characterize the movement. The phrases pile up, crowd in upon each other, and subside again over the persistent passage in the bass. In the last five measures, over the words "suffered and was buried," a series of downward inflected harmonies produce a moment of restrained anguish (see Example 2). There, after a brief pause for phrasing, the harmony turns in another

Example 2 **Bach, "Crucifixus," B minor Mass**

Grave se - pul - tus est,

pas - sus et se - pul - tus est.

se - pul - tus est, se - pul - tus est.

col 8va

direction and the movement virtually dies away and ends in an unexpected key, G major. One of the simplest of musical devices, this change from a minor key to a major is also one of the most magical. The grief implicit in the text is miraculously transformed into hope and courage. The power of faith seems to become incarnate at this great moment.

For quite the opposite musical experience, we turn to the third "Brandenburg" Concerto, also by Bach. The second movement of that work is alive, bustling, and vigorous. Throughout the sparkling, energetic passage that begins the movement (see Example 3) the momentum and driving exuberance are nowhere relaxed. Every measure is filled with its rising and falling scale figures in rapid tempo; every measure carries the listener along with relentless, invigorating force. The enthusiasm engendered is irresistible. For more than two minutes—which is a long time for rapid

Example 3

motion to be sustained—the exuberant passage is continued without a break. And then the exuberance is increased, for the rapid motion is compounded, on three occasions, by the addition of a few tones twice as fast (see Example 4). This is the tiniest of details and may easily be overlooked in hearing the piece. Yet its effect upon the attentive listener, or upon one who knows the passage and lies in wait for it, is profound. The tiny modification of the rapid motion comes as a revelation of Jovian humor; gone in the winking of an eye, it remains in the memory as one of the most delightful and heart-warming details in all of Bach's works. This is no long-faced or serious music: its youthfulness, zest, and drive put it in a category all its own.

Example 4

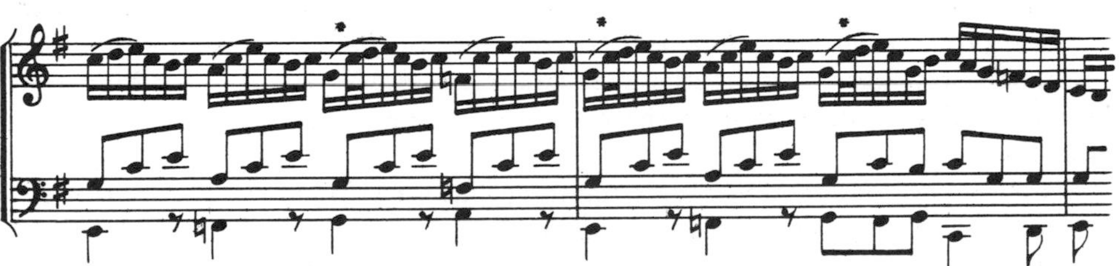

Many other passages containing moments of profundity, charm, humor, and beauty lie ahead for the observant listener. The search for them is rewarding; every composition he hears may contain such moments, and repeated hearings of familiar works will often disclose details that had previously been overlooked. What, now, is the prerequisite for having musical experiences of the kinds mentioned above? It is primarily the desire to listen to music and the willingness to realize that listening is an activity that requires the listener's participation. It must be borne in mind that *listening* is not synonymous with *hearing,* and hearing music is not the same as listening to it. The difference between the words is worth considering: *hear* does not necessarily imply attention or application; *listen* always does. Throughout the course of this book we shall be concerned with listening as a conscious, thoughtful activity whose purpose is to enrich the reader's musical experiences.

The mass of sound that comprises a piece of music is, of course, the raw material toward which the listening activity is directed. The purpose for which one listens is to observe or detect the shape, color, and arrangement of the strands and groups of tones that make up the whole. Music does not exist in pure sound itself, no matter how attractive the sound. Music consists of the organization and manipulation of particular sounds, arranged in a particular manner to serve particular purposes. The composer has chosen and manipulated his tonal material in a certain way in order to produce a certain expressive result. When we listen to and understand what the composer has done, we react in response, and that reaction may be the musical experience we are seeking.

It is logical that the more we are able to observe, the more our experience is likely to be heightened and enriched. This is true of any art, of course. To illustrate, let us consider the field of sculpture.

Sculpture may be enjoyed on a number of different levels, depending upon the observer's interest, background, and good will. Let us look at a piece of representational sculpture. At first we may see only how lifelike the sculptor has made it. Then, if we call upon our feeling for proportion, we may see how skillfully the sculptor has filled out the three dimensions of the space he has utilized, and our enjoyment increases. And if we know something about art history, we can add still more to our enjoyment by recognizing the style in which the sculptor has worked and the relationship of that sculpture to works in other styles.

Further, if the subject of the sculpture is taken from the fields of history or mythology, our pleasure increases to the extent that we recognize what the artist is portraying. We are then in a position to evaluate the point of view he is expressing. And if we are familiar with the artist's materials—wood, stone, clay, or any other—we may profit from seeing how artistic creations are influenced by the nature of those materials. Sometimes an artist may be limited by his materials, but more often he takes full advantage of their characteristic textures, grains, and other physical qualities.

Each level of information or understanding that we bring to a work of art carries its own kind of enjoyment. For on each level of observation we accumulate more sensory data to which we can respond, and on each succeeding level our enjoyment is enhanced. The greater the number of details we notice, the more material there is available for us to enjoy. The sum total is appreciation of the art itself.

So it is with music. In order to progress beyond the level of sensory enjoyment, the listener must know something about the purposes, structures, and techniques of music. Music is not only a collection of pleasant or exciting sounds; it, too, has

Music heard in an informal setting: the Metropolitan Opera in an outdoor concert in Central Park, New York City.

principles, materials, subject matter, and history. Further, music requires instruments and voices to bring it to life; without such performing media, we would have nothing more than composers' intentions expressed in symbols on printed or manuscript pages.

The nature of its materials influences the way music is put together, and this in turn affects the emotional response awakened in the listener. The instruments determine how the music will sound; they give it richness, variety, and color, and thus further influence the listener's response. Consequently, an understanding of musical materials and instruments is essential to the appreciation of music, not only because materials and instruments are worth knowing about in their own right but also because some knowledge of them will give the listener another vantage point from which to enjoy music.

The implications of the foregoing are clear. A person who merely hears a composition cannot rise far above vague feelings of pleasure or displeasure. The very essence of the composer's thought, with its subtleties and its refinements, will escape a person who only hears; for it is in the details of a composition that such elements are expressed. Only clarity of observation and attention to details on the part of the listener will allow him to experience the full flavor of the composer's expressive intentions.

There is a technique that makes it possible for the newcomer to music to single out the musical elements from the tonal mass, and thus gain a clear impression of what is being expressed. The technique may be called *selective listening,* and it is safe to say that everyone who listens to music employs it to some extent. Think of any composition you know fairly well. You can, no doubt, reproduce the melody and perhaps a few details of the rhythmic accompaniment. To that extent you have employed this technique in your listening, for you have lifted out ("selected") those elements each time you have heard the piece.

But do you understand how the instruments are employed, how the melodies depart and return, how separate tonal strands are used below the melody, or any other details of the composition? These, too, are capable of being listened to selectively—one at a time. And with a bit of practice in singling out the different elements, you acquire the ability to "listen in layers"—to concentrate on one melodic line or another, to *listen to* the rhythmic or harmonic effects even while you *hear* the composition as a whole.

Listen, for example, to any recording you have available. One feature of the composition will attract your attention—most likely the melody. But the melody may be so much on the surface or so prominent that it requires no further attention on your part; you can respond to it directly. Listening only to the melody is likely to take your attention away from the music's other components. Try now to concentrate on the lowermost tones of the piece; select the bass line for closer attention. Very quickly you will find yourself able to listen to the two lines—melody and bass together. A recording of a string quartet will prove most rewarding here. In a quartet by Haydn, Mozart, or Beethoven, say, only two or three melodies are heard at any one time. These separate lines of tones, which can be heard clearly, provide suitable material for developing skill in selective listening.

Music heard in a formal setting: the New York Philharmonic, Leonard Bernstein conducting, at Lincoln Center, New York City.

In another composition, an outstanding rhythm may be selected for closer attention. Listen, for example, to the "Habanera" from Bizet's opera *Carmen,* the G minor Prelude, Opus 23, No. 5, by Rachmaninoff, or the second movement from Beethoven's Symphony No. 7. Each of these pieces is built upon a rhythm used so extensively that it may be called a *rhythmic pattern* (see Example 5). In each case, an awareness of how the pattern is used, how it is transformed, and when it returns after an absence lends insight into the composer's methods and purposes, and hence lends depth to the musical experience. The discussion of rhythmic patterns will be elaborated in Chapter 2.

In similar fashion, other details may be concentrated upon. In an orchestral piece, one instrument may be followed throughout the composition—the flute in Debussy's *Afternoon of a Faun,* for example. In a song, some striking and recurring detail of the piano accompaniment may serve. On a more advanced level, a particular voice such as the alto or tenor may be singled out in a choral piece. The essential procedure is

Example 5

Bizet

Rachmaninoff

Beethoven

consciously to select one element, listen attentively to it, and thus quickly acquire the ability to roam at will within the tonal mass. The end result will be this: by quickly shifting your attention from one detail to another, by "scanning" the composition much as an electronic beam scans every part of a picture that is being transmitted, you acquire the ability to listen to a great variety of details at once, to organize them in your mind, and to react to them as a whole. You will have added a third dimension to your listening and will be in a position to respond fully to the composer's expressive intentions.

The foregoing paragraphs list only a few of the details that can be singled out by the selective listening technique. Certainly the details thus selected for closer attention should be significant ones; but the term "significant details" is not to be taken as referring only to musical technicalities. The search for such technicalities, no matter how interesting they may be in their own right, is by no means a sufficient reason for listening to music. In a broader sense, a significant detail is one that provokes both an emotional and an intellectual response of the kinds spoken of in connection with Examples 1–4, above, and it is this response that the informed listener seeks. In other words, it is not only awareness of the detail itself but also the emotional response to the detail that should animate your listening activity.

It would be possible to name here a number of other types of details that are amenable to selective listening, and even to mention specific effects in particular compositions—musical effects that generations of listeners have found especially moving. One of the great rewards of listening to music, however, is for each listener to discover independently the details and elements that have most meaning for him. The work thus belongs to him, in a sense, and becomes something to which he may develop a lifelong personal affinity. It is safe to say that an individual's deepest or most enjoyable musical experiences are arrived at through such personal discovery.

The consistent application of the selective listening technique will supply you with a large number of details to which you will respond emotionally and intellectually. In the process of gathering these details, you will necessarily make a number of observations about the principles and practices of musical creation. Those observations, in turn, will enable you to answer questions that may arise in your own mind as you listen. Questions about why your favorite composer is different from others, about why you feel attracted to a particular kind of music, about why one composition is considered good and another is not—such questions need no longer be impossible to answer.

It is likely, too, that you will come to associate certain musical devices with particular composers. This is natural, for every major composer has a distinctive style of writing, the style being the sum of the devices he habitually employs. It becomes desirable at that point to systematize this mass of details and observations and to make generalizations about the compositions you hear. This not only simplifies the process of recognition and recall but also opens the door to the enjoyment of the entire body of music. One of the greatest of pleasures lies in reliving a musical experience, in mentally recreating the music insofar as possible, and in responding retrospectively to its emotional power.

Finally, it is likely that you will find your most enjoyable experiences in the discovery that musical compositions have meaning in terms of music itself. In other words, you will discover that lasting musical satisfaction is not to be found by calling up fanciful images that have nothing to do with music. No pink clouds, haunted castles, children at play, or other extramusical images are necessary or helpful in listening to music—except in the relatively few cases where the composer has specifically referred to such images. Even in such cases, the music must be judged for its *musical* effect on the listener.

The ordered arrangement of tones, the selection of musical material for musical reasons, the manipulation of that material for the same reasons—these are what the overwhelming majority of significant composers are concerned with, and what you will discover in listening to music selectively. The listener who wishes to enjoy his musical experiences to the fullest hampers himself by looking for things the music does not and cannot contain. Listen to what the composer has written: listen selectively so that you may respond fully to what is there. Then you will find in music a lifelong source of enjoyment, filled with rich emotional experiences.

Listening Suggestions

The following compositions are chosen to illustrate a few of the moods that music can express. They are arranged roughly in an order that may be called "light to dark." Although each listener will respond differently to the works listed here, he will probably find that the music suggests moods that range from jubilation through resignation to deepest gloom.

The recordings of these works, further, will supply ample material for listening selectively. The brilliant violin passages in one, the rhythmic pattern in another, the bass line in a third—such elements can be "selected" for closer attention even as the moods of the various compositions are experienced.

Bach, "Brandenburg" Concerto No. 3, second movement
Mendelssohn, Symphony No. 4, Op. 90 ("Italian"), first movement
Beethoven, Symphony No. 7, A major, Op. 92, finale
Haydn, Symphony No. 101, D major ("The Clock"), finale
Mendelssohn, Nocturne from *A Midsummer Night's Dream,* Op. 61
Schubert, Symphony No. 8 ("Unfinished"), second movement
Beethoven, Symphony No. 5, C minor, Op. 67, first movement
Schubert, Symphony No. 7, C major, finale
Handel, "Hallelujah" Chorus, from *Messiah*
Wagner, *Tristan and Isolde,* Prelude to Act III
———, "Siegfried's Funeral March," from *Die Götterdämmerung*
Bach, "Crucifixus" from Mass in B minor
Beethoven, Symphony No. 3, Op. 55 ("Eroica"), second movement

Chapter 2

THE MATERIALS OF MUSIC

The basic material of all music is tone, which is itself a particular variety of the psychophysical phenomenon known as sound. Sound is the result of vibrations or waves in the atmosphere, waves that strike the ear and give rise to sensations in the brain. If the waves are irregular, we interpret the sensation as noise; if regular, we call it tone. How are the vibrations set in motion? By a physical object that is itself capable of vibrating. This object then disturbs the atmosphere that surrounds it and thus indirectly is the source of the tonal sensation.

Perhaps the most obvious fact about a tone is that it possesses certain characteristics that differentiate it from any other tone. An awareness of tonal differences is probably among our very earliest experiences. Not until later do we realize that the differences between tones can be only of four kinds; in other words, a tone has only four characteristics.

Tone Characteristics

PITCH

Let us begin by examining a few well-known melodies, such as the three fragments given in Example 6. Now, whether or not one is experienced in reading musical notation, he will discover that music has a vertical dimension; that certain tones may be

Example 6

placed higher or lower than others, or that a tone may be placed on the same level as another. One may also experience the vertical dimension by singing the fragments, although here the terms "high" and "low" are only conventions. High singing requires greater muscular effort than does low, and one may think of *high* as implying tension and *low* as relaxation. Thus one may both see and feel that the fragment of Example 6*a* begins at a high level and that thereafter each tone is lower than the preceding one. This vertical component is also present by implication whenever one speaks of the "high tones" (right end) and "low tones" (left end) of the piano keyboard.

Imagine now the entire possible series of tones arranged in order from lowest to highest. In our musical system the place of each tone in the series is defined, and in locating that place we speak of the *pitch* of the tone, the first of the four characteristics of tones. The pitch of a tone defines its height or depth in relation to the whole series of tones the ear is capable of hearing.

Certain overlapping sections of that series are given special names. It is obvious that the singing range of a woman is higher than that of a man, and equally obvious that there are differences in pitch range among women's voices, as among men's. Thus four overlapping sections suggest themselves. A woman's voice of comparatively high range is called *soprano;* of low range, *contralto,* but usually abbreviated *alto.* A man's voice of high range is called *tenor;* of low range, *bass.* In addition to these four principal ranges, two intermediate ranges are often referred to: *mezzo soprano* and *baritone.* The limits of each range are approximately as shown in Example 7; those limits are greatly exceeded, of course, by trained singers and by those with special vocal ability.

Example 7

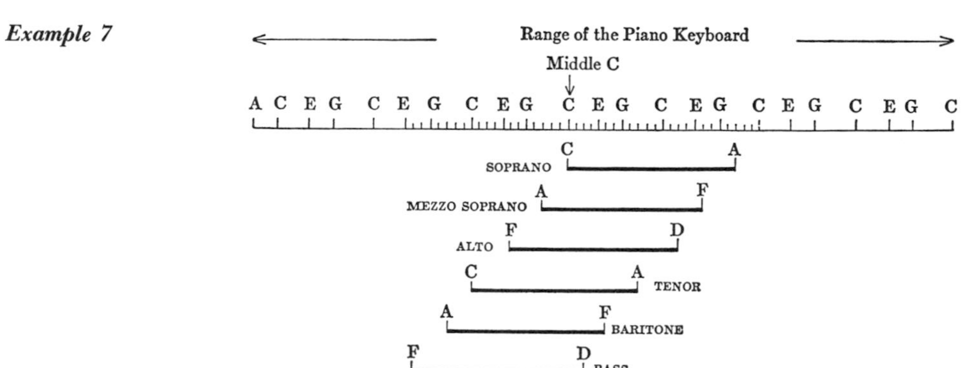

This combination of four voices (excluding the intermediate ranges) is known as the *vocal quartet,* and it has had great influence on the course of music. Not only is much vocal music of small dimensions written in four parts (hundreds of the standard hymns, for example), but four-part writing is an important technique in all branches of musical composition. Further, as we shall see later, many instruments are organized into families that correspond roughly to the four voices of the vocal quartet.

DURATION

Music differs from the arts of painting, sculpture, and architecture in that it cannot be separated from the element of time; a measurable period of time elapses between the beginning and end of a piece of music. In musical notation the time element is pictured by the horizontal dimension. Reading from left to right, we become aware of the passage of time as the music progresses on the printed page. But simultaneously we also realize that the tones we perform or read are not all of the same length.

Thereby we call attention to the second characteristic of tones: *duration.* A tone may exist for an established period of time, a fraction of that period, or a multiple of it. Various notational symbols indicate how long a tone should be in relation to a pre-established beat or pulse that is basic to music. It may be pointed out here that all matters connected with the duration of tones are related to *rhythm,* one of the most important of musical factors.

INTENSITY

The third characteristic of tones is equally obvious. Imagine any tone performed very loudly, very softly, or at any level of volume between these extremes. A single tone may be strongly emphasized at its beginning and gradually decrease in volume; or it may begin softly, swell out, and again diminish in degree of loudness. This characteristic is referred to as *intensity,* and it too is provided for in musical notation. Symbols and terms called "dynamics" indicate particular levels of intensity or volume. Symbols for a gradual increase or decrease of tonal volume, for accents on single tones, and for a variety of other changes in intensity are employed also. (See Appendix III for a list of dynamic symbols.)

QUALITY

Imagine a single tone played on the piano, then the same tone sung by a tenor, hummed by a soprano, and blown by a trumpeter. Imagine further that this tone is equally loud and equally long in all four versions. Three characteristics of the tone are thus identical—pitch, duration, and intensity; yet no one will deny that a major difference between them is still apparent. This difference is one of *quality* or, in technical terms, *tone color* or *timbre.* And quality is the fourth and only remaining characteristic of tones.

Tone quality permits the listener to distinguish between the sound of a flute and that of an oboe, a violin and a clarinet, or a cello and a bassoon, for example. Even beyond that, the experienced listener can detect differences in quality between the voices of a lyric soprano and a dramatic soprano; between a violin of poor quality and one made by Stradivarius; or even between pianos made by different manufacturers. It is the difference in tone quality between various instruments that gives an orchestra or band its rich variety of sound.

If we reflect briefly on any piece of music we know, we come to realize that its very existence depends upon the four characteristics that tones possess—namely, *pitch, duration, intensity,* and *quality.* Composers in a real sense are bound by these characteristics when they create music out of tones. They manipulate the raw tonal material in ways they find meaningful, and they have available a variety of well-established musical formulas to help them organize that material. This process gives rise to the elements of melody, rhythm, and harmony.

Melody

Throughout the centuries many kinds of music have developed. They have varied from country to country and from one century to another; they have existed on many different cultural levels, from the primitive to the most civilized. And yet, however different these kinds of music may have been, they have had one element in common—*melody.* Other musical elements may be rudimentary or present by implication only; melody of some kind is rarely missing.

Of all the components of a piece of music, the melody is usually the most immediately appealing. Melody lies on the surface of the music; it is given a favored acoustical position by the composer, and thus becomes the element first to attract the listener's attention. In most cases it is the melody that we carry away, hum, and remember. It is the element that most often gives a composition its distinctive character or special qualities. A particular rhythm may be shared by hundreds of compositions; a particular set of chords may fit equally well into dozens of works. Only the melody is unique.

We may define melody, first of all, as a meaningful series of tones. This definition is broad enough to include all possible types of melody; however, because of its broadness, it may seem vague. Few people will agree, for example, upon the definition of the term "meaningful," and the unspecified length implied by the word "series" is also subject to some dispute. Yet the very nature of melody justifies the apparent looseness of the definition; a more exact description will not cover all melodic types.

MELODIC REQUIREMENTS

To be meaningful, a melody must first of all be coherent and built with a plan or purpose. An aimless or formless collection of tones, such as might result from a person's humming idly to himself or from a child's striking piano keys at random, would scarcely qualify as a melody. Melody is one aspect of musical communication, just as the sentence is an aspect of verbal communication. An aimless string of vowels and consonants is not likely to be mistaken for a series of words that carry verbal meaning; nor does an aimless string of musical sounds carry the musical meaning that a melody does.

A melody must also have emotional meaning. That is, it will evoke a mood, arouse an emotional response, or suggest an emotional state. A particular melody may be called stirring, for example; or it may soothe, cheer, or depress the listener. Exactly how or why a melody exercises this remarkable power cannot be explained to everyone's satisfaction. It may be due in part to the speed at which the melody is performed, to its pitch level and contour, and to the way its rhythmic components are arranged; such technical elements can of course be analyzed and classified. But in addition, there is likely to be an elusive quality—lyric or dramatic or humorous or pensive—that results not from any one element, but from several elements acting together. It is this quality that gives a melody its distinctiveness, its emotional meaning, and its effectiveness. And while that quality is identified and felt in the same way by most listeners, it is not something that can be pinpointed and defined.

A third element of meaningfulness is found in the melody's relationship to its surrounding musical material. A melody may become fully meaningful, for example, when we notice its connection with other melodies in the same composition or when we hear the melody together with the chords that support it. Its meaning may depend upon the melody's place and function in a large composition or upon the way it exemplifies a particular kind of musical treatment.

Another aspect of melody is its tonality. The feeling of tonality is associated with the nature and quality of the chords that accompany it, and with the particular scale or tonal arrangement upon which it is built. This point will be amplified in Chapter 3.

All these aspects of melody are elusive and are not easily subject to exact verbal description. We must recognize that the attractiveness of a melody is largely a matter of feeling, and that it is possible that the feeling for a particular melody will be influenced by any associations it brings to mind. A well-remembered performance, a pleasant occasion, a personal relationship—such events may impart additional meaning to a particular melody.

Characteristics of Melody

In spite of the somewhat elusive nature of the melodic element and one's subjective reactions to melodies in general, it is possible to examine that element a bit more closely and to discover certain characteristics that tend to give melodies their coherence and meaningfulness. Among those characteristics are contour, cadence, organization, the relationship of melodies to what surrounds them, and function.

Example 8

MELODIC CONTOUR

Perhaps the most obvious way in which one melody differs from another is in deviation from a single level of pitch. This deviation establishes a melodic *contour.* In Example 8 we can distinguish three types of contour. One type (Example 8*a*) approaches a static or passive state; another (8*b*) is considerably more active insofar as vertical movement is concerned; and a third (8*c*) lies between the extremes of passivity and action.

The outstanding feature of a passive melody is that it contains a number of tones on the same pitch or in the same general range. This reliance on horizontal movement rather than vertical often evokes moods of quietness, repose, or restraint—especially when the melody is performed slowly and is heard after a vigorous or fast-moving section.

An active melody is characterized by a considerable amount of vertical movement (see p. 284 for an extreme example of this type). The vigor of such movement most often suggests moods of energy and forcefulness: quiet energy when the speed is moderate, and an energy that becomes explosive as the speed increases.

By far the greater number of melodies, however, lie between the active and passive extremes. A melody most often rises and falls gently, or hovers around a single tone to which it periodically returns, or contains only a moderate amount of leaping motion. Examples 35*b* (p. 75), 40 (p. 80), 45 (p. 136), and 53 (p. 167) may be taken at random to illustrate this most usual type of melodic motion. Other examples are numerous in musical literature, and the emotional responses will be as varied as the melodies themselves.

The perceptive listener will notice that virtually all melodies contain what may be called a *climax.* Essentially, the climax is the moment of greatest listener-attraction, but many different types of climaxes may be found. For example, a climax may occur at the highest point of the melody; or it may result from the fact that a long tone is surrounded by shorter ones. It may be felt at the moment of greatest melodic activity, or may be brought about by a wide leap in the melodic line. It may occur near the beginning, middle, or end of the melody.

Often, in addition to one great climax, an extended melody will contain one or more moments of lesser climax. Such moments create a rise and fall of attention; they draw the listener along from point to point and provide the variety of interest necessary in a satisfying melody.

MELODIC CADENCES

The question may well arise: How, in an extended composition, does the listener know when one melody has ended and another has begun? The rise or fall of the melodic line in itself may not give a clue, for such motion is not confined to the ends of melodies. The answer is found in the cadences that are spread liberally through a composition.

A *cadence,* in this instance, may be tentatively described as a melodic fragment that gives a feeling of rest or suspended movement. It is the musical counterpart of the punctuation mark. Semicolons, periods, and other symbols in prose imply differing degrees of rest or movement, and in reading aloud the competent reader inflects his voice and makes short pauses (during which he may breathe) in carrying out the implications of the punctuation.

Similarly, the musical performer observes the cadences; he inflects tonally, and takes a musical breath, so to speak, allowing the successive sections of the composition to be recognized separately. If cadences did not exist, or if the performer ignored the implications of cadences, a melody would be little more than a long series of tones strung together without apparent reason, giving little musical satisfaction to the listener. In Chapter 5 we shall discuss how the observance of cadences is vital to the proper performance of a piece of music.

A typical cadence contains two factors: first, a progression of tones in the melody (the melodic factor) to a point where either a degree of repose or the need for onward motion is felt; and second, a set of at least two chords (the harmonic factor) that amplify that feeling, and relate the cadence to a particular key or tonality.

Examples 9*a*, 9*b*, and 9*c* show the final cadences of three well-known melodies. These are all cadences that give an undeniable feeling of finality. Two elements are common to each of them: the final tone is the first scale step of the key in which the melody is written, and the final tone occurs on a strong beat. (Scales will be discussed in the next chapter, and strong and weak beats later in this chapter.) Those two elements combine to produce the feeling of finality, and the strongest cadences almost invariably contain them.

A lesser feeling of rest is felt when the final tone is not the first scale step, or when that tone is not on a strongly accented beat (see Examples 9*d*, 9*e*, and 9*f*). Many other types of cadences occur in music and in all of them the *harmonic* factor (discussed below, p. 44) is the important element.

Example 9

MELODIC ORGANIZATION

In the preceding pages we have used the term "melody" in a rather general way. We have discussed melodic types and contours, melodic climaxes and cadences. In addition to these characteristics, a melody also has a form or structural plan. That is to say, its tones are arranged according to a particular scheme that gives a sense of completeness and order to the whole. The resulting melodic form or plan plays an important part in making the melody meaningful.

In one type of plan, the cadences that occur in a melody will divide it into sections or parts. If the melodic section is long enough to constitute a single musical thought—

that is, long enough to give the impression of being unified and somewhat complete in itself—it is called a *phrase.* Phrase lengths are usually dependent upon tempo (discussed below, p. 31); for example, a phrase in slow tempo usually consists of two measures, in moderate tempo four measures, and in fast tempo eight measures. But phrases that contain an irregular number of measures—three, five, or six, for example—exist in profusion also.

The tones of a melody may also fall into groups smaller than a phrase, but in such cases they are not separated by cadences. These melodic groups are called *phrase members, melodic figures,* or *melodic motives,* depending upon their length and function. A complete melody may consist of two or more phrases (arranged according to principles that will be discussed in Chapter 5); these phrases are roughly comparable to sentences in a paragraph. Such a group of phrases of "paragraph" length is called a *period, double period,* or *phrase group.*

The whole of *America* admirably illustrates the interdependence of the various melodic sections (see Example 10). The first strong resting point occurs in measure 6, and the first six measures of the tune form the first phrase. The next resting point is at the end, and measures 7–14 form the second phrase, which roughly balances the first. Also, each two-measure group has a degree of independence, caused in part by the identical rhythmic patterns (discussed below pp. 29–31) in measures 1–2, 3–4, 7–8, and 9–10, and the related patterns in the other pairs of measures. In summary, *America* consists of a phrase group divided into two phrases, one six and the other eight measures long; and each phrase includes several two-measure phrase members.

Example 10

This analysis of a single melody allows us to make three general observations that apply to large numbers of melodies: (1) a satisfying melody gives evidence of being constructed according to a plan; (2) the presence of a rhythmic pattern produces to a high degree the melodic unity that is an important factor in listening pleasure; and (3) the balance of phrases likewise tends to supply a degree of unity to the phrase group, for balance implies relationship and relationship is one element of unity.

TEXTURES

Most of the melodies mentioned thus far have been taken out of their contexts and discussed in isolation. Normally, melodies are not heard in this way; they are usually heard as part of a tonal complex that includes a set of supporting chords, or of a complex made up of several melodies heard simultaneously. Only in a few small areas of music are melodies designed to be heard alone, without any kind of accompaniment.

It is customary to use the term *texture* to describe the situation in which a melody is found; and three different textures may be distinguished. The first and simplest is called *monophonic texture;* it is composed of a single unaccompanied melody (see Example 11*a*). Illustrations of this texture include unaccompanied chants that form parts of the worship service in many churches, folk songs sung by a single voice without instrumental support, and military bugle calls played by a single instrument.

The second is *homophonic texture,* which consists primarily of a single line of melody and a supporting set of chords, the latter adding a harmonic accompaniment to the melody (see Example 11*b*). Hymn tunes, accompanied songs, operas, many portions of symphonies, and a great variety of other works are constructed in this fashion.

The third type, *polyphonic texture,* consists of a web of intertwined melodies (see Example 11*c*). Two or more melodies, heard without supporting chords, form the tonal substance of compositions in this category. Rounds such as *Three Blind Mice,* works called *fugues* (which we shall discuss later), many vocal compositions of the Renaissance known as *madrigals* and *motets*—these are examples.

In general, two kinds of polyphonic texture exist. One kind is composed of melodies that, in contour and rhythm, resemble each other only slightly or not at all; the alto and tenor melodies of Example 11*c* are of this type. Dvořák's *Humoresque* and Foster's *Old Folks at Home* are sometimes sung together; this results in the same general kind of polyphonic texture. One melody is a *countermelody* to the other; in technical language, it is a *counterpoint.*

The other kind of polyphonic texture contains a principal melody and a countermelody that begins like the principal melody but that enters the texture after the first melody has begun and thereafter runs its own course. Often a number of melodies are employed, each one having the same beginning contour but perhaps entering at a different pitch level (see Example 12*a*). In other cases, the second melody may be an inverted version of the first, with every interval of the original turned upside down; or it may be set with halved note values, thus acquiring a speed twice as great as that of the original (see Example 12*b*).

Every new melody in this kind of texture imitates the others and this technique is appropriately called *imitative technique,* or simply *imitation.* The amount of melodic freedom given to the imitating fragments may be considerable; but if the perceptive listener takes note of the beginning of each fragment and hears its relationship to the fragments that surround it, he will feel the balance between unity and variety made possible by the use of this technique.

Example 12

Imitative techniques of several other kinds exist also, and they represent far more than dry intellectualizing on the part of composers who employ them. Imitation allows a composer to unify his composition even as he provides melodic variety for the listener. It is a technique that calls forth the balanced activities of heart and mind; and it is such a balance that music requires if it is to serve a useful and enjoyable purpose.

We may now make a large historical generalization about the musical textures themselves. Monophonic texture found its greatest usefulness in the long period before the tenth century. From about the tenth through the sixteenth centuries, polyphonic texture was used most widely in music designed for the Church, and homophonic texture found considerable use in the smaller field of secular music. Since the seventeenth century, polyphonic and homophonic textures have existed side by side, but homophonic texture has probably been the more widely used.

We find often that compositions are written in more than one texture. Works that are homophonic in some sections and polyphonic in others exist in great profusion; for expressive reasons, the major composers have never hesitated to mix these styles.

Music written in monophonic texture may be thought of as being one-dimensional (horizontal); homophonic or polyphonic music adds a second (vertical) dimension to the whole. The vertical relationships between a melody and its accompanying chords, or between the simultaneously heard melodies in polyphonic texture, constitute the element of *harmony,* which is the subject of a later section (see p. 41).

MELODY AND THEME

The role of memory—or at least short-range recall—in the enjoyment of music is often overlooked. Many minutes (and in the case of an opera or other lengthy work, several hours) may elapse between the beginning and end of a composition. In almost every extended composition, bits of melody and other musical material are reworked, manipulated, and organized within a space of time. Any one section of the composition thus bears a calculated relationship to the other sections, and full enjoyment depends upon how well the listener recalls what he has heard previously.

The process is simplified through the fact that an extended composition contains one or more melodies that are raised to a higher level of importance and that play significant parts in the structure of the whole. If those important melodies can be grasped and recalled, the listener gains an insight into the construction of the work and the relationships between its parts. This, as we have seen earlier, is directly related to the enjoyment of the music. Melodies of this kind are called *themes;* and since an understanding of musical themes is vital to an understanding of the ways in which music is organized, the function of a musical theme may appropriately be discussed here.

In the world of literature, *theme* has a distinct meaning—one quite different from its musical meaning. In a novel, an author's theme may be based on a fundamental truth, such as the power of love or the clash between two forces. In a real sense, the theme is what his novel is about. The same meaning of "theme" applies to a sermon, a term paper, or a political speech.

Relatively few compositions embody a theme in this sense. The theme of Beethoven's Ninth Symphony is universal brotherhood; that of his Sixth or "Pastoral" Symphony is impressions of the countryside; and the themes of various descriptive compositions, songs, and operas are the impressions or stories they attempt to recreate in musical terms. But the majority of musical works are not "about" anything. They are artistic abstractions, with no stories to tell and with no purpose other than to express musical ideas that do not have counterparts in verbal experience. In the literary sense of the term, they have no themes.

In the musical sense of the word, however, they do have themes; themes are melodies raised to positions of structural importance. A musical theme has the same relationship to a composition as a *single character* has to a literary work. In the course of a composition, the theme's nature is revealed; it is related to or comes into conflict with other themes, which then become transformed as a result of the musical conflict. While a short story may require only one or two characters, a novel may require many; in a similar way, a musical composition may require one theme or a dozen.

In light of this, the importance of recognizing and recalling musical themes during the course of a composition becomes obvious. If we are to recognize and enjoy fully the adventures and transformations of the themes, we must be able to recall the original versions. To do this we must first gain a clear impression of the melody's shape, contour, or other characteristics. In the very process of gaining that impression we necessarily formulate thoughts about what we are hearing; and the recollection of the melody is a result of applying thought to the sense impression we have received.

Every noticeable feature of a melody acts as an aid in recalling the whole. The contour of a melody, the arrangement of the tones that constitute it, its range and direction, the way it is organized—these and other factors can be observed even at first hearing. In the very act of becoming conscious of such factors we briefly memorize them, and this act greatly simplifies the process of recalling the melody when we hear it again or hear it in a transformed version.

Rhythm, Meter, and Tempo

A great variety of everyday experiences illustrates the essential nature of rhythm. Rhythm is present in the rising and setting of the sun, in the act of breathing, in the sequence of waking and sleeping. Rhythm is seen in the breaking of waves on the seashore, in the arrangement of windows in a building, in the pattern of pickets in a fence. Rhythm is felt in the sentences of a good speaker, and in the performance of a piece of music. Yet, even though the manifestations of rhythm are familiar to everyone, rhythm is elusive when one attempts to define it in simple terms.

The illustrations given above have several elements in common: (1) a "background," which may consist of either time or space; (2) an event or detail that recurs repeatedly; (3) a divisive factor that separates one event or detail from the next; (4) some form of relationship between each repetition. On the basis of those elements, a partial characterization of rhythm can be given—partial because any definition broad enough to cover rhythm in all its manifestations would be so broad as to be meaningless.[1]

Rhythm results from the consistent recurrence of an event or detail that breaks up the formless background of time or space into convenient units. Rhythm is a principle that enables us to organize or bring order into our perceptions of time and space.

RHYTHM AND ACCENT

In music, the unit of time is called a *beat.* In order to establish a feeling of rhythm, the beat must reappear often enough to establish a series; obviously, one beat alone will not do this. Since the beat is essentially a small fragment of time, it need not be heard; it is enough that it be felt, sensed, or thought.

Now, let us imagine a series of beats and notice how difficult it is to avoid emphasizing some beats more than others. When we hear the ticking of a clock, or the drip of water from a tap, or any other similar series of sounds, we tend to combine the successive beats into groups containing two, three, or four; and we impart to the first member of each group a stress or accent to mark the grouping. This psychological fact suggests that rhythm and *accent* are closely linked, and that consequently the one cannot be considered quite apart from the other.

Accents may differ in relative strength, of course. We have only to listen to a sentence of prose or a line of poetry to realize that accents may range from very strong to very weak. Notice that the speech sounds attract attention roughly in proportion to the amount of accent they carry; that is to say, a strong accent attracts attention more than a weak one does.

The same variety in quantity of accent is also found in music. One of the most fundamental musical experiences comes from realizing the infinite variety of accents that come to expression in a good performance. Listen to the rhythmic pulse of any stirring march, or a waltz, or of any other piece that is well accented. Notice that in a very subtle way the strongest beats pull you along and the weaker beats let you relax a bit. The flow of strongly accented and less accented beats is pleasurable, and any arbitrary or willful disturbance of beat or accent (as in jerky performance, for example) is likely to be less pleasant.

In any series of rhythmic beats, accents may be spaced in a variety of ways. This fact makes it possible to classify rhythms according to the type of spacing employed. Whether or not the accents are spaced evenly, the flow of beats is likely to continue

[1] The definition given in Willi Apel, *Harvard Dictionary of Music,* Harvard University Press, is typical: "Rhythm is everything pertaining to the temporal quality (duration) of the musical sound." That definition helps us not at all.

unaltered; consequently, there need not be any lessening of the enjoyment that the rhythm brings. There are several basic types of rhythm that are established by various ways of spacing accents.

METER

In one type of music, evenly spaced accents occur on every second or fourth beat. Each strong beat (S) is followed by one weak beat (w), and a rhythm of S-w S-w, or S-w-s-w S-w-s-w is established; in the second of these cases the second strong beat (s) is likely to be given less stress than the first (S). Since the strong accents are spaced equally, they are capable of being measured and reduced to a formula. Hence the rhythm of music that embodies this type of evenly spaced accent is called *metrical rhythm;* and the above formula, one of the most common in our music, is called *duple meter.* Duple meter is the metrical basis of a march, for example, and is carried out by the "LEFT-right, LEFT-right" of the marching men. Countless compositions other than marches employ duple meter. This meter is also an ingredient of one type of poetry, as the following lines show (the strong beats are indicated by accents):

> Tíger! Tíger! búrning bríght
> Ín the fórests óf the níght:
>
> WILLIAM BLAKE

In another type of music, each strong beat is followed by two weak beats, and metrical groups consisting of S-w-w S-w-w are established. or two such groups are combined, in the form S-w-w-s-w-w S-w-w-s-w-w, and again the second strong beat is stressed less heavily than the first. Because of the threefold nature of the resulting groups, this is called *triple meter.* Perhaps the best-known example of triple meter is the waltz, in which a "ONE-two-three, ONE-two-three" grouping of beats is characteristic. Triple meter is also common in poetry, as in the following lines:

> I spráng to the stírrup, and Jóris, and hé;
> I gálloped, Dirck gálloped, we gálloped all thrée;
>
> ROBERT BROWNING

In a third type of music, the strong beats are not equally spaced, as they are in metrical music of both the duple and triple variety. Irregular numbers of weak beats may intervene between the accents, and a common measurement or formula cannot be determined. This type, somewhat more rare than the metrical type, illustrates what may be called *unmetrical rhythm.* But it is definitely incorrect to think of unmetrical rhythm as being unrhythmical; for a succession of strong and weak beats is still present, the beats create a rhythmic flow, and they have the power to carry the listener's interest forward.

Unmetrical rhythm is found most often in plainsong, or Gregorian chant, to give it a more familiar name (see Example 11*a*, p. 21). It is closely analogous to the rhythm of prose, where an irregular number of unaccented syllables may intervene between the accented syllables that resemble the beats in music:

> Whén, in the Cóurse of húman evénts, it becomes nécessary
> for óne peóple to dissólve the polítical bánds . . .
>
> THOMAS JEFFERSON

We may recapitulate the foregoing very briefly. *Rhythm* has to do with a succession or flow of beats. *Meter* results from imposing a pattern of accents upon the flow of the beats. A rhythm that employs a regular accentual pattern is said to be a *metrical rhythm;* one in which no regular pattern of strong and weak beats is present constitutes an *unmetrical rhythm.*

The great majority of the music we shall be concerned with is metrical music, of either the duple or triple variety. Marches and dances are of this type, of course; the regular spacing between strong beats is one of the most obvious characteristics of this kind of music. Also included in this category are orchestral and choral music, songs and short pieces—in fact, almost all the music composed after about 1600.

Only four groups of Western music embody the unmetrical rhythmic type to any extent: (1) the centuries-old Gregorian chant of the Roman Catholic church mentioned above; (2) portions of the vocal music composed between about 1300 and 1600, especially that which is based on prose texts; (3) the short passages in opera and oratorio that we shall later come to know as *recitatives;* (4) parts of many compositions written after about 1913, especially works by Igor Stravinsky and other contemporary composers. In other words, metrical rhythms prevail in most of the music written in the past 350 years; and unmetrical rhythms are characteristic of the majority of earlier music and of some contemporary works.

Quite apart from the grouping of beats to form duple meter, triple meter, or unmetrical rhythm is the matter of distributing the tones on, between, or across the beats. It is possible, of course, for a melody to be written so that every one of its tones coincides with one of the beats that establishes the rhythmic flow. Hymn tunes in general most closely approach this condition; but even in that branch of music perfectly regular examples are rare. One of the very few hymns that exhibits full agreement between tones and beats is *All Praise to Thee* (see Example 13).

Example 13

The overwhelming majority of our music, however—whether metrical or unmetrical—shows that tones do not always coincide with beats. True, the rhythmic background is present; it is established by the flow of beats in time. Above that background, however, and attracting the listener's attention on another level, are the long and short tones that constitute the melodies and harmonies. It is these tones that give the piece its musical identity. The tones of the melody may at times coincide with the beats that establish the rhythmic background, as they do in the first and third measures (but not in the middle of the second and the fourth measures) of *America* (see Example 10, p. 20).

At other times, however, the tones may fall between the beats, or extend past them, or be quite independent of them. Such deviations, taken in a group, serve to create a second rhythmic structure which is superimposed upon the basic rhythmic background. This inevitably brings to the listener a sense of rhythmic conflict, which is one of the most enjoyable aspects of music. Several types of tonal deviation from the rhythmic flow of beats are noted here.

(1) More than one tone may occupy the space of a single beat; the beat is in effect divided. (2) The opposite case may occur also: a tone may extend over more than one beat, resulting in a moment of repose in the melody. (3) The amount by which a tone is lengthened need not be a full beat or several beats, but can be a half-beat or a still smaller fraction. (4) In the rhythmic device called *syncopation,* a tone may be sounded on a subdivision of a beat and extend past the following beat; or it may be placed on a weak beat and extend past the beginning of the next strong beat. Syncopation gives the effect of tones starting between the beats, as it were, and it results in a brief conflict between two rhythmic patterns (see Example 14). (5) A beat or several beats may go by in silence without a tone's being sounded, and again the rhythmic flow of

Example 14

the beats is undisturbed. (6) An accent may be placed anywhere in the measure (which is the group of tones between two strong beats), to give added stress to a strong beat or to give a weak beat or a subdivision of a beat the strength of a strong beat. (7) Any or all of these devices for disturbing the even flow of tones may appear in combination. In fact, few extended passages do not make use of more than one of them. For example, the first four choral measures of Handel's "Hallelujah" Chorus from *Messiah* employ no fewer than a dozen deviations from a regular ONE-two-three-four beat (see Example 15).

In the majority of such cases, the deviations assure more rhythmic variety than a regular succession of tones can provide. Often, especially in the case of syncopation, the conflict of accents (one heard, the other felt) gives music much of its rhythmic interest. It is important to realize that in all such cases the rhythmic pulse is not affected; all the beats are felt in regular succession, even though no new tones may be sounded on some of them.

Handel, *Messiah*, "Hallelujah" Chorus **_Example 15_**

(a) First beat lengthened by half
(b) Beat subdivided
(c) Quarter rest on fourth beat
(d) Eighth rest and two sixteenth notes on weak beat
(e) Eighth rest and eighth note on fourth beat
(f) Brief syncopation; the second tone is heard on a subdivision of the first beat, and the second beat is unheard

RHYTHMIC PATTERNS

Rhythm, as was pointed out above, provides one of the most fundamental musical experiences. Whether the rhythm is embodied in the stirring beat of a march, the lilt and swing of a waltz, the motion of a quiet expressive melody, or the driving force of a large orchestral work, it underlies all music. The nature of the rhythm becomes apparent when we listen selectively to the succession of strong and weak beats—whether metrical or unmetrical, regular duple or triple meter, or irregular compound meter. Once the rhythm has been consciously established, then the conflicts between tone and beat—subdivisions, lengthened tones, syncopation, expressive accents, moments of silence—can be fully perceived and enjoyed. The observance of these deviations and rhythmic conflicts results in the greatest response on the listener's part to the strength and forcefulness of the rhythm.

The examples that we have shown of rhythmic deviations, which have been taken out of context, may have led to the thought that the deviations themselves exist only in isolation, or that they are rare. Such a conclusion is not justified, for the examination of almost any extended composition will reveal that a specific pattern of deviation will recur repeatedly through large sections or an entire movement. Other compositions may contain patterns that coincide with the beats, instead of deviating from them. The first movement of Beethoven's Violin Concerto, for example, contains a pattern of four quarter notes, repeated many times. Such a reiteration of a rhythmic device, whether it coincides with the beats or deviates from them, may be called a *rhythmic pattern.* An awareness of rhythmic patterns, gained through listening selectively, will give depth and order to the listening experience; in fact, it is one of the essential ingredients of that experience.

Dance music provides the most obvious examples of rhythmic patterns; it is the rhythmic pattern that gives each dance form its identity and character. Example 16 shows a few of the basic dance patterns. It includes the familiar waltz and the rhyth-

Example 16

mic pattern found in the more common duple-meter dances, such as the two step. It includes also the more exotic dances that appear primarily in other countries or in a sophisticated fashion on the concert stage.

Rhythmic patterns also abound in the standard concert literature. There is virtually no limit to the number of patterns that could be illustrated here. Several are given in Example 17, merely to show a variety of types that do occur; in each case the reiterated pattern is indicated by a brace. The repetition of the pattern may be verified by tapping out or singing the phrases that follow the fragments illustrated here; we then notice that in every case the pattern is basic to an extended passage or even to an entire composition.

Changes in *melodic contour* are to be expected, for we are speaking of *rhythmic patterns* and not *melodic motives* of the kind to be discussed later. The three recurrences of the

Example 17

(a) Handel, *Messiah,* "Hallelujah" Chorus
(b) Beethoven, Symphony No. 5
(c) Schubert, Symphony No. 8 ("Unfinished")
(d) Beethoven, Symphony No. 7
(e) Grieg, *Peer Gynt* Suite No. 1, "In the Hall of the Mountain King"
(f) Wagner, *Die Walküre,* "Ride of the Valkyries"
(g) Mendelssohn, *A Midsummer Night's Dream,* Scherzo
(h) Schubert, *Marche Militaire*
(i) Wagner, *Lohengrin,* Prelude to Act III
(j) Bizet, *Carmen,* "Toreador's Song"

rhythmic pattern in Example 17*h* illustrate this point. But as far as the rhythm itself is concerned, the pattern may recur dozens or hundreds of times without change, as it does in the first movement of Beethoven's Symphony No. 5 (Example 17*b*). It may be added to or subtracted from, as happens in the first movement of Schubert's "Unfinished" Symphony (Example 17*c*), or it may act as a seed out of which related patterns evolve, as seen in the Mendelssohn Scherzo (Example 17*g*). The pattern may be temporarily abandoned in one section of a composition (Examples 17*a* and 17*i*), only to return later with added effectiveness. Slight variants of the pattern may be expected at times also; such momentary departures add interest and variety to the whole.

To the degree that a composition is well made and has any degree of artistic unity, it will contain recurring and recognizable rhythmic patterns. Without these patterns, music would become rhythmic chaos. The search for and recognition of such patterns, through the process of selective listening, is one of the most rewarding of musical activities. The composer, in his handling of these patterns, reveals his mastery of one of the fundamental musical elements. And the listener, in recognizing them, gains additional material with which to enrich his musical experiences.

TEMPO

The matter of speed is an important one in music; a composition played at an incorrect speed may create an emotional effect quite different from that intended by the composer. For example, if a slow and serious work is played fast, it is likely to sound like a caricature of itself; a fast piece played slowly will drag and become boring. In order to guard against such distortions, it is customary for the composer to indicate the speed of the basic beats. This rate of speed is called *tempo.* When we speak of a slow tempo, a fast tempo, or any tempo between these extremes, we refer by implication to the actual speed of the beats as they pass by in time.

The tempo indication consists of a word—usually in Italian—set at the beginning of the piece; such an indication may also appear at any internal point where a tempo change is desired. The following are the most usual terms:

prestissimo	very quickly	*andante*	literally, "walking"; hence, moderately
presto	quickly	*adagio*	rather slowly
allegro	fast (lively)	*lento*	slowly
allegretto	somewhat fast	*largo*	very slowly (broadly)

The above tempo indications are often combined with a qualifying descriptive term, as follows: *moderato,* moderately; *cantabile,* singingly; *marziale,* martially; *con brio,* with spirit; *pesante,* heavily. These are only a few of the qualifying terms used. (See Appendix III for a more complete list.) The addition of these terms will normally affect the speed of a composition; for obviously *allegro marziale, allegro con brio,* and *allegro moderato* each imply a modification of the basic term, *allegro.*

Even at best, however, such terms must remain approximations, for "fast," "slow," and all other descriptions of speed are purely relative. A mechanical device developed by Johann Maelzel early in the nineteenth century has helped considerably to bring accuracy to the problem of determining tempo. This device, called a *metronome,* produces a series of clicks whose rate can be adjusted from about 40 to 200 per minute. By indicating the desired number of beats per minute the composer can state the tempo he wishes more accurately. The form used for indicating tempo in this way is shown in Example 18. The letters "M.M." sometimes used refer to "Maelzel's Metronome."

Example 18

♩ = 100 or 𝅗𝅥 = 60 or ♩ = M.M.160

Listening Suggestions

I

All music illustrates the four characteristics of tone discussed in this chapter, and none of the characteristics exists in isolation. In the following recordings, however, usually at or near the beginning, a single one of them is perhaps more clearly illustrated than the others; hence that characteristic may be lifted out for selective listening. The element to be selected is given in parentheses after the title in each case; and the listener, having formed an aural image of what he is listening for, will be led to realize how the characteristics of tone are fully exploited in a musical composition.

PITCH

Beethoven, Symphony No. 7, A major, Op. 92, second movement (many tones on the same pitch level)

———, Symphony No. 5, C minor, Op. 67, third movement (many groups consisting of three short tones and one long on the same pitch)

Mendelssohn, *Fingal's Cave,* Overture, Op. 26 (constant changing of pitch levels)

DURATION

Tchaikovsky, Symphony No. 4, F minor, Op. 36, finale (variety of length of tones)

———, Symphony No. 5, E minor, Op. 64, second movement (groups of short and long tones heard alternately)

INTENSITY

Mozart, Symphony No. 40, G minor, K. 550, finale (contrasts of loud and soft across short time spans)

Beethoven, *Egmont,* Overture, Op. 84 (alternation of loud and soft phrases)

QUALITY

Rimsky-Korsakov, *Capriccio Espagnol,* Op. 34, fourth movement (differences in the quality of the various solo instruments)

Tchaikovsky, *The Nutcracker,* Suite, Op. 71 (contrasts of quality between the various solo instruments and instrumental groups)

Brahms, *Variations on a Theme by Haydn,* Op. 56*a* (effect of contrasting string and woodwind groups)

II

All the compositions included in present-day repertoires illustrate one or more of the metrical types and tempos discussed in this chapter. The following works, however, are suggested as representatives of the various types; they have the virtue of being easily available on recordings.

METER

Gregorian chant, sung by the Monks of the Solesmes Abbey, or by the Benedictines of Beuron (unmetrical rhythm)
Stravinsky, *The Rite of Spring,* first and last sections (unmetrical rhythm)
Schubert, Symphony No. 8 ("Unfinished"), first movement (triple meter)
Wagner, *Die Meistersinger,* Prelude (duple meter)
Tchaikovsky, Symphony No. 6, Op. 74 ("Pathétique"), second movement (quintuple meter; combination of 2/4 and 3/4)
Debussy, *Fêtes,* from Nocturnes for Orchestra (compound meters; 9/8, 12/8, and 15/8)

TEMPO

Mendelssohn, Symphony No. 4, Op. 90 ("Italian"), finale (very fast)
Mozart, *The Marriage of Figaro,* Overture, K. 492 (fast)
Beethoven, Symphony No. 5, C minor, Op. 67, second movement (moderate)
Brahms, Symphony No. 2, D major, Op. 73, second movement (slow)
Dvořák, Symphony No. 5, Op. 95 ("New World"), second movement (very slow)

RHYTHMIC PATTERNS

Beethoven, Symphony No. 7, A major, Op. 92, first movement, after introduction (reiteration of one rhythmic figure)
Bizet, "Habanera," from *Carmen* (reiteration of one dance rhythm)
Ravel, *Bolero* (reiteration of one rhythm in the accompaniment)
Bach, "Brandenburg" Concerto No. 3, G major, first movement (the movement is based on one constantly recurring rhythmic pattern)

TEXTURES

Repertoire of Gregorian chants; unaccompanied folk songs; military bugle calls (monophonic texture)
Haydn, Symphony No. 101 ("Clock"), second movement (homophonic texture)
Tchaikovsky, Symphony No. 4, F minor, Op. 36, second movement (homophonic texture)
Bach, Fugue in G minor ("The Little") (polyphonic texture)
———, *Kyrie,* from Mass in B minor (polyphonic texture)

Chapter 3

TONAL ARRANGEMENTS

In this chapter we shall consider the ways in which the many possible tones are organized and made to serve the purposes of our musical system. The organization is both horizontal and vertical; tones may be arranged consecutively (horizontally) to create *scales,* which are basic to melodic construction, as well as simultaneously (vertically) to create *chords.*

Scales

Imagine all possible tones arranged in order of pitch from lowest to highest. Of all the possible tones that the human ear can perceive, a relatively small number have gradually come to be employed in our musical culture; they provide the material out of which our music is made. These few tones, when arranged in order of ascending or descending pitch according to a particular formula or pattern of pitch differences, constitute a *musical scale.* Each tone, counting from the first, is called a step or degree of the scale.

The term scale is derived from the Latin *scala,* which means "ladder"; in fact, the German word for scale is *Tonleiter,* which is translated as "tone ladder." Although we may safely assume that in a well-built ladder all the steps or rungs are equally spaced, in the most usual musical scales the steps are *not* all equidistant. Some steps are only half as great as others—a fact that is of tremendous importance in the development of our music. Thus we shall deal both with *steps* and *half steps* (see diagram below).

THE MAJOR SCALE

If all the different tones used in the fragments shown in Examples 6*a* and 6*c* (p. 13) are arranged in order from lowest to highest, the following set of eight tones results (see Example 19). These eight tones constitute what is called a *major scale.*

Example 19

It can be proved scientifically (by determining the vibration rates of the tones) that the distance between the third and fourth scale steps, and again between the seventh and eighth, is roughly half as great as the distance between any other pair of adjoining tones. These differences can be experienced by singing the series of tones in the scale; the degree of physical tension required to move up a half step is felt to be less than that needed for a whole step.

The pattern of whole steps and half steps revealed in this tune is like that shown by countless other tunes when their tones are taken out of melodic order and are arranged in order from lowest to highest. *America, Adeste Fideles, Jingle Bells*—these are only a few of the thousands of tunes that illustrate this major scale pattern. In each case the half steps appear between degrees 3–4 and 7–8; whole steps occur everywhere else. This pattern or formula is shown in the following diagram, which may be imagined as a ladder lying on its side. Some of the rungs of the ladder are spaced twice as far apart as the others.

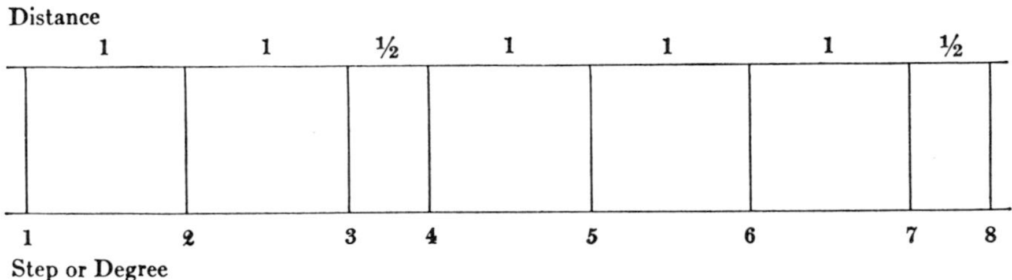

The eighth tone of this type of scale has a special characteristic. It appears, even though on a higher pitch, to flow into or fuse with the sound or value of the first tone, much as two different shades of the same color flow into each other. It gives rise to the feeling that the two tones are essentially the same—a result of the fact that the vibration rate of the eighth tone is exactly twice that of the first tone. This feeling is strong enough to warrant musicians' calling each pair of tones by the same alphabet name. Thus, both the first and last tones of Example 19 are called "C"; and every other tone is similarly related in feeling and alphabet name to the tone eight steps above it or below it (see Example 20). Since the upper tone is in each case the eighth step above the lower (or vice versa), it is called the *octave* (from the Greek word *okto,* meaning "eight").

The octave segment shown in Example 19 represents only a small portion of the total pitch range, of course. The segment may be extended by adding tones upward in alphabetical order, and downward in reverse alphabetical order, to the very limits of the pitch range. The same pattern of whole steps and half steps will result, to form a series of tones several octaves in extent. In each case, the same octave relationship between any two tones eight steps apart will be present (see Example 20).

Example 20

THE CHROMATIC SCALE

Referring to Example 19 and the diagram of the "ladder" again, we see that the half steps shown there are between E–F and B–C. Centuries ago musicians discovered that certain whole steps could be divided in half, and that the "between" tones thus produced could also be employed in music. This is analogous, in the ladder diagram, to placing an additional rung between any two widely spaced ones. In the course of time all of the whole steps were so divided, and the new tones took their places in the complete musical system.

Each of the new tones may have two names: when a new tone is *above* a neighboring tone it is given the alphabet name of its neighbor plus the term *sharp* (whose symbol is ♯); when it is *below* a neighboring tone it assumes that neighbor's alphabet name plus the term *flat* (♭). Thus the tone between C and D is named either *C sharp* (C♯) or *D flat* (D♭), depending upon the context in which it is used.[1] If this system of naming tones seems complex or illogical, it is because our musical system has a long and involved history and its growth was most often brought about by adding to older material.

A complete series of twelve half steps in the octave results from the process described above; this series may be illustrated by revising the ladder diagram, as follows:

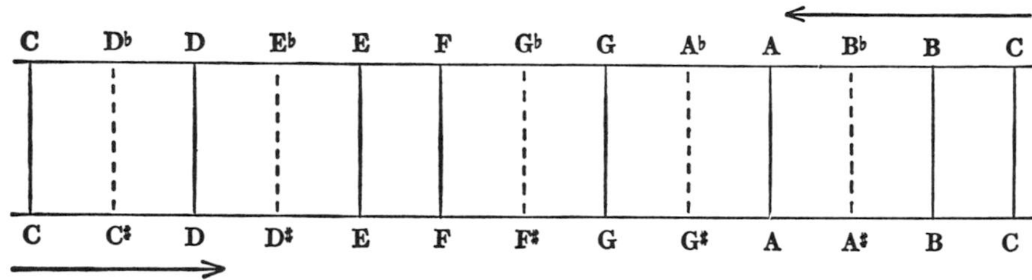

These twelve tones with their respective octaves constitute the *chromatic scale.* The places on the piano keyboard of the twelve tones of the chromatic scale are shown in the accompanying diagram. Notice that the tones that do not have sharps or flats (represented by the solid "rungs" in the diagram above) are played by the white keys; those with sharps or flats (the dotted "rungs") by the black keys. The entire keyboard embraces a range of seven and one-third octaves or eighty-eight (seven and one-third times twelve) tones.

[1] In the interest of simplification, the acoustical inaccuracy contained in this statement is permitted to stand. Actually, on all instruments except "tempered" ones (keyboards in general), a true C sharp is a few vibrations faster (and thus higher in pitch) than a D flat. In the process called "tempering" this and similar intonation problems are evened out.

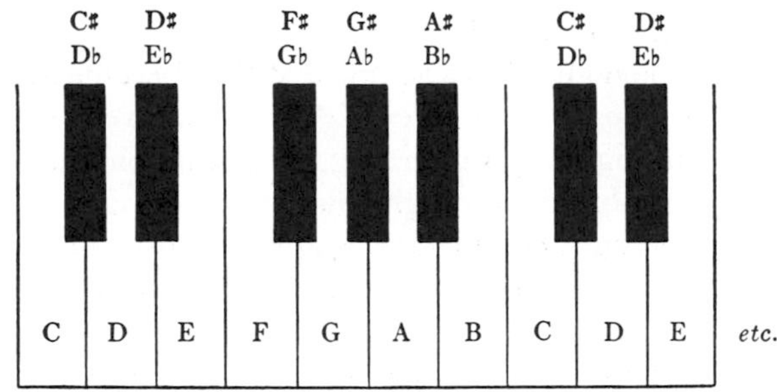

OTHER MAJOR SCALES

Of what use are the tones represented by the black keys? Why does the system require half steps between C–D, D–E, and the other whole steps? The questions can best be answered by pointing out that in our musical system a major scale can be formed beginning on any tone of the chromatic scale. In order to provide all the scales with the proper half and whole steps, these additional tones of the chromatic scale are necessary.

For example, suppose we wished to construct a major scale beginning on F, and we had available only the tones, F, G, A, B, C, D, E, F. We discover that we cannot use the tone B, because the distance between degrees 3 and 4 must be a half step, and A–B is a whole step; thus B flat becomes necessary. Likewise, a major scale built on G requires a half step between degrees 7 and 8; and since the interval F–G is a whole step, F cannot serve, but F sharp can. Similarly, scales on other starting tones require additional sharps or flats if the pattern of whole and half steps is to be maintained.

Thus twelve major scales are possible—one on each of the twelve tones. A composition that employs primarily the tones of one of these scales is said to be in the *tonality,* or *key,* of that scale. Thus one refers to the *key of C* or *key of B flat,* and so on.[2]

Why are compositions written in keys other than C, and why are other scales necessary at all? A number of reasons exist—some psychological, others merely practical. There is first of all the feeling, held by many composers and performing musicians, that each tonality or key has a characteristic mood value or emotional significance. For example, one key may be considered proper for forthright, majestic, or imposing utterance; another is felt to be bright in nature; a third is suitable for neutral expression; a fourth is an intimate key; and so on. Moreover, when a composer is collecting and working over his tonal material, he will usually find that the tunes and other musical fragments enter his consciousness firmly fixed to a particular tonality. In other words, a musical idea will occur to him in a definite key, and he will perforce honor that key while manipulating the material. To this extent, then, the need for a variety of keys is psychological.

Another reason for using keys other than C centers about the practical matter of range. A song written for a soprano, say, might be in the key of C and extend up to

[2] Appendix II gives a table of the twelve major scales, together with their respective key signatures.

the top of the normal soprano range. If that song were to be sung by an alto, the upper tones would be entirely too high, of course. It would then become necessary to shift the entire song down several steps, say to the key of A flat, G, or even F. This process, called *transposition* (that is, "shifting the position of"), is a common one, especially among singers. Many songs are published for high voice in one key and for low voice in another. To some extent the same considerations apply to instrumental music. A violin piece, for example, would probably be transposed to a lower key if the piece were to be played by a viola or cello.

It happens that a composition often carries the key in which it is written as an integral part of its title. We shall become familiar with many a "Symphony in D major," "Sonata in E flat," and the like. And in most cases we can expect the respective compositions to possess a mood content that is appropriate to the key in which they are written.

MINOR SCALES

To review, in all twelve major scales the half steps are found between degrees 3–4 and 7–8; all other intervals are whole steps. Now, there are a large number of melodies in which the half steps are not in the above positions, but appear elsewhere in the scale. The Christmas carols *God Rest Ye Merry, Gentlemen,* and *On Our Way* are in this category, as are the first few measures of Schubert's Symphony No. 8 ("Unfinished"), Beethoven's Symphony No. 5, and innumerable other compositions. Example 21 gives the beginnings of some of these tunes, along with the scales on which they are based.

Regardless of how liberally half steps seem to be strewn about in tunes of this type, one element is constant: there is always a half step between degrees 2 and 3. This element is enough to identify the tune as being based on a *minor scale* instead of a major scale. The whole matter of minor-scale formation is tightly bound up with the early history of our music and cannot be fully discussed here. For our purposes it will suffice

Example 21

to point out that three distinct forms of the minor scale are recognized by music theorists, that ascending and descending forms of the scale often differ, and that the key signature reflects the descending form but not the ascending.

Intervals

Let us now examine a number of different melodies: one that forms virtually a straight line (as seen in Example 22*a*), another that undulates widely (Example 22*b*), and one that is not extreme in either respect (22*c*). Some more convenient means of vertical measurement than counting half steps and whole steps is needed if we are to determine the distance between one tone and another. The concept of *interval* provides that means. We recall first that an "octave" was described as the eighth tone above or below another tone in a major or minor scale. But "octave" is also used in another sense to mean the *distance* between two tones eight degrees apart. In this sense, "octave" refers to an interval.

Example 22

Notice first that the "eightness" of this interval comes about when we count the lower tone of the interval as "one" and proceed to count each tone up to "eight," regardless of whether whole steps or half steps are involved. This same principle applies to the measuring and naming of all intervals in music: we begin counting with the lowest tone of the interval. Example 23*a* gives the main intervals that can be counted from C. Other intervals (that is, those not having C as their lowest tone) are counted in exactly the same fashion, as Example 23*b* shows. In each case the lower tone becomes "one" in the counting, and the number of the higher tone gives the name of the interval.

Example 23

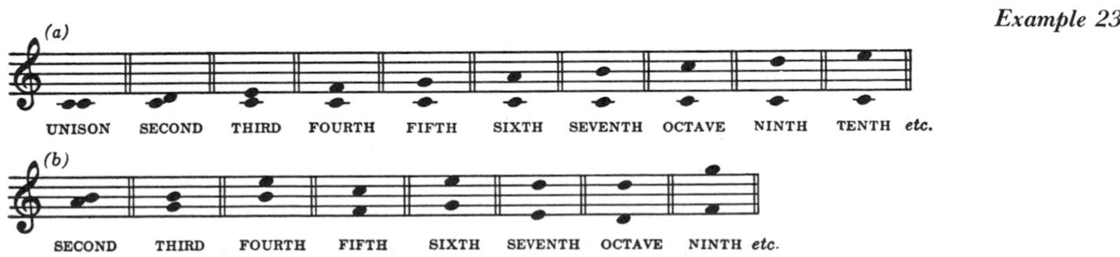

One qualification may be made here. Certain intervals are referred to as major or minor (a major third, for example, or a minor sixth); others are perfect, diminished, or augmented (as in a perfect octave, a diminished fifth, or an augmented fourth). These refinements have to do with the number of half steps within the interval (to illustrate, a minor third contains three half steps; a major third, four). This qualification is of great importance to the music theorist and composer, but it need not be pursued here.

Chords

Most of the musical examples we have referred to in the foregoing pages have been fragments of melody. As we saw in Chapter 2, however, melodies are seldom heard alone in that fashion. Far more melodies are accompanied by other melodies or supported by two, three, or more tones heard simultaneously. This immediately adds another dimension to music. It is both significant and historically true that composers of the Western world have been almost alone in employing both the vertical and the horizontal dimensions. For over a thousand years, European composers and those culturally related to them have worked with the sonorities brought about by the vertical support of melodies—something that composers of the East seldom did. A vertical group of tones of different pitch is called a *chord.*

The basic unit of chord construction is the interval of a third. Chords are built by placing one third above another, as Example 24 shows. A three-tone chord so constructed is called a *triad;* a similar four-tone chord is called a *seventh chord* (because the interval created by its outer tones is a seventh); a five-tone chord becomes a *ninth chord,* and so on (see Example 25).

Example 24

Two principles of chord manipulation are as follows: (1) A chord may be constructed on any tone of the scale (the tone on which the chord is constructed is called the *root* of the chord), as shown in Example 25*a*. (2) Any tone of a chord may be shifted from one octave to another; only in a few cases is the basic effect of the chord changed thereby. This process, called *chord inversion,* is of great importance in making possible rich and varied musical textures (see Examples 25*b* and 25*c*).

In the discussion above we saw that intervals could be qualified, according to the number of half steps they contained, as major or minor, perfect or augmented or diminished. Chords may be qualified and classified in a somewhat related manner. For example, a triad containing a major third below a minor third is called a *major triad.* The same principle holds good for taller chords: seventh chords may be major, minor, or diminished. A full account of the classification of chords, however, lies beyond the scope of this discussion.

Example 25

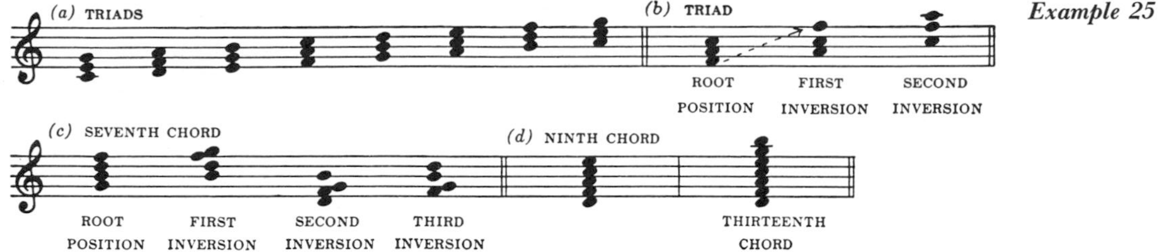

Harmony

In discussing melodic cadences in Chapter 2, we pointed out that a melody has the power to evoke feelings of tension and relaxation, or motion and rest. The degree of tension or relaxation is determined in part by the rise and fall of the melody, by the selection of certain tones at significant places in the melody, and by the relative lengths of those tones. Much of the expressive interest and emotional satisfaction that a good melody engenders is a result of this increase and decrease in emotional tension.

The interplay of melodic motion and rest can be strengthened and made more enjoyable for the listener when the melody is supplied with chords. One chord enhances the feeling of motion or tension, another adds to the sense of rest or relaxation. And a series of selected chords heard one after the other amplifies the feeling of ebb and flow of melodic motion in subtle gradations.

This practice of sounding groups of tones together with the tones of a melody gives rise to the concept of *harmony.* The effect of harmony upon music has often been likened to the effect of perspective upon drawing: an element of depth is added. In the centuries since harmony was first conceived, it has become one of the most effective and flexible means of evoking emotional response to music. Harmony may be thought of as the study of tones in vertical arrangements, and of the horizontal relationships between the vertical groups.

It should be pointed out that harmony in a musical sense is only incidentally related to what is usually called "harmonious." While the effect of a harmonized melody can be harmonious, the opposite is also likely to be true. Indeed, we can say that a composition is harmonious in moments of musical rest or relaxation, and unharmonious in moments of tension and motion.

The basic unit of harmony is the chord, introduced in the previous section. Composers have not customarily restricted themselves to using chords (triads, sevenths, and the like) in their simplest root position, but have manipulated them in various ways. One type of manipulation, chord inversion, has been mentioned. Other types may be briefly discussed here.

1. Any tone of the chord may be repeated (*doubled*) in another octave to increase the chord's sonority and to provide smooth connections between one chord and another. Such doubling is, of course, inevitable whenever a triad is placed below a melody tone. For example, when the tone F is in the melody and is harmonized by

the triad F–A–C placed an octave below, the entire tonal group then becomes F–A–C–F, and the F of the triad has been doubled in the upper octave by the F in the melody (see the final chord of Example 26). Any other chord tone may be doubled in this manner; the result is called *four-part writing,* made up of a series of triads plus a line of melody tones, each of which doubles a tone of its harmonizing triad. Four-part writing is typical of the great majority of hymns and is the usual harmonic texture (the homophonic texture) in many other types of music.

2. A tone may be omitted from a chord (but rarely the root) when the normal four-part texture is momentarily abandoned, or when other expressive considerations require the omission. For example, in the first complete measure of *The Star-Spangled Banner* (Example 26), the first "chord" consists only of two B flats (both doubled), the D and F of the triad being omitted. In the second chord, B flat and D are present, and each is doubled; but the F is still missing. In the last beat of the third full measure, on the syllable "-ly," the chord is actually C–E–G–B flat, but the G is omitted for the sake of providing a smooth melodic progression in the two inner parts (see p. 46 for an explanation of the E natural in this chord). By combining the principles of tone doubling and tone omission, a flexible and variable texture is produced.

Example 26

3. The three upper tones of a chord, whether doubled or not, may be spread across more than one octave without significantly altering their harmonic function. If the chord is so spread out, it is in *open harmony;* otherwise it is in *close harmony.* Example 27 shows three stages in the evolution of a satisfying open harmonic texture. In Example 27*a* the melody is supplied with appropriate triads in close harmony and in root position, but the musical effect is crude or coarse. In Example 27*b*, with the same close harmony, the two chords marked with asterisks have been placed in inverted position, and the aesthetic effect is somewhat better. In Example 27*c,* finally, a mixture of open harmony (the first three chords) and close harmony (the last two chords) results. It is well to note how the harmony gains in richness, resonance, and appeal when the chords are spread vertically in the texture.

Example 27 ***The Star-Spangled Banner***

4. Chords may be diffused or spread horizontally in the music and their tones made to sound one after the other. This procedure does not affect the harmonic integrity of the chords, for the memory of the sound of each tone is held long enough for the group of tones to be perceived as a chord. Many types of music often contain chords divided so that one tone of the chord appears on the strong beats and the other tones on the weak beats; Examples 28*a* and 28*b* illustrate the device. Example 28*c*, taken from Schubert's "Trout" Quintet, shows an expansion of the procedure; here the diffused chord tones take on something of a melodic function. And Example 28*d*, from the same work, illustrates a texture in which the chord tones establish a rhythmic pattern that is carried across many measures of the work. The types of chord diffusion shown in Example 28 are extremely common especially in piano music.

Example 28

Chord diffusion of this kind sometimes reaches a stage in which the functions of melody and harmony are in effect combined. In such passages, there is only a single line of tones, arranged so that it outlines triads and other chords. Several additional examples of the procedure are given in Example 29. It is almost impossible, in passages of this sort, to separate melody and harmony. A harplike configuration (arpeggio) is present and the line has a melodic effect, but its shape is such that it implies definite *chord progressions* also.

CHORD PROGRESSIONS

During the centuries in which awareness of harmonic principles developed, composers discovered that the function and effect of a chord differs according to the scale step upon which the chord is built. For example, a triad constructed upon the first step of the scale (the *tonic*, symbolized by the Roman numeral I) greatly enhances the feeling of rest or finality. One built upon the fifth step (the *dominant*, V) suggests a feeling of tension or onward motion. A dominant chord gives a sense of incompleteness to the melody; this makes it desirable to follow that dominant chord with

Example 29

another chord—usually the tonic—if a feeling of finality is to be established. Similarly, chords built on other scale steps differ in regard to the sense of motion or rest that they engender. A succession of chords that arouses a feeling of increasing motion or repose in this way is called a *chord progression.* The chord progressions in Example 30 illustrate a few of the gradations in motion that are possible. Examples 30*a* and 30*b* produce a feeling of finality or repose. Examples 30*c* and 30*d* are incomplete as they stand; they require an additional chord or group of chords to bring them to a state of rest, or to *resolve* them, to use the technical term.

Progressions of the kind shown in Example 30 are the material out of which the harmonic factor of the *cadence* is constructed. The cadence was described briefly on page 19 as consisting of two factors—the melodic and the harmonic. A series of tones in the melody progresses to a point where either a degree of repose or the need for onward motion is felt; and a set of at least two related chords amplifies that feeling and connects the cadence with a particular key or tonality.

The progression shown in Example 30*a* is called a *perfect cadence;* it might, because of its air of finality, be appropriate at the end of a composition. The IV–I progression shown in Example 30*b* is called a *plagal cadence* and is familiar from its use as an "amen" at the end of a hymn. The cadence in Example 30*c* suggests a feeling of unexpectedness wherever it occurs and is most useful within (rather than at the end of) a composition; it is, in fact, called a *deceptive cadence* and often has the same effect as a question has in speech. The progression shown in Example 30*d* is one type of *half cadence* and suggests a feeling of incompleteness.

Many other cadence forms exist, and each one carries its own degree of tension or relaxation. The construction of the proper cadence forms is an important aspect of the composer's art. If the cadences are badly made, his music will limp, halt, or tend to disintegrate into a number of unconnected sections. If they are well made, his work will pulsate with motion toward its harmonic goal, lead to climaxes at well-spaced

Example 30

intervals, and come to a satisfying conclusion. And the cadences within a work greatly influence the harmonic variety it reveals.

The concept of harmonic motion (illustrated by the cadences in Example 30) has been of the utmost significance in the development of our music. Throughout this development, the historian can trace a continuing effort to strengthen the resolution-seeking effect of chords. Many composers took part in that effort; and the history of music is in one sense the history of growing harmonic resources. While working at the problem of increasing those resources, composers made more and more use of *dissonance* in their music and gradually broadened the concept of key or tonality. Appreciation of the historical development of music is based largely upon an understanding of dissonance and tonality.

CONSONANCE AND DISSONANCE

It is customary to think of consonance and dissonance as related to pleasant and unpleasant musical experiences, respectively. Those meanings of the two terms are rather unsatisfactory, for music history shows that what were considered unbearable dissonances in one century often were accepted as pleasant a generation or two later. Many composers—Beethoven, Wagner, and Debussy among them—wrote dissonantly according to the standards of their times, and hence were charged with composing disagreeable music. Some listeners today may smile indulgently at this, for they find no harmonic unpleasantness in the music of those composers. Yet the same listeners may consider many contemporary composers guilty of writing disagreeable music—disagreeable because it is dissonant; and they do not admit the likelihood that another generation will feel quite otherwise.

A more satisfactory concept of consonance and dissonance is simply this: an interval or a chord is *consonant* when it arouses a feeling of repose or relaxation—when it is felt as being stable, as having arrived, and as not requiring resolution. Conversely, a *dissonant* interval or chord is one that suggests onward movement, that is unstable, and that, hence, does require resolution. The chord progression of Example 30*a* has achieved its goal, and the consonant tonic chord with which it closes gives auditory evidence of this fact. The progression in Example 30*d*, on the other hand, leaves us in a state of suspense; the dissonant VII chord suggests unrelieved tension that must be resolved if a satisfactory feeling of rest is to be attained.

Other chords vastly more dissonant than that VII chord are in common use in contemporary music, and with the increase in dissonance comes a greater degree of tension. It is possible to arrange chords in order of tension from the most stable and consonant tonic chord to the least stable and most dissonant group of tones. The use of such chords gives the composer a means of affecting the emotional response of his hearers. He may so control the forward motion of his music, through subtly or directly altering the tension of the harmony, that the listener is forced out of one emotional state into another. The calculated or intuitive control of harmonic resources is one of the criteria by which the worth of a composer may be measured. And the soul-stirring quality of a piece of great music is likely to be related to the varying degrees of harmonic tension and relaxation it evokes.

TONALITY

Another factor that has greatly influenced the course of music through the past several centuries is the gradual broadening of the concept of *tonality*. The feeling of tonality is first of all associated with a melody built upon a particular major or minor scale. As we have seen, the formula for a scale is calculated from its first scale step or tonic, and the tonic exerts a strong influence on the shape and emotional effect of the melody. The tonic often acts as a point of departure and return; it is present or implied harmonically at the beginning and end of the melody, and it allows us to identify the melody as being in a particular tonality or key: D major, for example.

We may now extend this description by pointing out that tonality is also the result of a chord progression centering around the tonic triad and moving from a dissonance (usually the dominant seventh chord) to the consonant tonic chord. Melody and chords interact to arouse a feeling of belonging to a particular scale or key; the contour of the melody and the motion of the harmony—both taking their departure from the tonic of the scale—move toward a point of relaxation, and that point is identified with a particular tonality.

For example, *America* is firmly in the tonality of G major (see Example 10, p. 20). Its chord progressions and cadences lead to that key, and every tone of its melody and all but one of the tones found in the harmony are found in the G major scale. *The Star-Spangled Banner* is just as firmly in B flat major; except for two tones and their repetitions, all of its harmonic and melodic material is found in the tones of the B flat scale. The two tones not found in that scale are F sharp in the second full measure and E natural in the third (see Example 31). Those tones and the chords in which they appear are "borrowed" from other scales; consequently, they momentarily affect the basic integrity of the B flat tonality to a small degree. Indeed, the fragment illustrated in Example 31 gives the impression of ending not in B flat major but in F major, for the last two chords form a V–I cadence in the latter key. However, the next phrase of the song firmly pulls the piece back to B flat.

A short composition entirely in one tonality is similar to a small painting in which shades of only one color occur—color, that is, in the usual sense and not in the sense of "instrumental color." A single unrelieved color is likely to require some contrast, if only to relieve the monochrome effect; a tint borrowed from a contrasting color scale will add vitality and variety to the painting. Similarly, the tones or chords

Example 31

borrowed from another scale help to vitalize a piece of music that is predominantly in one tonality—B flat in the case of Example 31.

If we now think of a larger painting, we can imagine that its greater size requires a greater amount or degree of color contrast if it is to contain pleasing variety. But we can also imagine that borrowed colors are introduced in such great amounts and with such degrees of contrast that the basic color is lost sight of. Then we can no longer speak of a red painting, or a blue one, but only of a painting executed in a number of colors, including some red or blue.

This analogy may be related to musical compositions. A small work can well afford to be entirely in one tonality. Many hymns and folk tunes, each based on one scale, contain not a single tone borrowed from other scales. This generalization may be tested by leafing through a hymnal or songbook; borrowed tones are indicated by *accidentals* (sharps, flats, or naturals) not found in the respective key signatures. A larger composition will almost invariably require some contrast of tonality; either a greater number of accidentals will appear in the music as evidence of borrowings, or the key signatures themselves will be altered. It is obvious that the strength of the basic feeling of tonality diminishes to the extent that such contrasts find their way into the music.

Since the early seventeenth century, about the time that the concept of tonality first began to be felt, composers have in general departed from the fundamental idea that a composition should be built entirely in a single tonality. In addition to borrowing a few tones and chords from other scales, as described above, composers of the seventeenth century often employed a series of tonalities in a single work. A composition beginning in one key *modulates* to another closely related key, remains in that key for a time, and returns to the original key only in the final portion of the work. With each passing generation the number and distance of such modulations increased.

Key relationship is measured by the number of tones one key has in common with another. The keys of C and G, for example, share all but one tone (F in the one, F sharp in the other), thus exhibit the closest relationship. Conversely, the keys of C and G flat, sharing only one tone (F), are the most distantly related. The concept of distance is illustrated in the diagram of the Circle of Fifths (see Appendix II).

Now, however far distant and numerous the modulations, and however many the borrowings in a piece of music written between the seventeenth and mid-nineteenth centuries, the work most often begins and ends in the same key. To that extent it does not desert a basic tonality, and to that extent we are justified in referring to a particular work as being written in a particular key. It is possible, of course, for a composer to increase the amount of borrowing and modulation to a point where all feeling of a basic tonality is lost. The history of music reveals that such an increase actually took place in the years after about 1870, and that tonality became so all-embracing that it virtually ceased to exist. Before discussing that development, which leads directly to contemporary music, let us examine one other harmonic tool which played an important part in that development.

NONHARMONIC TONES

From the earliest period of harmonic development, composers have written melodies containing tones foreign to the chords used to harmonize those melodies. Such tones are dissonant, in that they are not parts of the chords that underlie them; therefore they suggest onward movement or they require resolution (see p. 43–44). They serve variously to enrich or ornament the harmony, and they increase the harmonic tension of the piece in which they are used. They are appropriately called *nonharmonic tones.*

Normally, the chords coincide with the beats of a composition (as opposed to the subdivisions of the beats), and are spaced a short distance apart so that the ear has time to absorb one harmony before the next is sounded. The melody, however, may move at a faster pace and may contain unharmonized tones that lie between the beats. Those tones ride along on the harmonic momentum of the previous chord and establish fleeting dissonances, because they are not tones found in the chords.

Example 32*a* illustrates one such case (the nonharmonic tones are numbered). Example 32*b* contains the same chords without adornment. The difference in appeal between the two versions gives evidence of the importance of nonharmonic tones in achieving a rich sound.

The nonharmonic tones illustrated in Example 32*a* are tones of the scale upon which the chords are constructed, but not tones of the chords themselves. As such, they are representative of the use of nonharmonic tones in a large number of compositions—particularly those written before the middle of the eighteenth century. Later in that century, it became a common practice to borrow nonharmonic tones from the chromatic scale rather than from the major or minor scale upon which the surrounding chords were based. This practice gradually opened a new area of harmonic expressiveness to composers of the time. Bach and Mozart were among the first to make use of chromatic embellishment in their music, leading the way to *chromaticism.*

Example 32

By the nineteenth century such chromatic borrowing was well established. A typical case, shown in Example 33*a*, is drawn from Wagner's opera *Tristan and Isolde,* a work outstanding for its chromaticism. One chord underlies both measures of the example: B–D–F–A flat. The borrowed tones—that is, the tones not contained within the chord—are A natural, B flat, E natural, and E flat. Example 33*b* shows the same passage stripped of the borrowed tones; only the chord itself, in different inversions and in different open positions, remains.

The use of tones borrowed from the chromatic scale may broaden the concept of tonality, in the sense that the borrowed tones momentarily introduce harmonies that are foreign to the underlying key. The broadening may become so extensive that it is difficult or impossible to identify a passage as being in a basic tonality. One stage in the widening of the concept may be seen in Example 33*c*. This passage, also from *Tristan and Isolde,* begins in A flat and ends on the dominant-seventh chord of F minor. Between those points it is so fluid harmonically that it cannot be said to be in any tonality—it can only be said to change as the colors of a kaleidoscope change.

Beyond this stage, the tonality of a piece written in chromatic harmony virtually loses its identity. Or, from another point of view, the extensive borrowings become indistinguishable from the original harmonic framework. The concept of tonality is so much broadened and becomes so all-inclusive that it all but ceases to have any meaning in large portions of many compositions. The chromatic additions to the harmonic structure are almost always dissonant. Thus, the expansion of tonality, in which chromaticism plays so large a part, has gone hand in hand with the increasing use of tension-building dissonances spoken of earlier. The two are different aspects of the same situation.

CONTEMPORARY HARMONY

Shortly before the beginning of the twentieth century, the principal stream of music, already made turbulent by nineteenth-century practices, underwent a radical change of direction. A number of composers began to experiment with harmonic materials and soon several new styles of music emerged. Claude Debussy was in the forefront of this movement and became the founder of a new style of music called *Impressionism.* In this style, dissonant chords are treated as consonances—as tonal groups that do not require resolution. Thus one factor of music—namely, the alternation of different degrees of harmonic tension leading to harmonic relaxation—which had been paramount for many centuries now became of limited importance.

By the end of the following decade or two, one group of composers had removed themselves even further from the concept of tonality. In fact, they abandoned the idea of tonality so completely that their music came to be called *atonal*—that is, without tonality. At about the same time, in opposition to the atonalists, another group reaffirmed the principles of tonality in their music. However, they went even further than the traditionalists had done by writing in more than one tonality within a single work. In *polytonal* music, as this is called, a melody could be in B flat major, say, and the accompaniment in D major. Still other composers emerged with individual systems; new ways of arranging melodic material, new ways of constructing chords, with superimposed fourths instead of the traditional thirds—these and other novelties became common. The most important of those new practices will be discussed in Chapter 14. Debussy's use of unresolved chords, Schoenberg's invention of the twelve-tone system, Bartók's use of expanded tonality, and the polytonality employed by Stravinsky and others—these are among the practices that will be illustrated when the music of those composers is under discussion.

The immediate result of these experiments, dating approximately from the 1930's, was a body of music that is pungent and filled with unrelieved harmonic tensions and that avoids every possible expression of sentiment and warm feeling. It is objective to an extreme degree, percussive in its effect, and alien to many of its listeners. Out of these experiments, however, came a concept of tonality that went far beyond the nineteenth-century concept. A respect for consonance was restored, even though dissonance was raised to a higher level than ever before. Although the old distinctions among major, minor, and chromatic scales lost their force, the new music employed the twelve tones of the chromatic scale freely, both vertically and horizontally. Thus, the feeling of a tonal center still found a place in the new music.

One cannot yet generalize about the harmonic principles revealed in all contemporary music. The principles of chord construction, cadence formation, and scale use found in the works of one composer do not necessarily apply to those of another. In general, we may say only that a sense of tonality is usually basic to contemporary music, harmonic motion is everywhere present, and dissonance is resolved into consonance. The harmonic factor of contemporary music is a logical result of harmonic developments that began centuries ago. As such, it is worthy of being listened to with the same attention that we give to music of the Classical and Romantic periods.

Listening Suggestions

I

In the following compositions, one or more of the elements discussed in this chapter may be heard prominently in certain sections. The particular element may be isolated in each case by using the selective listening technique; and being thus heard in a musical context, it may be understood more fully.

Mozart, Symphony No. 41, C major, K. 551 ("Jupiter"), finale (ascending and descending major scales in fast tempo)
Beethoven, Violin Concerto, Op. 61, first movement (ascending scale passages in moderate tempo)
Brahms, Symphony No. 3, F major, Op. 90, finale (minor scale fragments)
Tchaikovsky, *Marche Slav,* Op. 31 (minor scale fragments)
Debussy, *Afternoon of a Faun* (chromatic scale fragments)
Schubert, *The Omnipotence* (chordal piano part)
———, *The Double* (chordal piano part)

II

Every composition written in either homophonic or polyphonic texture makes use of the element of harmony. A short composition may employ a particular harmonic type or may feature one harmonic device throughout; a longer composition is almost certain to include a variety of types and devices. The compositions suggested here are likely to include more than one type. Selective listening will allow the student to isolate one type from the others.

Bach, Prelude No. 1, C major, from *The Well-Tempered Clavier* (largely consonant chords set as arpeggios)
Beethoven, Sonata, Op. 53 ("Waldstein"), second movement (chord diffusion)
———, Symphony No. 5, C minor, Op. 67, last thirty measures of finale (reiteration of one harmony)
Chopin, Prelude, A major, Op. 28, No. 7 (consonant harmony)
Hindemith, *Mathis der Maler,* second movement (dissonant harmony)
Honegger, *Pacific 231* (dissonant harmony)
Schubert, Piano Trio, E flat, Op. 100, first movement (many modulations)
Stravinsky, *The Firebird,* Suite (mixed consonant and dissonant harmony)
Wagner, *Das Rheingold,* Prelude to Act I (static harmony)
———, *Tristan and Isolde,* Prelude to Act I (chromatic harmony)

Chapter 4

MUSICAL INSTRUMENTS

For many centuries, composers concerned themselves primarily with the human voice, the most fundamental of musical instruments. A majority of all music written before about 1600 was vocal music. We saw in Example 7 (p. 14) that a single voice covers only a small segment of the audible pitch range: a bit less than two octaves. When it is combined with three other voices of different pitch ranges, the resulting vocal quartet encompasses a range about twice as extensive, or slightly more than three octaves. The voice is, of course, capable of sustaining tones, of singing with different degrees of intensity, and even of modifying its quality to some extent, but its very nature imposes limitations upon the composer.

Even while working within these limitations, many composers found it desirable to go beyond them and exploit the characteristics of tone to the utmost. That is to say, they found it desirable to write music that went higher or lower, could be sustained longer, and could be more varied in quality than vocal music. Instruments make such music possible, and ever since the beginning of music history, instruments have been available to composers. Instrumental music existed in ancient times and played a part in the early phases of our culture, but it did not become a dominant force in the changing shape and sound of music until early in the seventeenth century. Since that time, more and more composers have concerned themselves primarily with writing for instruments. As a consequence, the relative quantity of vocal music declined even though its quality remained at a high level.

Musical instruments differ not only in quality and pitch range but also in the method of producing tone. They are commonly divided into three classes, in each of which a different method of sound production is basic: (1) *string instruments,* in which a stretched string is bowed or plucked; (2) *wind instruments,* in which an enclosed air column is blown into or across; (3) *percussion instruments,* in which a membrane, metal rod, resonant block, or disc is struck. In each case, the bowing or plucking, blowing, and striking causes the corresponding object to vibrate, and this vibration, transmitted by the surrounding atmosphere and transformed by the ear, results in the sensation of tone or noise, as the case may be. In addition to the three classes, there is a small mixed group of instruments whose characteristics set them somewhat apart.

The illustrations on pages 57–66 show the chief instruments of the string and wind classes, and those instruments are arranged in "families" in the chart on page 59. The correspondences between the instruments and the voice parts shown in the first column are only relative, however, for each instrument far exceeds the range of the corresponding voice. The voice usually has a range of less than two octaves, while an instrument ranges from two and one-half octaves to three or more. Thus each instrument extends both below and above the vocal part to which it is related.

String Instruments

The principal string instruments are those of the violin family. They exist in several sizes, of which the *violin*, corresponding roughly to the soprano in range, is the smallest. It has four strings, each tuned to a different pitch; each string is tuned by turning a peg, thus changing its degree of tension. The player's bow, held at right angles to the string, moves across it with the proper degree of speed and pressure, setting the string into vibration. A change in bow speed or pressure may change the width of the vibration and affect the intensity or loudness of the tone. But the pitch of the tone, determined by the rate of vibration, is not changed by means of the bow. In order to change the pitch, the string must be shortened.

This shortening is accomplished by placing a finger firmly on the string and pressing it to the fingerboard, thus preventing the portion of the string between the finger and the tuning peg from vibrating. Now, it is a fundamental law of acoustics that the shorter the string, the higher the pitch. The shortening, called *stopping,* may be done systematically by using all four fingers and shifting the hand higher or lower on the neck of the violin.

The violin has taken a dominant position in our instrumental music because of its extreme flexibility. It may be played at great speed, as well as in a vibrant, sustained style. It may soar eloquently, and it may be played in a sharp, pungent manner. The strings can be plucked (this effect is called *pizzicato*) to produce a dry, mandolin-like tone. By playing on two strings at once, two tones of different pitch can be sounded simultaneously; and by rolling the bow slightly across the strings, three- and four-tone groups can be played. Many other effects can be carried out, depending upon the manipulation of the bow. A series of tones smoothly connected by one long-drawn bow movement, a series of short, hammered tones, a succession of broad, semiconnected tones—these and many more are possible in the hands of a skilled player. Prized above all is the violin's suitability to melodies that express warmth, sentiment, and lyricism.

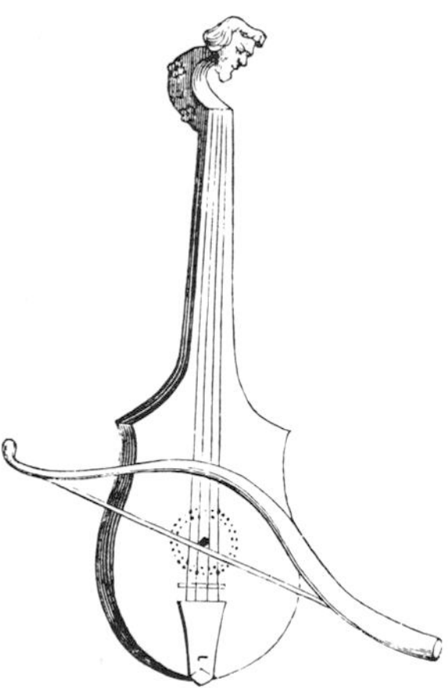

Rebec, ancestor of the modern violin.

It is a popular supposition that there is a difference between first and second violins. The instruments are identical; there is only a difference of function. Normally

The Guarneri String Quartet with Artur Rubinstein at a recording session.

the second violin plays a lower part than the first, but the player's instrument possesses the same tonal capabilities as that of the first violinist.[1]

Next in size to the violin, and only slightly larger, is the *viola.* It employs the same principle of tone production, as do all members of the violin family, and the same tonal effects are possible. The viola, however, being somewhat larger than the violin, is lower in pitch range; it corresponds roughly to the alto of the vocal quartet. Its strings are somewhat heavier as well as longer, hence its tone is a bit darker or more somber in quality. But it is capable of both fast and sustained melodic playing, and it adds a characteristic quality to the string group.[2]

[1] Prominent violin passages exist in great numbers in orchestral music, but a few characteristic passages at the beginning of the following works may be singled out: Beethoven, Symphony No. 1, last movement, and Symphony No. 3 ("Eroica"), second movement; Haydn, Symphony No. 94 ("Surprise"), second movement; Tchaikovsky, Symphony No. 4, third movement.

[2] Some of the outstanding passages for viola are found in Strauss, *Don Quixote;* Tchaikovsky, *Romeo and Juliet* and Symphony No. 6 ("Pathétique"), first movement; Beethoven, String Quartet, Op. 59, No. 3, fourth movement.

The string section of the Cleveland Symphony Orchestra. Reading clockwise from top: first violins, second violins, cellos, and violas.

Still lower in pitch range, and corresponding roughly to the vocal tenor or baritone, is the *violoncello,* or *cello,* as it is usually called. Here the increase in size is considerable—so much so that the instrument is held between the player's knees, and, by means of an extended end pin, rests on the floor. The cello is pitched eight tones lower than the viola, and has a correspondingly deeper quality. It is capable of expressing intense feeling. In sonority and flexibility of expression the cello ranks with the violin, and it is effective both in broad melodies and in resonant bass tones that support the melodies above it.[3]

The largest member of the string family is named variously the *contrabass,* the *double bass,* the *bass viol,* or the *string bass;* but among musicians it is called the *bass.* Its great size is something of a disadvantage. Not only does the player have to stand

[3] The cello is well represented in passages from the following: Beethoven, Symphony No. 5, second movement; Brahms, Symphony No. 3, third movement; Mendelssohn, *Fingal's Cave,* Overture; Wagner, *Tristan and Isolde,* Prelude.

Basses of the Chicago Symphony Orchestra.

while performing (or at least sit on a high stool), but he is hampered by the sheer weight, length, and thickness of the strings.

The bass is not capable of the speed and lyricism possible with its smaller relatives. The heavy strings are relatively slow in responding to the pressure of the bow; hence the same speed of playing is difficult to achieve. The large distances that the player's hand must cover to play an extended melody further cut down the flexibility of expression. But in compensation the bass is capable of a resonant tone that suits it ideally to its principal function—that of providing a solid tonal foundation above which the other string instruments may play speedily, eloquently, or dramatically, as the music requires. The bass is often used in connection with the cello; the two instruments then play the same passage eight tones apart, to lend a doubled bass sonority to the tonal mass.[4]

FRETTED INSTRUMENTS

Another group of string instruments (but not a family) differs in several respects from those of the violin family. The lute and the guitar are the most important representatives of the group. The bodies of the instruments are of various shapes: some, such as the lute, are elliptical (see the illustration on p. 105); others, such as the guitar, are shaped somewhat like the figure 8. Further, the tops of these instruments are virtually flat, while the backs may be gourd-shaped (such as the lute) or flat (such as the guitar). The fingerboards of the instruments are equipped with a number of thin bars or wires set at right angles to the strings. The *frets,* as the bars are called, are placed at half-step intervals and serve to indicate to the performer where his fingers should be placed in stopping the strings. The instruments are played by plucking the strings with the fingers or a pick (plectrum).

[4] Among many passages in which cello and bass are doubled in this fashion are those found in: Beethoven, Symphony No. 5, third movement, trio; Schubert, Symphony No. 8 ("Unfinished"), introduction and second movement. For another type of bass passage, see Dvořák, Symphony No. 5 ("New World"), last measures of second movement.

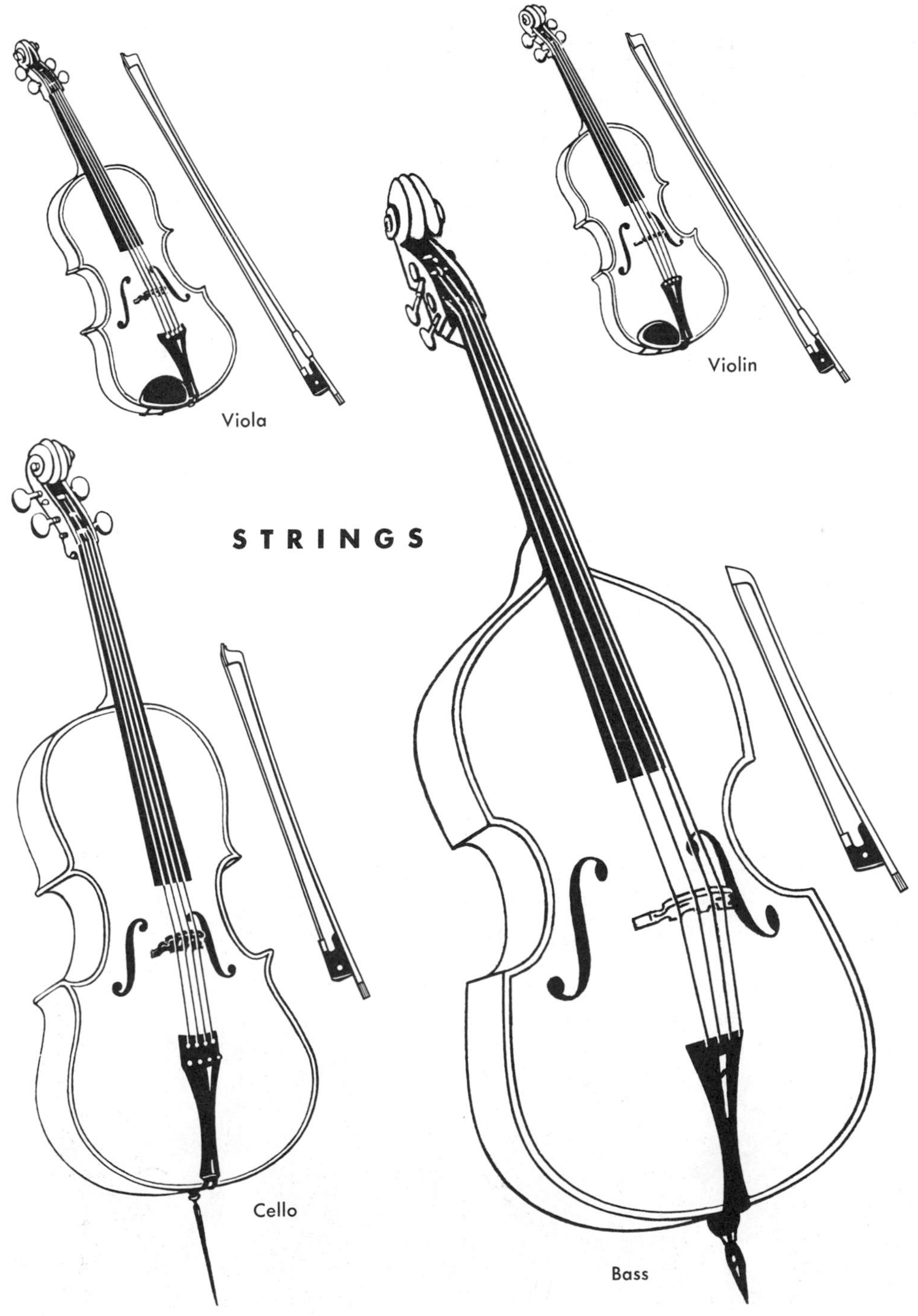
Viola
Violin
STRINGS
Cello
Bass

The lute played an important part in music of the fifteenth and sixteenth centuries. In the past few decades it has again come to the notice of performers and listeners. Although it is sometimes heard alone in sets of dances or in fantasies, for example, it is used more often to accompany songs. The guitar, too, has an ancient heritage. Used principally by Spanish and Moorish musicians during the Renaissance, it possessed a large repertoire of pieces in the smaller forms. Much of this music has been restored to the concert stage by the school of so-called "classical guitarists," and the literature has been augmented by contemporary compositions and by arrangements of earlier works composed for another instrument—for example, the Chaconne from Bach's D minor sonata for violin alone. The guitar is most widely used today as an accompanying instrument for singers of folk music, popular songs, and "rock." In the latter case it is usually electrically amplified.

Wind Instruments

The instruments of the second class are the *winds,* and here we encounter two divisions: the *woodwinds* and the *brasses.* In the woodwinds (so called because at one time all the instruments in this division were made of wood) we may distinguish three different families. In all of them a column of air confined in a tube is set into vibration by the act of blowing. The length of the tube determines the pitch of the tone produced.

Woodwinds of the New York Philharmonic. First row from left, flutes and oboes: second row, clarinets, bassoons, and contrabassoon.

Principal Instruments of the Orchestra

	Strings	Woodwinds			Brass
		Open-hole	Double-reed	Single-reed	
High soprano		Piccolo			
Soprano	Violin	Flute	Oboe	E flat clarinet	Trumpet or cornet
Alto	Viola	Alto flute (rare)	English horn	B flat clarinet	Horn
Tenor	Cello		Bassoon	Alto clarinet	Trombone
Bass	Bass		Contra-bassoon	Bass clarinet	Bass tuba

The tube contains a number of holes set at carefully calculated positions; the holes may be opened or closed by means of the player's fingertips or by means of pads operated by levers and keys placed convenient to his hands. If all the holes are closed when the instrument is blown, the air column within the tube vibrates at its full length and the instrument's lowest tone is sounded. If the hole nearest the lower end is opened, the tube is in effect shortened by the distance of that hole from the end, and a higher tone is sounded. A similar method operates throughout the entire tonal range; a systematic closing or opening of the holes alters the effective length of the air column, thus producing a large number of different pitches.

OPEN-HOLE WOODWINDS

The three families of woodwinds differ in the manner by which they are blown and in the device used to set the air column into vibration. In the *flute,* the upper end of the tube (that is, the end nearest the player) is sealed. A few inches from that end is a hole surmounted by a curved plate. The player blows across this plate and directs the stream of air so that it is split by the sharp edge of the hole opposite his lips; the process is similar to that used to produce a tone in a narrow-necked bottle. This stream of air under pressure vibrates within the tube in a complex manner. The end result is a tone whose pitch is determined by the position of the player's fingers. Modern flutes are almost always made of metal; a wooden flute today is a decided rarity.

The flute is held horizontally from the player's lips and off to his right. It can be played with extreme speed, and its tone is clear and limpid, ranging from "velvety" in its lowest register (that is, the lowest portion of its range) to piercingly sweet in its highest. The instrument corresponds to a soprano in range.

The flute has a relative, called the *piccolo* (simply a small flute), about half its size. The piccolo produces the highest tones in the orchestra, and its upper limit is very close to the upper limit of the piano. Larger flutes exist also, but they are rarely used. Thus the flute family is not represented in the four ranges (soprano to bass), as is the string family.[5]

The flute in its present form is a product of the late seventeenth century. It was preceded by an instrument known as the *recorder* (*block flute* or *fipple flute* are other names). In the recorder, a wooden block or fipple is inserted in the upper end of the tube, almost obstructing it. The player, blowing into the end of the vertically held instrument, directs the stream of air past the block, where it is compressed, toward a sharp edge. There the air is set into vibration. The resultant tone resembles that of the flute in quality, except that it has none of the brilliance and volume of that instrument. Recorders exist in several sizes from the sopranino, whose lowest tone is an octave above middle C, to the bass, which is actually in the tenor range. The instrument, made of wood, has at the most one key. It is capable, nevertheless, of playing the full chromatic scale across a two-octave range.

In the Renaissance and Baroque periods, ensembles of recorders were widely employed in chamber music. Sonatas and other works for one or two recorders and harpsichord were composed by many eminent composers of the early eighteenth century, and in many orchestral suites of the time the term *flauto* ("flute") referred to the recorder. The flute, if required, was designated by the term *flauto traverso,* or "transverse flute." In recent years, with the revival of interest in Baroque and earlier music, recorders have again come into their own (see the illustration on p. 105) as solo and ensemble instruments, and as accompaniment to small choral groups.

DOUBLE-REED WOODWINDS

The full quartet is found in the oboe or double-reed family. The *oboe* is the highest of the quartet. Here the tone is produced not directly by the player's lips but by two thin vibrating reeds made of bamboo. The reeds are less than a quarter of an inch wide, scarcely an inch and a half long, and are scraped to paper thinness at their upper end. They are bound together at their lower end and tied to a short metal tube, which is inserted into the upper end of the oboe. The tone that results from the reeds' vibration is nasal, often pungent in quality. The instrument can be played very softly as well as with a loud, penetrating tone. It is capable of considerable tonal variety and is especially effective in poignant, intense melodies. These characteristics make it one of the most valuable members of the orchestra.[6]

Next larger than the oboe is the *English horn,* essentially the alto of the double-reed family. Because of the instrument's greater size, the tube to which the reed is attached is bent slightly, so that the player's arms need not be stretched out uncomfortably before him. At one time in its history, the instrument itself was curved or bent near its mid-point; then it was called, in French, the *cor anglé,* meaning "angled horn."

[5] The flute is prominent in the following: Brahms, Symphony No. 4, last movement; Debussy, *Afternoon of a Faun;* Smetana, *The Moldau.* The piccolo may be heard in Sousa, *Stars and Stripes Forever;* Beethoven, Symphony No. 5, last movement, near the end.

[6] Typical oboe passages are found in the following: Beethoven, Symphony No. 3 ("Eroica"), second movement; Symphony No. 5, cadenza in first movement; Symphony No. 7, introduction and first movement; also, Tchaikovsky, Symphony No. 4, second movement.

Flute

Piccolo

WOODWINDS

Oboe

English horn

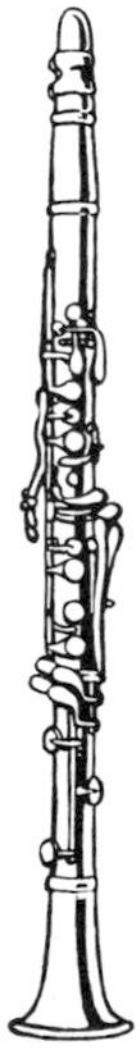

Bass clarinet

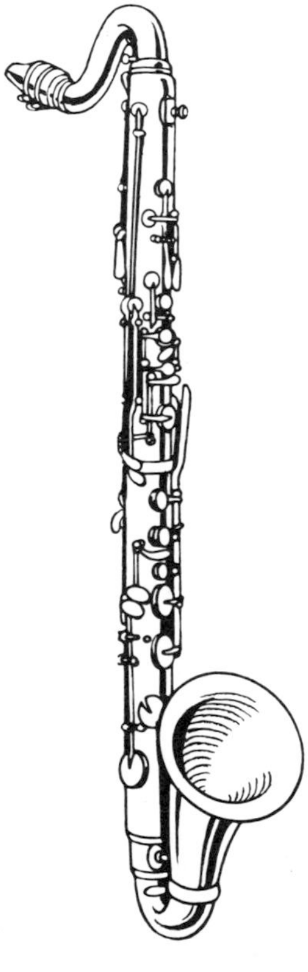

Clarinet

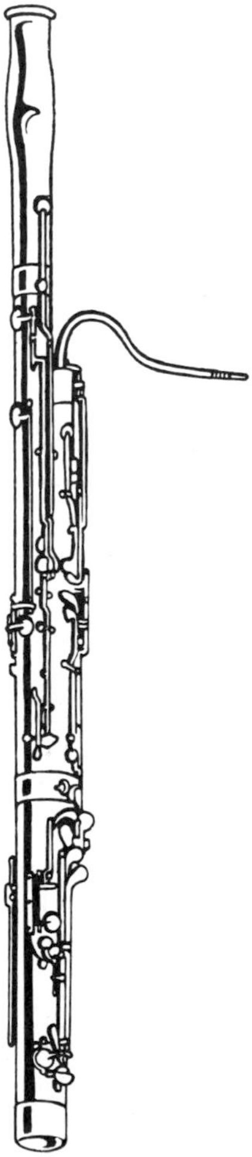

Bassoon

Contrabassoon

This was sometimes written (with the same pronunciation) *cor Anglais,* whence by translation the term "English horn." The instrument has much of the nasal quality of the oboe, but in addition it can suggest melancholy or nostalgic states; it is often used for pastoral tunes. What it lacks in flexibility it makes up for in distinctive tone quality.[7]

The tenor of the double-reed family is the *bassoon.* Here, because of its great length, the tube is bent back upon itself, so that the instrument resembles two tubes held side by side. In addition, the small metal tube to which the oboe reed is fastened has in the bassoon become a foot-long tube shaped like a question mark. The reed, too, is correspondingly larger—almost half an inch wide and two inches long. But in tone-producing principle, the bassoon is like the oboe. Flexibility of expression is still within the bassoon's capabilities, along with a dry utterance in the upper register and a somber or foreboding quality in the lowest tones. The bassoon, because of its great range and ability to leap easily from one part of the range to another, is one of the most useful instruments in the orchestra. It is used in melodies, in accompaniments, and as a provider of fundamental bass tones as well.[8]

The lowest and most ponderous member of the double-reed family is the *contra-bassoon;* its wood-and-metal tube is doubly bent upon itself, so that it is bulky rather than long. Pitched an entire octave below the bassoon, it is at its best in sustained tones near the very bottom of the orchestral range. It has the power to be felt as much as heard, so close to a floor-shaking rumble are its lowest tones. It is not much given to rapid playing and sounds somewhat pathetic in its attempts to play melody. But since it can blend equally well with string and wind tone, it serves the function of providing a resonant bass for other sections of the orchestra.[9]

SINGLE-REED WOODWINDS

There is still another family of woodwinds, the clarinet family—this time with a single reed acting as tone-producing device. In the *clarinet,* the reed is a flat piece of bamboo roughly half an inch wide and almost three inches long; this is attached at its lower end to the instrument's mouthpiece. As in the oboe family, the upper third of the reed is set in motion by the player's breath. A system of holes, pads, and levers similar to that on the other woodwinds makes pitch changes possible.

The clarinet exists in several sizes, of which four are in general use. The most common is the clarinet in B flat (see Appendix IV), the mainstay of the band and the most usual representative of the family in the orchestra. A close companion is

[7]The English horn is featured in the following works: Dvořák, Symphony No. 5 ("New World"), second movement; Franck, Symphony, second movement; Rossini, *William Tell,* Overture; Tchaikovsky, *Romeo and Juliet.*

[8]For typical bassoon passages, one may turn to the following: Rimsky-Korsakov, *Scheherazade,* second movement; Tchaikovsky, Symphony No. 4, second movement, Symphony No. 5, third movement, and Symphony No. 6, introduction.

[9]The contrabassoon is heard prominently in the following works: Beethoven, Symphony No. 5, last movement; Brahms, Symphony No. 1, first and last movements, and *Academic Festival,* Overture.

the slightly larger clarinet in A. The clarinet has a larger range than any other woodwind instrument—so much so that the B flat clarinet embraces the range of both soprano and alto. It is capable of tones that range from mere whispers to raucous shouts. It is nearly as flexible as the flute and possesses a variety of tone qualities. In its lowest register it is dark, brooding, or mellow; in the middle it can play with a variety of tonal effects; and nearer the top it tends to become strident or pinched. For easily flowing lyric expression and for general versatility, the clarinet has few superiors.[10]

Smaller than the B flat clarinet is the high clarinet in E flat. Its tone is rather shrill and lacks the variety of its larger relatives. It is used mainly in large orchestral works such as Strauss's *Till Eulenspiegel,* where its part expresses sardonic humor and caricature. The *alto clarinet,* also in E flat but an octave lower than the instrument just mentioned, is really in the tenor range. It is used mainly in the band, where its sonorous and slightly nasal voice adds richness to the middle parts of the ensemble. Its lower relative, the *bass clarinet* in B flat, finds employment in the band also, but since the time of Wagner it has been a valued member of the orchestra as well. Capable of more softness than the bassoon and having an effective range nearly as great, it is useful in supplying a bass voice in quiet woodwind passages, in carrying somber or mysterious melodies, and in filling out the resonance of the entire woodwind choir.

The *saxophones,* another group of wind instruments, are related to the clarinet in method of tone production; the beak-shaped mouthpiece and the single reed are used in both families. In other respects the saxophone is unlike the clarinet: its body is a widely flaring conical tube, and (except for the smallest size) its lower end is bent into a U-shape and its upper end into the shape of a gooseneck.

Saxophones were invented and produced by Adolphe Sax in Brussels about 1840. They are found in a variety of sizes from the smallest, the sopranino in E flat, to the largest, the bass in B flat. Each instrument has a range of about two and a half octaves. Saxophones were designed by their inventor to be used in military bands; in France and Italy the instruments found a quick foothold. The saxophone was used in a few operas near the middle of the century, and Bizet employed it in his incidental music to *L'Arlésienne.* A repertoire of concertos, sonatas, and the like has gradually built up in recent years, and the saxophone is sometimes heard as a serious concert instrument. Its widest use, however, is in concert bands, marching bands, and dance orchestras.

BRASSES

We come now to the second large division of winds, the brass instruments. Even though a variety of metals go into their manufacture, and the five instruments represented differ acoustically in several respects, it is customary to refer to them as one family.

[10] Outstanding clarinet passages are found in the following works: Brahms, Symphony No. 1, second movement; Rimsky-Korsakov, *Scheherazade,* second movement; Schubert, Symphony No. 8 ("Unfinished"), second movement; Weber, *Der Freischütz,* Overture.

Here again we are concerned with a column of air enclosed in a tube. But now, in place of a reed, as in the oboe and clarinet families, or an open hole, as in the flute, there is a cup-shaped mouthpiece. The player, blowing into this mouthpiece, allows his lips to vibrate; thus the air in the column is set into motion, giving rise to a tone.

Brass instruments have another characteristic that sets them apart from the woodwinds. The extreme length of the tube in relation to its diameter makes the air column relatively unstable. Consequently, not only can a player cause the column to vibrate in its entirety, but he can split it into a regular series of fractional vibrations. That is to say, he can sound not only the tone determined by the over-all length of the tube, as he does on a woodwind, but also a series of higher tones that are the result of the column vibrating in fractional lengths.

This can be demonstrated most clearly on a *bugle.* Imagine a bugle that in its total length produces the tone C (this is known as its *fundamental tone;* see p. 71). The player, by *overblowing*—that is, by forcing air under higher compression into the tube and changing the angle of his lips slightly—can produce a series of higher tones also. Example 34 gives the first seven tones of the series that it is possible to produce in this manner.

Such higher tones are known as *overtones,* or *harmonics;* and the entire series, of which Example 34 gives only the lower portion, is the *overtone series.* These tones are

Example 34

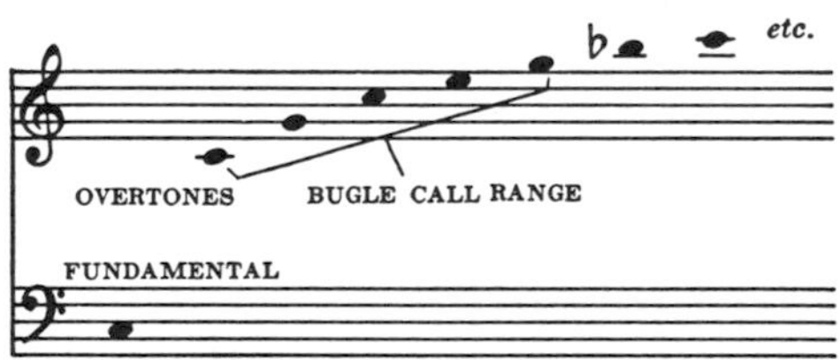

Brasses of the New York Philharmonic. First row, horns; second row from left, trumpets, trombones and tuba.

responsible for the melodic contour of all the standard military bugle calls, for such calls are composed of melodic alternations of the first few overtones in the series—nothing more. A comparison of the tones of "Taps," "Reveille," and "Mess Call," for example, with the tones enclosed by the brace in Example 34 clearly illustrates the point.

Modern brass instruments are similar to the bugle except in one important respect. In the *trumpet, French horn, tuba,* and several other instruments, short lengths of tubing together with devices called *valves* are attached to the main tubing at a point near the mouthpiece. With the valves open, the original series of tones (fundamental and overtones) can still be played, as on the bugle. When one of the valves is depressed, the stream of air is detoured into the short tube attached to the valve, and the whole instrument in effect becomes appreciably longer. As a consequence, the pitch of the fundamental and of each overtone is lowered to correspond to the amount of lengthening.

The majority of brass instruments are equipped with three such valves capable of lengthening the main tubing (and lowering the pitch of any overtone) by a half step, a whole step, and a step and a half, respectively. The three valves, used singly or in combination, thus make it possible to play all the tones that lie between one overtone and the next lower one. Through the right choice of valves and the right amount of overblowing, the player can perform the full scale of tones.

The soprano of the brass family is the *trumpet,* usually with B flat as its fundamental tone. A companion of exactly the same range is the *cornet.* Slight differences in the taper of the tube (the first is cylindrical, the second conical, through much of its length) cause differences in the tone quality of each instrument, and both are called for by many composers of large orchestral and band works. The instruments not only possess the stentorian "brassy" tone that is all too familiar but are also capable of sensitive expression, of extreme flexibility in level of intensity, and of smooth melody playing.[11]

Next in size is the *horn* (often called *French horn*), pitched usually in F. The horn embraces both the alto and tenor ranges, and can be used for soulful and romantic melody playing as well as for brilliant fanfares and all manner of accompaniments. It is one of the most eloquent instruments, one of the most versatile, and one of the most difficult to play.[12]

The *trombone,* next in size, employs a mechanical principle different from that of the trumpet and horn, although its method of tone production is identical to theirs. Instead of valves, it has a U-shaped slide of tubing that fits over two sections of the bent main tube (see the illustration, p. 66). With the slide in its closed position, the trombone produces the fundamental and overtone series of B flat. The slide can then

[11] Exposed passages for trumpet or cornet may be found in the following: Beethoven, *Leonore,* Overture No. 3; Debussy, *Fêtes;* Franck, Symphony, last movement; Strauss; *Ein Heldenleben.*

[12] Most symphonic works since Beethoven include rich horn parts. For a few examples, see: Brahms, Symphony No. 3, third movement; Dvořák, Symphony No. 5 ("New World"), first and last movements; Strauss, *Till Eulenspiegel's Merry Pranks;* Tchaikovsky, Symphony No. 5, second movement.

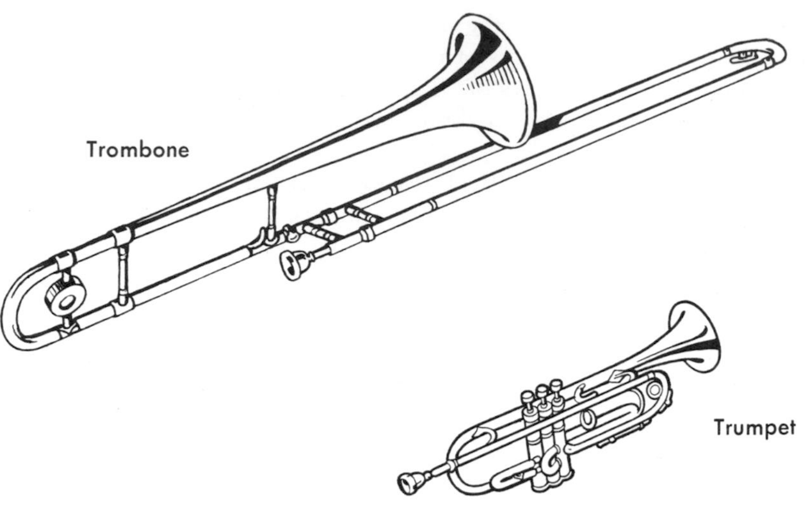
Trombone
Trumpet

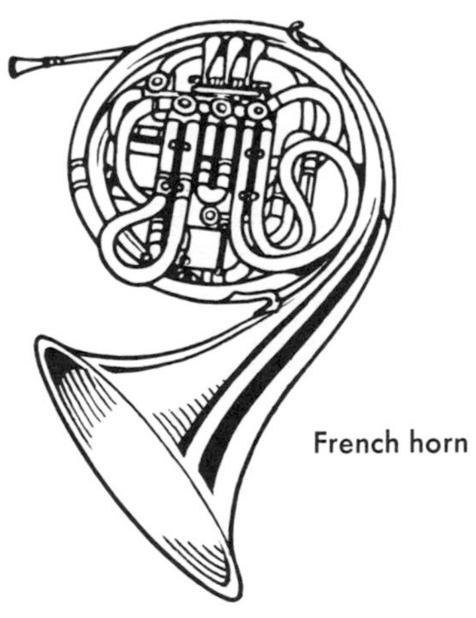
French horn

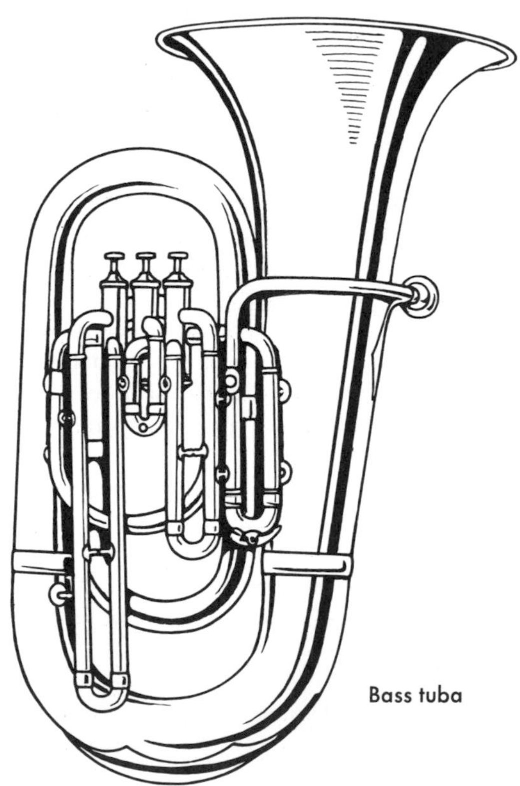
Bass tuba

BRASSES

be pulled out to lengthen the tube, and a series of fundamentals from A down to the E below can be produced. The overtone series of each fundamental follows suit, of course; thus the instrument has no need of valves to play the complete scale. This instrument is capable of dignified and powerful expression, along with a variety of blasting effects. Although the trombone is often reserved for the climactic moments of a composition, it is equally useful in quiet, sustained passages, where it blends well with the other brass instruments.[13]

The bass of the family is the *bass tuba,* or simply *tuba,* pitched variously in F, C, and low (or *double*) B flat. Here again the system of valves is employed to give this large instrument a full scale of tones. Great wind pressure is required to play the tuba, and the size of its air column causes difficulties in playing fast or in skipping from one register to another. The tuba is best employed to provide a solid foundation for the other brass instruments or for the full orchestra.[14]

Since the tuba can be carried only with difficulty and cannot be employed in a marching band, it is often replaced by another instrument of similar musical qualities but of different shape: the *sousaphone.* The tubing of this instrument is formed into a helical or circular shape, so that the sousaphone can be placed over the player's shoulder for purposes of marching.

Percussion Instruments

The third principal class of instruments is composed of the various drums, gongs, cymbals, chimes, and tuned blocks known collectively as percussion instruments. In the *bass drum* two membranes called *drumheads* are stretched across the ends of a wide but short wooden cylinder which is placed on its side. The drumhead is struck with a soft beater to produce a noise rather than a tone of definite pitch. The bass drum is used primarily to supply accents.

Somewhat similar in construction is the smaller *snare drum,* except that this instrument is placed on one end, and a pair of sticks, with which the player can produce a great variety of rhythmic effects, is used on the exposed drumhead. The snare drum also includes a set of cords, which lie parallel to each other just beneath the lower drumhead. These cords, called *snares,* may be brought in contact with the drumhead to produce the well-known rattle or "snarl" that is characteristic of this instrument.

The *tympani* or *kettledrums* are usually used in pairs or in sets of threes. Each one has a kettle-shaped metal body across the top of which a single drumhead is attached. Tympani are unique among drums in that they produce tones of definite pitch, and they can be tuned (by changing the tension of the drumhead) across the span of four

[13]For typical trombone passages, the following are noteworthy: Brahms, Symphony No. 1, last movement; Ravel, *Bolero;* Rimsky-Korsakov, *Russian Easter,* Overture; Wagner, *Tannhäuser,* Overture.

[14]The tuba probably plays fewer exposed passages than any other brass instrument in the orchestra. Its resonant voice may be singled out in the following: Mendelssohn, *A Midsummer Night's Dream,* Overture; Strauss, *Ein Heldenleben,* second section; Stravinsky, *Petrouchka;* Wagner, *Die Meistersinger,* Prelude.

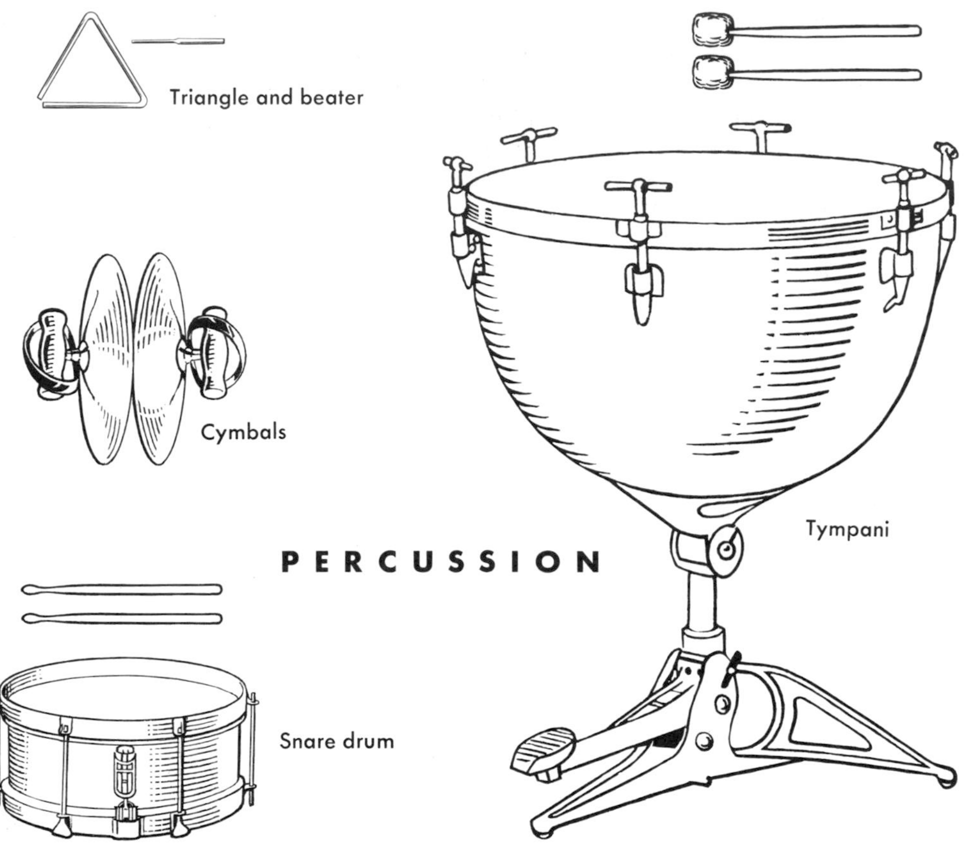

or five tones. Since a larger and a smaller drum constitute a pair, a range of about eight tones becomes possible. Tympani are used not only to supply accents, but also to provide bass tones for other instrumental groups in the orchestra. They are capable of being played very softly and can also bring forth a thunderous noise.[15]

A number of small percussion instruments—notably the *gong, cymbal, triangle,* and *tambourine*—have the function of providing accent or of supplying a rhythmic accompaniment for the rest of the ensemble. These instruments are most effective when sparingly used; consequently they are usually reserved for climactic points in the music, where they add immeasurably to the sonority of the whole.[16]

In one type of percussion instrument a set of resonant blocks, each tuned to a definite pitch, is laid out in the manner of a piano keyboard. These blocks are struck with small mallets; thus, melodies can be played on them, as well as chords and a

[15] Unusual examples of writing for tympani are found in the following: Beethoven, Violin Concerto, first movement, and Symphony No. 9, second movement; Sibelius, Symphony No. 1, introduction; Tchaikovsky, Symphony No. 4, first movement.

[16] However, they are not always reserved for climactic points; see Rimsky-Korsakov, *Capriccio Espagnol,* fourth movement.

variety of tonal effects. When made of hardwood blocks, the instrument is called the *xylophone.* Another instrument of the same type, but with high-pitched bars of metal, is the *glockenspiel.* The *celesta* is similar to the glockenspiel, except that it is supplied with a short piano keyboard and is enclosed in a case something like that of the old-fashioned parlor organ.

Many other percussion instruments exist. Various kinds of *tubular chimes,* each chime tuned to a definite pitch, are often employed. Sometimes in place of such chimes, flat bars of metal are used. Whistles, hollow wooden blocks, sheets of metal, chains, and even typewriters have been employed by composers to give variety and color to their compositions.

Independent Instruments

There remain the instruments that cannot easily be placed in the string, wind, or percussion classification. The *piano* is an outstanding example. It contains stretched strings, but the tone is produced by striking the strings with a hammer actuated by a key under the player's finger. It is obviously neither a string instrument of the violin type, nor a percussion instrument related to the xylophone. It remains outside the three classifications.

The *harpsichord,* too, is in a separate category. It usually resembles a small grand piano in its general outlines and, like the piano, it has a number of stretched strings that give it a range of several octaves (four to six, according to the date of the instrument). Unlike the piano, however, the harpsichord does not contain hammers; a

The percussion section of the New York Philharmonic. Top: tympani; center: xylophone and snare drum; bottom: bass drum and cymbals.

Two-manual harpsichord from the middle of the seventeenth century, showing the elaborate case typical of the time.

plectrum or quill attached to an upright "jack" plucks the string when the key is depressed, and the string is set into vibration. A system of "stops" or registers is employed. One stop, for example, causes the key to sound a tone an octave higher than normal; another stop brings into play a separate row of jacks equipped with quills made of softer material than the other quills, thus producing a different quality of tone. Larger harpsichords with two keyboards or *manuals* also exist; these have a greater number of stops (four-foot, eight-foot, lute stop, and so on) and a greater variety of tone colors.

The harpsichord was a favored instrument for over two centuries until about the middle of the eighteenth century. At that time the piano came into general use and drove the harpsichord into the background. In recent decades, however, the renewed interest in music of the Baroque period has brought the instrument back into public view. It is often heard in concerts of Baroque music, and it has also begun to acquire a small repertoire of contemporary works.

The *pipe organ* is another instrument that, because of its construction and method of playing, can scarcely be classed with conventional wind instruments. It contains hundreds of pipes of fixed length and various types (metal, wood, open, closed, etc.) into which air is forced under pressure; to that extent it is a wind instrument. But the player operates a keyboard to direct the air stream into one or more of the pipes, and he is powerless to alter the pitch or quality of the tone pre-established by the individual nature and dimensions of those pipes.

Similarly, the playing technique of the *harp* has little in common with that of the familiar string instruments. Each string, for example, is capable only of three different pitches; these are produced by a complex system of pedals that lengthen or shorten the strings by a half step. Further, the strings themselves are always plucked; the harpist, of course, does not use a bow as the violinist does.

Finally, there are the various electronic organs, in which electrically produced tones are amplified to bring them into the range of human hearing. These must likewise be considered as not belonging to the three major classes.

Now, these instruments—piano, harpsichord, organ, harp, and electronic organ—are also unique in another sense. On them one may play several melodies simultaneously, or a melody and a set of supporting chords. Thus they virtually duplicate the function of an orchestra. In addition, their ranges (each one embraces several octaves) come close to or exceed the range of the orchestra. Such instruments are truly independent; they can bring forth great quantities of tone. Thus they are complete in themselves; the members of the violin family, with their ability to play two or three tones simultaneously, approach this condition only in small part.

Tone Quality

We must finally consider the reasons why instruments differ so markedly in tone quality; and here we must look into the field of *acoustics,* the science of sound. One of the fundamental laws of acoustics is this: a stretched string vibrates not only in its over-all length to produce its fundamental tone, but also in regular fractions of that length. Even while it is vibrating as a whole, it is also vibrating in halves, thirds, fourths, fifths, or smaller fractions of that length. Each of these fractional or partial vibrations produces a tone faintly heard in its own right. The tones thus produced are called *overtones,* and normally the fundamental along with the whole series of overtones sound simultaneously. The same phenomenon is true of an enclosed column of air, such as is found in the tube of a wind instrument.

In the brass family, however, a special condition applies—namely, that each of the overtones at the lower end of the series can also be sounded separately. This condition was discussed in connection with the bugle earlier in this chapter, and Example 34 (p. 64) showed the tones so produced. A related effect can be produced on string instruments by touching a string lightly at the appropriate point—one half its length, or one third, or one quarter, etc. The corresponding overtone will then sound when the string is bowed. These special conditions, however, do not change the fact that the overtones and fundamental normally sound simultaneously.

Top to bottom: clavicembalum, lyre, clavicitherium, instruments of the early 16th century.

Under those normal conditions, what we hear as a single tone is actually a compound tone made up of the fundamental and several overtones sounding together. In various tone-producing bodies the relative loudness of each of these tone components may be different, and this accounts for the differences in quality between one instrument and another. Imagine a mixture of several flavoring ingredients: salt, lemon, catsup, and tabasco sauce, for example. The relative amount of any one

Andrés Segovia (b. 1893), who has led the way in reviving the classical guitar.

of these may be altered, and a distinct difference in the compound flavor results. By applying this analogy to a compound tone, we may see why tone quality differs from one instrument to another.

Imagine, for example, that the intensity or degree of loudness of the second to the fifth overtones is considerably greater than those higher in the overtone series; the resulting tone will resemble that of a violin. Or if the first overtone sounds out strongly and the upper overtones are almost silent, the tone of a flute will be approached. Or again, if the overtones above the seventh are stronger than those lower in the series, the characteristic tone of a clarinet is heard.

Referring back to the musical instruments themselves, we can now point out some important facts. The method by which a tone is produced (whether bowed, plucked, blown, etc.) greatly affects the resulting tone quality. In addition, the physical shape of the instrument is equally important in determining what the overtone pattern (and hence the tone quality) will be when the instrument is sounded. The shape of a violin (roughly that of a figure 8) produces a particular overtone pattern; it was developed, experimentally in all likelihood, in order to achieve a particular tone quality. This is likewise true of the cylindrical tube of a flute, the conical tube of an oboe, and the parabolic curve of a kettledrum. In each case, the physical shape of the instrument affects the shape of the atmospheric wave, the relative strength of the overtones within that wave, and the tone quality that the wave gives rise to.

If the arching of a violin were a bit higher, if the flare in the lower joint of a clarinet were a bit wider, or if the mouthpiece of a trumpet were a bit deeper—then the tone quality of each instrument would be modified accordingly. It is in this field that science and art come close together. Long experimenting with instruments on the basis of acoustical laws has led to the development of tone qualities that are aesthetically satisfying.

Listening Suggestions

The compositions referred to in the footnotes of this chapter are extended works in which particular instruments are heard prominently at one time or another. Below are listed other compositions so constructed that a number of instruments are featured singly within a relatively short time span. Such compositions make it possible for the listener to apply the selective listening process to instruments in concentrated fashion, and thus to become familiar more quickly with the tone qualities found in the orchestra.

Britten, *The Young Person's Guide to the Orchestra,* Op. 34.
Dohnányi, Suite for Orchestra, Op. 19
Prokofiev, *Peter and the Wolf,* Op. 67
Ravel, *Bolero*
Rimsky-Korsakov, *Capriccio Espagnol,* Op. 34
Schubert, Octet, F major, Op. 166, fourth movement
Tchaikovsky, *The Nutcracker,* Suite, Op. 71

Chapter 5

THE STRUCTURE OF MUSIC

Up to this point, we have been concerned mostly with taking music apart. We have examined various kinds of melodies, harmonies, and rhythms; we have seen how musical textures are created; and we have gained an idea of the instruments and instrumental combinations that are used most frequently in musical compositions. Now we shall reverse that process; we shall learn how a composer takes the isolated elements and combines them to create a piece of music.

It is safe to assume that a composer probably does not begin to write unless he has a musical or emotional or psychological purpose. He may wish to set a particular text to music; he may wish to translate into sound some emotional experience he has had; or he may wish simply to deal with tonal material in an abstract way—to manipulate it, or to fill out a particular design he has in mind.

Before he begins to write, it is likely that the composer will have a number of musical ideas—ideas suggested by the very nature of the musical material. The idea may take the shape of a rhythmic pattern that appeals to his imagination: Rachmaninoff's Prelude in G minor grew out of the pattern seen in Example 35*a*, for example, and Beethoven's Symphony No. 7 has the patterns shown in Examples 35*b* and 35*c* as the bases of two of its movements. The idea may be a melodic fragment, such as that in Example 35*d*, which Brahms used in his Symphony No. 2, or that in Example 35*e*, which is the nucleus for Liszt's *Les Préludes*. Similarly, the musical idea may be a series of chords, a particular tone color heard in the imagination, or one of many other musical entities. Thus, the composer may be expected to have a purpose and a number of musical ideas even before he begins to write.

Immediately he will come face to face with one of the most challenging of artistic problems: how to organize these ideas into a composition. Such organizing is necessary for a number of reasons, among them the following: the ideas must be related

Example 35

to each other if the composition is to have any artistic unity; those relationships must be grasped by the potential listener if the composition is to be satisfying; the presentation must avoid both monotony and excessive variety; and the end result must appeal to the sense of order that resides in the human mind.

In organizing the musical material to satisfy these requirements, the composer creates a musical form. It is within such a form that he solves the artistic problems we are concerned with here. In a real sense, the music is the form. The form provides the means by which the musical ideas may be worked over and expressed adequately. And the listener's perception of the form enables him to judge the composer's craftsmanship, his ideas, and the extent to which he has accomplished his musical purpose.

Now, musical form is not to be thought of as a rigid mold or series of molds into which the composer pours his materials. It is as flexible and free as he wishes to make it; in this sense it is like form in the other arts. For example, we are likely to know what is meant by a short story, or by a colonial house. But how many characters, or how many paragraphs, or how many episodes constitute a short story? And how many rooms, arranged in what plan, should be in the house? As many as the creator—writer or architect—finds necessary for his purposes. As many as suit the quantity and nature of the material he has available.

So it is with musical forms. Each has certain characteristics that distinguish it from other forms. But in each case the inner organization of details, the use or avoidance of certain features, is entirely subject to the composer's wish. That wish, it may be pointed out here, is not likely to be an arbitrary one if the composer knows his craft. It is far more likely to be determined by the nature and quantity of the musical material he is working with. In other words, the music dictates the form.

It is customary, in writing about musical form, to make use of schematic diagrams or to employ letters to symbolize the various form sections; for example, a specific form may be said to have an ABACA pattern. Such procedures are justified, in a sense, for they clarify a composition's inner relationships. But they also carry with them the danger of creating an impression of rigidity, as though the parts of a form were standardized and inflexible. When we see diagrams of that sort—in this book and elsewhere—we must keep this admonition in mind: a particular diagram may be right for an individual composition, but only in the most general sense will it be right for all the works of the type it represents.

Organizing Principles

Within these limits, then, and with the awareness that compositions that are similar in their larger parts may vary considerably in their inner details, musical forms can be classified. This becomes possible because virtually all such forms have resulted from the application and interaction of five organizing principles—*repetition, contrast, symmetry, variation,* and *development.* These principles have underlain the structure of Western music during the nineteen centuries of its existence; employed singly or in combination, they were at work in the plainsong of the early Christian church and are still potent today. The composer applies them in manipulating, combining, and organizing his musical material; the result is the musical form.

REPETITION

The most useful and easily recognized of the five principles is simple repetition, illustrated in Example 36. In Example 36*a,* the melodic fragment that is repeated is one measure long; in Example 36*b,* it is two measures long; and in Example 36*c,* four

Example 36

measures long. Repetition may extend across a span longer than four measures, as it does in *The Star-Spangled Banner.* Here the melody that is repeated is eight measures long, set to the following lines:

> Oh say, can you see by the dawn's early light,
> What so proudly we hailed at the twilight's last gleaming?

and the repetition of that melody carries the text,

> Whose broad stripes and bright stars through the perilous fight,
> O'er the ramparts we watched were so gallantly streaming?

There are innumerable compositions in which long or short portions are repeated exactly. Virtually every march includes four to eight lengthy melodies, each of which is usually repeated. Forms we shall later come to know under the names *minuet* and *scherzo* contain long repeated sections; the principle of repetition is found at work in many other forms as well.

In a musical sense, repetition need not always be exact. Unessential changes in contour, rhythm, orchestration, or other factors are to be expected. The last few measures of a repeated section are especially likely to be different from the corresponding measures of the original section, if only because the repetition progresses to a different cadence than the original does. In compositions in which imitative texture (see p. 22) is characteristic, a repeated section may contain a new disposition of the imitating voices—different enough so that variety is assured, but not so different that the total effect or intent of the repetition is new. All such examples may be grouped under the term "modified repetition," for there is little likelihood that they will fail to be recognized as containing material heard earlier.

Another kind of repetition, which is neither exact nor modified, is called "sequence repetition." In this type a short melodic figure, perhaps a measure or two in length, is repeated several times, but each time on a different scale step. The well-known "Morning" from Grieg's *Peer Gynt* Suite No. 1 is one outstanding example (see Example 79, p. 220), as is the "Anvil" Chorus from Verdi's opera *Il Trovatore* (see Example 29*a*, p. 44); and sequence repetition is seen in Example 42 (pp. 82–83) at measures 35–41.

CONTRAST

The composer introduces contrasting material in order to provide more variety than modified repetition permits. In doing so, he must see to it that the new material differs in some important aspect from the old—for example, in melodic contour, mood content, loudness level, tonality, texture, or relative speed. Example 37 contains three fragments that illustrate short-range contrast. In Example 37*a*, the syllables "ee-i, ee-i, oh" interrupt the narrative flow of the text and thus provide a contrast; Example 37*b* illustrates contrast of loudness level, in that the soft passages gives way to a sudden loud section; and Example 37*c* illustrates not only a loud-soft contrast but also a sudden change from forceful to lyric expression.

The fragments in Example 37 illustrate contrast in extremely small dimension; but just as in the case of repetition, the principle of contrast plays an even more important part across longer time spans. It appears most often in larger forms that are mentioned here, but that will be discussed more fully in later chapters after the remaining organizing principles have been illustrated. Among such forms is the *recitative* and *aria* pair, found most often in opera and oratorio; here the recitative presents a section of text in a style that imitates to some extent the prose rhythm of the speaking voice, while the

Example 37

aria is concerned with a contrasting text sung in lyric, poetic, or dramatic fashion. Another is the *prelude* and *fugue* pair, found often in the works of Bach. In the *sonata-form* with its complex of melodic material, one melodic group is likely to be dramatic or brusque, another lyric or suave.

SYMMETRY

Like the two foregoing principles, symmetry may be illustrated first in small dimension. Symmetry results from the union of the principles of repetition and contrast. For example, two repeated fragments or sections may be separated by a contrasting one, as in the form ABA. In this form, symmetry finds wide application in all the arts, of course. A pair of matching windows on either side of a door, automobile headlights to the right and left of a radiator grille—such examples of symmetrical arrangement can be found on every hand, and all lend themselves to being diagrammed as ABA.

In music, however, the principle of symmetry is often extended to include AABA forms—that is, forms in which the first element is itself repeated before the contrasting member is introduced. The familiar song *Drink to Me Only with Thine Eyes* is of this type; it is shown in Example 38. Note that the melody in the first four measures is repeated exactly in the second four and in the last four, and that the contour of B (of the AABA group) is altogether different.

Example 38

The same pattern of repetition, contrast, and symmetry is found in *Oh! Susanna, It Came Upon the Midnight Clear*, and many other tunes. In each case, the second phrase is a repetition of the first, the third provides melodic contrast, and the fourth is like the first—hence the whole is symmetrical. This interaction of the basic principles of organization is by no means uncommon, as we shall see when the larger forms are discussed. In fact, it is relatively rare for just one of these principles to appear in isolation for any length of time.

VARIATION

In a sense, variation is another kind of modified repetition; for in order to recognize a variation of what has gone before, we must observe that the later material has points of similarity with the earlier. But in the most typical cases, variation results in music that has an identity of its own even while its source or derivation is unmistakable. Further, the principle is likely to be applied to the earlier material more consistently or across a longer time span than is the case with modified repetition. The decision as to whether a piece of music illustrates variation or modified repetition must often be made on quantitative grounds.

As an illustration of true variation as opposed to modified repetition, consider Example 39; here the principle has been applied to the first four measures of *Adeste Fideles.* Four miniature variations result. The main tones of the melodic fragment, marked by crosses in the example, have been shifted, or the melodic skips have been filled in, or the basic rhythmic pattern has been altered, or (in the case of the fourth variation) the tune has been transferred from the major key to the minor. Yet the essential character of the fragment, as defined by its harmony and general shape, has been maintained. This can be demonstrated by singing, in each variation, only the tones that are marked by crosses.

Example 39

Example 39 is an illustration of variation at its simplest; it does no more than touch upon the many imaginative devices that the skilled composer employs. And perhaps because the principle makes its greatest appeal to a skilled composer, there are few examples of true variation consistently carried out in folk music or in other pieces organized on a simple level. We must turn to larger works for other examples; representative works illustrating the principle of variation will be discussed in later chapters.

DEVELOPMENT

The essence of the principle of development is that a group of tones or a rhythmic pattern—called a *motive* earlier—serves as a seed out of which larger entities grow or

Example 40

develop. In some cases the motive serves as a point of departure; the composer returns to the motive repeatedly and out of it fashions a series of phrases that bear a recognizable relationship to each other. Example 40*a* illustrates the principle; the motive is marked by a bracket, and in its third and fourth appearances it is modified slightly by having the interval between its tones expanded. The result is a number of phrases that begin with similar contours and that have grown one out of the other.

In Example 40*b* and Example 40*c*, the respective motives are treated similarly—except that here the repetitions come closer together, and in the Bach piece the motive is repeated sequentially and appears in an inverted position as well as in the normal position. In the applications illustrated here, the motive is employed like the links in a chain; and long phrases, with their components closely linked together, result.

In yet another application of the development principle, the motive is not repeated but is consistently manipulated. Examples of this procedure are found in highly organized works. As in the case of variation, musical development is not often found on the simple levels of organization. Haydn's String Quartet, Op. 33, No. 2, provides a clear example of this type of motive manipulation; its beginning is given in Example 41. Here the motive consists merely of the interval of a fourth (marked by the bracket). On successive appearances it is gradually expanded from a fourth to

Haydn, Quartet, Op. 33, No. 2 *Example 41*

an octave (starting at the end of the fourth measure and continuing through the fifth and sixth). Having reached this point, the expanded motive itself suggests another melodic figure to the composer, and the development proceeds in the seventh measure on the basis of that new figure.

Larger Formal Units

We return now to the use made of these five principles in organizing musical ideas. One point has been mentioned: the organizing principles are most often employed in combination with each other. One illustration of this interaction of the principles may be seen in Example 42, a portion of the first movement of Brahms' Piano Quartet in C minor, Op. 60 (see pp. 82–83). The full score has been condensed into a one-line score; the chief elements are shown, but accompanying parts and doublings have been omitted. This work is chosen because it is one of the few in which a set of variations is found *within* another musical form; normally the variation set constitutes a form in its own right.

In this example by Brahms, several kinds of *repetition* are illustrated (not all cases are indicated in the example). *Symmetry* is present in that measures 102–109 balance measures 70–77; *contrast* is achieved on both large and small scale; measures 70–109 illustrate *variation;* and *development* is seen at measures 5–9 and again at measures 44–59.

Now another point of equal importance may be made: the same principles apply not only in the smallest of details, as the examples have shown, but also on the highest and most complex levels of musical organization. Their application to successively larger musical units creates the musical form. The point may be illustrated by referring to any other hierarchical plan where smaller units are combined into successively larger ones. The typical infantry organization is an example. Individual soldiers are grouped into squads, squads into platoons, and platoons into companies. Several companies form a battalion, the latter are grouped into regiments, and a number of regiments comprise a division. In a sense, the larger prose forms exemplify the same plan of organization also; for words, sentences, paragraphs, sections, chapters, and parts are combined in a similar manner to form a book.

Example 42 Brahms, Piano Quartet in C minor, Op. 60

60
(VIOLIN)
p dolce
Modified imitation of meas. 60-63
(VIOLA)
Extension of meas. 66
(CELLO)
70
Theme and variations (contrasts with meas. 32-60)
Theme (in piano)
p
espressivo
Var. I
(VIOLIN)
p
80
Var. II
(CELLO)
p
(PIANO)
mf
90
Var. III, minor
(CELLO)
(PIANO)
espressivo
cresc.
Var. IV, like theme (meas.
100
f (PIANO)
70-77), hence symmetrical
p
Codetta (Violin)
110
p
Derived from introduction by development
(CELLO)
Repetition of meas. 110-113
120
End of first
part (exposition)
of first movement.

We have seen that motives or phrase members may be used to form phrases, and that a musical phrase corresponds roughly to a sentence of prose. Phrases may be combined in a number of ways, and specific names are given to the resulting larger units. For example, the union of two phrases is called a *period;* most usually the period illustrates the principle of contrast, as in a period diagrammed ab. Three or more dissimilar phrases, such as abc or abcd, form a *phrase group;* contrast again is apparent here. And other combinations of phrases may form *double periods* (aba′c or aba′b′), in which contrast and variation are exemplified.

Complete short compositions may consist only of the units that result from combinations of phrases. Many hymns and folk songs, for example, are constituted of no more than a period, phrase group, or double period. A unit of this kind may be recognized as containing a compound musical idea presented concisely. In this sense it is analogous to a paragraph of prose. But these units are also employed as components of more extended forms.

The next higher level of organization results from combining these units into still larger ones. These larger units are usually called *part forms* or *song forms,* although the term applies to instrumental as well as vocal music. A song form may consist of three phrases arranged symmetrically, such as aba; but most often a song form will include two or more periods, phrase groups, or double periods. These elements of a song form are usually called *parts.* The parts of a song form, like the parts of a phrase or period, are organized in accord with the principles of contrast, symmetry, variation, or development. At this level, however, changes of tonality are likely to occur.

The song form plays a double role in the hierarchy of forms. Like the musical period, it often appears as a short composition complete in itself. For example, many smaller piano pieces a page or less in length, as well as certain of Chopin's shorter *études* and preludes and various pieces from Schumann's *Album for the Young,* are all typical song forms. But again like the period, the song form is more often found as a component of still larger forms. The first section of a standard march, up to the section called the *trio,* is usually one song form; and the trio itself is another. Likewise, a song form serves as the first minuet (the section from the beginning of the movement to the trio) in the majority of Haydn's and Mozart's symphonies and string quartets. (These will be discussed more fully in later chapters.)

Technical differences between various kinds of song forms exist, but such differences need not concern us here. When the listener has observed the unity of the song form, when he has grasped the relationship between its phrases, and when he has sensed the extent of its periods, then he may feel sure that he has understood the essentials of the composer's ideas and purposes.

Single-Movement Forms

Compositions that are more elaborately organized (hence longer) than song forms may be divided into two classes: *monothematic forms,* in which a single theme and its manipulations provide the essential musical materials; and *polythematic forms,* in which two or more themes are employed. A composition in either of these classes normally requires from about five to twenty minutes of playing time; it proceeds from beginning to end without interruption, and may be considered to contain a statement and complete working out of the thematic material upon which it is based. Songs, marches, dance music, the larger instrumental pieces called *overtures,* and many additional types of compositions are included in these classes.

Such works usually contain two or more song forms. In certain of these forms the principle of symmetry applies in its largest aspects. They begin and end with the same or similar material, hence may be diagrammed as ABA, AABA, or ABACA, for example. Chief among such forms are the *minuet, scherzo, rondo,* and *sonata-form.*

Others among these forms are not characterized by the use of symmetry. They consist generally of a number of connected sections each of which is to a larger or smaller degree different from earlier sections; consequently they may be diagrammed as ABC, $AA^1A^2A^3A^4$, or AABBCC, and the like. Examples of these nonsymmetrical forms include the *variation set, canon, fugue, motet,* and *madrigal.*

Details and examples of all these forms will be discussed in later chapters, in connection with the historical period or with the music of the composer in which they come to prominence.

Compound Forms

The single-movement forms mentioned in the section above—minuet, rondo, sonata-form, variation set, and all the others—are complete in themselves. Any one of them may appear on a concert program as a separate musical entity, for each has a beginning and ending, a definite individual character, and an inner relationship between its parts. In the majority of cases, however, such forms do not appear alone but are combined with one or more similar or contrasting forms to constitute a still larger entity. Such an entity, consisting of two or more separate pieces, is called a *compound form.* Each of the separate pieces is then known as a *movement* in instrumental music and as an *act, scene, number,* or *part* in a vocal work.

The justification for grouping the various movements or parts of a compound form under a single title or descriptive term may be structural, psychological, or textual. In other words, the composer has a valid emotional or intellectual purpose in creating the compound form, and the form must reveal that purpose if it is to be successful. The various movements or parts are placed so that the effect of the whole is cumulative, emotionally satisfying, or otherwise indicative of the inner relationships between the parts and the whole. It will suffice here to call attention to the principles underlying such compound forms. The forms themselves—the sonata, symphony, opera, oratorio, and all the rest—will be described fully in later chapters, where typical examples will be discussed.

Thematic and Nonthematic Material

Let us recall a statement about musical themes in Chapter 2: The theme corresponds to a single character in a literary work. Now, just as the character may be given only a name and a few lines of description, so the musical theme may be set concisely and be no more than a phrase or two in length. Or, just as a character's inner and outer nature may be described across many pages of a novel, so may a theme extend across several musical periods and require the participation of many motives and phrases.

It becomes obvious, then, that the musical theme cannot be assigned a place in the hierarchical organization of forms. Sometimes it may exist on a higher level than that provided by the song form; at other times it may be contained entirely within the smaller units. As a composition progresses, the theme may appear in part only, just as the character in a novel may appear by implication only. In fact, considerable modification of the theme on successive appearances is evidence of one of the subtlest aspects of the composer's art. The larger musical forms are classified and described according to the number of themes they contain, the interrelationship of those themes, and the treatment they undergo. In other words, the manner in which the thematic material is treated determines what the form of the composition is called.

One distinction must be made between thematic and nonthematic material. A composition must obviously consist of more than themes, just as a literary work must contain more than character delineation. A stage must be set, a background must be sketched in, and means must be supplied to connect one section with another. It is the composer's responsibility to make the different levels stand out clearly. The listener must be led to distinguish between what is most essential to the composer's purposes —namely, the themes themselves and their elaboration—and what is subsidiary. All the subsidiary material is called *nonthematic;* and if the composition is well made, the distinction between the two types of material can be easily observed.

Sometimes the nonthematic material may be in the nature of an introduction. It may suggest a legendary "once-upon-a-time" mood, as do the first few measures of Richard Strauss's well-known piece for orchestra, *Till Eulenspiegel's Merry Pranks.* Or it may provide an imposing façade for the main structure which follows, as does the slow introduction to many a Haydn symphony. Or again, the introduction may serve as a kind of seed bed for the seedlings of themes that are fully presented later; this situation is seen, for example, in the introductions to the first and last movements of Johannes Brahms' massive Symphony No. 1.

Most nonthematic material, however, occurs in the body of a composition. There it serves as connective tissue between sections; and an instance where it is so used is called a *transition.* A transition may be recognized by the listener as being on a lower level of melodic interest than a theme. It is likely to be made of short melodic fragments, or a set of repeated tones, or a reiterated chord progression; and it will often suggest a mood of "marking time" until the next thematic entrance.

Example 43, taken from Haydn's "Surprise" Symphony, shows one type of transition: here the high violins mark time while the lower strings repeat a short melodic

Haydn, Symphony No. 94 ("Surprise") *Example 43*

figure until the theme re-enters. Other types of transition may be seen in measure 31 and measures 64–69 of Example 42. Each of those passages has a single function: to provide a connection between the theme out of which it emerges and the theme to which it leads. And in context, that function is clearly sensed.

In summary, the composer's musical ideas may be presented singly or expanded into phrases. The composer has available five organizing principles: repetition, contrast, symmetry, variation, and development. Using these principles, he works the phrases into periods, song forms, and larger musical entities, and presents this material in orderly fashion. He works on two different levels—thematic and nonthematic; and those levels allow him to differentiate between "main characters" on the one hand, and backgrounds and transitions on the other. The listener finally hears, recognizes, distinguishes, and evaluates these elements. The composer thus communicates his ideas and their elaborations to the listener through the vehicle of the musical form.

Listening Suggestions

As the text has made clear, no one of the five principles under which music is organized is likely to appear alone in a composition of even moderate length. Yet by listening selectively, one may observe the activity of each principle in isolation. In each of the works listed below, one of the principles is employed more consistently than the others.

REPETITION

Grieg, *Peer Gynt,* Suite No. 1, Op. 46 (many examples of sequence repetition)
Ravel, *Bolero* (frequent repetition of the theme, each time with changed orchestration)
Tchaikovsky, Symphony No. 5, E minor, Op. 64, first movement (considerable repetition of short phrases)

CONTRAST

Mozart, *The Magic Flute,* Overture, K. 620 (two sections contrasting in tempo and mood)

Bach, Prelude and Fugue, B flat minor, *The Well-Tempered Clavier,* Vol. 1, No. 22 (two movements contrasting in texture and form)

SYMMETRY

Haydn, Symphony No. 101 ("Clock"), third movement, minuet (ABA symmetrical form; moderate tempo)

Beethoven, Symphony No. 7, A major, Op. 92, third movement, scherzo (ABABA symmetrical form; fast tempo)

Bach, *Passion According to St. Matthew,* final chorus (large ABA form)

VARIATION

Each work or movement is a set of variations on a theme.

Beethoven, Symphony No. 3, Op. 55 ("Eroica"), finale

Brahms, *Variations on a Theme by Paganini,* Op. 35

Elgar, *Variations on an Original Theme* ("Enigma Variations")

Schubert, Quartet, D minor ("Death and the Maiden"), second movement

DEVELOPMENT

These typical sonata-form movements contain an unusual amount of development of their respective first themes.

Beethoven, Symphony No. 3, Op. 55 ("Eroica"), first movement

———, *Coriolanus,* Overture, Op. 62

Brahms, Symphony No. 2, D major, Op. 73, first movement

Rachmaninoff, Symphony No. 2, E minor, Op. 27, introduction and first movement

Chapter 6

INTERPRETATION

One of the outstanding facts of concert life is that various equally competent musicians may perform the same composition and affect their audiences quite differently. One performer, for example, is able to move his listeners, another leaves them cold and unmoved. One performer is able to command the respect of all who hear him, and another is merely tolerated. Inequalities in technical proficiency are not likely to be among the causes of these differences; for with the high standards of performance that exist on the concert stage today, no professional musician can afford to be deficient in the sheer mechanics of playing or singing. The differences lie, rather, in the way each musician interprets the music he performs.

Although interpretation is the activity for which the performer exists, it is also of vital importance to the listener. The degree or kind of musical pleasure a listener derives from a performance is most often directly related to the quality of the interpretation. Yet the principles of interpretation are seldom discussed, except among performers themselves or in the studio of a great teacher. Musical reference books and textbooks are usually silent about these principles; and newspaper reviews of performances are more concerned with the effects of interpretation than with the principles.

A working definition of interpretation as it affects the performer and listener is, in the simplest terms, as follows: the act of bringing to expression the musical ideas of the composer. These ideas are both notated and implied in the pages of the composition. The note symbols and their implications must be properly translated into auditory phenomena that produce significant emotional experiences. The musical ideas embodied in those symbols must be projected in the way the composer has indicated.

The composer's ideas, as we have seen in the previous chapter, are usually manipulated in accord with the organizing principles of music. A musical idea may be repeated; it may be set opposite a contrasting idea that is designed to show the original idea in perspective; it may be developed—which is to say that new musical ideas are derived from it. No matter how the idea is treated, its manipulation is designed to create a piece of music that has unity, variety, musical logic, expressive power, and emotional effectiveness. These elements must be in proportion to each other if the composition is to be satisfying. And the factor that holds them all together is the musical form.

The form thus provides the setting not only for the composer's musical ideas, but also for their elaboration and development. It is the form that permits the composer to communicate his ideas to the listener. And it is the musical form that the interpreter utilizes above all in creating or working out his interpretation. In essence, therefore, interpretation is the art of clarifying and explaining the musical form.

Clarification of the Form

The question might be asked: In what way does the form need clarification? We have seen that every musical form consists of smaller units combined into successively larger ones, and that the nature and inner relationships of these formal units determine the name given to the form. The connections between one part and another are often subtly or obscurely made and need to be brought to the attention of the listener. This is perhaps the most obvious way in which the form needs to be clarified.

But also, the basic tempo at which the units are played bears directly upon the intelligibility—and therefore the emotional effectiveness—of the musical ideas that the units embody. Changes in the basic tempo likewise alter the impact that the successive ideas make upon the listener. In a similar manner, the basic dynamic level at which the units are performed, as well as deviations from that level, are factors in properly expressing the ideas they contain. It follows that basic tempo, dynamic level, and any deviations from a single tempo or dynamic level also may act to clarify or obscure the musical form.

In addition, the duration of individual tones is directly related to the emotional effect of the musical idea expressed by those tones. Further, the quality with which a tone or group of tones is performed has a formative effect upon the mood engendered by the musical passage. Thus the tonal characteristics of duration and quality must be considered in clarifying the form; for, as we shall see below, they affect the style of the performance.

These, then, are the elements with which the performer works in interpreting a musical composition; tonal and unit connections, tempo, dynamic level, tone duration, tone quality—all play essential parts in interpretation. Singly or in combination, these elements are influential in outlining structure and establishing mood.

PHRASING

In an earlier chapter a phrase was described as analogous to a sentence of prose; in this sense, the phrase may be seen as the embodiment of a musical idea. The phrase is, in effect, the unit out of which a musical form is created; it is by means of the phrase that successive emotional states are reflected. And the performer works most directly with the phrase in arriving at his interpretation.

We saw also that the phrase endings are indicated by cadences. The performer, concerned with explaining the musical structure, first of all gives due weight and stress to the cadences, so that phrases may stand out clearly. In addition, he connects all the tones of one phrase (or phrase member or half-phrase, if these small units together with their own smaller cadences are present within the phrase), pauses slightly, and then begins the next phase. This activity—stressing the cadences and connecting the tones that lie between cadences—is called *phrasing;* and it is phrasing that strengthens the listener's awareness of the musical structure.

Phrasing, in addition to its role in delineating the elements of form, serves another need as well. The slight retardation of melodic motion, brought about by the phrasing as well as by the form of the cadence itself, is attractive to the listener; for it is just sufficient to disturb the regularity of rhythmic flow that might otherwise become monotonous.

In many cases, the music is supplied with curved lines written above certain tones (see Examples 33*a* and 33*c*); these lines, called *slurs,* enable the composer to indicate where and how he wishes the phrasing to take place. In other cases, especially in music with accompanying texts, symbols resembling commas or inverted carets are inserted at phrase ends or at other natural breathing places; these symbols also throw light upon the phrase structure of the piece. Often, however, phrasing indications are used sparsely or not at all; this is largely true of music composed before about 1720.

TEMPO

The tempo at which a composition is performed is an essential element of interpretation. In an extended composition, each part or section may require a specific tempo, which may be a slight modification of the tempo basic to the whole. Whether the tempo is fast or slow depends upon the musical content of the section, the length and complexity of its phrases, the types of musical ideas it brings to expression, and the underlying mood.

A failure to choose the proper tempo will, in extreme cases, make a caricature of the music being performed. This applies also to verbal interpretation; to test the truth of this statement, experiment with a few sentences of Lincoln's Gettysburg Address, speaking them at various speeds. Noble expression (in music as well as prose) becomes trivial if the performance is too fast; liveliness becomes dull at too slow a tempo; and every other kind of expression is distorted if the tempo is wrongly chosen.

The interpreter must go far beyond a general tempo indication such as *allegro* or *adagio,* and even beyond a refinement of general tempo, of which *allegro moderato* and *adagio ma non troppo* (slowly, but not too much so) are examples. He must search for the exact degree of speed, testing the music against different tempos, until he finds the one that best reflects its expressive content. And having found that tempo, he must be able to maintain it, deviating only for musical or structural or expressive reasons.

One of the most usual kinds of deviation from a pre-established tempo is the very slight retardation that often accompanies phrasing. Phrasing, as we saw earlier, is a means of revealing the inner structure of a composition; in effect, phrasing separates a work into its component parts. The retard is one of the performer's means for accomplishing the separation—and inevitably the forward motion of the music is slightly impeded thereby.

Even the slight retardation of tempo at phrase joints is sufficient to affect the tonal inertia of the composition. *Inertia* is that property of matter by which it tends to remain in an existing state of motion or rest unless acted upon by an external force; and a tonal mass, too, is subject to the law of inertia. The *retard* is the "external force" that the interpreter may employ to alter the music's state of motion. It is the performer's means of "applying brakes" to a composition, both at internal points and at its end. A composition of great tonal mass—for example, a long work for large orchestra—requires more "braking" to bring it to a stop than does a small folk song for voice and piano.

When an automobile is stopped smoothly, the retard has been properly made; the passenger is not thrown forward in his seat. Similarly, when a musical retard is prop-

Cellist Jacqueline du Pré in rehearsal.

erly carried out, the listener's sense of rhythmic motion is not violated. If, on the other hand, a phrase seems to stop abruptly or arbitrarily and gives the effect of having been chopped off, a faulty retard is likely to be the cause. The same is true of a phrase that seems to be prolonged unduly, that seems to linger and die.

Exceptions to the foregoing occur often, however, and are valid factors of musical interpretation. A car driver may find it necessary to jolt his passengers with a sudden stop. In a similar manner a musical passage may be performed so that it ends suddenly, or it may even be accelerated as its end approaches—both for purely expressive reasons. The hastening may lead to a feeling of growing excitement, or it may take attention away from a long passage of nonthematic material, or it may be employed to enhance a musical climax.

DYNAMIC LEVELS

The degree of loudness with which a composition is performed vitally affects the expression of its musical ideas. An idea that expresses a forceful emotional state at one dynamic level, for example, may seem trivial or empty if performed softly; conversely, if an intimate or subtle idea is shouted out at a *fortissimo* level, it may lose all feeling of intimacy and become bombastic. In this sense, a musical passage or melodic fragment that expresses a musical idea can be as flexible or as versatile as a spoken word or phrase.

For example, a quietly spoken "yes" may, in one context, imply simple agreement; a forceful "yes" may serve as a positive statement in an argument, or as an imperative; and a shouted "yes!" might suggest forced compliance in a critical situation. Composers often take advantage of this flexibility of musical material by employing identical passages to express a variety of ideas. Through choice of context and degree of loudness they then make plain the nature of the contrasting ideas embodied in the identical musical material. (See, for example, the first movement of Schumann's Symphony No. 4, discussed on pages 206–07.)

Since the performer interprets the musical ideas expressed in the composition, it follows that he must perform all parts of the work at the dynamic levels that reveal the nature of their respective contents. Thus, basic levels of loudness as well as deviations from those levels (all of which are included in the musical term *dynamics*) become additional factors in clarifying a musical form.

A composition might be so constructed that all of its parts could justifiably be performed at the same level of loudness, of course. An unyielding *forte* (loud), for example, might be appropriate to all the ideas contained in the work, and that dynamic level would then be one factor that unified the whole. But unrelieved unity might easily become monotonous; the factor of variety is also an essential if monotony is to be avoided. The interpreter then would virtually be compelled to modify the dynamic level at appropriate places, and to a degree appropriate to the nature of specific passages.

It is far more likely that a satisfactory composition will contain contrasting ideas—ideas that provide variety; we have seen that contrast is a potent element in the organization of musical forms. The different ideas normally include contrasting dynamics as well as melodic or harmonic or textural contrasts, and the performer is guided accordingly. These differences are not arbitrary, however; they grow out of the nature of the music. A lyric section, for example, may be played softly because of its nature, range, and texture. It may be succeeded by a dramatic section; drama implies emotional conflict, of which loudness is sometimes the musical counterpart. The performer will then play the dramatic section more loudly than the lyric one. Variety has been achieved, and the contrasting ideas have been performed in accordance with the emotional states they express.

DURATION AND QUALITY

Musical notation provides symbols that permit the composer to indicate how long a tone is to be held: whether for a beat, several beats, or a fraction of a beat. The interpreter, guided by the notation, performs so that these respective tonal lengths are properly observed. But even without violating the notation, he can alter the length of successive tones. He can shorten or lengthen them; or he can connect some of them smoothly and sharply separate others. By employing these various means of altering the exact length of the tones he plays, the performer can control the emotional effect of his performance.

Similarly, the tone qualities revealed by a composition are predetermined by the composer. He has scored the work for instruments, for voices, or for a combination of them. Basic tone qualities can be expected, for in performing a work it is not usual to depart from the indicated scoring. But instruments and human voices alike are each capable of more than one tone quality. A violin, for example, normally produces violin-like sounds; but the violinist may so alter the quality of those sounds that he can suggest an array of moods ranging from light and gay to dark and foreboding. It follows, then, that since tone quality can become a factor in suggesting moods, it is a factor in musical interpretation. The exact duration of tones, together with the qualities of the tones themselves, play vital roles in expressing emotional states. Duration and quality, both understood in the sense of the above paragraphs, are the principal ingredients of what is usually called *style.*

Assume, for example, that a musical passage suggests the darker moods of pessimism or discouragement; the performer must modify his style of performance to express those moods. He may sustain the individual tones, letting one connect with the next; he will play or sing with a dark or dull tone color, avoiding all suggestion of brilliance. (The roles that tempo and dynamics play in the matter of style may be disregarded for the moment.) Were he to shorten the individual tones and permit short pauses to appear between them, a martial or marchlike mood might be expressed. Were he to play with a warmer tone quality, the connected tones might suggest a sentimental mood.

The composer usually employs a number of musical terms that aid the performer in interpreting moods properly and that help him in adjusting his style to the music. *Giocoso* (joyously), *amoroso* (lovingly), *sostenuto* (sustained)—these terms and many others may appear in connection with the initial tempo indications themselves (as *allegro giocoso,* for example); or they may appear within the composition whenever the mood of the music requires (see Appendix III).

The Interpreter's Problems

A summary of the above discussion reveals that phrasing, tempo, dynamics, duration, and quality are among the principal musical elements subject to interpretation. A musical passage may express a specific idea at one tempo and dynamic level, and another idea if the speed and loudness are modified. Deviations from a pre-established tempo or dynamic level also play important roles in the expression of musical ideas. Phrasing clarifies the structure of a composition, and style directly affects the moods suggested by the passages.

The performer thus has at his command various means for expressing musical ideas that directly affect his listeners. The source of those ideas is, of course, the composition itself; and the ideas contained in the composition are the ideas the composer has sought to express. One of the problems the interpreter faces, therefore, is to distinguish between his own ideas and the composer's, and to let himself be guided by the latter.

There is also the problem of quantity. The amount, kind, and effect of every expressive shading must be carefully considered by the performer. The problems of how much deviation in tempo, how much contrast in dynamics, what kind of phrasing, and what style of delivery must all be solved correctly if the interpretation is to be authentic, or if it is truly to express the composer's ideas. The performer must bring to these problems such diverse elements as knowledge of the composer's style in general, familiarity with the traditions of performance, and the good taste that is a part of artistic sensitivity. And he must have an objective attitude toward his own temperament.

Responsibility to the composer, the question of the amount and kind of expressive factor, knowledge of the composer's general style, and a consideration of his own temperament are the chief problems that face the interpreter. Although they are related and cannot be completely separated from the others in performance, they may be discussed separately.

RESPONSIBILITY TO THE COMPOSER

The composer is rarely present in the concert hall to interpret his own music; the performer, acting as an intermediary between composer and audience, assumes the responsibility of clarifying the composer's ideas. These ideas, as we have seen, are expressed in the symbols of musical notation and in the intangibles surrounding those symbols. The expressive factors applied to that notation, however, can radically alter the ideas it seeks to communicate. The performer is thus able to amend or distort the composer's ideas and to substitute his own—without doing violence to the notation itself.

Bruno Walter, at a recording session, clarifying a point of interpretation.

Unfortunately, the performer sometimes forgets that he is only an intermediary—the composer's agent, as it were. In extreme cases he performs as though he himself had written the music. His tempos may be chosen so that the joy or nobility or sentiment the composer sought to express are transformed into other emotional states; his dynamic levels may ignore the composer's subtlety and substitute prosaic expression. His choice of style may change light-heartedness into clumsiness. All such arbitrary distortions of the composer's communication represent, of course, a violation of the performer's first responsibility—namely, to serve as the interpreter of the *composer's* ideas.

AMOUNT AND KIND OF EXPRESSION

In all musical details, the matter of quantity cannot be long absent from the interpreter's thinking. How heavily, how much louder, what kind of accent, how much acceleration—all such questions must be answered correctly. No two composers are alike in the ideas they express and in the ways those ideas are projected; few composers employ dynamic markings, tempo changes, and the other expressive factors in the same fashion. The performer, therefore, must be aware of these individual differences between composers, and must read into the music not only the proper kind but the proper amount of expressive shading.

The single element of dramatic effect may be taken as an illustration. Haydn, for example, is usually straightforward and direct in his music. Dramatic effects occur in his works, but they are controlled and employed discreetly in proportion to the nondramatic elements. The musical devices that suggest drama (sudden accelerations, impulsive surging of tone, unexpected alteration of texture and instrumentation) are treated by Haydn with care and economy. The interpreter must treat them just as carefully. He must avoid reading drama into passages that do not contain it. He must not make a feature of the dramatic elements that do occur, but must keep them properly subdued and related to the contexts in which they are found. Above all, he must

avoid a sensational type of expression, for that type is completely foreign to the style of Haydn.

Richard Wagner, on the other hand, is more generous in the use of dramatic detail than Haydn. This is probably caused in part by the fact that Wagner dealt mostly with opera and Haydn with abstract music. Spectacular instrumental effects, the piling up of great masses of sonority, the use of a greater variety and number of instruments—all are more common in Wagner's music. Thus, when dramatic moments offset nondramatic moments in this music, the interpreter makes full use of the opportunity to be dramatic. He may make broad tempo changes, radically increase the amount of tone from one moment to the next, and employ great intensity of expression.

IMPLIED EXPRESSION

It is very probable that many of the expressive shadings the performer imparts to his interpretation are not specifically indicated, but only implied. In the works of both Haydn and Wagner, for example, the basic expression marks are sure to be present. However, the refinements of shading, the small variations of volume that the phrase structure demands, the many kinds of accents, the indications for changes of mood—these are probably employed more copiously by Wagner than by Haydn. Music literature contains many similar examples, for the use of expression marks has varied from composer to composer.

Some composers, notably Beethoven and Brahms, spread these markings lavishly across their pages and clarify their intentions at every turn. Other composers are less explicit, or are even inconsistent, and rely strongly on the good sense of the performer. A few are careless, or seem not to have understood fully the function of such terms. And although expression marks have existed for several centuries (they appear frequently in vocal music of the 1600's), they did not come into general use until about the 1720's. Early instrumental composers rarely made use of them beyond basic indications of loud or soft, fast or slow.

Thus, in large quantities of music, the performer is faced with the problem of interpreting sparsely marked music. The problem would be difficult to solve were it not for the fact that the rhythmic, dynamic, and other expressive indications are often inherent or implied in the music itself. In other words, the way the music is written often gives a clue to how it must be performed; the markings are in a sense only reminders for the performer. In the case of unmarked or sparsely marked music, then, he must determine what kind of expression is implied and play the music in accordance with that implication. To do this, he needs to have an exact knowledge of the composer's style in general, as well as of his place in music history. Awareness is either the intuitive possession of a good performer or the result of training and experience. It is the essential element of "being musical."

FUNCTION OF EXPRESSION MARKS

In a strict sense, all expression marks exist to aid in clarifying the musical form. This clarification is directed toward the listener, of course. The listener's span of attention is extremely short; he has a mind and thoughts of his own, and sometimes must be recalled to the music. He is not likely to shut out all extraneous thoughts and feelings, and in the process of letting his mind wander he may overlook an important part of the composer's communication.

Thus, an indirect function of expression marks is to reattract the listener's attention from time to time. Any rhythmic pulse, once established, tends to become monotonous or uninteresting; any series of tones on the same level of loudness will not long hold the listener's attention. These extreme cases probably do not often occur in music; the composer's interest in variety of expression is in itself a safeguard. But in many cases the variety must be forcefully projected; the differences in content or texture or instrumental color must be emphasized. And performing with variety in tempo, dynamic level, and all the other expressive factors is one means of assuring that the listener will attend to the progression of the composer's musical ideas.

It is with this indirect function of expression marks in mind that the performer approaches sparsely marked music. In the absence of an indicated dynamic level, he will select a level that allows the musical ideas to be perceived. If he feels that an undeviating dynamic level or a strict tempo will allow his listener's attention to wander, he will not hesitate to emphasize the contrasts that are implied (but not specifically indicated) in the music. These are practical procedures of the successful interpreter; and however little place they may have in an ideal or theoretical system of musical aesthetics, they cannot be disregarded by the performer who considers the musical welfare of his listeners.

TEMPERAMENT

The performer, at some point in working out his interpretations, must solve the problem of personal temperament. If his temperament is well balanced and controlled, it will not offer a serious problem in his interpretation of the music. If, however, it is

A chamber music rehearsal at the Marlboro Music Festival. Reading clockwise, Alexander Schneider, violin; Rudolf Serkin, piano; Mischa Schneider, cello; Boris Kroyt, viola.

extreme in any way or is characterized by one-sided reactions, it may stand in the way of achieving a satisfying and authentic interpretation.

Two extreme temperamental types are relatively common among performers. One performer, for example, may be a romanticist at heart. His tone will be warm and intense, his deviations from rhythmic regularity will be impulsive and extreme. He will be at his best when playing *con amore* or *con sentimento,* and his playing may lack self-discipline. His performances of Schumann, Liszt, and Chopin will be more satisfactory than his performances of Haydn, Debussy, or Hindemith. His temperament will impel him to play all music with the warmth and fervor that are appropriate only to certain Romantic composers.

Another extreme type is the reserved and controlled individual. Coldness or austerity will characterize his playing, even though it may be refined, well proportioned, and "correct" in all details. But the absence of an essential warmth or of affection will make it difficult for his performance to move his listeners. Dramatic conflicts, exuberant strains, vigorous expression will all be minimized and refined until little more than the notes is left.

Between these extreme types are the many performers whose temperaments are well suited to the music they are called upon to interpret. But they too must be on guard against specific characteristics that may adversely affect their interpretations. One performer may be a rhythmic perfectionist, for example, and will play in a mechanically precise way that borders on rhythmic monotony. Another may possess a pedantic attitude; he will play in the style that he believes will best disclose the historical aspects of the music being performed, and in so doing may leave his listeners unmoved.

A performer must be able to modify his temperament in the direction required by the music; otherwise his interpretation is sure to be false in some details. There are those who would argue that no harm is done thereby, and that such a musician is simply expressing himself or is giving his "personal" interpretation. To this argument we must point out that each composition is written in a particular style and with a specific set of ideas that must come to expression. A basic distortion of these ideas at the hands of a performer whose temperament allows him to alter the composer's communication cannot be called anything other than false. A single composition cannot be, and is not intended to be, a dozen different things at the hands of a dozen different interpreters.

Two basically different points of view are outlined in the above paragraph. Each view has its adherents, and it is doubtful that the two positions can be reconciled. The first position holds that the composer has written his music so that only *one* interpretation is right; any other interpretation may be right in some details but will be wrong in others. The other position holds that one satisfactory personal interpretation is as valid as another; a performer acts not only as the composer's agent but as the re-creator of the composer's ideas.

Every performer must come to grips with these opposing points of view, adopt one of them, and be judged accordingly. Every sensitive listener will eventually do likewise, for a vital factor of his musical enjoyment is the ability to evaluate the worth of the performances he hears.

Listening Suggestions

A comparison and critical evaluation of several performances of the same work may often lead to a better understanding of the principles of interpretation. Many compositions of the standard repertoire are available in more than one recording; listening selectively to any one detail in different performances can be revealing and rewarding. For example, the basic tempo of each movement may be compared in a number of different versions of the same work and an attempt made to determine which tempo best reveals the true spirit of the music. Likewise, the amount of accent, the spacing between phrases, the deviations from one tonal level, the mood of the performance itself—all such elements may profitably be compared in records of the following works.

Beethoven, Sonata, Op. 13 ("Pathétique")
Grieg, Concerto for Piano, A minor, Op. 16
Mendelssohn, Violin Concerto, E minor, Op. 64
Mozart, Symphony No. 38, K. 594 ("Prague")
Sibelius, Symphony No. 2, D major, Op. 43
Strauss, *Till Eulenspiegel's Merry Pranks*
Tchaikovsky, *Romeo and Juliet*
———, Symphony No. 6, Op. 74 ("Pathétique")

Chapter 7

MUSICAL PERFORMANCE AND HISTORY

The art of interpretation, as discussed in the foregoing chapter, is a relative newcomer to the musical scene. It is the result of a development that began probably no farther back than the middle of the eighteenth century and that culminated late in the nineteenth with the rise of the virtuoso conductor. In a sense it is a by-product of the intense subjectivity that marked the middle 1800's. Interpretation by its very nature begins with a subjective attitude toward music; the performer is declaring, in effect, "This is how I feel about it." Only much later, after the interpretations of a large number of performers have been observed, can objective principles be established.

There is little historical evidence to show that interpretation, as the term has been used here, played a major part in music before about 1750. The sparseness of musical expression marks, the content of the music itself, and the objective attitude that is known to have prevailed prior to that date lend strength to that belief. But it is equally clear that musicians before 1750 approached their work thoughtfully and developed their own performance practices. The practices of the early eighteenth century were not necessarily those of the seventeenth; and the latter differed considerably from the practices of the sixteenth. Each period developed its own types of performance; and in each case the type was conditioned by the content of the music being played, by the composition of the performing groups that existed, and by the aesthetic nature of the period itself.

It is possible to approach this subject of performance practices with an erroneous belief—namely, that the practices of earlier centuries were inferior to ours, simply because they belonged to a period farther back in time. Such a view is widely held, unfortunately; and it is often accompanied by an equally erroneous belief that earlier music is less highly organized or less significant than later music. Both of these beliefs are contrary to the facts.

Seen from the historical point of view, music does not exhibit a long straight line of development from simple to complex, from small to large, from naïve to sophisticated, or from primitive to civilized. For a relatively short time, it is true, music may seem to have followed one of these tendencies. From a more distant vantage point, however, we see simple works following the most grandiose, and loose, insignificant pieces following carefully constructed masterpieces. Changes in the manner of writing and performing music have been manifest everywhere, but the changes cannot be interpreted as constituting "growth" or "improvement." One century's music is not "better" than another's.

In spite of this seemingly undisciplined series of changes, a certain historical principle has been apparent for many centuries: namely, that two tendencies exist in music, one revolutionary and experimental, the other reactionary and conservative. For a period of time one tendency is dominant, after which it declines and the other comes to the fore.

About 1600, for example, a large number of composers discarded their musical heritage, set out on untried paths, and devised a new way of composing. The performance practices of the time were altered accordingly. After a period of conscious experiment, another group modified and refined the new manner, and brought back into music some of the balance and order the earlier composers had abandoned. Soon after 1700, however, the settling process resulted in a decline of vitality, expressiveness, and other qualities; many composers of the next generation revolted against the then-established musical order and began a new series of experiments that led to a new kind of music and a new kind of performance.

This alternation of the two tendencies—experimental and conservative—has been repeated many times in the history of music. The alternations were most forceful and effective at three-hundred-year intervals; the years about 1300, 1600, and 1900 mark the most radical changes in musical tendencies. Series of less experimental changes took place at intervals of approximately 150 years; the dates about 1450 and 1750 are examples. And the principle operated in a still lesser degree about seventy-five years after each of the larger alternations became effective—namely, 1375, 1525, 1675, and 1825 (see the chart on p. 104).

The music written between the dates when musical changes take place usually has many elements in common. We are justified in making generalizations about the style of that music, and setting it apart from music written at other times. Thus the concept of periods of musical style comes into being.

The style periods that we shall examine in detail in the second to fourth parts of this book are shown with their approximate dates in the following chart. In this chapter the various periods are discussed in chronological order, so that an orderly view of the major changes in music across the centuries may be obtained. The later chapters, in contrast, are arranged not chronologically but in a sequence that presents more familiar styles and more available music before it discusses the more remote styles and less familiar works. Here we shall only outline the characteristics of each period, describe the most prominent types of performing groups, and mention briefly the performance practices that prevailed.

It need scarcely be said that performing groups in music have been of the most diverse kinds. Music has been composed for single performers and for combinations

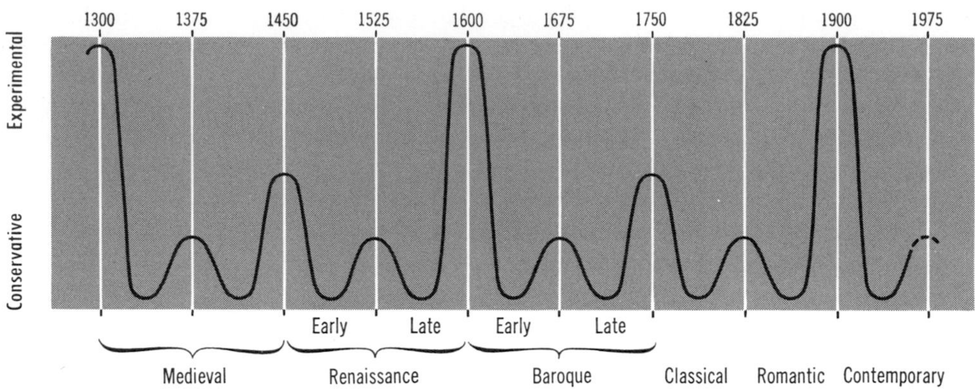

ranging from two to a hundred or more performers, as well as for a great number of different combinations of voices and instruments. However, certain instrumental and vocal combinations have proved more satisfactory than others and have to a large extent become standardized; that is, for a long period a particular combination of instruments has met the needs of its time and has had much music written for it. With the passage of time, however, even such a standardized combination may outlive its usefulness to composers. It may then become modified to meet new conditions (although it may still bear the same name), or it may be replaced by another combination.

The Renaissance Period (1450–1600)

Historically, the term "Renaissance" refers to the period of the rebirth of culture and learning after the many centuries often called the Dark Ages. In music this period began when Christopher Columbus was a boy; its midpoint was marked by the activity of Martin Luther in solidifying the Protestant Reformation; and it ended about the time when such figures as Sir Walter Raleigh and Sir Philip Sidney flourished at Queen Elizabeth's court in England, and when Shakespeare was at the height of his dramatic powers.

Music in the Renaissance served one principal function: to contribute to worship in the Church service. Its secondary function was to express worldly emotions, needs, and satisfactions. The first function gave rise to a large body of choral literature, which, being directed toward God, is called *sacred music.* The second contributed to the formation of a somewhat smaller literature which is directed toward man; this is consequently called *secular* ("worldly") *music.* Although the secular literature was primarily written for choral groups, a considerable amount of instrumental music was written also. The latter, however, did not become truly independent of vocal forms until well into the following period.

The *chorus* came into being shortly before the beginning of the Renaissance period. Choruses of that time were often modest groups containing perhaps a dozen singers, whereas today a chorus may include several hundred. Through much of history the choral group has been divided into four parts—the familiar soprano, alto, tenor, and bass; it is then referred to as a mixed chorus. Late Renaissance music often calls for a fifth part, either second soprano or second tenor—and works for six-, eight-, and even sixteen-part choruses are found.

Choruses in the Renaissance generally sang with instrumental or organ accompaniment, even though parts for the accompanying instruments were not written out. The practice of *doubling* prevailed: that is, an instrumentalist was assigned to perform the vocal part that lay within the range of his instrument, merely to give support to the singers of that part. However, choruses often sang in chapels where instrumental accompaniment was not available or not desired; they were then said to be singing "in chapel style," the Italian for which is *a cappella.* That term is rather generally used today for any choral singing without accompaniment.

Originally, a distinction existed between a chorus (a group that performed secular music) and a choir (one restricted to sacred music). However, that distinction has not always been maintained. Many a chorus today will sing, for example, an unaccompanied church work on occasion, and at that moment it becomes an *a cappella* choir.

The principal function of the choral conductor in the Renaissance period was to keep his vocal forces together. The unmetrical rhythm that prevailed in the music of that time (see pp. 317ff.) made a regular duple, triple, or quadruple beat unrealistic; therefore a Renaissance conductor made little regular use of the metrical patterns employed by the conductor of today. Instead, he showed merely the passing of background beats in an unaccented series, such as, "beat, beat, beat, beat" and not "one, two, three, four." The beat, called a *tactus,* was indicated by a series of up-and-down motions of the hand, and the conductor often held a rolled-up sheet of paper to

A group from the University of Maryland Madrigal Singers, dressed in costumes of the Renaissance period. From left: alto recorder, soprano recorder, lute, tenor and bass recorders, krumhorn, and portative organ. Singers in the background.

Some Comparative Dates in Music History

HISTORICAL EVENTS	CULTURAL AND HISTORICAL PERSONAGES	COMPOSERS AND MUSICAL EVENTS
1492–1504 Voyage of Columbus	1452–1519 Leonardo da Vinci	1501 First printed part-music (Petrucci)
1513 Machiavelli, *The Prince*	1483–1520 Raphael Sanzio	c. 1450–1521 Josquin des Prez
1517 Beginning of Protestant Reformation	1473–1547 Copernicus	1524 Publication of first Lutheran hymnal in Wittenberg
1535 Printing press introduced into Spanish America	1491–1547 Henry VIII, King of England	1547 Publication of Glareanus' *Dodecachordon*
1541 Mississippi River explored (De Soto)	1475–1564 Michelangelo Buonarroti	1545–63 Council of Trent
1568 Revolt of the Netherlands	1533–1603 Elizabeth I, Queen of England	c. 1526–94 Giovanni Pierluigi da Palestrina
1588 Defeat of the Spanish Armada	1564–1616 William Shakespeare	c. 1595 Performance of first opera, *Dafne* (Peri)
1607 Founding of Jamestown Colony	1564–1643 Galileo Galilei	1607 Monteverdi, *Orfeo*
1620 Landing of Pilgrims in Massachusetts	1596–1650 René Descartes	c. 1613 Decline of the Elizabethan madrigal
1618–48 Thirty Years' War	1609–69 Rembrandt von Rijn	1637 First public opera house opened in Venice
1653–58 Protectorate of Oliver Cromwell	1608–74 John Milton	1642 Monteverdi, *L'Incoronazione di Poppea*
1683 Siege of Vienna by the Turks	1638–1715 Louis XIV, King of France	c. 1682 Beginning of *concerto grosso* form (Corelli)
1687 Newton's *Principia*	1644–1737 Antonio Stradivari	1709 Handel, *Agrippina*
1707 Founding of Great Britain	1688–1744 Alexander Pope	1721 Bach, "Brandenburg" Concertos
1769 Invention of steam engine (Watt)	1694–1778 François Arouet (Voltaire)	1762 Gluck, *Orfeo ed Euridice*
1775–83 American Revolution	1712–78 Jean Jacques Rousseau	1787 Mozart, *Don Giovanni*

1789–91 French Revolution	1706–90 Benjamin Franklin	1791–95 Haydn, "London" Symphonies
1796–1815 Napoleonic Wars	1729–96 Catherine the Great, Empress of Russia	1803 Beethoven, Symphony No. 3 ("Eroica")
1807 First successful steamboat (Fulton)	1788–1824 George Gordon, Lord Byron	1824 Schubert, Quartet No. 14 ("Death and the Maiden")
1832 First successful telegraph (Morse)	1749–1832 Johann Wolfgang von Goethe	1828–30 Berlioz, *Symphonie Fantastique*
1848 Karl Marx, *The Communist Manifesto*	1809–49 Edgar Allan Poe	1846 Mendelssohn, *Elijah*
1859 Darwin, *On the Origin of Species*	1812–70 Charles Dickens	1857–59 Wagner, *Tristan und Isolde*
1861–65 American Civil War	1796–1875 Jean Baptiste Corot	1871 Verdi, *Aïda*
1876 Invention of the telephone (Bell)	1812–89 Robert Browning	1873 Brahms, *Variations on a Theme by Haydn*
1877 Invention of the phonograph (Edison)	1819–1901 Victoria, Queen of England	1888 Rimsky-Korsakov, *Scheherazade*
1887 First successful automobile (Daimler)	1853–90 Vincent Van Gogh	1892–94 Debussy, *Prelude to the Afternoon of a Faun*
1895 Invention of wireless telegraphy (Marconi)	1828–1906 Henrik Ibsen	1896 Puccini, *La Bohème*
1903 First successful airplane (Wright brothers)	1856–1939 Sigmund Freud	1898 Strauss, *Ein Heldenleben*
1914 Panama Canal opened	1858–1919 Theodore Roosevelt	1913 Stravinsky, *The Rite of Spring*
1914–18 First World War	1870–1924 Nikolai Lenin	c. 1915 Rise of jazz
1927 First successful transmission of television signals	1863–1947 Henry Ford	c. 1925 Introduction of twelve-tone music (Schoenberg)
1939–45 Second World War	1899–1961 Ernest Hemingway	1928 Weill, *The Three-Penny Opera*
1945 Founding of the United Nations Organization	1874–1965 Winston Churchill	1945 Bartók, Concerto No. 3 for piano and orchestra
1957 Launching of Sputnik I	1929–68 Martin Luther King, Jr.	c. 1950 Introduction of electronic music

make the indication of the beat more visible. It was then left to the individual singers to count the proper number of rests or to hold sustained tones for the proper length of time, as well as to determine the timing of their own musical entrances and exits.

The Baroque Period (1600–1750)

The Baroque period was one of the most eventful in music history. It paralleled the rise of our own country from a wilderness to an established system of colonies. Shakespeare was still alive when the period began, and George Washington was a young man when it ended. Early in the course of this century and a half, the modal system (see pp. 307 ff.) was discarded by many composers and the modern system of major and minor scales slowly took shape.

The polyphonic style, which had risen to heights of expressiveness in the previous period, was abandoned for several decades as a result of the revolutionary urge of the early Baroque. Many composers felt that music written in polyphonic style "lacerated the poetry"; for at any given moment of vocal polyphony each voice of the chorus was likely to be engaged with a different word of the text. The composers experimented toward making the text intelligible; their work led to a new style of writing and performing, out of which opera emerged. The development of opera, in the years just before 1600, was one of the most significant events of early Baroque history.

Instrumental music came of age at this time also, and began to cast off the last traces of vocal idioms and vocal forms. Early in the Baroque period small groups

Seventeenth-century musicians performing on treble and bass viols.

of three or four musicians often replaced the organist in the Church and provided appropriate music for the service. Other groups of about the same size provided light musical entertainment in rooms ("chambers") of the palaces and private residences of their aristocratic employers. Those activities soon gave rise to a new musical medium: *chamber music.* When the performances were more pretentious or the rooms larger, the instrumental groups were augmented: here we find the beginning of the orchestra as the term is understood today.

Sacred choral works continued to be written in the period that saw the emergence of independent instrumental music and the domination of the opera. Indeed, several new sacred forms were introduced in the early Baroque period, notably the *oratorio* and the *sacred cantata;* and the composers of these works gradually developed a new version of the polyphonic style that the early Baroque composers had discarded. Secular music, however, and especially secular instrumental music, became more and more popular, until near the period's end a majority of the compositions served man's purposes rather than God's.

BAROQUE OPERA

In the course of three and a half centuries, standards of operatic production have been considerably altered, but the essential requirements in operatic personnel are now what they were in the early 1600's. The mainstays of an operatic production are the vocal soloists—from three to a dozen—who sing the parts of the principal characters. Supporting the dramatic action is the chorus; and amplifying it, in many cases, is a ballet. The orchestra that ties the vocal forces together may consist of a dozen players or may require as many as the largest symphony. Costumes, lights, scenery, and a fully equipped stage are essential parts of an operatic performance also; and the whole provides a musico-dramatic spectacle unequaled in our culture.

Occasionally today an opera is performed on a concert stage without costumes or scenery, but with participants in conventional dress; this is called a *concert version* of the opera. Certain operas that call for a minimum amount of physical action on the stage (Wagner's *Tristan and Isolde,* for example) are sometimes performed in this fashion.

The new style in which the first operas were written required a new approach to performance. The style itself and its components will be described later (see pp. 334 ff.); it will suffice to say here that the style brought a new musical practice to prominence—namely, *improvisation.* The performer of the keyboard part in an opera orchestra had before him a bass line supplied with figures and other symbols. The symbols and the bass notes together served to outline the harmonies desired by the composer. And from those symbols the performer improvised the chords and the entire accompaniments to the various vocal or recitative numbers.

The practice of improvising from the figured bass or "realizing the figured bass," as it was called (see p. 335), soon spread to other musical media. For a century and a half, keyboard players were required to improvise accompaniments in opera, sacred music, chamber music, and smaller works; as late as the 1850's, figured-bass parts were written occasionally.

A concert in a Baroque church in Munich; detail from an eighteenth-century engraving.

BAROQUE CHAMBER MUSIC

Chamber music is among the oldest of Baroque instrumental media. Its traditional distinguishing marks are these: there is only one player for each instrumental part, as opposed to the dozen or more players of the same part in an orchestra; and a conductor is not required, as he is in an orchestra, opera, band, or chorus. In observing these traditions, chamber-music composers have been challenged and stimulated by the self-imposed limitations to do their best work. A type of music that is intimate, clear, and enjoyable has resulted. Much of the finest music in the world's repertoire is found in this field. In spite of its clarity, chamber music is often felt to be "difficult" by lay listeners. True, it is not a spectacular medium, nor is it often sensational in effect. But its unique values emerge after even slight acquaintance.

One chamber-music form, which served both the Church and the aristocracy through the entire Baroque period, dominated all others; this was the *trio sonata.* It required four players (not three, as its name would indicate). Two violins and a bass or cello formed the trio; and in addition, a player at the harpsichord, organ, or other keyboard instrument improvised an accompaniment over the figured-bass line in the manner described above. From about 1600 until the death of Bach in 1750, an extensive literature in this form was composed; and such works by Corelli, Handel, Bach, Telemann, and other lesser-known Baroque composers are still heard in concerts today.

THE BAROQUE ORCHESTRA

The orchestras that accompanied the earliest operas at the beginning of the Baroque period scarcely resembled our present-day combinations. Twenty to thirty instruments supplied a variety of tone colors, a few flourishes or fanfares, and a few chords for vocal accompaniments. Many of those instruments—viols, lutes, recorders—have since become almost obsolete.

At about the same time, the orchestras of the nobility contained a dozen or two string instruments whose function was to provide music for dancing or to accompany ballet performances. Viols of various sizes formed the bulk of these orchestras, but as the modern violin family developed in the seventeenth century, violins, violas, and cellos soon began to supersede the viols.

As the Baroque period progressed, both types of orchestras grew in size. Members of the violin family, with basses added, formed the nucleus of the group. A few wind instruments were also usually present—flute, oboe, bassoon, sometimes trumpet or horn, and sometimes a pair of tympani. The instrumentation varied from work to work, however, and standardization was unknown. (See p. 365 for the diverse instrumentation of Bach's six "Brandenburg" concertos.) It follows that one cannot generalize about the personnel of the Baroque orchestra.

Orchestral works of the time were supplied with figured-bass parts, as were virtually all Baroque compositions. The conductor (often the composer) sat at a harpsichord in the midst of the orchestra and improvised the harmonic accompaniment for the work at the same time as he vigorously indicated the rhythm and tempo. The practice became so general that it became a tradition long after the need for a figured-bass accompaniment had ended.

The Classical Period (1750–1825)

Early developments in the Classical period were contemporary with the American Revolution and the formation of the United States. Washington was born in 1732, a year that also saw the birth of Haydn, whose music contributed so largely to the formation of the Classical style. The last years of the period followed closely upon the end of the Napoleonic wars, and the general cultural tumult in Europe at that time was one of the factors that led to the decline of Classicism.

The Classical period is one in which the balance shifted in favor of instrumental music. Operas, sacred and secular choral works, and songs continued to be written, but the majority of the principal composers occupied themselves primarily with chamber music, orchestral, and other instrumental works. As in earlier eras, the changes in style and content of the period's new music brought forth a new set of performance practices. The figured bass began to fall out of favor, and all voices of a composition were now written out fully. The improvisatory attitude toward performance died out, except in the cases of the freely improvised solo sections called *cadenzas* in concertos, and began to be replaced by the approach to interpretation described in Chapter 6.

CLASSICAL CHAMBER MUSIC

During the beginning of the Classical period the transformation of musical style caused the trio sonata to be virtually abandoned as a musical form; a new form, the *string quartet,* took its place. This most widespread of chamber-music forms required four instruments—two violins, a viola, and a cello; and with that combination the

Chamber Music Media

The names of sonata combinations are generally shortened; in each case the presence of the piano is implied.

Violin sonata: violin, piano
Cello sonata: cello, piano
Clarinet sonata: clarinet, piano

The most usual combinations of string instruments

String trio: violin, viola, cello
String quartet: violin I, violin II, viola, cello
String quintet: violin I, violin II, viola I, viola II, cello
String sextet: violin I, violin II, viola I, viola II, cello I, cello II

Combinations for piano and strings

Piano trio: violin, cello, piano
Piano quartet: violin, viola, cello, piano
Piano quintet: violin I, violin II, viola, cello, piano

The most usual combinations of woodwinds

Woodwind quartet: flute, oboe, clarinet, bassoon
Woodwind quintet: flute, oboe, clarinet, bassoon, horn
Woodwind-piano quintet: flute, oboe, clarinet, bassoon, piano

string quartet has remained unchanged to the present day. Virtually every major composer from Haydn to Hindemith has written one or more significant works for this combination. (Haydn wrote eighty-three quartets, for example, Mozart, twenty-six, and Beethoven, seventeen.)

The decline of the Baroque trio sonata had the effect of greatly curtailing the role of the harpsichord in chamber music. The piano, which had been developed earlier in the eighteenth century, thereupon became a favorite instrument, and a new literature for piano and strings camc into being. The combination of piano, violin, and cello proved to be most attractive to composers, and was exceeded in popularity only by the string quartet itself. The name of the new combination, in essence a trio for piano and strings, was shortened to *piano trio,* and that name is still in use today. It must be emphasized that in the musical world generally the terms "piano trio" and "piano quartet" do not refer to combinations containing several pianos, as they do in one area of commercial entertainment, but signify the combinations mentioned above.

The role of the piano also gained in importance early in the Classical period. In Baroque chamber music the keyboard player was an accompanist; the musical weight of every composition in which he played lay in the string parts. In Classical chamber music, on the other hand, that condition was radically altered; for now the piano was no longer cast in an accompanying role. Musical responsibilities were equally divided and the piano became an equal partner of the string instruments. As a consequence of this, distinctions between soloist and accompanist cannot be made in Classical and later chamber music.

Combinations of woodwind instruments also found their way into the field of chamber music. The most usual group is the *woodwind quintet* (see table opposite). Music for two or three woodwinds, with or without piano, exists in relatively limited quantities. The combinations of wind instruments interested the great masters only rarely; consequently much of this literature is by lesser-known composers.

In addition to the foregoing media, which include the combinations for string instruments that are most numerous and musically most important, a few isolated masterpieces for unusual combinations fill out the literature. Mozart's Quintet for clarinet and strings, K. 581, and Quintet for woodwinds and piano, K. 452; Beethoven's Quintet for piano and woodwinds, Op. 16, and Septet for strings and woodwinds, Op. 20; and Schubert's Octet for strings and woodwinds, Op. 166—these are among the Classical period's principal works of this mixed category.

THE CLASSICAL ORCHESTRA

As the Baroque period gave way to the Classical, and the orchestral literature grew in size and importance, the orchestra itself acquired more color and flexibility. The unstandardized ensemble of the Baroque period fell out of fashion early in the Classical era, and composers began regularly to include parts for pairs of flutes, oboes, bassoons, and horns in their scores. However, the five-part string division remained the mainstay of the group. For example, the orchestra for which Haydn wrote over half his 104 symphonies (up to about 1780) seldom included more than the following:

6 violins I	2 flutes	2 horns
6 violins II	2 oboes	2 trumpets
4 violas	1 or 2 bassoons	2 tympani
2 cellos		
2 basses		

And much of the time the flutes, trumpets, and tympani were optional.

Toward the late 1780's the size of the orchestra increased. A pair of clarinets was added, and bassoons were always specified in pairs. An orchestra of this size, with perhaps thirty string players divided among the five string parts, and with one player on each of the wind instruments, is called a "Classical orchestra." Virtually all the orchestral works (symphonies, overtures, and concertos) of Haydn, Mozart, and early Beethoven can be performed by a group no larger than the Classical orchestra.

Occasionally Beethoven in his middle- and late-period works called for a few additional instruments. He required three horns in the "Eroica" Symphony, for example, and trombones, piccolo, and contrabassoon in his Symphony No. 5. But the greatest development of the orchestra's resources was delayed until the middle of the Romantic period. (See p. 116 for a table of the orchestra's growth.)

The Romantic Period (1825–1900)

About the time that Napoleon's ravaging of Europe ceased, a new attitude toward music began to make itself felt. Walter Pater characterized a similar new attitude in the other arts when he wrote: "It is the addition of strangeness to beauty that constitutes the romantic character in art; and the desire for beauty being a fixed element in every artistic organization, it is the addition of curiosity to this desire of beauty that constitutes the romantic temper."[1]

The interest in "strangeness" led composers of the time to concern themselves with Oriental stories, supernatural tales, mythology, and folklore. These exotic elements inspired both operatic and instrumental composers; and Eastern legend and literature became the source for many compositions. "Curiosity" took the form of experimenting with new means of expression appropriate to the new subject matters. A consuming interest in the sheer *sound* of music developed—sound, that is, quite apart from other musical factors such as melody, harmony, and form.

The outstanding characteristic of Romanticism is its intense subjectivity. Well-balanced and proportioned forms were no longer the goals toward which composers strove; miniatures and vastly inflated compositions appeared side by side. Sentiment was often reduced to sentimentality in these new forms. Tender emotion, morbid depression, hysterical enthusiasm, impulsiveness—these and many similar moods were

[1] Walter Pater, *Appreciations,* V (Macmillian & Co., London, 1931), p. 246.

expressed. And whatever the emotion, its mode of expression was garbed in glowing instrumental colors.

THE ROMANTIC ORCHESTRA

One of the most significant results of the new interest in sound was the change in the nature of the orchestra. The Romantic period was scarcely on its way before additional instruments began to be specified by forward-looking composers; in this development, Beethoven had preceded the Romanticists, as we have seen. The inclusion of piccolo, contrabassoon, bass clarinet, trombones, and tuba, as well as additional horns, made a larger number of string instruments necessary (see table, p. 116), and by the end of the Romantic period the modern symphony orchestra was an accomplished fact.

This orchestra differed from the Classical orchestra in other respects than size, however. Wind instruments in the earlier group had been limited in a mechanical sense. In general, rudimentary fingering systems were used in playing the woodwinds; and trumpets, and horns resembled bugles, in the sense that they were not equipped with valves (see p. 65).

Between about 1830 and 1885, a number of inventions were applied to wind instruments. New mechanisms and new fingering systems were developed for the woodwinds that extended the range, increased the flexibility, and improved the tone quality of these instruments. Both rotary and piston valves were developed for use in the brasses, to give them the use of the full chromatic scale (see p. 36).

The end result was the flexible, powerful, and colorful orchestra we know today. Composers of the Romantic period made increasing demands upon the technical skill of performers; the latter, together with the instrument manufacturers, met the challenge of the composers. The level of skill that had formerly been confined largely to the virtuoso soloists gradually became typical of any competent orchestral performer.

ROMANTIC PERFORMANCE PRACTICES

The Romantic period also saw the rise of the piano as a favorite solo instrument in public concerts. Previously confined largely to private salons or to appearances as soloists with an orchestra, virtuoso pianists now began to appear before a larger public. They performed sonatas, short pieces, and transcriptions of songs and operatic airs in what came to be called *piano recitals.* And at about the same time the piano became a familiar piece of parlor furniture in modest homes as well as in the most palatial ones.

It is at the hands of these piano virtuosos of the Romantic period that subjective interpretation took on the status of an art. Pianists such as Mendelssohn, Liszt, and Bülow gradually developed the principles of interpretation that are valid today. Many of Europe's leading pianists were orchestral conductors as well, and interpretation soon became the conductor's principal function.

The transition from the composer-conductor at the harpsichord to the baton-wielding virtuoso of the Romantic period was not made directly. For a time the orchestra's leading violinist conducted with his bow from his place in the violin section. Soon he moved to the center of the stage and substituted a thin wooden wand for the violin bow (orchestra players as well as listeners objected to this novelty). Still later the "sensa-

Instrumentation of Five Selected Compositions Between 1795 and 1913*

Haydn, Symphony No. 104 ("London") 1795	Schumann, Symphony No. 1 1841	Franck, Symphony in D minor 1888	Strauss, *Symphonia Domestica* 1903	Stravinsky, *The Rite of Spring* 1913
2 flutes 2 oboes 2 clarinets 2 bassoons	2 flutes 2 oboes 2 clarinets 2 bassoons	2 flutes 2 oboes 1 English horn 2 clarinets 1 bass clarinet 2 bassoons	1 piccolo 3 flutes 2 oboes 1 oboe d'amore 1 English horn 1 clarinet in D 3 clarinets 1 bass clarinet 4 bassoons 1 contrabassoon	2 piccolos 2 flutes 1 flute in G 3 oboes 2 English horns 1 E-flat clarinet 3 clarinets 1 bass clarinet 4 bassoons 1 contrabassoon
2 horns 2 trumpets	4 horns 2 trumpets	4 horns 2 trumpets 2 cornets 3 trombones 1 tuba	4 saxophones 8 horns 4 trumpets 3 trombones 1 tuba	8 horns 4 trumpets 1 bass trumpet 3 trombones 2 tubas
2 tympani	2 tympani 1 triangle	3 tympani 1 harp	4 tympani assorted percussion (2 players) 2 harps	4 tympani 1 bass drum 2 cymbals 1 triangle 1 tamtam
violins I violins II violas cellos contrabasses	violins I violins II violas cellos contrabasses	violins I violins II violas cellos contrabasses	violins I violins II violas cellos contrabasses	violins I violins II violas cellos contrabasses

*The table reveals graphically the extent to which the resources of the symphony orchestra increased in little more than a century. A definite pattern of instrumentation for the orchestra was first established in Mannheim, Germany, in the 1740's. In the following decades that pattern was adopted by other European orchestras; and beginning about 1790, instrumentation became somewhat standardized. Within a short time, however, the orchestra grew beyond the standard list of instruments, and the nineteenth century was marked by a great increase in the orchestra's size. However, since 1930, a tendency toward fewer instruments has been observed.

tional" conductor became a familiar sight on the concert stage. The most prominent of such performers, Louis Jullien, pomaded his hair afresh for each concert, wore elaborately embroidered vests and white gloves, and sat in a velvet-upholstered chair facing the audience rather than the orchestra—so that his gestures and grimaces could be properly appreciated.

The Contemporary Period (1900-   )

About the turn of the century another major revolution in musical style was set in motion—one as far-reaching as those of 1300 and 1600. It began with the feeling that the tonal system of major and minor scales and the chords related to them, which had served composers for three centuries, had outlived its usefulness. The tones of the chromatic scale were employed in new ways, and several theories of how to combine those tones into a new kind of harmony were developed. Many other musical factors were radically revised; subjective feeling was frowned upon, and a new kind of modern, nonsentimental objectivity was sought.

In spite of the new sound of the new music, however, the performance practices of the present day are not essentially different from those of the Romantic period. Virtuoso conductors have flourished mightily, and have successfully impressed their own interpretations upon everything in their respective repertoires. Orchestras, opera companies, choral groups, and all the other musical combinations are largely as they were in the late nineteenth century. And a very large portion of the music heard today is music that was heard seventy-five or more years ago. The Romantic repertoire still is a basic part of today's performances.

One new performing medium has appeared in recent decades, however, and that is the tape recorder. Composers in the field of electronic music (see Chapter 18) manipu-

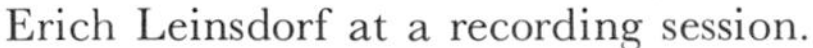

Erich Leinsdorf at a recording session.

Erich Leinsdorf and the Boston Symphony in concert.

late either conventional musical tones or electronically generated sounds, recording the results on magnetic tape. The tape recorder thereby takes over the role traditionally given to the living performer, for the recorder is the only intermediary between composer and listener. The impact of this activity on the total field of music is yet to be assessed. At the moment it is a new development that challenges the attention and interest of everyone concerned with music.

With this exception, musical performing groups have not changed materially in form or method in the twentieth century. Although this is so, much of the activity of these performing groups comes to listeners through media that were unknown in the Romantic period: recordings and broadcasts. And insofar as the United States is concerned, the economic situation in regard to performance today is different from that of any other period.

Before the beginning of the twentieth century, music in Europe was financially supported in a number of ways: by the Church, by the aristocracy, or by the state. Such kinds of support have not been general in the United States. It is true that for a time, and in certain areas of this country, a few wealthy individuals provided the financial means that enabled music to be performed. In recent decades, however, performance has depended more and more upon the support of the audience itself; as never before, the individual ticket purchaser has become necessary to the welfare of music.

This fact suggests that listening to recordings and broadcasts is not enough, and that financial support on a broad popular basis is essential to the survival of "live" musical

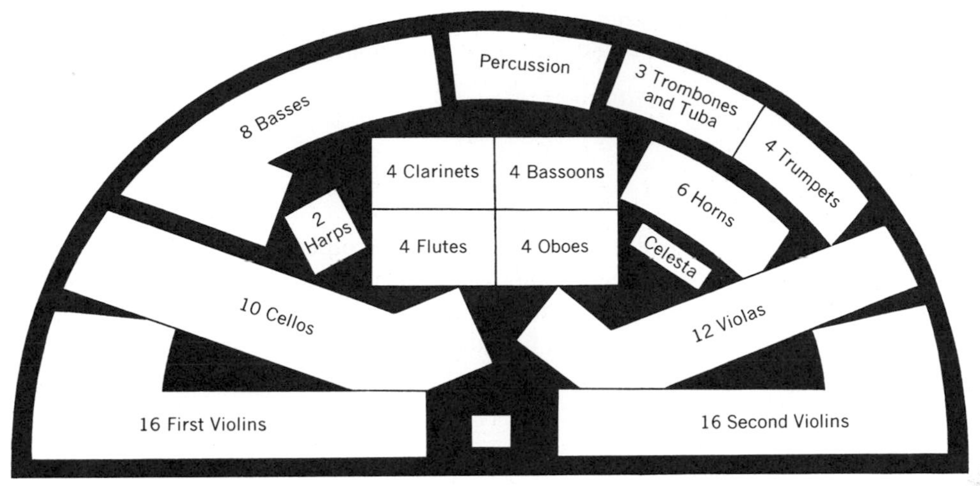

One Seating Plan for a Modern Symphony Orchestra

16 Violins I	6 Horns
16 Violins II	4 Trumpets
12 Violas	3 Trombones
10 Cellos	1 Tuba
8 Basses	2 Harps
	1 Piano
3 Flutes	1 Celesta
1 Piccolo	
3 Oboes	Tympani
1 English Horn	Bass Drum
3 Clarinets	Snare Drum
1 Bass Clarinet	Cymbals
3 Bassoons	Assorted Percussion
1 Contrabassoon	Instruments

performance. Live performances are no longer confined to the largest cities, as they were until quite recently. Community orchestras exist in many parts of the country; world-famous recitalists and chamber-music groups often appear in very small communities. Opportunities to hear music performed by living musicians are everywhere available, but the opportunities are not always fully taken advantage of.

Phonograph recordings and broadcasts are convenient means for awakening an interest in music or for recapturing a musical experience, but they cannot long substitute for live performance. The listener can advance his interest in the best and most natural manner by attending concerts and recitals whenever the opportunity offers. He will then contribute to his own welfare as a music-lover, and do so in a concrete way.

By supporting live performance whenever he can, he will do his part to assure the continuance of one of the noblest and most enjoyable of human activities—making music.

Listening Suggestions

The following compositions are representative of their respective historical periods. The student will find it helpful to select one particular element, listen for the element in compositions of different periods, and make a comparison of the way it is employed in the successive periods. For example, first the melodic element may be isolated in a Renaissance, a Baroque, and a contemporary composition; then the element of texture may be compared; and so on.

RENAISSANCE
Byrd, Mass for Four Voices
Josquin, *De Profundis*
Palestrina, *Missa Papae Marcelli* ("Mass of Pope Marcellus")

BAROQUE
Bach, "Brandenburg" Concertos, Nos. 1–6
———, "Italian" Concerto (for harpsichord)
Corelli, Concerto Grosso, Op. 6, No. 8 ("Christmas Concerto")
Handel, *Water Music*
Monteverdi, *The Coronation of Poppæa*
Vivaldi, Concerto Grosso, Op. 3, No. 8

CLASSICAL
Beethoven, Sonata, Op. 53 ("Waldstein")
Haydn, String Quartet, Op. 76, No. 4 ("Sunrise")
Mozart, *The Marriage of Figaro,* K. 492

EARLY ROMANTIC
Chopin, Nocturnes
Mendelssohn, Symphony No. 3, Op. 56 ("Scotch")
Schumann, *Frauenliebe und Leben,* Op. 42 (song cycle)
———, Symphony No. 3, Op. 97 ("Rhenish")

LATE ROMANTIC
Borodin, "Polovtsian Dances" from *Prince Igor*
Rimsky-Korsakov, *Scheherazade,* Op. 35
Schoenberg, *Verklärte Nacht* ("Transfigured Night")
Sibelius, Symphony No. 1, E minor
Strauss, *Don Juan*
Wagner, *Siegfried Idyl*

CONTEMPORARY

Copland, *Appalachian Spring*
Hindemith, *Nobilissima Visione*
Sessions, Symphony No. 2
Stravinsky, *The Firebird*, Suite
Ussachevsky, *Piece for Tape Recorder* (Composers Recordings, Inc., No. 112)

PART TWO The Traditional Repertoire

Chapter 8

THE CLASSICAL PERIOD

Artists in all media and in all centuries have faced the problem of imposing a sense of order or an organizational scheme on their material—whether that material consisted of verbal images, ideas, shapes, spaces, colors, tones, or any other matter subject to aesthetic treatment. That problem has been solved in many different ways through the course of history, for each change in the nature of the material employed has required changes in the way it was ordered, organized, or presented. The style periods discussed briefly in the previous chapter are themselves manifestations of those various solutions; each new style represents the collective work of a generation or more of the poets, painters, architects, or musicians who sought to organize in aesthetic fashion the material that was available to them.

The composer's material is the conglomerate of tones, tone colors, harmonies, and rhythms that he uses to express his musical ideas; the order or organization of that material is represented by his manner of connecting, relating, and contrasting one bit of material to another. The material is *content;* the manner of treating it results in a *form.* Either one may be approached in ways ranging from experimental or radical to conservative or reactionary. At various times in past centuries some composers have attempted to adapt radically new expressive content to traditional forms or have tried to force traditional material into experimental forms. In most cases the music that resulted has seldom lived past the lifetime of its composers. Other composers have found an aesthetically satisfying relationship between form and content; traditional material has been meshed to traditional patterns of organization, or new types of material have been cast in new patterns. When the creative forces were balanced in this way, the term "classical" has been applied, for that term carries connotations of excellence, clarity, proportion, dignity, and beauty.

In the present chapter we shall be concerned with the period about 1750 to 1825. During that period, new melodic types, new textures, and new expressive ideas inherited from composers a generation earlier were refined, clarified, and invested with dignity. These changes took place under the influence of a kind of formal principle that was being developed simultaneously. Thus forms were adapted or newly created to fit the new expressive content, and a perfect balance of content and form resulted. So striking were those results, and so excellent the majority of the music composed during that time, that historians have applied the term "Classical period" to the seventy-five years under discussion here.

An example of what Classicism is *not* may be helpful in clarifying this balance. Imagine a speaker intoning, with exaggerated dramatic utterance and in a voice filled with pathos, remarks such as: "Today is Wednesday," or "The weather is improving." Or again, imagine him delivering the Gettysburg Address in a flippant, superficial fashion that has no bearing on the depth and dignity of the sentiments in those inspired paragraphs. In neither case has the speaker found the proper relationship between the thing expressed (content) and the way of expressing it (form).

The existence of the careless designation of "classical music" as opposed to "popular music" may be disregarded here, for it has value neither in fact nor in history. It tends to legitimize the curious anomaly "semi-classical music," which seems to imply music too "good" to be truly popular and not "good" enough to be truly classical. And that, of course, is an absurdity. We shall therefore confine the term "Classical" (capitalized) to the historical period with which we are concerned here.

The composers who best represent the Classical period are Haydn, Mozart, and Beethoven, all of whom are closely associated with the city of Vienna. Haydn began his professional career in the Austrian capital about 1755, and Beethoven died there in 1827; these biographical facts determine approximately the limits of the Classical period. The previous style period, the Baroque, ended about 1750 and is represented in its latest style manifestations by Bach and Handel, who will be discussed in Chapter 16. Even before the Baroque style had reached its peak, another set of style elements, called *galant,* had come into being and existed contemporaneously with the Baroque. The *galant* style, providing the ground out of which the Classical was to grow, continued in use past the time that Classicism took its first definite shape. Thus the period in which *galant* elements flourished may be looked upon as a subperiod that overlapped both the Baroque and Classical eras (see the chronological discussion of the characteristics of these two periods in Chapter 7).

The Rococo Subperiod

In 1715 Louis XIV died; he had been King of France for seventy-two years and had influenced, through his nod or his frown, virtually all French art and cultural affairs. During his long reign, art had become characterized by massive proportions, formal dignity, and an elaborate if austere style. The King had exerted conservative authority on many artists and architects of the time, especially those associated with the palace at Versailles. With his death that authority ended and a new architectural style was born. Formal gardens were enlivened by statues of nymphs and other mythological figures. Artificial ruins made of carved stone dotted the landscape. Stucco decorations and delicate traceries of sculptured rock became typical architectural ornaments. The new style flourished in France during the time of Louis XV, who reigned from 1715 to 1774. It spread quickly to other parts of Europe and became especially popular at the courts in Germany and Austria. The Nymphenburg Palace, near Munich, and *Sans Souci,* the home of Frederick the Great in Potsdam, are outstanding examples. The new architectural style was gay and lighthearted, reflecting a search for entertainment. It thrived on freedom from rules and soon degenerated into extravagance. Its name, "rococo," is derived from the French *rocaille*, which refers to the sculptured rockwork itself.

Influenced by the new architectural style at the courts, a new kind of music soon emerged. Dilletantism became fashionable; noble lords and ladies took up the violin and the flute, and composers adjusted their style to the tastes and abilities of their patrons. The music was elegant and pleasing, but often trivial; the application of the term *galant* to this music is appropriate. Homophonic textures predominated, with ingratiating melodies set in the most obvious place, at the top of the tonal fabric. A host of minor French and German composers supplied the needs of the times by writing in the new *galant* style; many of them had brief moments of prominence, then sank into near oblivion.

Italian composers remained relatively free of these French and pseudo-French developments. The fresh air of novelty crossed the Alps, however, and a number of significant events took place in Italy. A style that had been formalistic and heavy gave way to one that was melodious and thin-textured; the beginnings of symmetry or recapitulation appeared in the forms. These elements were refined and carried further by later generations and became the basic ingredients of the Classical style, which began to take shape primarily in Vienna in the years after 1750.

In the decades between about 1730 and 1750, operatic performances became extremely popular with masses of people who had had little previous contact with music. This interest in turn greatly increased the demand for music of all kinds. In the following years, the number of public orchestral concerts and the size of the general audience grew steadily.

The producers of orchestral concerts were faced at first with the lack of a suitable repertoire. In general, three musical forms were available: the orchestral dance suite, the concerto, and the *sinfonia* (plural, *sinfonie*). The dance suite, a set of unconnected movements each in a different dance rhythm (*allemande, courante, gigue,* and *bourrée* are typical), was especially popular in France and southern Germany. It became obsolete shortly after the middle of the century, however, and was replaced by the *divertimento*—somewhat similar to the dance suite but less regular in form and less bound to dance rhythms. Divertimenti for small ensembles of string or wind instruments appeared, and these in turn prepared the way for present-day chamber music forms. The concerto, a work usually in several movements and set for one or more soloists and orchestra, provided the nucleus of the programs. And the sinfonia, originally a curtain-raiser (overture) for one type of Italian opera, was transformed in both content and form and eventually became the most important orchestral form of the emerging Classical period.

In about 1740 the sinfonia was separated from the opera and was often used as a concert-program form in its own right. In addition, an enormous number of separate sinfonie were written by minor German and Italian composers and were presented in public concerts to fill out the spaces not occupied by concertos, arias, and various smaller forms. The typical sinfonia was short, and its three movements, in fast-slow-fast tempo, were seldom of more ambitious scope than other typical Rococo music. It became desirable, then, to deepen the content and enlarge the scope of the sinfonia (especially of its first movement) so that it could compete with the concerto, whose brilliance and virtuoso appeal were important factors in increasing the concert audience. One important step in this direction was taken by a few Austrian and German composers in about 1740: the minuet was borrowed from the dance suite and inserted in the sinfonia. The four-movement form known today as the symphony and described below (see p. 132) was the result.

The Neapolitan opera orchestra for which the earliest of the sinfonie were written was modest in size. Composed mainly of string instruments, it occasionally employed an oboe and a bassoon to reinforce the strings, and on special occasions a pair each of trumpets and tympani were added. But soon after the sinfonia left the opera house and entered the concert hall, its orchestral personnel became more numerous. Pairs of oboes and horns joined the orchestra; flutes were often called for; and in certain of the larger establishments—notably in Paris and in Mannheim—clarinets were substituted for the oboes on occasion. Before 1750 the instrumentation of the orchestra had not been standardized (see p. 111); after that time, standardization became relatively more common, and orchestras in the various countries began to approach uniformity as to number and distribution of instruments. The composer of a sinfonia in Mannheim, say, could be reasonably sure that an orchestra in London, Berlin, Vienna, or Milan would include all the players his work required.

At this point in history the stage was set for the arrival of the masters who were to usher in and formulate the Classical style. Further refinements in the *galant* style took on secondary importance. Homophonic textures dominated virtually all compositions, and a typical piece seldom consisted of more than a series of pleasant melodies supported by chords. And certain forms that had been introduced in the Rococo subperiod now completed their development.

Musical Forms of the Classical Period

In Chapter 5 the place of the song form in the hierarchy of forms was discussed. Consisting of a group of phrases arranged with regard to symmetry or contrast, the song form may appear as a short composition complete in iteself or as a component of a larger form. In the Classical period it most often assumed the latter function.

MINUET AND SCHERZO

In almost every case the *minuet* as written by Haydn and Mozart consists of two dances. The first dance, called simply "minuet," is usually of song-form length and comes to a definite close. It is followed by a second dance, the "trio"—also of song-form length and with a definite close—which is most often set in a contrasting key. Then comes a return, or *recapitulation*, of the first dance. The whole is consequently a symmetrical form of three separate song forms and may be diagrammed as ABA. Its full name is "song form with trio and recapitulation."

In the majority of cases the first dance consists of two parts, each of which is repeated; the trio is constructed similarly but may be shorter than the first dance. The recapitulation is seldom written out. A symbol, *da capo* or *D.C.*, placed at the end of the trio indicates to the performer that the piece is to be played again from the beginning to the end of the first dance (which thus becomes the third). It has long been customary not to observe the repeat signs on the second playing; thus the entire piece is performed as shown in Example 44. The minuet from Haydn's "Sunrise" String Quartet is given in outline on page 139.

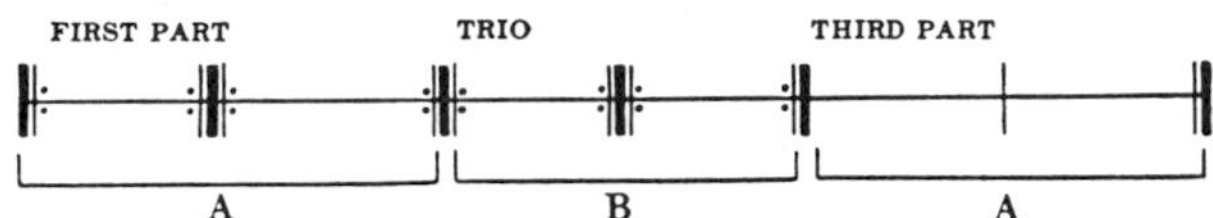

Example 44

Ever since its inception in the seventeenth century, the minuet has most frequently been a dance in triple meter. In the minuets of Haydn and Mozart a stately quality that had characterized the dance since its origin is usually preserved. In the works of Beethoven and later composers, however, as well as in a few of Haydn's string quartets, the tempo of the minuet was often increased, and with the greater speed an element of humor or vitality came to replace the stateliness. The symmetrical form was not altered, even though on occasion a repetition of the trio and a second recapitulation were added, to make the form ABABA. The new, faster, and more humorous version is known as the *scherzo*, and it practically replaced the minuet in much orchestral and chamber music composed after the early 1800's.

RONDO FORMS

The *rondos* are a class of forms whose diagrams may be similar to those of the minuet and scherzo, but whose content and mood are quite different. First, the rondo is likely to be continuous from beginning to end, and normally will not have the breaks in continuity that occur at the end of the first part (and often at the end of the trio) in the minuet. Further, the rondo often is written in fast duple meter, as opposed to the triple meter of the minuet. And finally, the rondo generally displays a lively, rollicking, or brilliant mood, unlike the stateliness of the minuet.

The rondo is based on the principle of alternating themes, of which at least one is of song-form length or greater; these themes are arranged in the order ABA, ABABA, ABACA, or ABACABA. The principle is seen to involve a periodic return to a thematic statement after a contrasting theme, which is generally in a related key; and the number of returns determines whether the form is to be called a first, second, or third rondo. In highly organized examples of the rondo, transitions, modulations, and even short sections of development appear between the various thematic sections. The presence of such "connective tissue" ensures that a rondo will be perceived as a unit, and not as a set of three or more separate pieces—the effect often produced by a minuet or

A chamber orchestra at Sans Souci, Potsdam. Carl Philipp Emanuel Bach at the harpsichord, Frederick the Great playing the flute in the foreground.

scherzo. (Beethoven's use of transitions in the scherzo of the Symphony No. 7, as seen in Example 56, is unusual for his time.)

A rondo is often found as the last movement of an eighteenth-century symphony, string quartet, or sonata, although Beethoven in the early nineteenth century continued to employ the form, as did Brahms and many other composers later in that century. A typical example is diagrammed below: it is the fourth movement of Haydn's "Clock" Symphony, No. 101. The humor, energy, and formal freedom displayed by that movement are quite characteristic of rondos in general. Another of Haydn's rondos, from his String Quartet, Op. 76, No. 4, is outlined on pages 139–40.

SECTION	KEY	CONTENT
A	D major	a, b, a
B	A major	c
A	A major	a, with new countertheme
b	D and A	derived from b, above
A	D major	variations of a and b
C	D minor and G minor	d, with development of a
A	D major	fugal treatment of a, with new counterthemes
Coda	D major	a, with development

SONATA-FORM

The most highly organized of all musical forms is the *sonata-form.* It is usually found as the first movement in symphonies and other instrumental works by Haydn and other

Classical composers; for that reason it is sometimes called *first-movement form.* It is generally performed at a moderately fast tempo; thus an alternate name, *sonata-allegro,* is sometimes justified. But it is found in positions other than the first movement; it appears often as a single-movement form (for example, as the so-called *concert overture*); and it may appear in a variety of tempos other than allegro. In such cases, neither of the alternate names is appropriate. The term *sonata-form* meets all the conditions under which the form is found, and it is the term we shall use throughout this book.

Sonata-form is a vehicle for expressing drama and conflict in music and has been used as such for more than two centuries. Although great changes in musical style and taste have taken place in that interval, the basic principle of sonata-form has remained unchanged. The content, proportions, and details of the form have varied from one generation to the next, but the element of musical conflict between groups of themes has remained and continues to be utilized by composers writing in sonata-form.

The basic principles may be stated simply: (1) two or more contrasting themes are presented; (2) the contrasting characteristics and potentialities of the themes are brought into the open and a dramatic conflict ensues; (3) the themes are heard again and revealed in a new light as a result of the conflict. Thus three large sections suggest themselves: thematic exposition, development, and recapitulation; to these an introduction and a coda are often added.

As is true of other musical forms, the greatest possible freedom is practiced by composers writing in sonata-form. Among the many details revealed by an examination of standard works written in that form, the following may be singled out: the number of themes and theme fragments may vary from two to a dozen or more; several themes are often combined into a theme group, which generally exhibits similarity of mood, style, and tonality; transitions are liberally used, and sometimes become miniature development sections; the recapitulation of the themes is not always in the same order (or as complete) as in the exposition; and the coda or closing section often summarizes or continues the development and the conflict.

While we should keep in mind the extent of freedom that is typical, we may use the following outline to illustrate what we may expect to find in many examples of the sonata-form.

EXPOSITION

Introduction.
First theme or theme group, in tonic key, and often dramatic in mood.
Transition, with modulation to key of second theme.
Second theme or theme group, in contrasting key, and in a lyric mood that contrasts with the mood of the first theme.
Codetta or third theme, in key of second theme.

DEVELOPMENT

Free manipulation of the thematic material (see Example 41, p. 81).
Themes may be reduced to fragments, the fragments may be recombined, and out of them new ideas may grow.
Major climaxes may occur, to illustrate the conflict between lyric and dramatic moods.
(The section is called "free fantasy" in German, and this gives a clue to its nature.)

RECAPITULATION

First theme or theme group (perhaps in part only), most often in the tonic key.
Retransition, designed to suggest that the second theme will be presented in a contrasting key.
Second theme or theme group (perhaps in part only), but now in the tonic key.
Coda, which concludes the entire movement, and which often takes on the function of a second (terminal) development section.

SONATA TYPES

In the three and one-half centuries since the term *sonata* was first introduced, it has been applied to several different compound forms. We shall use it here in its most common meaning—a composition containing three or more contrasting movements, composed for one or two instruments—but we shall immediately expand that definition to include various *types* of sonatas that are written for more than one or two instruments. The *sonata,* which is under discussion here, and *sonata-form,* discussed immediately above, are by no means synonymous. In the interest of accuracy and clarity, it is well to keep in mind the fact that *sonata-form* is a single movement that appears most often as a part of the compound form called *sonata.*

The sonata as a compound or multi-movement form is a means of expressing a variety of related or contrasting moods within a flexible framework. Tradition has long decreed that if the composition is written for one or two instruments, the form is called a sonata, as defined above. But the identical form may also be used in writing for three or more instruments; in fact, up to a hundred or more instruments may be involved with little more than a change in the name and size of the resultant form. When written for three to about nine instruments, the form is found most often in the field of chamber music; the various names attached to such compositions indicate both the number and classification of the instruments involved (see p. 112). As we will see below, both Haydn and Mozart, along with their minor colleagues in the Classical period, employed this type of sonata extensively in their chamber-music works.

Even a work that requires from two dozen to a hundred or more instruments—namely, the *symphony*—is essentially a sonata type for orchestra. And the *concerto* is likewise in most respects a sonata for solo instrument and orchestra. Even though the concerto usually introduces an element of competition between its two performing entities—in the sense that the solo instrument is often given its own thematic material—it generally makes use of sonata-form movements in the manner of a symphony. (An earlier type of concerto that flourished for a century before about 1750 and that made use of other types of organization will be discussed in Chapter 16.)

One quantitative difference between the symphony and the other sonata types may be noted. The symphony is likely to be longer, to contain more thematic material in its respective movements, and to be more elaborately organized, than other sonata types.

Most typically, the first movement of a symphony is written in sonata-form and in moderately fast tempo. The second movement, usually in a contrasting key and in a slow tempo, may be a set of variations, a slow rondo, a sonatina-form (that is, a sonata-form with its development section replaced by a short transition), or even another sonata-form. If the work contains four movements, the third movement is most often a minuet or a scherzo of the type described above; the tempo is then animated or fast, and the key is usually that of the first movement. The last movement, almost invariably in fast tempo and in the key of the first movement, is likely to be a rondo or a sonata-form.

If the symphony is well made, it will be emotionally satisfying; that is, it will provide both unity and variety and will embody a feeling of direction, a sense of striving toward and reaching a goal. In addition to unity of style, a sense of unity is often felt because of the fact that two (or three) of the movements are in the same key. This unity is strong enough to justify designating that key as the distinguishing mark of the work, thus: "Symphony in E flat," or "Symphony in G minor," and so on. Such terms are appropriate, even though at least one movement is in a constrasting key and large sections of the sonata-form movements are themselves in keys other than the main key of the work.

The variety in a symphony is provided by the contrasts of tempo, mood, and emotional content between the several movements. The intense expression and dramatic conflict characteristic of a sonata-form movement, for example, bring forth a response quite different from that evoked by a stately minuet, a humorous scherzo, or a buoyant rondo. And the composer, in assembling the compound form, takes into account the emotional effect resulting from the structural plans of the successive movements.

The feeling of direction suggested by a well-made symphony is a more subtle matter. It may be caused in part by the sequence of tempos the work reveals; for the most typical pattern is one in which the moderately fast first movement is followed by three movements that range from slow to animated to very fast. The sequence established by the changes in mood from concentrated, to profound, to light-hearted, to vivacious may be in part responsible. In some cases, a gradual lifting of moods from dark to light may be felt across the four movements. Occasionally, but seldom in the works of Haydn and Mozart to be discussed below, a symphony will imply emotional direction by suggesting a sequence of dark-light-dark, as one with a slow introduction, fast inner movements, and slow finale may do.

Such then, are the single-movement forms (minuet and rondo) and compound forms (the various sonata types, including the symphony and chamber-music media) that were developed near the beginning of the Classical period. The formal ingredients were at hand, awaiting only composers who could transform Rococo music into something significant and lasting. Those composers were primarily Haydn and Mozart.

Haydn

Franz Joseph Haydn (1732–1809) was born in Rohrau, an Austrian village near Hungary. His father, a wagonmaker, enjoyed singing but had no formal training in music; the same was true of his mother, who had been a cook before her marriage. Haydn was gifted with an excellent voice even as a boy; at the age of eight he was engaged for the choir of St. Stephen's Cathedral in Vienna. He remained in the choir until his voice changed; then, at the age of seventeen, he was discharged.

His instruction at St. Stephen's had included a few lessons on the violin and the harpsichord, voice training, a grounding in musical theory, and an introduction to Latin and other subjects. But Haydn was observant, willing to experiment, and eager to learn; he had gone far beyond the limits of his formal instruction even as a choirboy. He had gained vocal experience and an insight into the choral repertoire. From that point onward, he was largely his own teacher.

At the time that Haydn was thrown upon his own resources, Vienna was probably the most musical city in Europe. It was the cultural center of the Austrian empire and it lay at the crossroads of Europe. Hungarian, Turkish, German, French, Italian, and other influences appeared in Austrian music, and Haydn was exposed to them all. It is not altogether accidental that Vienna became the spiritual home of the emerging Classical style, nor that Haydn became its first principal exponent.

He spent several desultory years, both as a performer and as a composer, with various bands of strolling serenaders, and for three years he was a composer and a violinist in two aristocratic musical households. Then, in 1761, at the age of twenty-nine, he secured his first important position. He was engaged by the fabulously wealthy Prince Paul Anton Esterházy, in the service of whose family he remained for almost thirty years.

Under two princes (Paul died in 1762 and was succeeded by his brother Nicholas) and at two princely establishments (Eisenstadt, 1761–66, and the immense, newly built palace of Esterháza, 1766–90), Haydn served as second in command and later (1766) as director of all musical activities. In this establishment, which included both instrumentalists and singers, Haydn's responsibilities included administrative and disciplinary details as well as composing, rehearsing, and conducting for all palace functions.

During this long term of service, Haydn had little firsthand contact with other composers, except for a meeting with Mozart in the winter of 1781–82. (The meeting developed into a close friendship that was maintained during the remainder of Mozart's life, and that had beneficial results for both composers.) A few winter visits to Vienna offered him some stimulation, but in general he worked in isolation. He was further encumbered by an unsympathetic wife. Yet he composed incessantly, and his disposition remained serene and good-natured.

In 1790, having been retired on a pension, he was prevailed upon to go to London to compose and conduct for Johann Peter Salomon, an enterprising concert manager. His visit, which lasted almost two seasons, was successful both musically and financially. In addition, he was awarded the degree of Doctor of Music by Oxford University. A second visit, in 1794–95, was equally successful, and he returned to Vienna as the most famous composer of Europe.

The creative energy Haydn had demonstrated for forty-five years gradually lessened after the London visits. The stream of compositions that had flowed so copiously since about 1750 began to dry up—even though the two great oratorios, *The Creation* and *The Seasons,* were written in the last years of the eighteenth century. Increasing weakness made public appearances difficult, and Haydn lived in almost complete retirement for the last several years of his life. In 1809, with Napoleon's troops beginning the bombardment of Vienna, Haydn died.

Franz Joseph Haydn (1732–1809). His quartets of Opus 33 mark a turning point in the evolution of musical style. (From an engraving by Schiavonetti.)

INSTRUMENTAL MUSIC

Haydn was among the most prolific composers of the eighteenth century. The complete list of his operas and other stage works, Masses and other sacred music, symphonies, concertos, quartets, trios, divertimenti, and many smaller compositions totals almost a thousand works. Much of this music has been lost, many works have never been printed, and only a relatively small number of them are still performed. A scant dozen of his 104 symphonies, perhaps an equal number of his 83 quartets, two or three concertos, and one oratorio—these are his only works that are heard with a fair degree of frequency today. Yet the quality of Haydn's music is such that he must be numbered among the truly great composers.

The early symphonies reveal how closely Haydn adhered to the *galant* style then current. Not until about 1764, in his Symphony No. 20, did he regularly adopt the four-movement form. But even in his early works his fast melodies show little of the artificiality of the time; and in slow movements he avoided the excess of sentiment that often disfigures the works of his forgotten contemporaries.

As Haydn gained experience and confidence, he experimented endlessly in order to solidify the form and deepen the content of his symphonies. In about 1770, a new type of melody began to appear in his works; often consisting of short motives, rhythmically more striking, and possessing noteworthy contours, such melodies gave added strength and forcefulness to his music. He experimented with music written in remote keys: the well-known "Farewell" Symphony, No. 45 in F sharp minor, and No. 46 in B major are examples. And in about 1781 he arrived at a new technique of composition—that of thematic development. Haydn was conscious of the extent of this innovation; when he applied it to his six string quartets of Op. 33 (published in 1782), he described the works as "written in an entirely new manner."

The Haydn symphonies most often performed today are drawn from his last twelve—those he wrote for Salomon on the occasion of the two London visits; hence the names "Salomon" or "London" symphonies are often given to the twelve. Several of them bear individual nicknames as well: No. 94, the "Surprise" Symphony; No. 101, the "Clock"; No. 103, the "Drum Roll"; and No. 104, the "London." To the twelve symphonies mentioned above must be added the one that immediately precedes them: No. 92, the "Oxford," written in about 1788 but performed when Haydn received his doctor's degree at Oxford on his first trip to England.

The "Clock" Symphony is representative of the best in Haydn. It begins with a slow introduction, moody and remote. This is followed by the fast first movement in sonata-form, which presents lively and rollicking themes in a buoyant manner. Loud sections for full orchestra alternate with quiet passages given to a few strings, but the rhythmic lightness does not falter. Every note is made to count in the transparent texture, and the music is perfectly proportioned.

The "Clock" Symphony takes its nickname from a rhythmic figure in the second movement, a figure that suggests the ticking of a clock (see Example 45). Haydn's works give plentiful evidence of his delightful sense of humor, and this movement is an excellent example. The florid melodies flow on with grace and elegance above the pulsating "tick-tock" of the accompanying instruments; the charm of the one and the dry humor of the other are beautifully contrasted.

The minuet, with an unusual static accompaniment in its trio (see Example 46) is more vigorous than many of the hundreds of minuets Haydn wrote. It provides an appropriate contrast to the lightly humorous second movement and to the brisk fourth. The latter is a rondo (see outline, p. 130); it drives along at a rapid pace, with ap-

Example 45

Haydn, Symphony No. 101 ("Clock")

Andante

I BASSOON II

I VIOLIN II

CELLO BASS

p

pizz.

pizz.

Haydn, Symphony No. 101 ("Clock") *Example 46*

propriate relaxed moments and with many sudden changes from soft to loud. The sheer joyfulness of the music is vividly communicated to the listener, and Haydn's skillful manipulation of his orchestral forces keeps interest at a high level.

The qualities found so abundantly in Haydn's symphonies are found also in his string quartets. He had written some forty quartets up to 1772; he then wrote none for nine years, during which time he worked at improving the form of the symphony. Having achieved that goal, he returned to quartet writing, and composed about forty more between 1781 and 1803. In those works, now that he was equipped with the "new manner," he demonstrated an inexhaustible imagination in the construction and manipulation of melodies. He created a balanced texture in which all the instruments share equally. Melodious themes presented in a composite of homophonic and polyphonic styles, music that is clear and suitable to the four instruments, a form of expression without sentimentality—these elements combine to create the true quartet style of which Haydn was the earliest master. Moods ranging from broad humor to profound seriousness occur in these quartets. With the sonata-form fully established and the quartet style an accomplished fact, Haydn set the standards for other composers to follow.

One of the most successful of his quartets, in B flat, Op. 76, No. 4, was nicknamed "The Sunrise"—possibly because the main theme of the first movement suggests a gradually unfolding mood. The work is outlined below (see pp. 138–40). The outline may indicate that in the hands of a great composer a musical form is not a rigid mold into which musical ideas must be forced, but rather a flexible framework which can be freely adapted to the composer's purposes.

Title page of Haydn's last oratorio, The Seasons (1799).

In these quartets as well as in his later symphonies, Haydn revealed how mutually fruitful was his friendship with Mozart. We shall see below that the younger composer was directly influenced by his contacts with Haydn's music, even to the extent of imitating themes, textures, and phrase structures. In the years after 1785 the influence was reversed, and Haydn made use of devices and elements he had learned to know through Mozart. The type of introduction seen in the "Clock" Symphony, for example, was directly inspired by what Mozart had done in his own symphonies. And the melodic chromaticism that became a feature of Haydn's music in the years between about 1785 and 1790 is also traceable to the impression Mozart's music made upon the older composer.

String Quartet, B flat major, Op. 76, No. 4 ("Sunrise"), by Joseph Haydn

FIRST MOVEMENT, Allegro con spirito, B flat

Meas.	*Theme*	
1	1st	Two six-meas. phrases and a nine-meas. period (Ex. 1)
22		Transition

Example 1

37	2nd	In expected dominant key. Related to 1st theme (Ex. 2)

Example 2

50		Transition derived from meas. 22
60	Codetta	In expected dominant key
DEVELOPMENT		
69		Based on Ex. 1 (meas. 1) and transitional material (meas. 50)
96		Based on codetta theme (meas. 60)
RECAPITULATION		
108	1st	Two six-meas. phrases, as expected; but now nine-meas. period is extended to fifteen meas.
135		Transition similar to meas. 22 ff, but shortened
142	2nd	Theme (Ex. 2) in expected tonic key; but second part of theme (meas. 44–48) is omitted
152		Transition similar to meas. 50–59
162	Codetta	Four meas. similar to meas. 60–63; the rest is an extension
175	Coda	Derived from fragments of Ex. 1 (meas. 1). Movement ends in meas. 188

SECOND MOVEMENT, Adagio, E flat

Meas.	*Section*	
1	A	In E flat major (Ex. 3)

Example 3

17	B	Begins in C minor, thence to B flat (Ex. 4)

Example 4

35	A	Ex. 3, but in E flat minor
43	B	Modulating section; theme extended and ornamented
52	A	Ex. 3, in E flat major again, with extensions and imitations
69	Coda	In E flat; brief extension of two meas. of Ex. 3. Movement ends in meas. 74

THIRD MOVEMENT, Menuetto, Allegro

Meas.	*Part*	
FIRST MINUET		
1	a	In B flat, eight meas. repeated (Ex. 5)

Example 5 

9	b	Derived from first meas. of part a
29	a	Ex. 5, but with extensions. Meas. 9–50 repeated
TRIO		
51	c	In B flat. Eight-meas. phrase with repeat written out (Ex. 6)

Example 6 

68		Development of part c, beginning on dominant
80	c	Eight-meas. phrase, but without repeat
88		Extension of part c, Ex. 6, leading to codetta. Trio ends in meas. 105
MINUET DA CAPO		
1–50		Exact repetition, but without repeats

FOURTH MOVEMENT, Allegro ma non troppo

Meas.	*Part*	
1	a	Eight meas., repeated (Ex. 7)

Example 7 

9	b	Contrasting figure
25	a	Reprise of four meas., thence into codetta (meas. 29). Meas. 9–34 repeated
35	c	In B flat minor. Eight meas. repeated

Haydn, String Quartet (cont.)

35	c	In B flat minor. Eight meas. repeated
43	d	Contrasting figure containing portions of part c
63	c	Reprise of four meas. of part c
67		Transition
75	a	Return of Ex. 7 in B flat major (not repeated)
83	b	Contrasting figure
99	a	Reprise of four meas. of part a
103		Transition to coda
111		Transition continues, but tempo increased to *piu allegro*
129	Coda	Based on part a, Ex. 7, with extensions. Tempo now *piu presto.* Movement ends in meas. 175

VOCAL MUSIC

The many works Haydn composed for voices and instruments represent several types. Chief among them are about thirty works for the stage, almost two hundred songs, about a dozen Masses, and three oratorios. One of the latter, *The Creation,* represents Haydn at his finest, and we shall examine it in some detail. An oratorio is a compound form usually set for solo voices, chorus, and orchestra, and is based on a text that is often of Biblical origin. Portions of the text are traditionally set in a speech-like style and sung by a character called the "narrator"; other portions are divided between soloists and chorus; and the whole is raised to a high dramatic level by the interaction of the voices and instruments.

The Creation owes its existence to a suggestion made by Salomon, Haydn's London manager. A minor poet named Lidley had written a poem, employing the Book of Genesis and Milton's *Paradise Lost,* on the Creation. Haydn, stimulated by contact with Handel's works in England, readily agreed to Salomon's proposal that Lidley's verses be set to music. The completed oratorio was first performed in Vienna in 1798. Haydn was sixty-six at the time, yet the work is among the freshest and most youthful of his compositions. It abounds in wide-ranging harmonies, including chromatic writing of a kind new in his music Perhaps the most imaginatively scored work of the Classical period, it reveals a new sensitivity to the effect of the instrumental colors.

The traditional recitative part of the narrator is here divided among three archangels: Gabriel, Uriel, and Raphael, all of whom are also given arias to sing. Choruses are prominent in *The Creation,* but a traditional distinction between solo arias and massed choruses is broken down in several instances. Elaborate arias contain choral interludes, and choruses include sections sung by one or more soloists. Thus, while *The Creation* contains separate numbers (thirty-four in its three parts), these numbers approach a unity of form and medium. The accompaniment is of symphonic dimensions.

It does not simply double the voice parts as was often the case in other works, but leads an individual life of its own. This fact gives Haydn much greater expressive possibilities than the earlier oratorio composers allowed themselves.

The text of *The Creation* gave Haydn ample opportunity to write dramatically and descriptively. The work begins with an orchestral "Representation of Chaos," which leads into the first recitative, set to verses from the first chapter of Genesis. In that section, Haydn's use of a fortissimo C major chord in a C minor context is a master stroke (see Example 47).

Haydn, *The Creation* ***Example 47***

The section concerned with the creation of the animal kingdom is equally striking. A unison trill depicts the roaring lion; a short series of scale passages denotes the leaping tiger; an angular running figure describes the noble steed; a tremolo in the strings stands for the hordes of insects; and to an undulating chromatic line in slow tempo "in long dimension creeps the sinuous worm . . ." (see Example 48).

Elsewhere Haydn succeeded in combining diverse forms and textures with happy results. Operatic arias in brilliant coloratura style are contrasted with polyphonic choruses. Quiet, limpid melodies are set off by dramatic choruses of praise to the Creator. And unifying the whole are the wealth of melody, the perfect proportions, and the moods of optimism and faith that animate all of Haydn's works. Some commentators declare certain sections to be naïve, but this criticism is based on a misunderstanding of the style. Those sections reflect Haydn's ability to cast aside sophistication and compose music that sparkles as the newly created earth sparkled. *The Creation* is as delightful now as it was in 1798.

Haydn's background was essentially nonmusical. He worked in isolation, and the quality of his music is the result of his own experimenting. When he arrived at musical maturity he was already in his forties. And although he sang and played the violin and harpsichord acceptably, he never became an outstanding performer. In all these respects he was the complete opposite of Mozart.

Example 48

Haydn, *The Creation*

Mozart

MOZART'S LIFE

Wolfgang Amadeus Mozart (1756–91) was born in Salzburg. His father was composer, violinist, and later vice-chapelmaster to various Archbishops of Salzburg. He was also a well-qualified teacher: in 1756, the year of his famous son's birth, he had published his method of violin teaching—a work that was widely used and that for many years was the only fundamental one of its kind. Thus he was in an excellent position to develop his son's enormous talent. At the age of three, Wolfgang began the serious study of music. His father supplied him with music of every kind: old and new, by great and small composers, and in all styles. Each work, each style left its mark upon Mozart and eventually influenced his own style of composition.

After three years of study, in his sixth year, Mozart set out on the first of many concert tours with his father and his sister, the latter also a musical prodigy. Extended stops were made at cities on the route. At public concerts and private performances for the nobility, Mozart played the harpsichord, violin, and organ; he also read difficult compositions at sight and played his own works. In all these activities his sister carried her full share of the musical burden. Auditors were delighted with the unspoiled, gifted children, and the tours were a success both musically and financially.

The trips lasted variously from a few months to three and a half years. By the time Mozart was sixteen he was known in Munich, Vienna, Paris, London, Milan, and other cities. Everywhere he went he had opportunities to hear the music of other composers, obscure and famous alike. And what Mozart heard, he absorbed and remembered. His feats of memory were fabulous. Nothing passed him by; every work he heard made an impression on him. Composing continually, he derived elements that he could use from others' music. Some of these were discarded, others were refined or improved upon—for his critical sense was highly developed.

As he grew older, and his dazzling years as a child prodigy lay behind him, he found that interest in his talents and accomplishments waned. The tours continued, however, until Mozart was twenty-three. He received commissions for operas and other compositions, but the results, even though musically satisfying, did not endure. His many commissions did not lead to the goal Mozart sought above all—a permanent position as a court composer. He was eventually able to secure a position as concertmaster and organist to the Archbishop of Salzburg in 1779, but less than two years later, after a series of disagreements with the Archbishop, he was forcibly ejected from the position.

In 1781 he moved to Vienna; he married Constanza Weber in 1782, and Vienna became his permanent home for the nine years that remained to him. A rewarding feature of his life there was the friendship with Haydn. Mozart had long admired Haydn's music from afar. When he came into closer contact with it and became well acquainted with its genial composer, he reacted to it as he had to the music of other composers. The "new manner" of Haydn made a strong impression upon him, and he exerted himself to master the technique of thematic development—without ever employing it as consistently as did Haydn.

Many commissions came his way, and he presented his own works in public concerts. But his income was uncertain, and since both Mozart and his wife were incompetent in financial matters he was constantly in debt and they often lived in poverty. His works were often coldly received at first, their full stature being beyond the comprehension of audiences of his time. Along with his precarious financial state, this lack of appreciation often brought him to a mood of bitter discouragement, but that mood is seldom reflected in his music. In the last year of his life, when his good friend Haydn

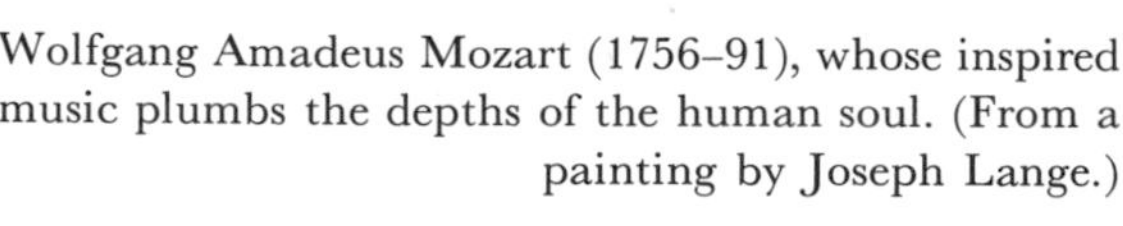
Wolfgang Amadeus Mozart (1756–91), whose inspired music plumbs the depths of the human soul. (From a painting by Joseph Lange.)

was far away in London, his health became undermined. He died in December, 1791, at the age of thirty-five. A few friends accompanied the body part of the way to the cemetery but turned back because of the inclement weather. Mozart, one of the greatest musical geniuses the world has ever known, lies in an unmarked pauper's grave.

MOZART'S MUSIC

Mozart did not use a consecutive set of opus numbers to enumerate his works; as was customary. Many compositions were printed by various publishers; some remained unpublished during his lifetime; and few of them bear identifying marks other than their date of composition. These conditions made it desirable to devise a systematic arrangement of his hundreds of works, so that the order of their writing could be related to the events of his life. The most complete and most valuable of such attempts was made by Ludwig von Köchel, an Austrian nobleman; Köchel published his *Chronologisch-thematisches Verzeichniss* ("index") in 1862. In its sixth edition (1964, edited by Franz Giegling and others), the *Verzeichniss* lists all known works of Mozart, as well as the doubtful ones, together with thematic indexes and other valuable bibliographical information. Mozart's works are referred to by the letters "K." or "K.V." corresponding to their place in the Köchel index, instead of by opus numbers, as are the compositions of most other composers. The numbers of the authentic works range from K.1, a minuet for piano of 1762, to K.626, the Requiem Mass of 1791.

Among Mozart's compositions are about twenty operas and various other stage works, fifteen Masses and many other sacred compositions, almost fifty symphonies, over forty concertos, more than sixty sonatas of various kinds, twenty-six string quartets, almost three dozen other chamber music works, and several hundred large or small compositions for a variety of media. The various styles Mozart employed in these works are indirectly the result of the impressions garnered through two decades of traveling. In some cases the influences become apparent years after the impressions had been made. For example, the dark and tempestuous music of Johann Schobert deeply impressed Mozart as a child in the early 1760's, but not until the 1780's did Schobert's characteristic moods find a place in Mozart's music. In other cases the influence was more quickly mirrored, as, for example, the imitation of Haydn's quartet style of 1772 in Mozart's quartets of the following year.

Mozart's genius is clearly revealed in the way he responded to external musical stimuli. He sensed immediately what was worthwhile in the music of every composer with whom he had any feeling of kinship. An expressive device, an innovation in form, a turn of phrase—whatever the musical element, Mozart found a way of using or refining it. If it failed to live up to his expectations, he discarded it at once and turned elsewhere. If it proved worthy, he modified it to serve his purposes and brought it into proportion by means of his immaculate taste and sense of musical fitness. Thus his music is in a sense the synthesis of everything that musical Europe had to offer, but purified and brought into order by the most extraordinary musical mind of all time. We have already spoken of the way his music in turn influenced Haydn in the years after the two men became friends. There are few happier examples of reciprocal influence in the history of music.

THE LATE SYMPHONIES

Mozart's last three symphonies are among the most universally beloved of all his works. They were completed in the summer of 1788, along with seven other compositions. This almost incredible speed of writing was well within Mozart's capabilities; he is said to have composed music as easily as other people write letters. Yet no sign of haste mars the symphonies; they are perfect in every detail. Listed (in the complete edition of his works) as Nos. 39, 40, and 41, they are completely unlike in mood and in type of thematic material.

The first of the three (K. 543, in E flat) begins with a slow and solemn introduction that provides a striking contrast to the melodious, almost romantic first movement. The andante is calm and suggests a mood of repose; only in its middle section does it approach an agitated state. The third movement, a minuet, stands as a model of what the Classical minuet should be; stately and dignified, it also breathes an air of well-being. The finale is economically written; one melodic figure serves both as the first theme and as a counterpoint to the second. The movement is predominantly in E flat; but it departs widely from that key, and its harmonic freedom counteracts the blandness of the basic key itself.

The Symphony No. 40 (K. 550, in G minor) is one of the most passionate and stormy of all Mozart's works. Its first movement is pessimistic and restless; short, downward-inflected melodies are carried over a pulsating accompaniment, and a mood of apprehension is strongly suggested (see Example 49). The quiet second movement provides a welcome contrast to the gloomy first, but even here the lyric melodies are chromatically twisted and not far removed from expression of grief. In the third movement, a traditional minuet, extreme emotions are held in check; but they come to wild and almost brutal expression in the fast finale. That movement runs on with relentless fury. Sudden outbursts of tone (see Example 37*b,* p. 77), abrupt changes of key, dark instrumental colors—these contribute to the melancholy and anguished mood that dominates the movement. That mood also permeates the entire symphony to a degree seldom found elsewhere in Mozart.

Mozart, Symphony No. 40 ***Example 49***

The third symphony of the set (No. 41 in C major, K.551) provides the greatest possible contrast to the other two. It was nicknamed the "Jupiter" Symphony by an unknown admirer, and it is called by that name even today. Here is revealed a straightforward, optimistic Mozart—one who is neither resigned nor pessimistic but who simply expresses his joy in the creation of a musical work. One charming melody follows another in a unique blend of formality and intimacy. Counterpoint, brought to life again after a long sleep, and *galant* elements, a heritage of the Rococo period, are here wonderfully combined. Routine rhythmic figures in the first movement are transformed by Mozart's magic touch into lively, bustling patterns that animate every section in which they appear.

The concluding movement of the "Jupiter" Symphony, which is cast in sonata-form, is without doubt one of Mozart's finest achievements. Near the end of the movement four different melodic fragments, all previously heard at separate times, are combined in an intricate polyphonic passage—a contrapuntal tour de force rare in Mozart's symphonies (see Example 50). The lively mood and brilliant sound here rise to a great climax; and the joyous, effervescent tone of the music makes light of the accomplishment. This is a perfect example of Mozart's ability to conceal the marks of his musical tools; no trace of effort nor of labored effect mars the apparent spontaneity of the music. The "Jupiter" Symphony is one of Mozart's many masterpieces.

Example 50 **Mozart, Symphony No. 41 ("Jupiter")**

THE CHAMBER MUSIC

Mozart's chamber music parallels his symphonic writing in its growth and scope. Early works reflect his impressions of the music he was hearing at the time—whether in London, Paris, or Italy. The influence of Haydn first appeared in the works of the 1770's, and in 1782 Mozart adopted Haydn's "new manner." In the interval between 1782 and 1785 he composed six string quartets (K. 387, 421, 428, 458, 464, 465), dedicating them to the older composer with the inscription, "the fruit of a long and laborious work." This testifies both to the novelty of Haydn's achievement and to the difficulty even Mozart had in mastering the new technique of thematic development. Yet so quickly did the innovation become a part of Mozart's style that his later works even transcend Haydn's in imaginative, eloquent expression. Heart and mind are perfectly balanced here, as they are in all of Mozart's works written in the last ten years of his life.

THE CONCERTOS

Since the mid-eighteenth century the form known as the *concerto* has most often been a three-movement sonata type (see p. 132) for a soloist and orchestra. Concertos for two or more instruments have been written, notably by Mozart, Brahms, and Bartók, and occasionally more than three movements occur, as in the four-movement Piano Concerto No. 2 by Brahms and in the five-movement *Symphonie Espagnole* (which is a violin concerto in spite of its title) by Edouard Lalo. The typical concerto of the Classical and later periods, however, is a three-movement compound form consisting of a moderately paced first movement in modified sonata-form, a slow second movement, and fast final rondo or sonata-form.

One may find that the sonata-form movements of a concerto are somewhat more free than the corresponding movements of a symphony or a string quartet. The presence of the solo instrument traditionally requires that opportunity be given the soloist to play alone at times, and a concerto movement may contain two expositions—one for the orchestra and one for the soloist. Moreover, a free improvisatory section called a *cadenza* is often inserted near the close of of movement; during the cadenza the soloist ornaments or develops the themes further without benefit of orchestral support.

The widely held feeling that a concerto for solo instrument and orchestra exists primarily to display the soloist's technical proficiency is, in the case of the major composers, likely to be false. The availability of a competent solo performer may lead a composer to write in a more brilliant style than he finds necessary in a symphony, but this is only so that he may make full use of the medium at his disposal. It is doubtful whether any serious symphonist from Haydn to the present day was animated only by the desire to compose spectacularly when he wrote in the concerto form. The more than forty concertos composed by Mozart—many of them for his own performances—offer eloquent testimony that he was animated by the highest ideals in writing them.

Mozart's twenty-one concertos for piano and orchestra include some of his most profound works. The relationship between solo instrument and orchestral accompaniment is not rigid; in some works or some passages the solo part leads brilliantly, while in others it is merged with the orchestra or even serves in an accompanying role. An old tradition of the concerto, namely, the use of contrasts of solo and *tutti*, was known to Mozart. Occasionally he revived the old tradition even while employing the sonata-form of his own time.

The D minor Piano Concerto, K. 466, perhaps the best-known of all Mozart's works in this form, provides a case in point (see pp. 148–50 for an outline of the concerto). Externally the work is similar to many other Classical concertos, including many of Mozart's own. The first movement, in sonata-form, contains a double exposition—one for the orchestra, the other for the piano; the second and third movements, too, fall into the accepted patterns of rondo and sonata-form, respectively. Throughout the work, however, one senses that the orchestra does not merely accompany the solo instrument but leads a life of its own. Orchestra and piano often have themes in common, but the developments of those themes and the transitions that connect them follow divergent paths in the two instrumental media. The result is a passionate composition in which contrasts of lyricism and drama, of repose and agitation, of pessimism and equanimity, are presented in a moving fashion. The variety of moods expressed in the D minor Concerto is scarcely exceeded in any other of Mozart's instrumental works, yet all is brought into unity by the clarity of the texture and consistency of the style.

Concerto for Piano and Orchestra, D minor, K. 466, by W. A. Mozart

FIRST MOVEMENT, Allegro

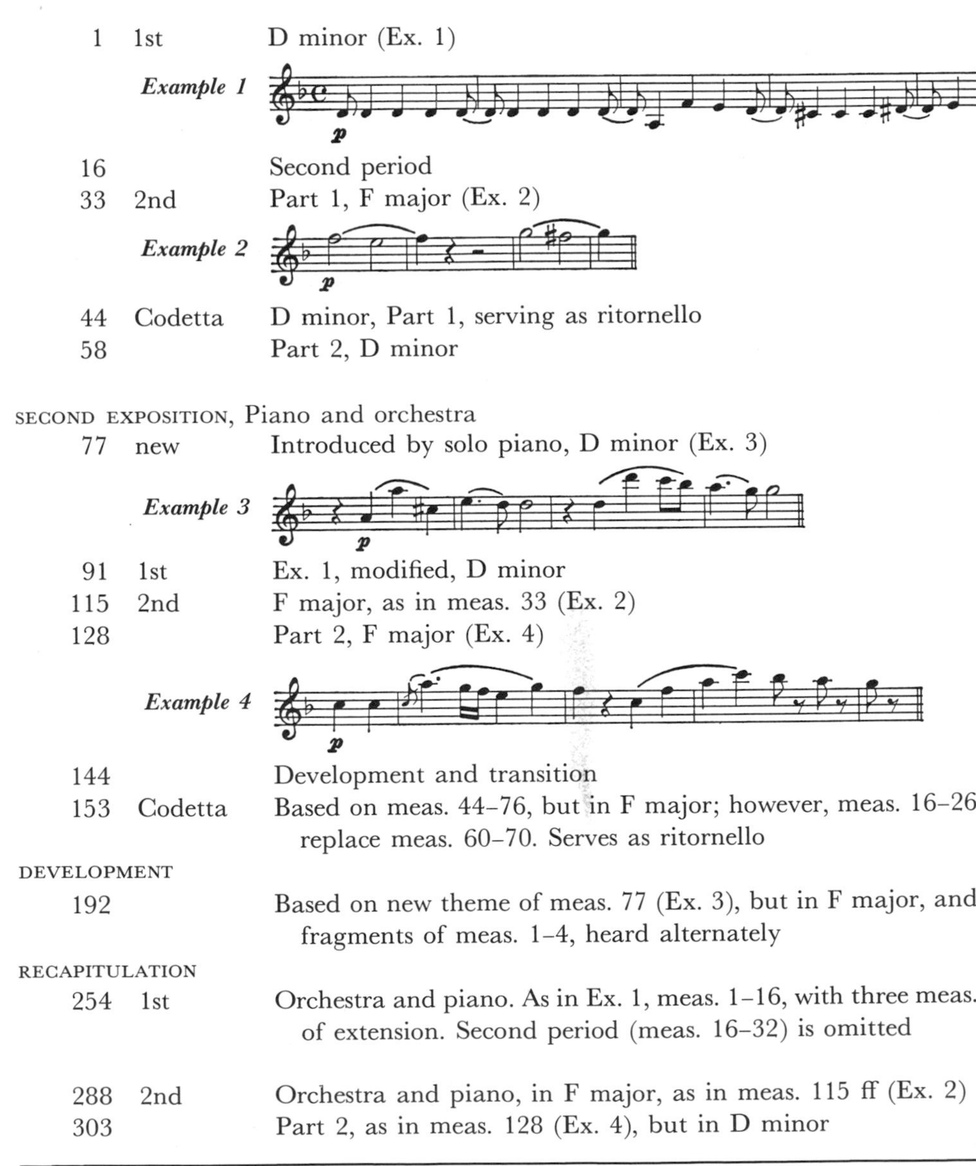

Meas.	*Theme*	
FIRST EXPOSITION, Orchestra alone		
1	1st	D minor (Ex. 1)
	Example 1	
16		Second period
33	2nd	Part 1, F major (Ex. 2)
	Example 2	
44	Codetta	D minor, Part 1, serving as ritornello
58		Part 2, D minor
SECOND EXPOSITION, Piano and orchestra		
77	new	Introduced by solo piano, D minor (Ex. 3)
	Example 3	
91	1st	Ex. 1, modified, D minor
115	2nd	F major, as in meas. 33 (Ex. 2)
128		Part 2, F major (Ex. 4)
	Example 4	
144		Development and transition
153	Codetta	Based on meas. 44–76, but in F major; however, meas. 16–26 replace meas. 60–70. Serves as ritornello
DEVELOPMENT		
192		Based on new theme of meas. 77 (Ex. 3), but in F major, and fragments of meas. 1–4, heard alternately
RECAPITULATION		
254	1st	Orchestra and piano. As in Ex. 1, meas. 1–16, with three meas. of extension. Second period (meas. 16–32) is omitted
288	2nd	Orchestra and piano, in F major, as in meas. 115 ff (Ex. 2)
303		Part 2, as in meas. 128 (Ex. 4), but in D minor

330	Codetta	As in meas. 153–164 with extensions, but in D minor. Serves as ritornello
356		Based on meas. 16–25; transition to cadenza
365	Cadenza	Piano alone
366	Coda	Orchestra alone, based on meas. 44 ff. Serves as ritornello
390		Based on Ex. 1. Movement ends in meas. 397

SECOND MOVEMENT, Romanze, B flat

Meas.	*Part*	
1	A	First phrase, piano alone (Ex. 5)

Example 5

8		Repeated in orchestra
17		Second phrase, piano alone
25		Repeated in orchestra, with transition
40	B	Piano and orchestra, B flat
68	A	First phrase of Ex. 5, piano alone
76		Repeated in orchestra
84	C	Piano and orchestra, G minor (Ex. 6); meas. 84–91 repeated

Example 6

92		Second part, piano and orchestra; meas. 92–107 repeated
108		Transition, piano and orchestra
119	A	Piano alone, Ex. 5; repetition (meas. 8–16) omitted
127		Second phrase, piano alone
135		Repeated in orchestra with extension (Part B, parallel to meas. 40–67, is omitted)
146	Coda	Piano alone, B flat
150		Orchestra, with nine-meas. extension. Movement ends in meas. 162

THIRD MOVEMENT, Allegro assai, D minor

Meas.	*Theme*	
EXPOSITION		
1	1st	Piano alone, D minor (Ex. 7)

Mozart, Concerto for Piano and Orchestra (cont.)

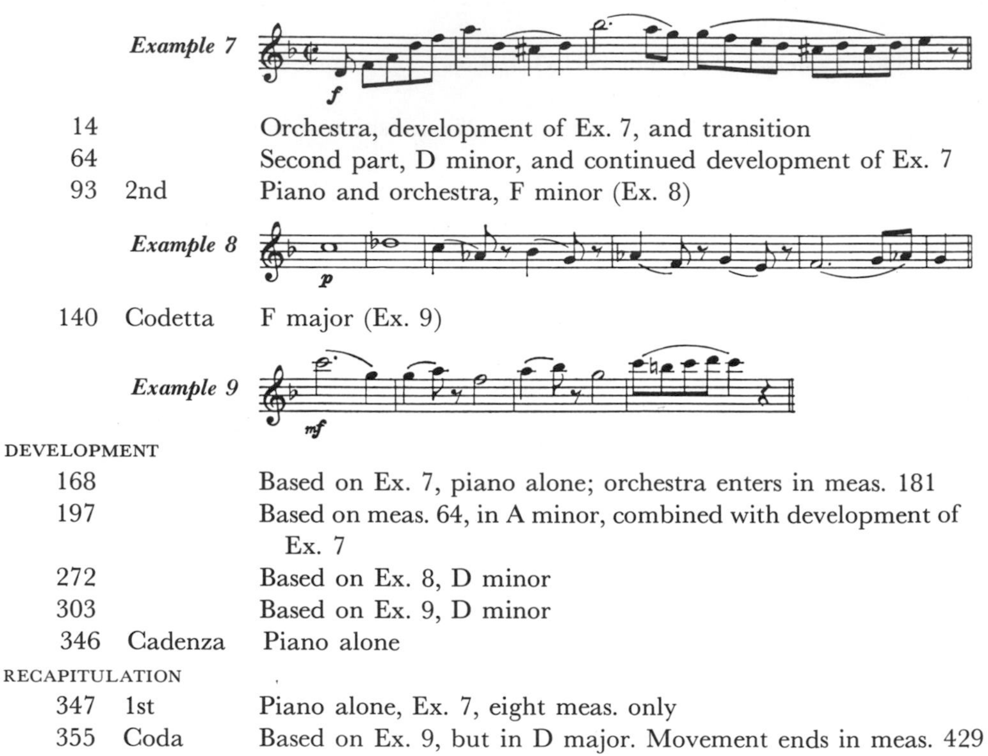

	Example 7	
14		Orchestra, development of Ex. 7, and transition
64		Second part, D minor, and continued development of Ex. 7
93	2nd	Piano and orchestra, F minor (Ex. 8)
	Example 8	
140	Codetta	F major (Ex. 9)
	Example 9	
DEVELOPMENT		
168		Based on Ex. 7, piano alone; orchestra enters in meas. 181
197		Based on meas. 64, in A minor, combined with development of Ex. 7
272		Based on Ex. 8, D minor
303		Based on Ex. 9, D minor
346	Cadenza	Piano alone
RECAPITULATION		
347	1st	Piano alone, Ex. 7, eight meas. only
355	Coda	Based on Ex. 9, but in D major. Movement ends in meas. 429

THE MASS IN C MINOR

In 1782 Mozart began to work at a Mass in C minor (K. 427), in fulfillment of a promise made to his wife. A year later the work was still unfinished; at its first performance it was filled out with music taken from earlier Masses, and Mozart found no occasion to return to it subsequently. Since early in the Christian era the Mass has included six separate texts: *Kyrie, Gloria, Credo, Sanctus, Benedictus,* and *Agnus Dei,* each of which was for several centuries set as a single movement. From about the middle of the seventeenth century, however, each movement was often divided into two or more contrasting numbers. Mozart adhered to the newer practice in the C minor Mass, but did not complete the task: about half of the *Credo* and the entire *Agnus Dei* are missing. The movements that do exist, however, constitute one of the most profound and moving works in the entire literature of choral music. No better approach to the mature Mozart can be made than through the C minor Mass; in the variety of its moods and the sheer beauty of its melodies it is unequalled.

The *Kyrie,* for chorus with interspersed soprano solos, is tender and full of supplication. The *Gloria* is divided into seven numbers, including settings for full chorus, for soprano solo, and for duet and trio of soloists: Mozart composed them to reflect his own feeling toward the text. The setting of "Qui tollis peccata mundi" ("Who takest away the sins of the world") in the *Gloria* is an eternal masterpiece (see Example 51). In the words of Alfred Einstein, a great Mozart scholar:

> The *Qui tollis,* for double chorus, in G minor, with the weightiest kind of orchestral accompaniment, in the broadest tempo, is, with its descending chromaticism, quite evidently conceived as a representation of the Saviour, making his way under whiplashes, and bearing the burden of the Cross, toward Golgotha. It is a movement that ranks with the *Kyrie* of Bach's B minor Mass and the opening double chorus of the St. Matthew Passion.[1]

The *Credo* is a jubilant song of faith. Its bright mood, made even brighter by the addition of trumpets and enlivened by the use of lightly pulsating rhythms, is a musical counterpart of the brilliant and colorful decorations with which the eighteenth century adorned its churches. Mozart set approximately half of the *Credo* text in one broad, concertolike movement. The "Et incarnatus est" is set separately in a soprano aria of surpassing beauty; the mood suggests the infant Jesus surrounded by angels, and reflects a personal rather than a traditional approach to the text. At this point the *Credo* breaks off, to be followed by an imposing choral *Sanctus* and a setting of the *Benedictus* for a quartet of soloists. The final "Osanna in excelsis," for double chorus, brings the incomplete Mass to a brilliant close.

Concert performances of the C minor Mass are relatively rare. The work has been recorded, however, and can be heard by anyone who wishes to encounter Mozart at his highest level of expressiveness. True, the Mass is not suited to liturgical use; it transcends the liturgy and stands, perhaps, as a statement of Mozart's personal faith. Listened to from a purely musical standpoint, it provides experiences of a kind found nowhere else in the available choral music of the Classical period. The work deserves to be known intimately.

The essence of Mozart's genius is to be found in his choral works, of which the Mass in C minor is the most profound. But it is also to be found, and in equal measure, in other categories of his compositions. In addition to all his other evidences of mastery, one must recognize his versatility. The symphonies, taken alone, reveal a Mozart whose sense of form was flawless, whose gift for melody never faltered, and who plumbed the depths of the human soul and expressed what he found there. But the chamber music reveals the same qualities; and the piano concertos do so in even greater measure.

THE OPERAS

In his operas, Mozart created yet another category of works that have no equals in music history. In musical quality they are on a level with his other works. Humor, lightness, seriousness, charming melodies, dramatic movements, perfect forms, variety of textures—all are well represented. But the operas are concerned with people: in depicting those people and describing their human problems, Mozart revealed yet another aspect of his genius.

[1] Alfred Einstein, *Mozart, His Character, His Work,* Oxford University Press, 1945, p. 348. Used by permission of copyright owner, Oxford University Press, New York.

Mozart's operas are of several types: *opera buffa,* essentially a comic opera, represented by *The Marriage of Figaro* and *Don Giovanni; opera seria,* or serious opera, of which *Idomeneo* is the finest example; and German opera, distinguished both by the language in which the text is written and by a warm, folklike melodic quality, of which type *The Magic Flute* is one of the best. Regardless of the type he was composing, Mozart revealed his insight into his characters as no composer had before him. The men and women who inhabit those operas come alive in them. Mozart's arias, ensemble numbers, and other sections are brilliant or somber or plaintive musical works, as the case may be; and they are more as well. They reveal the inmost natures of the characters who sing them. In humorous, or poignant, or dramatic strokes, Mozart created universal types and expressed universal emotions. His operas may well be listened to from this point of view.

Classicism

In the works they wrote after about 1782, both Haydn and Mozart abandoned the last traces of the frivolity of the *galant* style. The routine filling-in of standardized formal patterns, the rootless sentimental effect, and the surface charm akin to a "beauty patch" on an empty face—those elements disappeared. In their stead came a forthright or subtle (but honest) expression of a wide range of emotions, a clarity and economy in the use of musical materials, and intelligently devised proportions in all details.

The fully developed Classical style was the result. Boisterous well-being is appropriately presented in their works; drama is given dramatic musical treatment; profound harmonies are applied to profound sentiment; and simple utterances are set in simple musical style. In every case, a balance of form and content results. Haydn's temperament was such that he avoided the expression of gloom and pessimism; Mozart often preferred to express those emotions. Haydn and Mozart seldom ascended

Scenes from Mozart's *The Marriage of Figaro,* University of Michigan.

Example 51

to the truly heroic; Beethoven, as we shall see, did so repeatedly. Yet all three composers, in spite of the differences in their styles of writing, adjusted their musical means to their expressive purposes. All three wrote as economically—or as elaborately—as their purposes required. And that is the essence of Classical style.

Listening Suggestions

BACH, JOHANN CHRISTIAN

Sinfonia in D major

BACH, KARL PHILIPP EMANUEL

Concerto for Orchestra, D major

COUPERIN

Music for the Harpsichord (various short pieces and suites)

GLUCK

Alceste (opera)

HAYDN

Andante con Variazioni, F minor (for piano)
Concerto for Cello, D major
The Creation (oratorio)
Mass in D minor ("Lord Nelson")
String Quartets, Op. 33, Nos. 1–6
String Quartets, Op. 76, Nos. 1–6
Symphony No. 45 ("Farewell")
Symphony No. 92 ("Oxford")
Symphony No. 94 ("Surprise")
Symphony No. 101 ("Clock")
Symphony No. 104 ("London")

MOZART

Concerto for Piano, D minor, K. 466
Concerto for Violin, A major, K. 219
The Magic Flute, K. 620 (opera)
The Marriage of Figaro, K. 492 (opera)
Mass in C minor, K. 427
Piano Trio, B flat major, K. 502
Quintet for Clarinet and Strings, A major, K. 581
Requiem Mass, K. 626
String Quartet, D major, K. 575
String Quintet, G minor, K. 516
Symphony No. 39, E flat, K. 543

Chapter 9

BEETHOVEN

Beethoven's career as a composer marks one of the most important cultural events of our civilization. His impact upon the musical world of his time was tremendous. Within one generation after he first appeared as a pianist in Vienna, he had shown the way not only to a new kind of music but to undisclosed areas of the human soul. He is perhaps the only composer whose works have never suffered even a partial decline in popularity. His hold upon the affections of the vast musical public has never been stronger than it is today.

Although Beethoven was a child of the eighteenth century, and the direct heir of Haydn and Mozart, he was the figure against whom nineteenth-century musicians measured themselves. Composers as unlike as Berlioz, Wagner, and Brahms all believed themselves to be following in Beethoven's path. Lesser composers, viewing the magnitude of Beethoven's accomplishments in the field of instrumental music, grew discouraged at the thought of attempting to surpass him; they turned to other styles and other forms where his shadow did not reach.

The end of the eighteenth century saw a change in the attitude of society toward its members. With the power of the aristocracy broken by the French Revolution, and with a new liberal air blowing in many parts of Europe, the common people began to approach a state of freedom. Among musicians, Beethoven was the first to become free. Haydn had known and was reconciled to "his own place"—that of a servant employed by Prince Esterházy. He composed what was required of him, he wore a uniform, and he depended upon the good will of his patron for his professional well-being. Mozart above all wished to be a part of the same system, but he would not allow anyone to dictate how his music should be written. Too independent to allow himself to be bound, too dependent to strike out for himself, Mozart was crushed between the social forces of his time and his own temperament and died a pauper.

Beethoven became the first independent creative artist of the new century. He made use of patrons and at the same time ignored them. A group of wealthy aristocrats in Vienna guaranteed him an annuity—and he guaranteed nothing except that he would compose as he saw fit. Composers before him had written to order or for particular occasions; their music was functional in this sense. Beethoven wrote simply because he had the will to compose; scarcely any of his works serve a function other than to exist as freely conceived works of art. The practicability of what he wrote, the desires of people who commissioned him to write, the possibility of immediate performance for his compositions—these gave him little concern.

Beethoven's music came into being, was forced into being, only after long inner struggle. And having composed it, he compelled his audience to new levels of receptivity. To a world that recognized only the external charm and melodiousness of Haydn's and Mozart's music (a real appreciation of Mozart has come only in the past few decades) and that found even that music severe, Beethoven brought music that has not yet been equaled in forcefulness, sublimity, and universality of appeal. These miracles were accomplished by an undersized, pockmarked man who had no social graces and who suffered one of the worst of social afflictions—deafness. They were accomplished by a man who had only strength of character, spiritual greatness, and an imagination that knew no bounds.

Beethoven's Life

Ludwig van Beethoven (1770–1827) was born in Bonn. His grandfather was the chapelmaster at the court of the Elector in that ancient Rhine city and his father was a member of the local choir. His two brothers, Karl and Johann, were born in 1774 and 1776. Consistent musical training was denied Beethoven during his formative years, for his father was an alcoholic—harsh and unreliable. Severe discipline at home, desultory lessons with a few of his father's friends, and, beginning in 1781, three years of profitable study with a worthy local organist named Christian Neefe —this was the extent of his training in Bonn.

In 1784 Beethoven was engaged as viola player and harpsichordist in the orchestra of the Elector; in addition, he served as assistant court organist. For about three years the teen-aged boy successfully carried out the duties of his position, becoming acquainted thereby with large quantities of music in all categories. In 1787 he went to Vienna, where he played for Mozart. But his mother's serious illness recalled him to Bonn after only a few months. Her death in July of the same year deprived Beethoven of the only relative who had been sympathetic to his problems and aware of the magnitude of his talent. Moreover, her death placed upon him the full responsibility for the care of his two younger brothers and his drunken father. He took the obligations to heart: family loyalty was one of Beethoven's outstanding traits.

A resumption of his studies in Vienna was out of the question. He returned to his position in the Elector's orchestra, composed a number of works, and took every possible opportunity to educate himself. He made many good friends among the aristocracy of Bonn, and those friendships in part compensated for the unpleasantness he encountered in his own home.

Ludwig van Beethoven (1770–1827), master composer against whom nineteenth-century musicians measured themselves. (Lithograph by Klöber.)

When Haydn visited in Bonn on his way to and from London in 1790 and 1792, the Elector's orchestra entertained him. On the second visit Haydn was sufficiently impressed with the young man's ability (Beethoven was then twenty-two) to accept him as a pupil. Arrangements for a leave of absence from Bonn were quickly made, and in November, 1792, Beethoven set out for Vienna a second time.

But he had not solved his personal problems. In December his father died, after having wasted the money set aside to care for the younger boys. An invasion of Bonn by French forces threatened the existence of the Electoral court, and Beethoven's remittances from the court soon ceased. Political conditions in Vienna were confused also, and the time was unfavorable for launching a career. Beethoven's musical accomplishments, however, allowed him to surmount his financial difficulties. He quickly came into demand as a pianist and teacher: the unique quality of his improvisations at the piano was especially admired. His pupils and friends soon included some of the highest-ranking nobles of the Austrian empire. Characteristically, Beethoven moved among them as an equal and demanded that they accept him on his own terms.

His studies with Haydn proved unsatisfactory and were soon broken off. For a year or two he took lessons from Albrechtsberger, an esteemed contrapuntalist, and from Salieri, the official opera composer to the Austrian court. From that point on, Beethoven became his own teacher. He read, composed, experimented, and developed the high degree of self-criticism that became one of his most valuable assets. His career as a teacher and virtuoso performer provided a fair income, his compositions were becoming known and respected, and his chamber music works were often performed in the aristocratic circles in which he moved.

In about 1800, when Beethoven was thirty, he became aware of a deterioration of his hearing. By the middle of 1801 he realized that deafness was upon him and that he would shortly be facing the greatest calamity possible for a musician. Plunged into despondency, seeing his career as a performer cut off and life as a musician becoming impossible, he contemplated suicide. Soon, however, his enormous strength of will exerted itself: he would master his destiny and continue to compose in spite of the terrible affliction. By 1802 his mental stability had returned; and although Beethoven never became reconciled to the handicap, he rose above it. He composed energetically, and there is no evidence that deafness ever hampered his creative work. He made public appearances occasionally, but these became fewer as his hearing loss increased.

In 1815 came the second great crisis in Beethoven's life. Following the death of his brother Karl, and in accordance with the latter's will, Beethoven was made responsible for the care of Karl's son, then a boy of nine. Custody was to be shared by the boy's mother, whom, however, Beethoven despised and considered unfit to bring up her own son. He took steps to have young Karl removed from his mother's charge and placed entirely in his own. At first he was successful. But Karl's mother made repeated attempts to have her son restored to her, and in 1819 she won her case. Beethoven was equally determined to regain custody, and a year later a higher court decided in his favor. Litigation, public quarrels, and heartsickness occupied his time for these several years, and composition virtually ceased. Between 1815 and 1818 he wrote only five major works: two piano sonatas, two cello sonatas, and a cycle of six songs.

By 1819 this second great crisis had passed but Karl continued to be an additional responsibility with which Beethoven had to cope. Karl grew increasingly unreliable and shiftless, and his deaf bachelor uncle was quite unable to supervise him properly. In spite of this problem, Beethoven returned to his composing with full concentration. Secure in his growing reputation as the greatest living composer, he withdrew from the world almost completely. He received commissions, his published works were in demand, and his income was fairly stable. His general health, however, declined gradually, and his strength was not always equal to the demands he made upon it.

In 1826 Karl made an unsuccessful attempt at suicide. This unpleasantness cost Beethoven much of his remaining strength. He suffered a series of ailments, including a serious attack of pneumonia. Unwilling to use for himself the small sums he had saved for Karl and often unable to compose, he relied only upon a few faithful friends to care for his needs. Yet he composed his most profound string quartets under these unhappy circumstances: his last completed composition, a new finale for the String Quartet No. 13, Opus 130, is dated November, 1826. Early in 1827 his optimistic spirit looked forward to a renewal of health and strength, and he made plans for several new works. But even Beethoven's unquenchable will could not conquer his illnesses. Late in March, 1827, when he was fifty-seven, his suffering ended.

Beethoven's Music

Beethoven's compositions include nine symphonies, seven concertos, and about twelve overtures; seventeen string quartets; twelve piano trios and about as many miscellaneous chamber music works; thirty-two piano sonatas, fifteen sonatas for violins or other instruments and large numbers of piano compositions in a variety of forms; a few choral works, including the great *Missa solemnis;* one opera, *Fidelio;* and many other large and small works. There appeared during Beethoven's lifetime 135 numbered works or sets of works (for example, Op. 18 includes six string quartets). Many additional compositions, including those from his student days at Bonn, were published later, some with opus numbers and some without.

Measured by the number of his compositions alone, Beethoven was not as prolific a composer as were his immediate predecessors. His nine symphonies stand opposite Haydn's 104 and Mozart's forty-eight; his seventeen string quartets seem few compared to Haydn's eighty-three; likewise his seven concertos as compared to Mozart's forty-odd works in that form. But numbers provide no basis for comparison. Beethoven's works not only were larger and longer than those of his predecessors but also were created with more difficulty and were more demanding of their composer. Further, few of his compositions are examples of a standardized type, as are many works by his predecessors; Beethoven's stand as individual works of art, with individual characteristics. His highly developed sense of self-criticism forbade his offering compositions to the public until he was thoroughly satisfied that they could not be improved. Many compositions were written, rewritten, put aside for years, and finally revised again before Beethoven allowed them to be published.

In all of Beethoven's works, from Op. 1 (completed in 1793) to Op. 135 (finished in October, 1826), we can recognize stylistic traits that identify the works as being by Beethoven. But at the same time, they fall into three well-defined groups, each of which is stylistically set apart from the other two. The personal crises in Beethoven's life twice caused him to alter his attitude toward the world, and the changed attitudes are reflected in the content of his music. Thus it is necessary to recognize three distinct periods of composition, each with its own technical and emotional qualities.

The works of the first period were written between 1792, when Beethoven arrived in Vienna, and about 1802, at which time he realized that his deafness was incurable. In those works the influence of Haydn is notable, though the style of that master is suitably modified to reflect Beethoven's unique temperament. The second period extends from about 1802 to the years 1815 or 1816, when his creative activities were interrupted by the disputes with his sister-in-law. The most generally beloved works of Beethoven are compositions of the second period; they are characterized by power, eloquence, drama, and sheer beauty. Among them are the symphonies from No. 3 to No. 8, the "Emperor" Concerto, much of the chamber music, and the opera *Fidelio.* The third period, beginning in about 1818 and extending to his death in 1827, saw Beethoven turning away from the world and becoming introspective. The Symphony No. 9, the *Missa solemnis,* five of the piano sonatas, and the last six string quartets are the principal works of those years.

Perhaps the outstanding characteristic of Beethoven's music is the degree of individuality each work reveals. Stylistic elements that are uniquely Beethoven's are present in virtually everything he wrote; after we have become sufficiently familiar with his music we rarely mistake any of it for the work of another. Yet at the same time, each composition has a sound and shape of its own. It differs from his other works in either form, mood content, type of melodic material, rhythmic effect, or some other element. Probably no composer before him—or since, we are tempted to add—succeeded so wholly in giving each composition its own distinctive characteristics. There is not one Beethoven, but many. Therefore, there are no "typical" compositions in Beethoven, but only individual works of art.

VARIATION FORMS

In Chapter 5 the role of variation as one of the organizing principles of music was discussed briefly. Consistent application of that principle to a musical theme may result in a single-movement form, which may stand alone or form a part of a compound form such as a symphony, a sonata, or a string quartet. Both Haydn and Mozart composed many works embodying this principle, as did Beethoven. But in Beethoven's music the variation principle was used so often and resulted in so many outstanding works that a fuller discussion of the principle is appropriate here.

In the fragment of *Adeste Fideles* illustrated in Example 39 (p. 79) only the melody is shown as subject to variation. When the variation technique is consistently and successively applied to other aspects of the theme as well as to the melody, a variation form results. For example, imagine a theme made up of a melody with accompanying harmony, set in a particular texture, with particular tone colors, and embodying a particular phrase structure and rhythmic pattern. If that theme is presented a number of times, each time with one or more of its components altered, an extended composition built on both unity (the recurring theme) and contrast (the varied versions of the theme) is created. The form is called *theme and variations* or, alternately, a set of variations. While each variation may depart widely from the original character of the theme, the basic musical idea is seldom lost sight of. The number of variations is governed only by the musical possibilities disclosed by the theme—and of course by the quality of the composer's imagination.

The variation form is often found in orchestral compositions as well as in chamber music and piano works. Beethoven, for example, employed the form in four of his symphonies and several of his string quartets and piano trios; it appears often in his piano sonatas. The variations in Haydn's "Surprise" Symphony, No. 94, and his "Emperor" Quartet, Op. 76, No. 3, and in Schubert's "Trout" Quintet, Op. 114, and his "Death and the Maiden" Quartet are especially rewarding. Beethoven's *Thirty-three Variations on a Theme by Diabelli,* Opus 120, for piano, Brahms's *Variations on a Theme by Haydn,* Opus 56a, and Elgar's *Enigma Variations,* both for orchestra, are outstanding examples that exist as single compositions and not as parts of compound forms. In these works, as in many others, the variation principle has stimulated the respective composers to do their best work, and each composition has unique features. Often the variations go far afield, but usually some salient feature will be recognized in the successive variations.

Typical of Beethoven's works in this field is his *Thirty-two Variations in C Minor* for piano, without opus number. The theme consists of an eight-measure phrase whose stark outlines and characteristic harmony are well suited to variation treatment (see Example 52, in which only three of the thirty-two variations are given). In Variations I–III a running figure is heard first in the right hand, next in the left, and then in both hands together. Variations IV–XI introduce several different figurations and rhythmic patterns. Variations XII–XVI are transformed to the major key. Variations XVII–XXXI are based on a number of changed rhythms, figurations, counter-

Example 52

Comparative Table of Movements in Selected Compound Forms

I	II	III	IV
a. Introduction and sonata-form	Theme and variations	Minuet	Sonata-form
b. Introduction and sonata-form	Rondo (ABA) in slow tempo	Minuet	Rondo
c. Introduction and sonata-form	Sonatina-form	Minuet	Sonata-form
d. Sonata-form	Modified three-part form (abc-a-abc)	Minuet	Sonata-form, with fugal episodes
e. Sonata-form	Large ABA	Scherzo	Theme and variations
f. Sonata-form	Theme and variations	Scherzo	Sonata-form, with section of scherzo inserted
g. Sonata-form	Scherzo, with first song in sonata-form	Variations on two themes ($ABA^1B^1A^2A^3$)	Introduction, theme and variations with fugal interludes and subordinate themes
h. Sonata-form	Sonatina-form	Two movements only (see p. 181)	
i. Introduction and sonata-form	Rondo (ABA) in slow tempo	Rondo in moderate tempo	Introduction and sonatina-form
j. Introduction and sonata-form	Rondo (ABA) in slow tempo	Scherzo	Introduction and sonata-form
k. Sonata-form	ABA form	Minuet	Rondo
l. Introduction and sonata-form	Sonatina-form	Minuet	Sonata-form
m. Sonata-form	Sonata-form with suggestion of scherzo	Sonata-form (slow tempo)	Sonata-form (fast tempo)
n. Sonata-form	Large ABA form	(none)	Sonata-form
o. Sonata-form	Scherzo	Theme and variations	Rondo
p. Sonata-form	Large ABA	Scherzo	Rondo

WORKS LISTED IN ABOVE TABLE

a. Haydn, Symphony No. 94 ("Surprise")
b. Haydn, Symphony No. 101 ("Clock)
c. Mozart, Symphony No. 39
d. Mozart, Symphony No. 41 ("Jupiter")
e. Beethoven, Symphony No. 3 ("Eroica")
f. Beethoven, Symphony No. 5
g. Beethoven, Symphony No. 9
h. Schubert, Symphony No. 8 ("Unfinished")
i. Brahms, Symphony No. 1
j. Dvořák, Symphony No. 5 ("New World")
k. Haydn, Quartet, Op. 76, No. 4
l. Mozart, Quartet, K. 465
m. Beethoven, Quartet, Op. 59, No. 1
n. Mozart, Trio, K. 502
o. Beethoven, Trio, Op. 97 ("Archduke")
p. Schubert, Trio, Op. 99

---

melodies, and the like. And the final variation is expanded in length, developed, and led to a brilliant conclusion. Contrasting moods, a variety of textures, piano figurations that extend to the limits of the pitch range, striking rhythmic effects—such elements reveal how a simple phrase can be transformed through variation and become the nucleus of a lengthy and significant composition at the hands of a Beethoven.

Beethoven's extensive use of the variation form in several categories of his works illustrates how freely he treated the concept of the sonata (see p. 132); other major composers shared this characteristic. The basic element of one or more movements in sonata-form was retained, but the ordering of the movements and the inclusion of movements cast in other forms was seldom standardized. Formal plans of a number of well-known symphonies and chamber music works are given on the opposite page, where the flexibility possible within these compound forms may be seen.

THE SYMPHONIES

To realize completely the magnitude of Beethoven's accomplishments, we would need to become familiar with all his major works. It would obviously be impossible to touch even upon a representative selection of those works in this book. Since this is so, one category will be lifted out for closer attention, and a few lines of connection drawn between that category and others. This procedure may partially open the doors to a wider understanding of Beethoven's music. The nine symphonies constitute the most suitable category for this selection. They extend from his early period to late in Beethoven's life; they are accessible on recordings; they form the backbone of the standard orchestral repertoire; and they contain some of the most delightful, most profound, and most powerful music ever composed.

Beethoven's Symphony No. 1, in C major, Op. 21, was completed in about 1800. It takes its departure from the late style of Haydn, insofar as transparent texture, Classical balance, and objective expression are concerned. But where Haydn, as well as Mozart, had achieved a fine blend of elegance and energy, Beethoven often substituted rough vigor. The forms in which Beethoven wrote are the forms he had learned to know in Haydn's music. From the very beginning, however, those forms

Symphony No. 3 ("Eroica"), E flat, Op. 55, by Ludwig van Beethoven

FIRST MOVEMENT, Allegro con brio, E flat

Meas.	*Theme*	
EXPOSITION		
1	Intro.	Two chords, E flat
3	1st	Three versions of phrase (Ex. 1)

Example 1

45	2nd	Part 1, B flat (Ex. 2)

Example 2

57		Part 2
65		Transition (Ex. 3)

Example 3

83	3rd	In B flat
109	Codetta	In three parts, meas. 109, 132, and 144, in B flat
DEVELOPMENT		
152		Transition
166		Based on Ex. 2
178		Based on Ex. 1 and Ex. 3 together
220		Based on Ex. 2
236		Fughetta, F minor, derived from meas. 109
284		New theme, E minor
300		Based on Ex. 1, but in C major
322		Based on meas. 284, but in E flat minor
338		Transition, based on Ex. 1
RECAPITULATION		
398	1st	Four versions of phrase (Ex. 1)
448	2nd	Part 1, E flat (Ex. 2)
460		Part 2
468		Transition (Ex. 3)
485	3rd	In E flat
512	Codetta	In three parts, meas. 512, 535, and 547, in E flat

551	Coda	Based on Ex. 1, with new countertheme (derived from rhythmic figure of meas. 65) in meas. 567
581		Based on meas. 284, but now in F minor
603		Derived from accompanying figure in meas. 338
631		Based on Ex. 1 with second new countertheme (derived from rhythmic figure of meas. 65, Ex. 3)
673		Based on meas. 57. Movement ends in meas. 691

SECOND MOVEMENT, Marcia funebre, Adagio assai, C minor

Meas. *Theme*

EXPOSITION

1	1st	In C minor (Ex. 4); Part 2, meas. 17. Parts repeated in meas. 31 and 37

Example 4

51		Repeat of modified first part
56		Codetta
69	2nd	C major; Part 2 begins in meas. 80
98	Codetta	C major

DEVELOPMENT

105		Based on Ex. 4
114		Derived from meas. 5, with new countertheme
154		Based on Ex. 4
159		Transition

RECAPITULATION

173	1st	C minor (Ex. 4); Part 2, meas. 181
195		First phrase modified, as in meas. 51
200		Codetta, C minor
209	Coda	Derived from meas. 69; begins in A flat
223		Derived from meas. 25
238		Based on Ex. 1, now rhythmically modified. Movement ends in meas. 247

THIRD MOVEMENT, Scherzo, Allegro vivace, E flat

Meas. *Part*

SCHERZO

1		Introduction
7	A	In B flat (Ex. 5)

Beethoven, Symphony No. 3 (cont.)

Example 5

31		Quasi-development of Part A and introduction
93	A	Return of Ex. 5, with extension. Meas. 31–166 are repeated

TRIO

167	B	In E flat
199	C	Begins in A flat
225	B	And codetta, in E flat. Meas. 199–260 repeated

SCHERZO DA CAPO

259–422		Repetition of meas. 1–166 (written out), with one rhythmic modification in meas. 381–384
423	Coda	Movement ends in meas. 442

FOURTH MOVEMENT, Allegro molto, E flat

Meas.	*Part*	
1		Introduction of theme
12	Theme	But bass line only (Ex. 6)

44	Var. 1	Variation of bass
60	Var. 2	Variation of bass
76	Var. 3	Melody of theme is introduced (Ex. 7)

108		Transition
117	Var. 4	Fughetta on bass
175	Var. 5	Variation of melody, plus four measures of transition
211	Var. 6	Variation of bass, G minor
243		Transition
258	Var. 7	Variation of melody, C major
277	Var. 8	Fughetta on bass, begins in C minor
349	Var. 9	Variation of melody, E flat; change of tempo to *poco andante*
381	Var. 10	Variation of melody
396	Coda	In E flat. Movement ends in meas. 473

were expanded, the contrasts within them were heightened, and their harmonic relationships were considerably broadened. The symphony's third movement, still called *menuetto* as in Haydn's works, is a forerunner of the fast, often humorous movement that Beethoven was to develop under the name *scherzo.* It contains the sudden contrasts in mood and texture, the prevailing lighthearted expression, and the driving rhythm.

Beethoven. (After an original drawing by Lyser.)

The Symphony No. 2, in D major, Op. 36, was published in 1804. It reveals how completely Beethoven was able to rise above the anguish that filled his life. For it was begun at about the time he realized that his deafness was incurable—a time when he contemplated suicide—yet no trace of morbidity appears in the music. The symphony is boisterous in its first and fourth movements, and filled with calm lyric beauty in its slow movement. Its size makes it perhaps the largest symphony written up to that time. Three themes (instead of the customary two), each containing two distinct melodic ideas, result in a greatly lengthened first movement. Beethoven was equal to the organizational problem he set for himself; nowhere is the momentum allowed to sag, and nowhere does he falter in his manipulation of the many themes. The Symphony No. 2 is forceful and direct; it stands at the very threshold of Beethoven's second period, and is the last of his orchestra works in which the spirit of Haydn exerted any restraining influence.

With his Symphony No. 3, in E flat, Op. 55 (published in 1806), Beethoven opened the gates to a new world of music. The symphony, which he called the "Eroica," fully deserves that name, for it is heroic in every sense. Its length is almost double that of the Symphony No. 1; the nature of its dramatic conflicts, the variety of emotional states it reflects, and the concentration revealed in every measure—such elements remove it far from the plane on which all earlier works had been written. An outline of the symphony is given on pages 164–66.

The "Eroica" Symphony is distinguished first of all by the type of thematic material it contains. Instead of rather complete melodies such as Mozart usually employs, Beethoven introduces a number of fragments, each one capable of suggesting a different emotional state (see Example 53). Those fragments are then developed (Haydn's "new manner" of 1781 had long become the common property of all composers). New melodies grow out of them, and they are combined in a variety of ways.

The whole first movement reflects moods of suppressed excitement, concentrated purpose, and dramatic intensity. The second movement is a broadly sustained funeral

Example 53

march. Its moods suggest gloom and agony, but also courage and hope; Beethoven leaves it to the listener to determine which feeling is uppermost when the movement has ended. The wonderfully eloquent coda in effect summarizes the sentiments presented in the movement itself, and its last few measures are poignant beyond description. In that section the main theme of the movement is rhythmically transformed —dissolved—as if to symbolize the transformation that accompanies death. A comparison between the theme in its original form (Example 54*a*) and in its dissolution (Example 54*b*) will reveal how the noble expression of the one subtly gives way to the fitful, anguished tone of the other.

The last two movements of the "Eroica" offer a decided contrast to the first two. The scherzo discloses in full measure what Beethoven had been working toward in the corresponding movements of his first two symphonies. Here in the Third, the new type of scherzo stands fully revealed. The form (song form with trio and recapitulation, derived from the minuet) is retained, but the tempo has been increased, the entire movement has been lengthened, and the stateliness of the minuet has been replaced by a lively, humorous mood. The various melodic ideas are developed instead of merely being repeated; this results in a higher degree of internal organization.

Example 54

The finale is a unique set of variations. Instead of using a simple theme in the traditional manner, Beethoven presents the bass and the melody of his theme separately (see Examples 6 and 7 in the outline of the symphony, p. 166). A powerful introduction precedes the statement of the bass line; this is followed by three variations of that line, over the last of which the melody is introduced. Then follow five variations concerned with the two lines alternately; and in the last of the five the bass line is developed out of existence, as it were. The melodic theme has triumphed, and the rest of the movement is concerned with the melody alone.

Here we find a kind of symbolism that appears often in Beethoven. Two contrasting elements, one strong and the other weak, are brought into conflict; during the course of the conflict, the apparently weaker element drives the stronger one from the field. Beethoven had used the same melody and bass at the climax of his ballet, *The Creatures of Prometheus.* Prometheus, in Greek mythology, represents the triumph of human intelligence and freedom over the tyranny of the gods. And it is not without significance that what can be called the "Prometheus melody" in this symphony is treated so that it reveals the triumph of one element over another.

The year 1806 found Beethoven relaxing from the strain of producing and rewriting his opera *Fidelio;* the Symphony No. 4, in B flat, Op. 60, was begun at about that time. Perhaps as a consequence of that relaxed mood, the symphony is joyful throughout and is remarkably free from dramatic tension. It is perhaps the most approachable of Beethoven's second-period works; but probably because it does not represent the stormy, titanic Beethoven, the Fourth is played less frequently than any other of the nine symphonies.

It is likely that no work of Beethoven's is as universally esteemed as the Symphony No. 5, in C minor, Op. 67. Begun together with the Symphony No. 4 in about 1806, it was completed in the following year, but it is unlike the Fourth in every important respect. It is one of the most concentrated works in the entire literature; three themes in the first movement are based on the same four-note motive (see Example 55), and the concentrated pace of this movement is only once relaxed at a brief oboe cadenza in the recapitulation.

Example 55

Welcome relief from this tension is provided by the set of variations that constitute the slow movement. And although the movement is suave and lyric for the most part, it rises to a high climax on occasion: thus Beethoven avoids writing merely a passively beautiful work. The scherzo that serves as the third movement differs from every other scherzo Beethoven wrote. There is no humor here, but an air of foreboding, and the mutterings of cello and bass in the trio of the movement add to the disconcerting quality of the whole. The scherzo is connected to the finale by a long transitional passage in which the foreboding air is gradually dissolved to give way to the mood of triumph suggested by the finale.

If there is any truth in the often-expressed feeling that the Symphony No. 5 represents Beethoven's triumph over his own fate, the mood of the C major finale gives that view ample support. Joyful, clearcut expression of strong themes, a harmonic scheme that is forthright and direct, and a powerful rhythmic drive all give the finale its force and majesty. But by way of reminder that no victory is final, Beethoven introduces in the development section a portion of the foreboding scherzo; the effect is to suggest that dark forces are not completely destroyed, but vanquished only temporarily. After the interruption, the victorious mood returns, and now there is no question of its lasting quality. The coda of the movement presents jubilation at its highest level, and at the end of the coda the last thirty measures contain nothing but emphatic reiterations of the tonic (C major) harmony. The many repeated chords suggest that Beethoven was determined to leave no doubt in the listener's mind concerning the victory of personal will over fate.

Beethoven's music often allows itself to be treated symbolically: the above account of the Symphony No. 5 gives evidence of this. But only rarely is his music unmistakably descriptive. The Symphony No. 6, in F major, Op. 68, is one of these rare cases. Beethoven himself called it the "Pastoral" Symphony. Its five movements carry his own explanatory titles: (1) "Awakening of Cheerful Impressions on Arrival in the Country"; (2) "Scene at the Brook"; (3) "Merrymaking of the Peasants"; (4) "The Storm"; (5) "The Shepherds' Song: Feeling of Thanksgiving after the Storm." Moreover, there are realistic representations of a trio of birds in the second movement, a village band in the third, and thunder and lightning in the fourth. The Symphony No. 6 contains neither the psychological insights nor the power and drama that usually distinguish Beethoven above all other composers. Rather, there are a series of pleasant melodies, a consistency of style, and a relaxed pace—except, perhaps, in the fourth movement.

Example 56

Beethoven, Symphony No. 7, Scherzo

SECTION	LENGTH (IN MEASURES)	THEME
A	24, repeated 124, repeated	
B, Trio I	32 42, repeated	
Transition	14	
A	24 } 24 } (Now written out because of changed orchestration.) 124	
B, Trio I (repeated)	32 42, repeated	
Transition	14	
A	24 124	
Coda	9	

It was often Beethoven's practice to compose a relaxed work after an intense one; the fifth and sixth symphonies, be it noted, have consecutive opus numbers but are completely unlike in content and scope. The same is true of the Symphonies No. 7, in A major, Op. 92, and No. 8, in F major, Op. 93—both written between about 1809 and 1812 and both published in 1816. Where the Seventh is full of driving energy, the Eighth is a humorous, quixotic work that is leisurely and full of joy. The Seventh, in all its movements, is the embodiment of relentless rhythm: an exuberant mood animates the first movement (see Example 17*d*, p. 30, for the rhythmic motive that is basic throughout), and a wildness akin to fury characterizes the finale. The quiet second movement is based on a theme and variations (its theme is shown in part in Example 8*a*, p. 17), and the expansive scherzo has its trio repeated after the first recapitulation, thus constituting an ABABA form (see Example 56). Both movements come as a relief from the drama and tension of the outer movements.

The Symphony No. 8 has a first movement full of dry humor. The second movement, written in a precise and mechanical style that is purposely devoid of sentiment (see Example 57), symbolizes the rhythmic regularity of Johann Maelzel's newly invented metronome (see pp. 31–32); in fact, Beethoven used the theme of that movement in a humorous canon on the words "Ta-ta-ta, my dear Maelzel." A melodious minuet stands in place of the usual scherzo, and an enormous, rollicking finale in fast tempo, with many harmonic ambiguities and sudden fortissimo outbursts, concludes the symphony.

In spite of its good-natured, even boisterous air, the Symphony No. 8 is a profound work. Beethoven here comes to grips with a basic musical problem—namely, the conflict between tonalities—and he solves it brilliantly. An elaboration of this point cannot be attempted here, for it would lead into technicalities beyond the scope of this book. The Symphony No. 8 may be enjoyed on its own merits, nevertheless; it is a vital, buoyant composition that makes light of the harmonic subtleties it contains.

Example 57

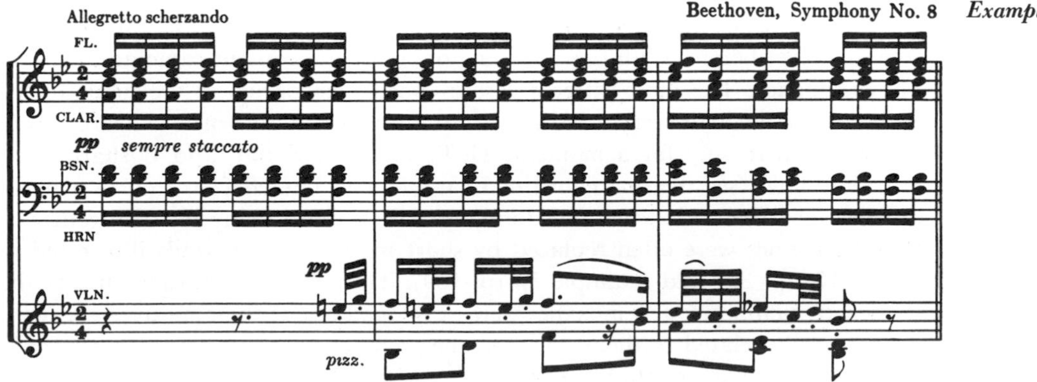

In about 1812, at the time that this symphony was approaching its final form, Beethoven sketched out some themes for a ninth symphony. Eleven years elapsed before the work was finished. In the interval he had passed through the second major crisis of his life. His attitude toward the world had altered and he had entered upon his third style period. The Symphony No. 9, in D minor, Op. 125, marks another milestone in the evolution of orchestral music. It is far removed from all earlier symphonies. It discloses a Beethoven who had turned inward, who had become an ethical philosopher, and who had completely mastered his tonal material in spite of total deafness.

A full chorus and a quartet of soloists are added to the large orchestra in the fourth movement. Beethoven selected for the vocal sections certain verses from Schiller's *Ode to Joy*—verses that proclaim the joy of mankind when universal brotherhood shall at last have been established under divine guidance. The long, brooding, and forceful first movement and the joyless, self-willed scherzo, however, express moods that are direct negations of the mood that animates the choral finale. Conversely, the sublime adagio transcends even the optimism of the last movement: peace, serenity, and sheer beauty are revealed here. The choral finale, a complex set of variations on the theme shown in Example 58, develops the sentiment of Schiller's *Ode* in a variety of joyful, eloquent, and vigorous moods, and it ends triumphantly. The manner in which Beethoven selected portions of Schiller's poem to express his own ethical philosophy may be seen in the outline of the symphony, given above.

Example 58

In the roughly twenty-five years that lie between the first and last of Beethoven's nine symphonies, the symphony itself had been completely transformed. Tension and conflict, fierce energy, and boisterous humor found expression to a much greater degree than ever before. With this widening of emotional content came an increased use of dissonance. The most extreme case in Beethoven occurs in the finale of the Symphony No. 9 where every tone of the harmonic minor scale of D is heard simultaneously, even if only for a moment: D, E, F, G, A, B flat, and C sharp, with several doublings (see the first chord of Example 59). The effect is that of a harsh roar, caused by the tonic triad and dominant ninth chord being heard together.

Melodic themes were often replaced by short motives of the kinds illustrated in Example 17*d* (p. 30) and Example 55 (p. 169). Through the consistent use of the development technique, new melodies were developed out of those motives and were thus organically related to them. Further, the technique was employed not only in the middle section of sonata-form movements, but virtually everywhere: in intro-

Example 59

ductions, in transitions, and in thematic statements alike. An increasing use of counterpoint also marked Beethoven's progress to musical mastery, especially in the third period. The result of all these practices is a kind of music in which intensity and concentrated expression are everywhere reflected.

The orchestra, too, had grown in size in the years between his first and last symphonies, and Beethoven occasionally made use of instruments that had been previously and primarily employed in the opera orchestra. The normal symphony orchestra of the late Classical period had contained two each of flutes, oboes, clarinets, bassoons, horns, trumpets, and tympani, and perhaps thirty string instruments (see p. 114). In Beethoven's symphonies that number was gradually increased and the way was prepared for the emergence of the massive orchestra of the Romantic period. The "Eroica" Symphony, for example, requires three horns; the Symphony No. 9, four. Trombones appear in Nos. 5, 6, and 9; contrabassoon and one piccolo are used in Nos. 5 and 9, and the latter calls for bass drum, triangle, and cymbals. Such additions made more string instruments necessary, and the turn-of-the-century orchestra of about forty-three players had become an orchestra of at least seventy by 1825.

Further, the woodwind instruments in Beethoven's orchestra gradually were given a much greater degree of independence, and the lower strings also shared in the new freedom of expression. It had been the custom in Haydn's and Mozart's day to employ woodwinds mainly to double the string instruments; brass instruments had the primary function of sustaining the harmony tones and adding sonority at the climaxes. Occasionally, especially in Mozart's works, a flute, oboe, or clarinet had been given an independent melodic line. With Beethoven, however, such independent treatment became the rule rather than the exception, and as a result, the majority of instrumental parts became more difficult to play. It is revealing to listen to Beethoven's symphonies from this point of view. Thematic statements are given to unsupported woodwinds, the cello and the bass are employed melodically, and in the scherzo of the Symphony No. 9 even the tympani are used to introduce thematic material. The end result is a great increase in the richness of orchestral sound; in this area as in many others, Beethoven pointed the way to the future.

THE CONCERTOS

The expansion of form, the increase of drama and tension, and the greater technical demands made upon the players—such elements, illustrated so copiously in the sym-

Symphony No. 9, D minor, Op. 125, by Ludwig van Beethoven

FIRST MOVEMENT, Allegro ma non troppo, D minor

Sonata-form with introduction (meas. 1), exposition (meas. 17), development (meas. 164), recapitulation (meas. 315), and coda.

SECOND MOVEMENT, Molto vivace, D minor

Large scherzo with trio and recapitulation. Scherzo is cast in sonata-form with exposition (meas. 9), development (meas. 151), and recapitulation (meas. 272). Trio, in D major, is in duple meter (meas. 416). Scherzo da capo (meas. 531) is followed by coda.

THIRD MOVEMENT, Adagio molto, B flat

Theme (meas. 3) with four variations (meas. 43, 83, 99, and 137) and development. But the movement also contains a contrasting theme, which appears in D major (meas. 25) and G major (meas. 65).

FOURTH MOVEMENT, several tempos

For chorus, four soloists, and orchestra. The text is from Schiller's *Ode to Joy,* which is cast in the form of eight eight-line stanzas, each followed by its own four-line refrain. Beethoven, in employing only the first three stanzas and the first, third, and fourth refrains, selected the portions that prophesy that divine joy (first stanza) will come when universal brotherhood (first refrain) is achieved under the guidance of heaven (third refrain).

Meas.	*Tempo*	
1	Presto	D minor. Orchestral recitative serving as introduction
30		Review of themes from first, second, and third movments, and an anticipation of theme of fourth movement
92	Allegro assai	D major. Main theme followed by three variations (meas. 116, 140, and 164) and a transition
208	Presto	Recitative, baritone solo, similar to meas. 1–29. The text is Beethoven's: "O friends, no more these tones"
237	Allegro assai	D major. Baritone solo and chorus, first stanza, "Joyful, joyful." Theme is in effect Variation 4 of meas. 92–115
269		Variation 5. Three soloists and chorus, second stanza, "He who blessed by great fortune"

297		Variation 6. Two soloists and chorus, third stanza, "All are nourished by joy"
331	Allegro assai vivace	B flat. Variation 7, for orchestra alone
367		Variation 8. Tenor and chorus, fourth refrain, "Glad as suns in heav'nly orbit"
431		Fugue for orchestra alone, on theme of meas. 237
543		D major. Variation 9. Chorus, return of first stanza, "Joyful, joyful"
595	Andante maestoso	G major. Chorus, first refrain, "Embrace, ye millions," on a new theme
627		G minor. Chorus, third refrain, "Why bow ye down?" on another new theme
655	Allegro energico	D major. Variation 10. Chorus, first stanza, "Joyful, joyful," and first refrain, "Embrace, ye millions," combined on themes from meas. 237 and 595
730		Transition. Chorus, third refrain, "Why bow ye down?" followed by first refrain, "Embrace, ye millions"
763	Allegro ma non tanto	D major. Four soloists and chorus, first stanza, "Joyful, joyful"; modification of theme from meas. 237, with two interpolated sections, *poco adagio* (meas. 810 and 832), in which the theme is further developed
851	Prestissimo	Chorus, first refrain, "Embrace, ye millions"; theme is a compressed version of meas. 595
904		Chorus, portion of first stanza, "Joyful, joyful"; further development of theme from meas. 595. Movement ends in meas. 940

phonies, are also found in other categories of Beethoven's instrumental music. Of the five concertos for piano and orchestra, for example, the Concerto in C major, Op. 15, and the one in B flat, Op. 19, represent his first period. The third work in this form, in C minor, Op. 37, stands at the threshold of his change in style. And the Concerto in G major, Op. 58, along with the "Emperor" Concerto, in E flat, Op. 73, are among the finest compositions of Beethoven's second period.

In the two last-named works, as well as in the masterful Concerto in D major for violin and orchestra, Op. 61, the orchestra far exceeds the function of mere accompaniment. Music of symphonic scope and depth is assigned to the orchestra, and the solo instrument becomes an equal partner in presenting and developing the eloquent melodies with which the concertos are filled. These works are no longer mere display pieces for a virtuoso soloist, as are many concertos by minor composers, but great works of art which happen to include a part for a solo instrument.

Example 60

Many examples of this new stature could be mentioned: a passage in the G major Piano Concerto is typical. That work's first movement is noble and reserved; one of its unique features is that the piano itself announces the opening theme without orchestral support. The second movement contains another of the magical transformations of mood that Beethoven achieved so superbly. Two conflicting elements are presented, as in the finale of the "Eroica" Symphony. In the concerto, however, the elements are a harsh, imperious phrase given to the orchestra alone (see Example 60*a*), and a quiet, yielding passage for the piano (Example 60*b*). During the course of the short movement (it contains only seventy-two measures) the forceful phrase is softened and broken down, until it eventually gives way to the quiet eloquence of the piano's melody. The conflict that was resolved brilliantly in the "Eroica" Symphony is here resolved subtly, with the utmost refinement. This movement represents Beethoven at his most appealing.

After the quiet and peace of that movement, the brusque and robust finale comes as a shock. This may very well have been Beethoven's intention. He often delighted in bringing his listeners down to earth again, after his tenderest improvisations at the piano, with a loud chord or something equally disconcerting. The contrast between the second and the last movements in the G major Concerto serves the same aesthetic purpose.

THE SONATAS

Beethoven's thirty-two piano sonatas range from Op. 2, of 1795 to Op. 111, of 1822; they reveal a course of growth and expansion similar to that taken by the symphonies. The influence of Haydn and other composers is felt in the earlier compositions. Forms are restricted in length and type of contrast, the emotional content of the works is "normal" for the period, and objective expression dominates.

The sonatas dating from about 1802 to 1816 (roughly from Op. 27 through Op. 90) are filled with the expressive content associated with Beethoven's second period.

Dramatic contrasts, a wider range of emotion, the use of a greater portion of the keyboard, "thundering" and "whispering" closely spaced—such features are typical. The great Sonata in D minor, Op. 31, No. 2, follows soon after the "Moonlight," Op. 27, No. 2. The "Waldstein" Sonata, Op. 53, and the "Appassionata" Sonata, Op. 57, are worthy neighbors of the "Eroica" Symphony, Op. 55, and deserve their high places among the works of the second period. (The "Appassionata" is the only one of these sonatas that Beethoven himself named.)

In the years after 1816, beginning with the Sonata in A major, Op. 101, and including four others of even greater stature, Beethoven shows an introspective content, a greater use of polyphonic textures, and a power and profundity unmatched earlier. His forms are more free, in keeping with the plastic, flowing nature of his melodic ideas. The development of the thematic material reaches new heights of eloquence, and a rare beauty pervades the quiet passages.

THE QUARTETS

What has been said about the expressive variety, emotional power, formal freedom, and profundity of Beethoven's symphonies applies in equal measure to his seventeen string quartets. The six quartets of Op. 18 are, like several other compositions of the years 1798 to 1801, first-period works that give hints of what the second will reveal. The five quartets between Op. 59 and Op. 95 correspond roughly to the six symphonies between Op. 55 and Op. 93; drama, subtlety, fierce joy, and pathos are expressed in them. And the six quartets from Op. 127 to Op. 135, composed after the Symphony No. 9, exceed even that great work in majesty, expression of optimism, forcefulness, and humor.

In four of the last six quartets, Beethoven attained his highest level of musical organization. Those quartets are the ones in A minor, Op. 132; B flat, Op. 130; C sharp minor, Op. 131; and the Great Fugue in B flat, Op. 133. They not only stand at the very peak of Beethoven's music as individual works but they also form a connected cycle. The four works together comprise nineteen movements, and one four-note motive and its transformations provide a large part of the thematic material for every one of them. On various occasions the motive is reversed, twisted, inverted in part, expanded, or shortened. Example 61 shows the original form of

Example 61

the motive as it appears at the beginning of the A minor Quartet, and several of the transformations.

Technically, this achievement of Beethoven's is capable of being analyzed and "explained." But musically and emotionally, one can only stand in awe and admiration of what has been accomplished here. The quality of the music, its sheer beauty, and its power to suggest hidden states of the soul are indescribable. The quartets must be listened to, and listened to repeatedly, if one is to gain even a portion of what the composer has to share with us. And that, in the final analysis, is true of virtually everything Beethoven wrote.

Listening Suggestions

BEETHOVEN

Concerto for Piano, No. 5, E flat major, Op. 73 ("Emperor")
Concerto for Violin, D major, Op. 61
Egmont, Overture, Op. 84
Leonore, Overture, No. 3, Op. 72*a*
Piano Sonata, C minor, Op. 13 ("Pathétique")
Piano Sonata, C sharp minor, Op. 27, No. 2 ("Moonlight")
Piano Sonata, F minor, Op. 57 ("Appassionata")
Piano Trio, B flat major, Op. 97 ("Archduke")
String Quartets, Op. 18, Nos. 1–6; Op. 130, 131, 132
Symphony No. 3, E flat, Op. 55 ("Eroica")
Symphony No. 5, C minor, Op. 67
Symphony No. 6, F major, Op. 68 ("Pastoral")
Symphony No. 7, A major, Op. 92
Symphony No. 9, D minor, Op. 125
Thirty-two Variations, C minor (no opus number)

Chapter 10

THE EARLY ROMANTIC PERIOD

Beethoven's death in 1827 in effect marked the end of the Classical period. The balance of content and form, which had concerned Beethoven as well as his great predecessors, Haydn and Mozart, ceased to be a major concern in the thinking of many of the composers who succeeded the Classical masters. A new style and a new content began to emerge in about the second quarter of the nineteenth century. Both the period and those who flourished at that time are called "Romantic." The musical elements that were to come to fullest expression in that period find their first considerable use in the works of Franz Schubert and Carl Maria von Weber, both of whom died before the Romantic period was well under way.

Schubert

Franz Peter Schubert was born in Vienna in 1797. His father, a schoolmaster with a large family and a meager income, was able to provide only a rudimentary education for the future composer. Before Schubert was in his teens he had received some instruction on the violin and piano, in voice, and in harmony. Soon he was able to take part, as a viola player, in the informal chamber music sessions that were a regular feature of the family life. There he learned to know the string quartets of Haydn and Mozart, and those composers provided the models for his first efforts at composition.

From his eleventh to his sixteenth year he sang in the choir of the Imperial Court; as a choir member he received some additional instruction in music. When his voice changed, in about 1814, he became an assistant in his father's elementary school. He had no interest in teaching, however; in fact, nothing other than composing ever interested him. Nevertheless, he remained in the school until 1816, when he was nineteen. In the following year he left his home and occupied a succession of inexpensive lodgings in various parts of Vienna. He had no regular source of income, and he was not a virtuoso performer on any instrument. Thus he was often forced to rely upon the hospitality of friends who were temporarily better off than he. This precarious way of life continued for more than ten years.

For a few months in 1818, and again in 1824, Schubert was engaged as piano teacher to the two daughters of Count Johann Esterházy on the latter's Hungarian estate. Those intervals represent the only professional position he ever held. He lived only to compose, and he spent a large part of every day at his desk. "When one piece is finished, I immediately start another," he said on one occasion, and the great number of his compositions gives evidence of his industry.

A few of his songs were performed by an excellent baritone named Vogl, whom Schubert numbered among his friends; those songs brought the composer to such public notice as he enjoyed during his lifetime. Many of them were published in the years after 1818. Although Schubert's arrangements with his publishers were thoroughly unsatisfactory, the small income from the sale of those songs and of some piano music stood between him and utter destitution. The situation in regard to his instrumental works was quite otherwise. Few of them came to public performance; and except for some commissioned works, none of them became a source of financial security.

Lack of performances, however, seems to have had no effect upon Schubert's zeal. Ignoring his financial state, he composed continually, but he made little effort to bring to the attention of the public the compositions that flowed so copiously from his fertile mind. Only once was he able to give a concert devoted entirely to his own works: that concert was held in the spring of 1828, when Schubert was thirty-one. The months that followed were full of illness, yet several of his greatest works were written during that period. In November of the same year, following an attack of typhus, he died.

Schubert occupies an unusual place in music history. He was a younger contemporary of Beethoven's, walked the same streets at the same time as the older composer did, and worshipped him from afar. Almost his entire creative work was done within the limits of the Classical period. But he was not a Classicist at heart or by temperament; nor do his most characteristic works adhere to the principles of Classicism. His early works, it is true, follow the models of Haydn and Mozart, but he seems not to have been interested in building upon those models, as Beethoven had done so successfully. We do not often find in Schubert's larger works the logically organized forms, the concentrated textures, and the perfect balance of heart and mind that distinguish the music of the great Classical composers. In Schubert the heart dominates, and the feelings of the heart are expressed in some of the most wonderfully wrought melodies that have ever been composed.

In the seventeen years between 1811, when he was fourteen, and 1828, the year of his death, Schubert composed about a thousand works. Among them are over six hundred songs; eight (or nine) symphonies; about two dozen chamber music works; as many piano sonatas, and innumerable shorter works for piano; large quantities of music for the stage, including several operas and operettas; six Masses and more than two dozen other works for the church; and almost a hundred choral compositions. Only a small fraction of those works were published during his lifetime, and many were not discovered and made known to the musical world until decades after his death.

INSTRUMENTAL WORKS

By the year 1818, when Schubert was twenty-one, he had written six symphonies, seven overtures, and about a dozen chamber music compositions. They are youthful works modeled upon Haydn, Mozart, and even Rossini. Many are full of structural faults and reveal that Schubert's self-critical sense was not as well developed as his interest in musical self-expression. But these early compositions also point the way to what Schubert was to become. Charming, graceful melodies that express deep feeling fill the pages of those works; dramatic, colorful harmonies and many unexpected changes of key give evidence of Schubert's originality even as a youth. Few of those early compositions, however, have survived on the concert stage.

The so-called "Unfinished" Symphony in B minor, composed only slightly later than those youthful works, is in another category altogether. Written in 1822, it was not found until 1865. It is utterly different from his earlier symphonies and their Classical models, and it is also unlike the majority of other symphonies in that it contains only two movements (see chart, p. 162); this fact is responsible for its bearing the label "Unfinished." More important, however, is its unique melodic content.

We have earlier described the symphonic type as being based on a contrast between dissimilar moods—between the lyric and the dramatic, for example. In Schubert's B minor Symphony lyricism has become the essential element. The orchestral instruments "sing" here as they do in no previous work. Even in its dramatic moments, of which the symphony has its share, drama and lyricism are wonderfully fused, and the lyric quality of the melodies shines through. Its very first measures of introduction (see Example 21*c,* p. 38), as well as the first and second themes of the first movement (see Example 36*b,* p. 76, and Example 22*c,* p. 39, respectively), are melodious above all. And the long melody in the second movement, given first to the clarinet and later to the oboe over a pulsating accompaniment (see Example 62), represents Schubert at his finest.

The first movement is pessimistic in tone in spite of its melodic beauty; the second expresses resignation. This emotional unity explains, perhaps, why Schubert did not write the usual two additional movements (he began a scherzo, but broke it off after

Schubert, Symphony No. 8 ("Unfinished") *Example 62*

a few measures). Had he composed a conventional scherzo and finale resolving the first movement's pessimism, or one in which the pessimism descended to morbidity, the mood of resignation expressed in the second movement would have been false. Two moods, or two aspects of the same mood, are expressed: the symphony is complete as it stands. It is fortunate that Schubert realized this in time and allowed the two movements to carry his message. The work is unique, but it points directly to the Romantic style that was to mark all music in the decades following his death. Rather than being unfinished, it is a perfect work of art in a new form.

Schubert's last symphony, in C major, was written in 1828. Here again is an instrumental work that is original in every respect, even though it contains four movements and approaches the size and intensity (if not the content) of Beethoven's Symphony No. 9. The slow introduction leads into a world compounded of sheer melodic beauty and relentless driving rhythm. Many of the symphony's themes and motives are related, in that they are based on the interval of a rising or falling third (see Example 63). These relationships allow Schubert to express enormous rhythmic vitality and driving force in concentrated fashion. Although the symphony is long, it develops great momentum as it carries the listener along relentlessly.

Schubert's thematic development, in the C major Symphony as well as in other works, is quite unlike that used by the majority of other composers. His method is to repeat melodies in a variety of keys, to present them several times virtually unchanged except in harmony. This is seen in the first movement of the symphony, where the second measure of Example 63*a* is used to introduce a series of melodies each of which touches upon many different keys—D flat minor, E major, and C minor among them. In the last movement, the melody shown in Example 63*e* is similarly employed. In these cases, as well as in many others in Schubert's works, the element of harmonic color becomes more important than close organization.

Example 63

The effect of such remote keys as B major, D flat major, D flat minor, and E major in passages having a harmonic background of C major is overwhelming. One commentator calls such passages "Schubert's purple patches."

Franz Schubert (1797–1828).

Among Schubert's most important chamber music works are two string quartets, in A minor and D minor, respectively; a string quintet in C major, in which a second cello is added to the regular string quartet; and the unique "Trout" Quintet for piano, violin, viola, cello, and bass. Those four works alone would earn Schubert a high rank among instrumental composers.

The Quartet in D minor especially is a masterpiece; popularly known as the "Death and the Maiden" Quartet, it is, like the Symphony in C major, a work full of rhythmic intensity, rich harmonic color, and profound expression. The popular title is appropriate in that Schubert used his own song of that name as a theme for the set of variations that constitutes the quartet's slow movement. In successive variations the melody is modified in enchanting fashion: it is given to each of the instruments in turn, or it is supplied with countermelodies, or it is altered rhythmically.

The "Trout" Quintet similarly contains a set of variations on Schubert's song *Die Forelle* (*The Trout*). But that movement is light in mood and graceful in its contours, as befits the sentiment of the song whose melody is used. In fact, the entire quintet, with five movements instead of the usual four, is a pleasing, entertaining work in the best sense. It contains none of the dark moods or the pensive tones that mark the other three great chamber music works of Schubert.

SCHUBERT'S SONGS

Schubert is known to have composed 603 works of the special category called *art songs.* Their unique qualities set them apart from works in this form by other composers. Songs for voice and piano had existed before Schubert's time, but such songs were usually written to focus on the vocal part. The piano, playing a subordinate role, provided only the necessary harmonic and rhythmic support. The songs of Mozart, Haydn, and their contemporaries and predecessors were of this type. With the composers who came after Schubert, the song often became a miniature drama. The piano part became descriptive, conveying specific moods, and sometimes even gaining ascendancy over the vocal part. In many cases the vocal line took on a static quality resembling a kind of declamation rather than a lyric melody. Thus the songs of the period between 1840 and 1900 often completely reversed the principle upon which eighteenth-century songs were composed.

In Schubert, a different type of song appears, for the two elements of melody and accompaniment are balanced. The melody gives full expression not only to the sense of the text but to the moods suggested by it. And the piano part, no longer a mere accompaniment, establishes those moods either by means of a short introduction, or by providing the appropriate atmosphere throughout the composition, or by going beyond the power of words to express emotions. These magical effects are kept from being extravagant by Schubert's use of appropriate musical motives. His sense of self-discipline, not always apparent in the instrumental works, is clearly shown in the way the piano parts of the songs are organized. The poignant motive that runs through *The Organ Grinder* (Example 64*a*) and the descriptive running figure that is found in almost every measure of *Gretchen at the Spinning Wheel* (Example 64*e*) are typical of the many devices that animate the piano parts of these masterpieces.

Even where such motives are not employed, the piano part is marvelously adapted to the mood of the text, and the melody provides the perfect complement. For ex-

Example 64

ample, the eerie quality of *The Double* (Example 64*c*) is carried not only by the somber chords in the piano but also by the tentative, halting melodic line. The naïve, folk-song-like *Hedge Rose* (Example 64*d*), on the other hand, is appropriately simple, clear, and unassuming in melody and accompaniment. And again, the majesty and power suggested in *The Omnipotence* (Example 64*b*) are carried by a resonant, pulsating series of repeated chords that perfectly amplify the eloquence of the flowing melodic line.

Many of Schubert's songs illustrate the various types of song forms discussed in Chapter 5. It will be recalled that the song form may exist both as a separate entity and as a component of compound forms. The latter was illustrated in connection with minuets and rondos as found in the Classical period (see pp. 128–30); Schubert's songs exemplify the use of the form as a separate entity. As a single short piece, the song form may exhibit different formal plans: two-part, three-part, and the like; and each part usually consists of phrases, periods, or both. In order to avoid monotony of harmonic color, the second part in the three-part form is often set in a contrasting key.

This plan is found in many of Schubert's finest songs, *Gretchen at the Spinning Wheel* (mentioned above) and *The Fishermaiden* among them. With first and third parts predominantly in one key and the second part largely in another, the songs reveal a high degree of unity in spite of their contrasting middle parts. In others, a variety of different formal plans are found. And occasionally in Schubert's three principal song cycles (*The Maid of the Mill, A Winter's Journey,* and *Swan Song*) a degree of thematic connection between one song and another occurs.

Drama, intense feeling, childlike trust, dark moods, heartbreaking sorrow, and many other states of emotion are reflected in Schubert's songs. The innate musical qualities of those works set them apart from "songs" in the ordinary sense; hence the appropriate term "art songs" is applied to them. The songs of similar quality composed later in the century by Schumann, Brahms, and Wolf, among others, are also given that name. Art songs are often referred to by their German name, *Lieder;* and a "Lieder singer" is then a performer who specializes in German art songs. Likewise, a "Lieder recital" is confined to songs of this type.

Weber

Carl Maria von Weber, born at Eutin, Germany, in 1786, was the son of the director of a traveling theatrical company. The elder Weber (a man of dubious reputation, occasionally given to shady practices) was the uncle of Mozart's wife; thus the future composer and Mozart were first cousins by marriage. Weber's boyhood was spent wherever his father's company happened to be situated; his musical education was a matter of a few months with one teacher, a half-year with another, and so on. But as he grew older he became thoroughly familiar with the techniques and requirements of the theater; that knowledge helped him enormously in his later career as an operatic composer. In addition, he showed great aptitude for the piano, and at the age of thirteen he appeared in public as a concert performer. He later became one of the most brilliant virtuoso pianists of his time.

As a composer, too, Weber was precocious. By his sixteenth year he had written three operas, but they proved unsuccessful. A series of minor positions, several concert tours, and a two-week term in prison (on the charge of embezzlement, a charge that properly should have been brought against his father) preceded his appointment in 1813 as conductor of the National Opera Theater in Prague. Throughout this period, he continued his activities as a composer.

Weber was an excellent conductor and a competent administrator. Under his direction the National Opera Theater was completely reorganized and gained a notable position among the opera houses of Europe. Weber's success in Prague resulted in his being called to Dresden in 1817 by the King of Saxony, to assume the directorship of the Royal Opera. He remained in that position until his death in 1826.

Shortly after arriving in Dresden he began the composition of the opera that was to bring him international fame and a secure position in music history. That opera, *Der Freischütz* (*The Free Shooter*), required three years for its completion. At its first performance, in Berlin in 1821, it became an immediate success. *Der Freischütz* was followed by two other operas: *Euryanthe* (1823) and *Oberon* (1826). Two months after the first production of *Oberon* in London, Weber died. Overwork, fatigue, and tuberculosis brought his career to an end.

The qualities that set Weber's late operas apart from other works in that form are the qualities that have come to be known as "Romantic." These works show first of all a concern with exotic, fantastic, or magical elements. *Der Freischütz* deals with enchanted bullets directed by the Devil; *Euryanthe* is set amid medieval castles and

C. M. von Weber conducting an opera at Covent Garden. (Lithograph by Hullmann, after J. Hayter.)

is peopled with noble lords and huntsmen; *Oberon* bears the subtitle "The Elf-King's Oath" and is compounded of fairies, Oriental characters, magical visions, and a storm at sea. A search for new subject matter—a search that was to preoccupy many later Romantic composers—is largely responsible for this choice of content. Mythology, folk legends, and stories from non-European cultures provided the new material for Weber, as they were to do for his successors.

The second major characteristic of Weber's operas is the new kind of dramatic effects they brought to expression. The magic and superstition upon which the plots depended made possible many unexpected situations and episodes that led to dramatic tension. Those and similar elements permitted Weber to introduce sudden changes of key, richer and freer harmonic schemes, and a variety of melodic and rhythmic types, all of which expressed the mysterious, gloomy, or supernatural moods called for by the plots.

Of more lasting importance was the use Weber made of the orchestra in establishing those moods. The evidence of his originality in this respect must today be sought largely in the overtures to the three late operas. The operas themselves are only seldom performed, whereas the overtures are standard fare in the orchestral repertoire. Weber's originality in orchestration is one of his most noteworthy accomplishments.

The exciting or sinister-sounding tremolo of the violas found in the slow section of the *Euryanthe* Overture (see Example 65*a*) does much to create an eerie mood in spite of its brevity. The short staccato passage for winds in the *Oberon* Overture (Example 65*b*) and the restless, syncopated accompaniment to the tense, surging cello melody in the Overture to *Der Freischütz* (Example 65*c*) are similarly well adapted to suggesting the emotions expressed in greater detail within the operas themselves. To these qualities may be added Weber's deftness and imagination in scoring, so that new tone-color combinations and new sounds permeate the orchestra. Passages in which the extreme ranges of the instruments are effectively used (for example, the lowest tones of the clarinet, or the highest tones of the flute) give Weber's orchestra a rich and varied sound. It is here, in his use of instruments for their own particular sounds, that his link with later nineteenth-century music is seen most strongly.

In earlier music, and in some contemporary with Weber's own, the instrumental sound had been varied and the different instruments had had appropriate music written for them. But the concern with sound itself—with sound considered separately from the melody, harmony, and rhythm in which it became audible—had not loomed large in the thinking of earlier composers. In the Baroque period, for example, a piece was often written with the instruments themselves unspecified; any instruments of the proper range were then acceptable. The Classical composers had gone far beyond that point, it is true, and had called for specific instruments in all their works. But now (and here we include the music of both Weber and Schubert) the sound of a particular instrument or of an instrumental combination achieved greater importance than ever before. The way a piece sounded became as important as its content or the emotions it expressed. And the new sound of Romantic music is one of its most striking characteristics.

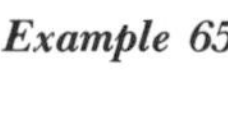

Example 65

(a) Largo — Weber, *Euryanthe*, Overture

pp (4 SOLO VIOLINS)

pp (4 SOLO VIOLINS)

(VIOLA) pp

(b) Adagio sostenuto — Weber, *Oberon*, Overture

(FLUTES) pp *staccato*

(CLARINETS) pp *staccato*

(HORN)

(c) Molto vivace — Weber, *Der Freischütz*, Overture

pp *cresc.*

pp

The Romantic Period

In the period that began in about 1825 and lasted until about 1900, the majority of composers exploited the new elements so eloquently introduced by Schubert and Weber. Those elements may be summarized as follows: in opera, a new type of subject matter, which included a variety of magical, exotic, or fantastic effects; in vocal music, a new type of song in which the piano part took on greater independence and often served to establish the mood; in instrumental music, many new orchestral effects along with great flexibility and variability of texture; in all categories, richer harmonies than had been used previously, more freedom in key relationships, and greater attention to the sheer sound of the music.

In addition to those elements came an outspokenly experimental attitude toward all musical matters. Many composers saw in music a means of describing or illustrating objects, situations, and emotional states. Music became for them a medium for telling stories or painting pictures, and they experimented with new effects that might make their works descriptive or "realistic." Thus, *program music,* as it is called, reached heights never before attained by earlier composers. Other composers, in their search for new materials, turned to national idioms, folk songs, legends, and the like for inspiration. A variety of national schools arose: musicians were no longer universal composers, but specifically Czech, Russian, Norwegian, and so on.

The enthusiasm with which all the new elements were employed was often accompanied by a lack of discrimination. In their lavish use of dissonance and varied harmonies, composers often lost sight of the balance of emotion and intellect that is a requisite of great music. The expression of feeling became a new watchword, with a consequent increase in subjectivity and a decline of self-discipline. Forms were loosely constructed, and good proportion was often neglected in the interest of giving expression to subjective emotions. With Schubert, as we have seen, harmonic color contrasts became more important than planned organization, and many of Schubert's successors expressed rhapsodic or impulsive moods in disorganized fashion.

With Classical considerations of form virtually abandoned, the unspoken restrictions on the size of various musical forms tended to disappear. Symphonies inflated beyond all previous dimensions emerged; Schubert's Symphony in C major, twice the size of the average Haydn symphony when played without "cuts," is an early example. Conversely, brief works that do no more than convey a momentary state of feeling were also written. The art songs of Schubert are themselves examples, and, as we shall see below, the short preludes of Chopin, the *Songs Without Words* of Mendelssohn, and the many piano pieces entitled "Album Leaf," "Moment Musicale," and "Morceau" fall into the same category. (A parallel to this is seen in our own time: novels that run to a thousand pages are not unknown, and "short short stories" of a page or two are common in Sunday newspaper supplements.)

It will become clear in the following chapters that the full weight of those new elements was not felt until the Romantic period was well on its way—that is, from about 1860 on. From that time one can distinguish three groups of composers: (1) those who wrote descriptively and who became exponents principally of program music; (2) those who employed the folk melodies, rhythms, and legends of a particular nation as source material for their compositions; (3) those who stood aloof from both programmatic and nationalistic concerns and wrote primarily abstract (that is, nonrepresentational) music in the forms they had inherited from the Classical period. To those three groups may be added a small fourth group of composers who seemed equally at home—or equally uncomfortable—in all three areas.

In the early part of the Romantic period—the period of time with which we shall be concerned in the rest of this chapter—the three areas were not yet clearly distinguished. The music written in the years between about 1825 and 1855 was in general not programmatic, or nationalistic, or anything other than purely Romantic. Yet four composers flourished in those years, each of whom revealed his kinship with one of the groups mentioned above; in a sense, they stand as heralds of what was to come. A tendency to write programmatically is seen in Hector Berlioz; Frédéric Chopin inclined at times toward the nationalistic; Felix Mendelssohn remained within the field of abstract music; and Robert Schumann seemed uncertain of his direction and worked programmatically, nationalistically, and abstractly at various times. In that very uncertainty, in his enthusiastic support of all the new trends then becoming apparent in music, Schumann was perhaps the most typically Romantic of all the period's composers.

Berlioz

Hector Berlioz, born near Grenoble, France, in 1803, was the son of a prosperous physician. In his early years he received a well-rounded education, including some rudimentary instruction in music. He became fairly proficient on the guitar and flute, but made little progress in piano playing. He was sent to Paris in 1821 to study medicine; however, music soon became his major interest. He neglected and later abandoned his medical studies, and eventually entered the Paris Conservatory for a short time. Even there he exhibited the rebelliousness, fantastic imagination, and energy that were to distinguish him throughout his lifetime. He began to compose in 1825: a Mass, several overtures, a number of choral compositions, and his best-known work, the *Symphonie Fantastique,* were written between that date and 1830.

In 1830 after having competed unsuccessfully several times, he won the *Prix de Rome;* the prize enabled him to live and study in Italy for eighteen months. Return-

Hector Berlioz (1803–69), who revolutionized the art of orchestration. (From a painting by Signol.)

ing to Paris, he became a music critic in 1835. Even though he often expressed dislike of the occupation, he rose to an influential position in the musical life of the city. He became an assistant to the Conservatory librarian in 1839, composing whenever time permitted, and from about 1842 to 1867 he traveled widely as a conductor and as propagandist for his own compositions. A number of concert tours through Germany, England, and Russia met with mixed success. Many controversies arose about the originality, extravagant nature, and monumental size of his works, but Berlioz was never at a loss in defending his creations verbally.

In 1864, the earnings from a series of performances of his opera, *The Trojans,* permitted him to give up his hated position as music critic. A number of ailments, some real and some imaginary, had undermined his health. Having outlived two wives and his only son, he declined rapidly after his last tour (to Russia in 1867), and he died in March 1869.

Berlioz' compositions do not always conform to the usual classification of musical types. For example, it is true that his *Symphonie Fantastique* is a symphony, but it contains five movements, is subtitled "Episode in the Life of an Artist," and is a descriptive work. Another symphony, *Harold in Italy* (1834), contains an extended part for viola solo: according to the composer's memoirs, the viola portrays "a sort of melancholy dreamer, in the style of Byron's *Childe Harold.*" Still another work, *Romeo and Juliet* (1839), he called a *"symphonie dramatique";* in it he included parts for vocal solos, choruses, and a prologue in choral recitative. Another hybrid work, *The Damnation of Faust* (1846), is called a *"légende dramatique";* it contains vocal solos, choruses, and orchestral numbers and is close in form to a secular oratorio.

Although Berlioz' works bear descriptive titles and are supplied with explanatory material in the form of programs, they can be listened to purely as music. The addition of the programs represented his concession to the romantic belief that music must have an underlying purpose—that it must describe a poetic idea, illustrate a succession of emotional states, or do something of that sort. Music was asked to serve as a source of stimulation for the typical man of that period, who was no longer content to live within himself. Excitement, vicarious passion, and other feelings induced by external experience were the rewards the concert-goers of the Romantic era sought in the music they heard. And Berlioz gratified those desires by superimposing involved programs upon his works.

To this task Berlioz brought a keen ear for new orchestral effects, great skill in handling the orchestra, and an unbridled imagination in creating spectacular, monumental, and bizarre musical situations. He visualized an orchestra many times larger than any in existence: he thought in terms of several hundred instrumentalists and choruses of a thousand. And even though the orchestra needed for the *Symphonie Fantastique* includes only about a hundred players, it calls for many instruments that had not found regular places in the ensemble before his time. Clarinets in several sizes, four bassoons, cornets as well as trumpets, the English horn, two harps, a piano, an expanded percussion section including four tympani instead of the usual two—these are among the additional instruments Berlioz required in this work.

Symphonie Fantastique, Op. 14, by Hector Berlioz

FIRST MOVEMENT, "Reveries, Passions," Largo, Allegro agitato

Meas.	*Theme*	
1	Introduction	
EXPOSITION		
72	1st	First part, in C major. The *idée fixe,* which will recur throughout the symphony (Ex. 1)

Example 1

119	2nd	First part, in C major
133		Second part, in F minor
152	Codetta	Contains fragments of first theme, but in G major (Ex. 2)

Example 2

DEVELOPMENT		
166		Based on Ex. 1, meas. 72
191		Based on Ex. 2, meas. 152
198		Transition
RECAPITULATION		
239	1st	Ex. 1, but in G major instead of the expected C major
278		New material loosely related to meas. 133. Not a true return of 2nd theme
311	Codetta	As in Ex. 2, meas. 152; begins in G major, but modulates to C major when the section is repeated at meas. 322
329	Coda	Based on 2nd theme, meas. 119
358		Based on Ex. 1, *idée fixe* (meas. 72) with a new counterpoint
409		Again based on *idée fixe*
462		Modulating section leading to final statement of *idée fixe.* Movement ends in meas. 525

SECOND MOVEMENT, "A Ball," Allegro non troppo

Meas.	*Section*	
1	Intro.	Begins in A minor, gradually approaches main key of movement
39	A	First part, in A major (Ex. 3)

Example 3

56		Second part
69	B	A major, but with contrasts of texture and melodic outline
94	A	As in Ex. 3, meas. 39, but more richly orchestrated
121	Quasi-Trio	Return of *idée fixe,* Ex. 1, in F major
163		Transition
176	A	First part, as in Ex. 3, meas. 39–55
193		Second part, as in meas. 56–68
206	B	A major, but with changed orchestration
233	A	Ex. 3, again in A major, with more elaborate orchestration
257	Coda	Based on new themes that suggest the rhythms of meas. 57 and 69
302		Return of *idée fixe,* Ex. 1, now in A major
320		Final section. Movement ends in meas. 368

THIRD MOVEMENT, "Scene in the Country," Adagio

Meas.	*Section*	
1	Intro.	In F major
20	A	In F major, with repetition in meas. 33
49	B	Suggests A minor. Developed and extended
69	A	In C major
79		Transition
88	C	In B flat, with portions of *idée fixe* inserted between phrases
113		Transition
119		New theme, in F major, instead of expected return of Section A
132	A	In F major, with theme of meas. 119 as a counterpoint. Developed, with theme of Section A and the *idée fixe* heard together
175	Coda	Based on introduction. Movement ends in meas. 199

FOURTH MOVEMENT, "March to the Gallows," Allegretto

Meas.	*Section*	
1	Intro.	Begins in G minor
17	A	In G minor, repeated in E flat, and extended (Ex. 4)

Example 4

ff *dim.* *p*

62	B	Part 1, in B flat
78		Part 2, in B flat
89		Part 1
105		Part 2, first phrase only, followed by transition

Berlioz, *Symphonie Fantastique* (cont.)

123	A	Ex. 4, first phrase only, followed by transition
140	Coda	Part 1, in G minor
164		Part 2, return of portion of *idée fixe*
169		Part 3. Movement ends in meas. 178

FIFTH MOVEMENT, "Dream of a Witches' Sabbath"

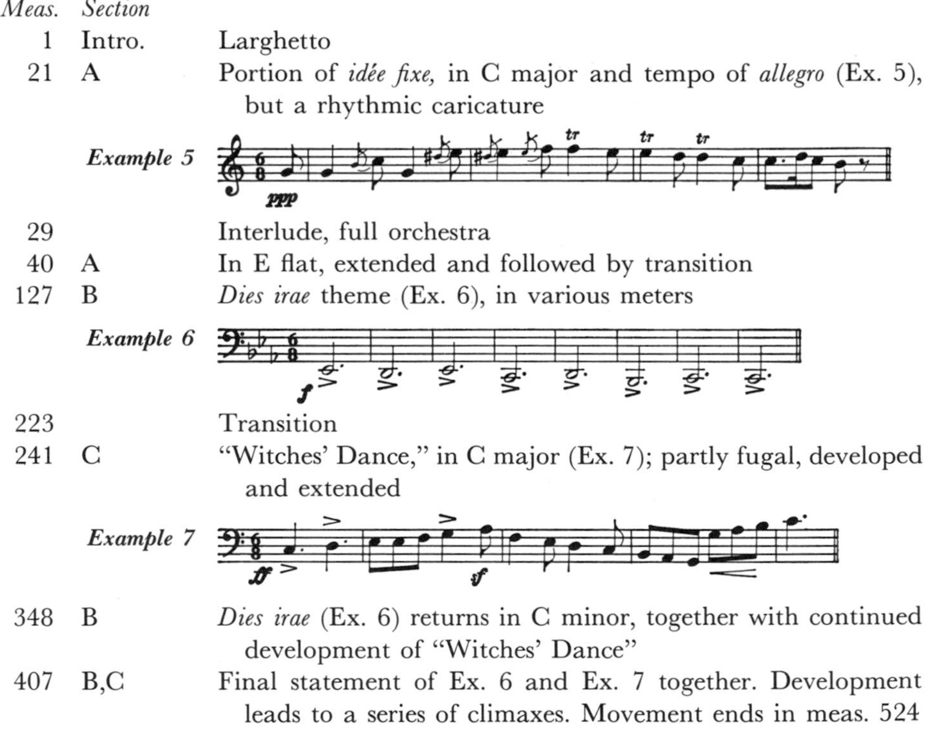

Meas.	*Section*	
1	Intro.	Larghetto
21	A	Portion of *idée fixe,* in C major and tempo of *allegro* (Ex. 5), but a rhythmic caricature
	Example 5	
29		Interlude, full orchestra
40	A	In E flat, extended and followed by transition
127	B	*Dies irae* theme (Ex. 6), in various meters
	Example 6	
223		Transition
241	C	"Witches' Dance," in C major (Ex. 7); partly fugal, developed and extended
	Example 7	
348	B	*Dies irae* (Ex. 6) returns in C minor, together with continued development of "Witches' Dance"
407	B,C	Final statement of Ex. 6 and Ex. 7 together. Development leads to a series of climaxes. Movement ends in meas. 524

The program that Berlioz supplied for the *Symphonie Fantastique* runs as follows: "A young musician of unhealthy sensitivity and feverish imagination has poisoned himself with opium in a fit of lovesick frustration. The poison is too weak to kill him, but it plunges him into a drugged sleep which is accompanied by weird visions. His emotions, sensations, and imaginings, passing through his sick mind, are transformed into musical thoughts and images. The beloved one herself becomes a specific melody (*idée fixe*) which he hears everywhere."

In carrying out the details of this program, Berlioz gave the following titles to the symphony's five movements: (1) "Reveries, Passions"; (2) "A Ball"; (3) "Scene in the Country"; (4) "March to the Gallows"; (5) "Dream of a Witches' Sabbath." Moreover, each movement has a detailed program of its own. In making this concession to the romantic spirit of his time, Berlioz found it unnecessary to abandon the forms of Beethoven's generation. The thematic outline of the symphony, given on pages 192–94, reveals how closely he adhered to the structural principles of the Classical period. Sonata-form, quasi-scherzo with trio and *da capo,* large rondo form —all are represented. Only in the last movement did Berlioz depart widely from a symmetrical, unified form.

The employment of the *idée fixe* is one of Berlioz' great contributions to musical form; it provides the possibility of unifying a work, no matter how long or how diffuse its content. In this symphony, the *idée fixe* appears first as a long, irregular melody in the first movement (see Example 66). Subsequently it appears at least

Example 66

once in each movement; each time it is suitably transformed to fit the emotional content of the movement, or else to serve as a clue to the events described in the program at that point. Thus, in the second movement the *idée fixe* takes the shape of a waltz melody (Example 67*a*); a pastoral theme is suggested in the third movement (Example 67*b*); the grisly fourth movement, full of dramatic surprises and

Example 67

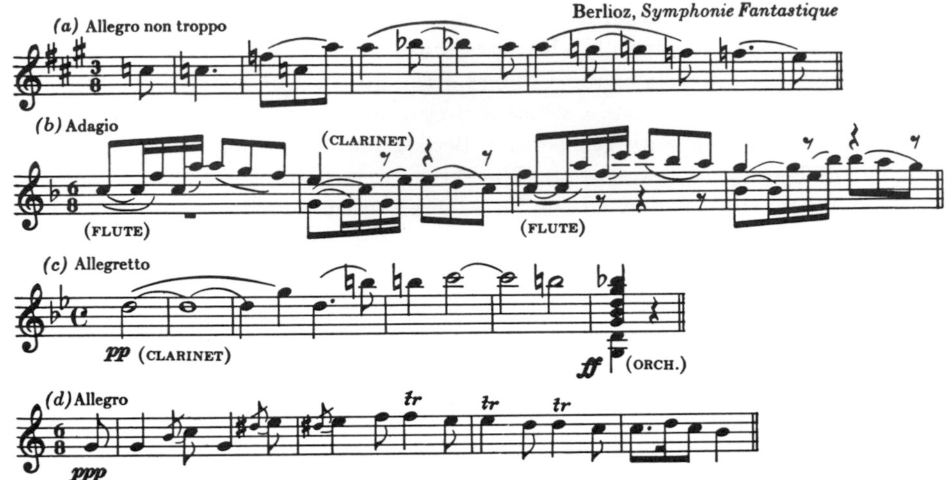

sharp contrasts, uses a fragment of the *idée fixe,* suddenly breaking off, to provide a climax (Example 67*c*); and the fifth-movement version, finally, is a caricature that suggests the unholy dance of the witches (Example 67*d*).

Since the dramatic, even fantastic, elements in Berlioz' music are sensational, they have always attracted attention. In so doing, they have tended to obscure the controlled, refined moments which are equally characteristic of Berlioz. The second movement of the *Symphonie Fantastique,* for example is a brilliant waltz, and the third is a quiet, reflective piece; neither has any trace of the excitement or forcefulness of the last two movements. Yet it is customary to think only of Berlioz' spectacular effects and to ignore those that reveal true beauty.

Berlioz, above all previous composers, thought of instruments as individuals, not as representatives of families. In his music the unique colors of single instruments or the mixed colors of a new grouping were lavishly used. The *Symphonie Fantastique,* for example, contains such effects as a flute accompanied by two horns; an oboe and English horn duet over a tremolo in the violas; a clarinet solo over an accompaniment of bass drum and tympani (the solo given in Example 67*d* has a tympani accompaniment); and an English horn solo heard above four tympani. Elsewhere, the utmost flexibility in writing for all the instruments gives his music a tremendous vitality and variety of sound. In this respect, Berlioz was one of the greatest masters in the new art of orchestration.

Chopin

Frédéric Chopin was born near Warsaw in 1810, the son of a French schoolmaster and a Polish mother. He received a thorough education in his father's private school and was given instruction in piano and composition from his earliest years. He made his first concert appearance at the age of nine, and his first compositions were published when he was fifteen. In 1829, already qualified as an outstanding pianist and a composer of great originality, he set out on his first important concert tour (after having played in many German cities) to Vienna, Paris, and ultimately London. After a successful stay in Vienna and Munich he traveled to Paris in 1831. His playing and his music were so well received in the French capital that he altered his plan of proceeding to London; he remained a resident of Paris for the rest of his life.

His concerts became fewer as his interest in composition grew; within a few years he gave up public performances entirely. He was in great demand, however, in the *salons* which were a feature of Parisian social life, and he moved in aristocratic circles almost entirely. His income was derived largely from the lessons he gave to children of French and Polish aristocrats, and his earnings from this source were considerable.

In 1836 Chopin met the novelist George Sand (the pseudonym of Aurore Dudevant) and formed an attachment that persisted, through many crises, until 1847. He spent the winter of 1838 with her at her home on the island of Majorca, attempting to overcome a severe bronchial infection. The prolonged illness, however, undermined his strength, and Chopin never completely regained his health. He resumed his feverish activity of giving private concerts, composing, and teaching; to this was added a full social life among the Parisian aristocrats. Two concert tours to London, in 1848 and 1849, brought him to the point of physical exhaustion; he died of tuberculosis in 1849, at the age of thirty-nine.

Chopin devoted himself almost entirely to music for the piano. His many compositions for that instrument have never been surpassed for originality of expression and for their insight into pianistic possibilities. His music represents not a reaction to the music of the Classical period, but a new departure. He created new forms, new textures, and new varieties of sound, and he accomplished this on an intimate, subjective level that never made use of bombastic, spectacular effects, or theatricality.

Fŕedéric Chopin (1810–49) playing for the Prince Radziwill. (From a painting by Siemisadszki.)

The majority of Chopin's works are single-movement forms, many of them quite brief. They include sets of preludes, waltzes, nocturnes, *études,* and mazurkas. He also made use of other single-movement forms such as the polonaise, the scherzo, the ballade, and the impromptu. Among his works in compound form are two sonatas for piano, two piano concertos, and a small number of other works for piano and strings. A few songs complete the list.

Chopin was the first composer who consistently spread the chord tones of an accompaniment in open position—that is, spread them so that they span more than an octave (see the bass lines of Example 68 and Example 69*d*). In addition, the broadly rolling chord passages that are typical of his music are given added sonority and richness by the extensive use of the *damper pedal*—a device that lifts the damper or mute from the piano strings and allows them to vibrate fully and richly. Thus, the bass tones sound resonantly even after the keys themselves are released (see Examples 68, 69*c*, and 69*d*). The use of the pedal also made a number of new sonorities possible—sonorities compounded of mixed or overlapping chords, of one harmony combined with another. In this interest in achieving new blends of sound, Chopin was a typical Romantic composer.

Chopin's melodies are of several types, all of them distinctive. The melodies in slow tempo usually rise and fall in gentle curves (see Examples 69*a* and 69*b*, and the portion of the well-known "Funeral March" shown in Example 68); they evoke nostalgic or mournful emotions—and they are incredibly beautiful. The fast melodies often dissolve into brilliant cascades of tone—into a rush of rapid notes that usually cover two or three octaves in a short space of time; these melodies rise and fall impetuously, and reflect exuberance and vitality (see Example 69*c*). Or again, the melody may culminate in a rapid scale passage to a climactic point (see Example 69*d*).

The melodies, of whatever type, are richly harmonized. Chopin's harmonic system is more flexible and more free than that of his predecessors; his harmonies range widely, depart far from the original key, and are often chromatically thickened to a point where the tonality is obscured. The end result of his skill and imagination in this area is an unlimited variety of harmonic effects, from the simplest effects to those that were generations in advance of his contemporaries. The variety of Chopin's harmonies is still one of his most attractive features.

Chopin's contributions to musical nationalism are seen in the almost sixty mazurkas and the dozen polonaises he composed. Both these dance forms are in triple

Example 68

Lento

Chopin, Sonata, Op. 35

not

Example 69

meter: the mazurka is in moderate tempo and was probably derived from folk festivities, while the polonaise is stately in character and was originally (in the sixteenth century) an element of court ceremonials. In raising the mazurka to the level of concert music and in recapturing, in the polonaise, the chivalry and pomp of earlier Polish court life, Chopin expressed the spirit of Poland. The intimate and concentrated moods of this music range from melancholy to gay; its appeal may be aristocratic or humble. It serves as a poetic reminder of departed national glories, and it has become a patriotic symbol of the life that the country once enjoyed.

Mendelssohn

Felix Mendelssohn was born at Hamburg in 1809 of wealthy and cultured parents. Three years later the family moved to Berlin, and there the future composer grew to maturity. His talent showed itself early: his pianistic debut was made at the age of nine, and he began composing when he was eleven. Few musicians have enjoyed a more favorable home life than Mendelssohn. A private orchestra played regularly in his parents' home, and he was able to hear his youthful works performed professionally and to hear them criticized by eminent musicians. His musical style reached a point of maturity in 1826, when he was seventeen. In that year he wrote one of his finest works, the *Midsummer Night's Dream* Overture; for the rest of his life he remained true to the style revealed in that masterpiece.

In 1829, against much opposition from the musical authorities, Mendelssohn succeeded in conducting a performance of Bach's *Passion According to St. Matthew*—the first since the then-forgotten composer's death seventy-nine years before. With that performance Bach was restored to the attention of the general public, and his music began slowly to take its important place in concert repertoires the world over.

Mendelssohn traveled widely as pianist, organist, and as conductor of his own works. A journey through Austria and Italy in 1830–32 was followed by many visits to England where he became especially beloved. He visited England no less than nine times, was received by Queen Victoria, and achieved great musical success whenever he performed his compositions there.

In 1835 he was appointed conductor of the Gewandhaus Orchestra in Leipzig; and in 1842 he founded the Leipzig Conservatory, an institution that became one of the most notable of Europe's music schools. Those activities in no wise interfered with his creative work. He composed continually, made repeated appearances as a concert artist in many parts of Western Europe, and in doing so, drove himself without rest. Depressed by the death of his favorite sister and fatigued beyond endurance, Mendelssohn died in 1847, in his thirty-eighth year.

Refinement, melodiousness, and sentiment characterize all of Mendelssohn's compositions. Just as there were few conflicts in his life, there are few conflicts in his music. Energy, enthusiasm, perfection of form, and technical mastery are everywhere apparent; but the deeper emotions are seldom touched. All this is particularly true of one of Mendelssohn's most enjoyable works, the Symphony No. 4, in A major, called the "Italian." Begun during the Italian trip of 1830–32, the symphony reflects Mendelssohn's pleasant memories of that country, but it is not to be construed as program music.

The first movement, in sonata-form, is in fast tempo and contains brilliant, sparkling melodies set in Mendelssohn's happiest vein. The bustling air and the impul-

siveness that animate the first theme are only slightly relaxed in the second; the development and recapitulation follow the usual course, and the movement ends in exciting fashion. The bright restlessness of mood revealed here was something new in orchestral music; it represents one of Mendelssohn's contributions to the possibilities of musical style.

The andante that follows is charming and serene. An eloquent melody accompanied by a "walking" bass moves leisurely through the movement (see Example 70), and is interrupted on occasion by a more animated theme. The writing is simple, yet the simplicity is of the kind that conceals great artistry. The third movement, easygoing in the style of the German folk dance called a *Ländler*, makes magical

Felix Mendelssohn (1809–47), who imbued the Classical style with Romantic spirit. (Pencil drawing by Marianne Hummel, née von Rohden-Kassel, in the collection of the Louis Spohr Memorial and Research Institute.)

use of the wind instruments in its middle part (see Example 71). A simple set of chords dispersed in a simple rhythmic pattern provides the content of the passage. The sheer beauty of the instrumental sound here is Romanticism at its best. The finale is in the mood and style of a *saltarello*, a fast and energetic dance popular in Italy at the time of Mendelssohn's visit. The movement is in sonata-form; its several themes go by at a lightninglike pace and lead to rousing climaxes (see Example 72).

The melodic types, the mood contrasts, and the textural clarity seen in the "Italian" Symphony are in general typical of all Mendelssohn's instrumental works. Speed and lightness characterize the Overture and Scherzo from the well-known *Midsummer Night's Dream* music, as well as the first and last movements of his equally popular Violin Concerto in E minor. The string quartets of Op. 44 and the several concertos for piano and orchestra also contain many movements showing the same light and airy texture. Conversely, the eloquent type of melody in moderate tempo is seen in the Nocturne from *A Midsummer Night's Dream,* in other instrumental slow movements, and in many of the short, sentiment-filled *Songs Without Words* for piano. The famous *Fingal's Cave* Overture is related to this type also.

Mendelssohn's best-known choral work is the oratorio *Elijah.* Similar in size and scope to the massive oratorios of Handel, *Elijah* has the Old Testament prophet as its central figure. Soloists, chorus, and orchestra are employed in a great variety of

Example 71

Con moto moderato — Mendelssohn, Symphony No. 4 ("Italian")

(HORNS AND BASSOONS) *p* *cresc.* *p*

Example 72

(*a*) Presto — Mendelssohn, Symphony No. 4 ("Italian")

p leggiero

(*b*) Presto

(*c*) Presto

pp

dramatic and lyric settings. The choruses range from the quiet trio for women's voices, "Lift Thine Eyes," to the thunderous and majestic "Behold, God the Lord." Mendelssohn's choruses in imitative style are among the finest written since Handel. Among them, "Help, Lord," "Be Not Afraid," and "He, Watching over Israel" are masterpieces. They contribute to the esteem in which *Elijah* has been held ever since its first performance in 1846.

In all his works Mendelssohn revealed his adherence to Classical ideals. Perfection of form, balanced phrase structures, refinement of detail, over-all sensitivity of expression, proper relationship between form and content—these elements of Classical music are found again in Mendelssohn's. The few descriptive titles or nicknames that serve to identify some of his works—the "Reformation," "Italian," and "Scotch" symphonies, for example—do not make those works into representatives of program music. They do no more than call attention to the historical or geographical source of his inspiration. Mendelssohn's interest lay in writing absolute or abstract music, similar in purpose and scope to music of the Classical period. His Romanticism is seen primarily in his sensitive and imaginative use of instruments, a use that places his works among the most colorful and enjoyable compositions of his time.

Schumann

Robert Schumann, the son of a bookseller, was born at Zwickau, Saxony, in 1810. Although he began to study the piano in his seventh year, and composed several works when he was eleven, his wholehearted interest in music did not develop until 1830. In that year, neglecting the study of law which had occupied him for two years, he became a piano pupil of Friedrich Wieck, at whose home in Leipzig he lived, and whose daughter, Clara, he eventually married in 1840. In an effort to hasten the development of his pianistic technique, Schumann employed a mechanical device that lamed his hand permanently. With the career of a piano virtuoso thus closed to him, he turned to composition and musical journalism.

As editor of the *Neue Zeitschrift für Musik,* a periodical that he founded in 1834, Schumann exerted great influence upon the musical public of Germany. He fought against superficiality, insincerity, and other manifestations of musical philistinism in performers and composers alike, and did much to raise the standards of musical taste of his time. He became a teacher at the Leipzig Conservatory in 1843, one year after it was founded by Mendelssohn, but resigned that position as well as the editorship of the periodical in 1845. With his family he moved to Dresden in that year, in the hope that a quieter life would improve his state of mental health: he had been subject to periods of severe depression and attacks of extreme irritability since about 1830.

From 1847 to 1853 Schumann held a series of positions as a conductor, first in Dresden and then in Düsseldorf. He was unsuccessful in that activity, however, for the signs of mental aberration now became stronger and he found it almost impossible to communicate verbally with anyone outside his immediate circle of family and friends. Early in 1854 he attempted suicide; he was committed to an asylum and died in 1856 with symptoms that strongly suggest schizophrenia.

When Schumann turned seriously to music in 1830, he discarded a number of juvenile works he had composed earlier and until 1840 he devoted himself entirely to the composition of piano music. Within ten years he had written about two dozen works, including some of his best-known sets of pieces—among them *Carnaval, Fantasiestücke,* and *Kinderscenen.* In 1840, the year of his marriage to Clara Wieck, he composed songs almost exclusively. About 120 songs, among them his finest song cycles (settings of short lyric poems by a single author, connected in subject matter), were written in this fruitful year. The famous cycles *Myrthen, Frauenliebe und Leben,* and *Dichterliebe* are among the works of 1840. Thereafter, from 1841 to 1853, his compositions were in a number of different categories: chamber music, orchestral works, choral works, and many more short pieces.

Robert Schumann (1810–56), the personification of German Romanticism.

Early in his career as a musical journalist, Schumann had adopted two pen names, and with them, two personalities: "Florestan" was vigorous, forthright, and energetic; "Eusebius" was dreamy, introspective, and romantic. The turn from one personality to the other became characteristic of Schumann's music also. For example, in the *Fantasiestücke,* Op. 12, *Aufschwung* ("Soaring") is representative of the Florestan strain, and the next piece in the set, *Warum?* ("Why?") is typical of the sensitive Eusebius. Similar contrasts of mood in other successive short pieces are often apparent, and in longer works the contrasting moods are sometimes introduced impulsively and without structural justification. It is unfortunate that performers often overlook the duality of moods that is one of Schumann's outstanding characteristics. The varied, impulsive, and typically Romantic qualities of his music thus are not always fully expressed.

Many of the art songs Schumann wrote in the incredibly fertile year of 1840 are dramas in all but size. Building upon the foundations laid down by Schubert, Schumann invested his piano parts with a variety of functions. Sometimes the piano accompanies, as it does in the charming *Sunday on the Rhine* (see Example 73*a*). At other times it establishes the mood of the piece, as it does, for instance, in *By Moonlight* (see Example 73*b*). And in the famous *The Two Grenadiers,* the piano also serves to enhance the mood of the text, which in this instance is martial (see Example 73*c*).

Example 73

Schumann's Symphony No. 1, in B flat, is also a product of his happiest years; it was written in 1841 and was named the "Spring" Symphony by Schumann himself. It is a joyful work, full of enthusiasm and optimism. Melodious, rhythmically alive, and clear in form, it represents the healthiest side of Schumann's nature. The lively first movement is followed by an andante that suggests moods of noble sentiment and controlled melancholy. The scherzo is one of Schumann's masterpieces. A number of short melodies—fast, vigorous, and restless in turn—are set with skill and imagination (see Example 74); this movement contains two trios (one of them in

duple meter) and a masterful coda that summarizes the whole. The finale is equally enchanting, and is full of humor and vitality.

Another symphony was begun in 1841, revised in 1851, and eventually published as the Symphony No. 4, in D minor. This work represents a considerable innovation in form, one that prepares the way for the symphonic poem. Schumann directed that it be performed without pauses between the movements. This by itself is no real innovation, but in this case the movements are thematically related, and the joining of the movements is structurally justified.

The symphony consists of the usual four movements, with a slow introduction to the first movement and a transitional passage between the third and fourth. (Example 75 shows the principal themes of the work.) A quiet, undulating melody first heard in the introduction (Example 75*a*) reappears in the slow movement (Example 75*e*). The second part of the introduction contains a wide-ranging, slow-moving figure (Example 75*b*) that gradually increases in speed; this is employed in both themes of the first movement proper (Examples 75*c* and 75*d*). The same slow-moving figure is found in the transition that appears after the scherzo (Example 75*i*), and it also plays an important part in the first theme of the last movement (Example 75*j*). In addition, the middle part of the slow movement contains a graceful melodic line (Example 75*f*) that later, in a faster tempo, serves in the trio of the scherzo (Example 75*h*). And finally, both melodies in the introduction (Examples 75*a* and 75*b*), which are otherwise unrelated, contain a similar melodic turn (shown by the brackets marked "a" in the examples) that is repeated or modified in all subsequent versions of the melodies that are derived from the introduction.

Such consistent use of related material throughout the course of a long work had not been common before Schumann's time. It represents a technical tour de force of the first rank. And yet, in spite of these close inner relationships between its parts, the symphony impresses one primarily through the variety of its moods; that is Schumann's great achievement here. For instance, the running figure of Example 75*b*, heard in various tempos and in different contexts, conveys moods that range from agitated to serene, from powerful to limpidly graceful. Although in this composition Schumann departed widely from the form of the Classical symphony, he succeeded in writing a balanced, well-proportioned work. The Symphony in D minor remains one of his masterpieces. Moreover, it provided the technical basis upon which other composers could superimpose a program; thus it was the forerunner of the symphonic poem.

Title page of Schumann's cycle *Songs for the Young.*

Schumann's Piano Concerto, Op. 54 in A minor, is roughly contemporary with his D minor symphony. It is not built along similar lines, however, for the cyclical form and the thematic interrelationships found in the symphony are not present in the concerto. The latter has a first movement in sonata-form, an intermezzo in a symmetrical ABA form, and a finale that contains elements both of sonata-form and rondo (see the thematic outline, given on pp. 208–10). Yet within these traditional forms Schumann embodied a wealth of Romantic ideas; the work is poetic, honestly sentimental, and warmly expressive. Piano and orchestra are equal partners here. And although the solo part is brilliant and effectively written, it is free of the

Example 75

empty virtuosic figuration that marred so many concertos by his lesser contemporaries. The Schumann piano concerto richly deserves the affection that generations of performers and concert-goers have given it.

The concerto and the D minor symphony, like the majority of Schumann's orchestral and chamber music works, remained within the field of abstract music; they thus represent the same ideal to which Mendelssohn adhered. But Schumann also showed himself to be a nationalist akin to Chopin. He interested himself in German

Concerto for Piano and Orchestra, A minor, Op. 54, by Robert Schumann

FIRST MOVEMENT, Allegro affetuoso, A minor

Meas.	*Theme*	
EXPOSITION		
1	Intro.	For piano alone
4	1st	First part, A minor (Ex. 1), wind instruments
	Example 1	
12		Repetition of first part, piano alone
20		Second part, A minor
32		Third part, G major, piano alone (Ex. 2)
	Example 2	
42		Extension and transition based on Ex. 2, F major
59		Transition, C major, derived from Ex. 1
67	2nd	In C major, (Ex. 3), again derived from Ex. 1
	Example 3	
95		Repetition of meas. 67 ff
134	Codetta	Derived from meas. 32 (Ex. 2), but in C major
DEVELOPMENT		
156		A flat major, change of tempo (*andante*) and meter (6/4). Based on Ex. 1, meas. 4
185		Return to tempo and meter of beginning. Based on meas. 1, but in A flat
205		Derived from Ex. 1, meas. 4; modulating section
RECAPITULATION		
259	1st	First part, Ex. 1, A minor, wind instruments
267		Repetition of first part, piano alone
275		Second part, A minor
287		Third part, G major, piano alone
297		Extension and modulation, beginning in B minor
312		Transition similar to meas. 59 ff, but in A major
320	2nd	Similar to Ex. 3, meas. 67 ff, but in A major

348		Repetition
385	Codetta	Similar to meas. 134 ff, but in A major; then a transition to the cadenza
402	Cadenza	Based on new figure and on 1st theme
458	Coda	Change of tempo (*allegro molto*) and meter (2/4). Movement ends in meas. 544

SECOND MOVEMENT, Intermezzo, Andante grazioso, F major

Meas.	*Part*	
1	A	Divided between piano and orchestra (Ex. 4), F major
	Example 4	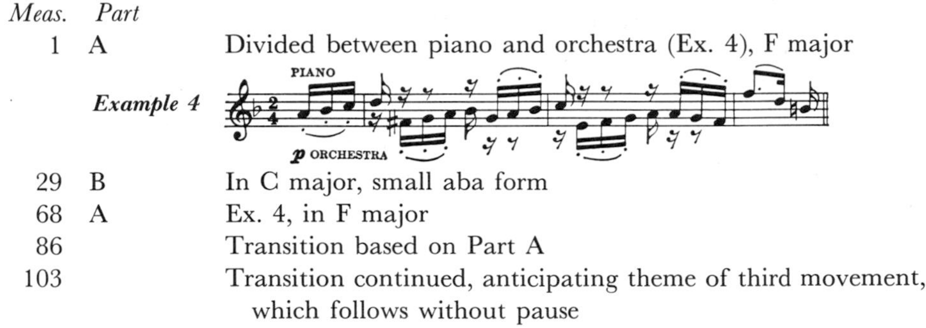
29	B	In C major, small aba form
68	A	Ex. 4, in F major
86		Transition based on Part A
103		Transition continued, anticipating theme of third movement, which follows without pause

THIRD MOVEMENT, Allegro vivace, A major

Meas.	*Section*	
109		Introduction, based on forthcoming Section A
117	A	In A major (Ex. 5). Repeated in meas. 132 ff
	Example 5	
149		Second part, C sharp minor
189	B	Quasi-waltz (Ex. 6), E major
	Example 6	
228		Second part, G sharp minor
252		Third part, E major
286		Transition, begins in C major
327	A	In A major, as in Ex. 5
347		Development

Schumann, Concerto for Piano and Orchestra (cont.)

391	C	New theme (Ex. 7), F major, developed and extended
	Example 7	
497	A	Ex. 5, but now in D major
529		Second part, F sharp minor
569	B	As in Ex. 6, but now in A major
608		Second part, C sharp minor
632		Third part, A major
666		Transition and development
707	A	Ex. 5, again in D major
727		Transition
739	A	Return of Ex. 5 in A major, as in meas. 117 ff
771		New second part, D major
811	Coda	First part derived from Section A by compression
835		Based on Section C, meas. 391 (Ex. 7)
859		Based on meas. 771
883		Based on Section A, Ex. 5, meas. 117
927		Derived from Section C, meas. 391. (Ex. 7). Movement ends in meas. 979

folk songs and attempted to recapture the German folk idiom in many of his songs and short piano pieces; he also wrote a few works that appeal openly to German patriotism. Finally, there are many descriptive titles among his piano works: butterflies, a happy farmer, and dreams, for example. These titles testify to Schumann's awareness of and interest in program music. He moved from one field to another with equal ease—or perhaps with lack of conviction about where his true calling lay.

Unlike the majority of other composers, Schumann did his best work at the beginning of his career. Enthusiasm, vigor, imagination, and technical skill were present in abundance until about 1845. As his mental illness became progressively more severe, his power of self-criticism declined and the schizophrenic split into the "Florestan" and "Eusebius" moods became more pronounced. His later works are often episodic and badly proportioned. Thus it happens that few of Schumann's late works are performed regularly. The compositions that are heard frequently—the two symphonies discussed here, the wonderfully eloquent Piano Concerto in A minor, a few of the songs, the Piano Quintet, Op. 44, and the cycles of early piano works—reveal a composer who represented all that was noble, warm, and exuberant in the early Romantic period.

Listening Suggestions

BERLIOZ

Harold in Italy (symphony with viola obbligato)
Requiem Mass
Roman Carnival, Overture
Symphonie Fantastique

CHOPIN

Concerto No. 1, E Minor
Études, Op. 10 and Op. 25
Nocturnes
Preludes

MENDELSSOHN

Concerto for Violin, E minor, Op. 64
Elijah, Op. 70 (oratorio)
Fingal's Cave, Overture, Op. 26
A Midsummer Night's Dream, Op. 21 and Op. 61 (orchestral suite)
Symphony No. 4, A major, Op. 90 ("Italian")

SCHUBERT

Fantasia, C major, Op. 15 ("Wanderer")
Piano Quintet, A major, Op. 114 ("The Trout")
Die Schöne Müllerin (song cycle)
String Quartet, D minor ("Death and the Maiden")
String Quintet, C major, Op. 163
Symphony No. 7, C major
Symphony No. 8, B minor ("Unfinished")

SCHUMANN

Carnaval, Op. 9 (cycle of piano pieces)
Concerto for Piano, A minor, Op. 54
Frauenliebe und Leben, Op. 42 (song cycle)
Piano Quintet, E flat, Op. 44
Symphony No. 1, B flat major, Op. 38, ("Spring")

WEBER

Der Freischütz (opera)
Euryanthe, Overture
Oberon, Overture

Chapter 11

PROGRAM MUSIC AND THE NATIONALISTS

The Romantic idea that music must have external meaning, that it must be based on poetic content—in short, that it must be descriptive or programmatic—continued to gain force as the nineteenth century neared its midpoint. Berlioz, as we have seen, adhered to this idea in part, but did so by remaining more or less faithful to the forms he had inherited. The *Symphonie Fantastique* was still a symphony, with its first movement in sonata-form and its subsequent contrasting movements suggesting a series of related emotional states. Berlioz was unable or unwilling to give up the framework of the symphony, and his most successful orchestral movements are those in which musical considerations of form and balance take precedence over programmatic or illustrative elements.

Shortly before 1850, Franz Liszt created a new form that allowed the full development of program music to take place. Liszt's purpose was to express musically his feelings toward literary, historical, or other extramusical subjects. He carried out that purpose in twelve symphonic poems composed between 1848 and 1857. Later composers strove to be more descriptive, and even literally realistic, in their adoption of the program music idea; many symphonic poems of this type were written until well into the twentieth century.

At about the same time that the symphonic poem was being developed, a series of political events led to the formation of national schools of composition. One action of the Congress of Vienna (the peace conference held in 1814–15 at the end of the Napoleonic wars) was the ruthless redistribution of the boundaries of European nations without regard for the wishes of the people concerned. This action provoked a number of uprisings and rebellions—some successful and others not—on the part of patriots who saw their cultural and political borders violated. In the entire period from about 1830 to the outbreak of World War I in 1914, political unrest fed the flames of national feeling in one part of Europe or another. The peoples turned to their folk culture, legends, and literature both as means of self-expression and as denials of their national inferiority. The musical aspects of that nationalism grew to maturity in about the

1860's. And in taking refuge in their cultural heritage, nationalistic composers adopted the ideals and methods of the writers of program music.

Thus, two separate but related musical philosophies existed side by side in roughly the second half of the Romantic period. It is interesting to note that composers in the politically stronger nations—primarily Germany, Austria, and France—took relatively little interest in nationally inspired themes and subject matter. Nationalism became primarily the province of composers in the politically less fortunate countries: Bohemia (now Czechoslovakia), Norway, Russia, and later Spain and Finland.

The Symphonic Poem

Occasionally in the music of the Renaissance and Baroque periods, thematic material employed in one movement of a compound form reappears in a later movement as well. In Bach's Mass in B Minor, for example, the text "Dona nobis pacem" from the *Agnus Dei* is set to the same music that is used in the "Gratias agimus" of the *Gloria* (see p. 370). In the same composer's *Musical Offering,* one theme pervades the entire work and appears, with modifications, in all of the sixteen movements (see p. 359). Many other examples of this *cyclical principle,* as it is called, abound in the literature.

Not until the nineteenth century, however, did the cyclical principle prepare the way for a new form. Beethoven, in his Symphony No. 5, introduced a theme from the Scherzo into the Finale, thus linking the two movements. In his Symphony No. 9, thematic fragments from the first three movements pass in review in the fourth (see p. 174). Hector Berlioz, in his *Symphonie Fantastique,* established one theme as an *idée fixe* (fixed melody), and out of it derived thematic material for the work's five movements. Robert Schumann, in his Symphony No. 4, employed three or four different thematic ideas in a variety of contexts throughout its four movements (and introductions to the first and fourth); further, he directed that all four movements be played without pause (see Example 75, p. 207).

This series of technical innovations in the compound form of the symphony provided the basis for the characteristic nineteenth-century form called the *symphonic poem.* That form, introduced by Franz Liszt in the mid-nineteenth century, has a descriptive purpose; it recounts a legend or describes a series of scenes or expresses the composer's feelings about an extramusical subject. In other words, it tells a story, and thus it belongs to the large and important branch of musical composition called *program music.* Program music, as opposed to abstract or absolute music, had existed in earlier centuries, but not until the second quarter of the nineteenth century did it become an important —almost dominant—element in music history.

The symphonic poem consists essentially of several connected sections, each one in a tempo and mood that contrasts with the others. In the most typical examples, one set of themes appears, with modifications or transformations in various sections, and thus unifies the work. The thematic transformations are appropriate to the particular event in the "program" that is being illustrated or suggested at that point. Many symphonic poems are so constructed that their various sections suggest the compound form of a

Franz Liszt (1811–86), one of the greatest pianists the world has ever known.

symphony whose movements are connected as they are in Schumann's Symphony No. 4. Liszt's well-known symphonic poem *Les Préludes* is an example.

Following Liszt's innovation, other composers wrote symphonic poems designed to tell a great variety of stories. Bedřich Smetana's *The Moldau* describes the course of that river through the Bohemian countryside. Richard Strauss's *Death and Transfiguration, Don Juan,* and *Ein Heldenleben* (*A Hero's Life*), Paul Dukas' *The Sorcerer's Apprentice,* Camille Saint-Saëns' *The Spinning Wheel of Omphale,* Ottorino Respighi's *The Pines of Rome,* César Franck's *Le Chasseur Maudit* (*The Accursed Hunter*), and dozens of other works disclose by their very titles the nature of the programs upon which they are based.

The playing time of a typical symphonic poem may range from perhaps fifteen minutes to almost an hour. Strauss's *Ein Heldenleben,* schematically outlined on pages 284–86, is over forty minutes in length, for example. Although the form is treated as an extended single-movement composition by some commentators, we have treated it as a derivative of the compound, multiple-movement forms. For if we consider a symphonic poem to be the result of condensing and connecting the movements of a symphony, as we have shown here, we can relate it to the historical stream from which it emerged. Further, when we listen to it we can better understand the relationships between sections and can learn how the descriptive material and the musical form have influenced each other.

Liszt

Franz Liszt, born in Hungary in 1811, was a child prodigy who became one of the greatest pianists the world has ever known. To further his musical education, the boy's family took him to Vienna in 1821 and to Paris two years later. Liszt made rapid advances as a virtuoso performer and composer; an operetta he wrote in 1825 was successfully performed in Paris. He also made several concert tours, and in 1827, at the age of sixteen, widely known as a masterful performer, he returned to Paris to live.

His playing brought him into close contact with the aristocratic patrons of music in the French capital. He became a friend of Chopin and Berlioz, and saw in the latter's music a hope for the future. Berlioz' instrumental and technical innovations, as well as the ideals of Romanticism in general, worked formatively on the young Hungarian, and he became an outspoken exponent of the modern elements in music.

In 1831 he heard Paganini, the fabulous violinist who at that time appeared in Paris after dazzling Italy and Germany with his stupendous technical feats. Paganini's virtuosity inspired Liszt to achieve a similar virtuosity on the piano. Within a few years he had developed an unheard-of technical facility and had written a number of brilliant compositions for the piano—works that combined sensational technical display with a poetic strain reminiscent of Chopin's.

From 1835 to 1839 Liszt lived in Geneva with the Countess Marie d'Agoult. (One of the three children born to them was Cosima, who later became the wife of Richard Wagner.) In 1839 he began a series of enormously successful concert tours that took him to all of the European musical centers and firmly established him as the superman of the piano. The tours continued until 1848, when Liszt became musical director at the court at Weimar. His fame, both as a pianist and teacher and as the foremost spokesman for the progressive attitude in music, attracted many like-minded musicians to the little town; Weimar again became one of the cultural centers of Europe, as it had been in the time of Goethe.

At Weimar, supported in his resolve by the Princess Sayn-Wittgenstein, Liszt changed his artistic goals completely. Although still at the height of his mastery, he virtually gave up public performances as a pianist and devoted himself to orchestral composition. His symphonic poems are the most important results of the new activity. He also became the champion of composers whose works could not be performed elsewhere; he extended himself generously to help others less fortunate, and he became a strong supporter of Wagner's controversial music.

In 1859, musical differences with the court forced his retirement. He left Weimar and took up residence at Rome, where he became active as a teacher. In 1870 he was restored to the favor of the court at Weimar and five years later he accepted a

Caricature of Liszt.

position as director of the new Hungarian Academy of Music at Budapest. His last years were divided between Weimar, Rome, and the ancient Hungarian city. When he died in 1886, at the age of seventy-five, he was the most honored musician of his generation.

In developing a new form to give expression to his poetic ideas in regard to program music, Liszt was very much aware of Berlioz' principle of the *idée fixe.* The essential element in Liszt's music, however, is not a long melody but a short, incisive motive out of which a number of related themes are constructed (here the influence of Beethoven is seen). According to the needs of the program, such themes are appropriately transformed or modified. Transitions between sections are usually based on the motive also; thus a high degree of melodic unity becomes possible. Themes and theme transformations appear in contrasting tempos, in different keys, and in various ranges of the orchestra.

Of the twelve symphonic poems Liszt composed, the third has become by far the best known. Entitled *Les Préludes,* it was inspired by a portion of the *Méditations poétiques* by the French poet Lamartine. A section of that poem is quoted in Liszt's score: "Life is but a series of preludes to that unknown song the first solemn note of which is sounded by death." Elsewhere the poet writes about love, nature, and the trumpet's call to war. On so slender a program Liszt built his symphonic poem. It is clear that the detailed realism typical of one aspect of Berlioz' music finds no place in the later composer's plan.

The form Liszt employed in *Les Préludes* consists of six sections, the first of which is a quiet andante. In that section the motive and the first section of the principal

Example 76

theme are presented (see Example 76*a*). Later sections are majestic, pastoral (with a contrasting theme; see Example 76*e*), or martial in mood. In each case the theme of Example 76*a* is suitably transformed (see Examples 76*b–d* and 76*f–i*).

The six sections of *Les Préludes* are roughly analogous to the movements of a symphony that has an introduction and transitions, but one in which the movements are musically connected, thematically unified, and psychologically related to each other. A similar structural and programmatic plan is basic to the other symphonic poems of Liszt. The sources of his inspirations in those works are found in poems by Victor Hugo, Goethe, and Shakespeare, in patriotic themes, in myths (the symphonic poems *Orpheus* and *Prometheus*), and in a painting ("The Slaughter of the Huns"). Those symphonic poems reveal Liszt's fertile imagination and his ability to characterize ideas, sentiments, activities, or objects by well-chosen motives or themes. In spite of the technical devices that are common to all these works, a great variety of moods is expressed in them. Single chords, quick changes of texture, and abrupt dynamic contrasts were among Liszt's devices for expressing the poetic content of his programs.

In composing melodies that contained unusual intervals, and in harmonizing those melodies with imagination and skill, Liszt closely approached what later came to be known as *chromatic harmony* (see Example 77; see also pp. 48–49 and Example 33, p. 49). Liszt, however, did not use chromatic harmony exclusively; its primary function was to serve as a flavor—as an inflection. This is especially true of the chromatic passages contained in his best-known works such as *Les Préludes,* the *Hungarian Rhapsodies,* and the two piano concertos, in E flat and A major, respectively.

Example 77

The twenty-odd *Hungarian Rhapsodies* for piano solo are based on what passed for Hungarian folk music in the nineteenth century. Later research, especially that of Béla Bartók in the early 1900's, has shown that Romantic musicians failed to distinguish between truly Hungarian folk music and that of the Gypsies; Liszt's works are thus more Gypsy than Hungarian (this is true also of Brahms' well-known *Hungarian Dances*). Liszt's typical procedure was to introduce a series of folk melodies, to subject them to various kinds of melodic, rhythmic, and harmonic elaboration, and to arrange them in a loosely constructed sectional form. All the technical brilliance of which he was capable is reflected in the *Rhapsodies,* and although they were once enormously popular as piano recital pieces, increasing age (and perhaps a higher standard of musical taste) has dimmed their luster.

Smetana

Bedřich Smetana was born at Leitomischl, Bohemia, in 1824. Because of his father's opposition to a musical career, the boy remained largely self-taught in piano and composition. For several years beginning in 1848 he operated a successful music school and gained a reputation as a sensitive and capable pianist, although his compositions were largely ignored. In 1856 he accepted an offer to become the conductor of the orchestra in Gothenburg, Sweden; there he composed three symphonic poems in the style of Liszt.

Following the granting of political freedom to Bohemia in 1860, a surge of national pride resulted in the establishment of a national opera house in Prague. Smetana resigned his position in Gothenburg in 1861, returned to Prague, and wrote his first opera, on a Czech subject. Encouraged by its reception at its first performance in 1866, he composed the enormously successful opera *The Bartered Bride,* also based on a Czech subject. Thereupon he was appointed principal conductor of the National Opera and in the following years composed three more operas. Those works, however, were severely criticized: Smetana was accused of imitating Wagner, and a strong feeling of opposition grew up against him. The accumulation of difficulties affected Smetana's mental health; he resigned the conductorship early in 1874, and within a few months he became totally deaf.

Immersing himself in work, Smetana returned to the writing of symphonic poems which he had abandoned almost twenty years before. In the period between 1874 and 1879 he composed the cycle of six such works known collectively under the title *My Fatherland.* An autobiographical string quartet, *From My Life,* also was written during this period. Changes in the management of the National Opera brought about Smetana's return to favor; he regained his interest in the opera, writing his last three works in this form in the years between 1876 and 1882. His health continued to deteriorate, however, and he was placed in an asylum for the insane early in 1884. He died a few months later in a state of complete mental collapse.

Smetana was the founder of Czech national music. In his operas and his cycle of symphonic poems he expressed the spirit of his people. This was not always accomplished by the external, easy method of quoting from Czech folk songs or imitating Czech folk idioms; most often, it was done by creating an atmosphere in which the aspirations, pride, and cultural background of his country are reflected. In his successful operas, the apt musical characterization of Czech people and customs contributes to that atmosphere. In the symphonic poems, Czech legend, history, and geography are the areas from which Smetana's programs are drawn. In both categories, the temperament of the Czech people, with all their emotional vitality, is fully expressed.

Only the second of the six symphonic poems, *The Moldau,* is still heard with any degree of frequency. Its program is a musical description of Bohemia's largest river, following it from its source to the point where it flows past Vyšehrad, the ancient castle of the Bohemian kings. The music suggests the scenes along the river's banks. For example, near its source the river is little more than a murmuring brook; it passes a village where a festival is in progress, and a forest where the sounds of a hunt can be heard. A series of rapids is musically described, as is the broadening of the river. And as the stream nears Vyšehrad castle, that fact is suggested by an imposing musical motive that also appears in the first and sixth works of the cycle, *Vyšehrad* and *Blanik*, respectively.

Liszt's method of thematic transformation is employed here, in that the main theme of *The Moldau* is heard in a variety of shapes, textures, and tonalities. Each of the descriptive scenes is distinguished from the others by suitable changes of tempo and mood; yet the scenes are connected, and the entire work is in a sectional form similar to that introduced by Liszt. A polka in the village festival section adds a national rhythmic idiom to the work; elsewhere, the themes are Smetana's own.

Smetana's music is melodious, and its lyric quality perhaps prevents it from achieving great dramatic climaxes. Smetana was not given to rhapsodic utterances or to wild, extravagant bursts of sound. Thus his works are quite unlike those of Liszt. Writing intimately and with controlled emotions, Smetana succeeded in creating an individual style. And since the programs of his works are closely identified with subjects dear to the Czech heart, his music in effect stands for a Czech national style.

Grieg

Edvard Grieg was born at Bergen, Norway, in 1843; while in his teens, he became a student at the Leipzig Conservatory, where he studied piano and composition. The influence of Mendelssohn and Schumann was still strong in Leipzig, and the Romantic character of their music set the tone of the city's musical life. Grieg, however, did not become a pale imitator of those composers, as did many lesser musicians; he was able to preserve his individuality. He traveled extensively, studied with Gade in Copenhagen, and eventually returned to Norway in 1866. He became active as a teacher and conductor in Oslo but repeatedly visited Germany and Italy. In 1880 he returned to Bergen and made that city his home between concert tours to Germany and England. He died in 1907, honored as Norway's greatest musician.

Edvard Grieg (1843–1907), the foremost Norwegian composer.

Among Scandinavian composers, Grieg occupies a position similar to that of Smetana among the Czechs. In making use of national literary material (as in *Peer Gynt*), but without necessarily employing Norwegian folk materials in his works, he succeeded in developing an individual style that represents Norway. Dark or melancholy moods are often interrupted by flashes of brighter feeling; harmonies are often based on modal rather than tonal progressions. And his melodic lines, with their unique contours, usually hover around the fifth tone of the scale rather than the tonic (see Example 78). To the extent that such characteristics are reminiscent of Norwegian musical culture, Grieg's music is nationalistic in spirit.

Example 78

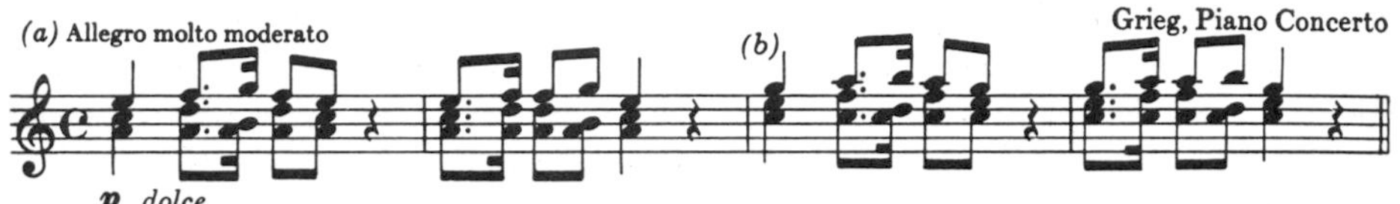

Grieg was primarily a lyric composer, and he was at his best in small forms. Many of his short pieces bear descriptive titles (*The Last Spring, Heartwounds,* and *Autumn* are examples), and they evoke the moods suggested by their names; to that extent they are descriptive. The incidental music he wrote for Ibsen's play *Peer Gynt* was later arranged into two suites, the separate short movements of which are similarly descriptive. The well-known *Peer Gynt* Suite No. 1 contains movements entitled "Morning," "Ase's Death," "Anitra's Dance," and "In the Hall of the Mountain King." In each case the music is so written that the title seems appropriate.

One characteristic of Grieg's music is his employment of the device called *sequence repetition.* In a typical Grieg work, a phrase or melody is repeated several times with its contour virtually unchanged, but each repetition begins on a different scale step. Examples can be found in the *Peer Gynt* Suite No. 1 (see Example 79), in the well-known Piano Concerto in A minor (see Example 78), in his Cello Sonata, in his single String Quartet, and elsewhere.

Example 79

Grieg felt most comfortable when writing short, single-movement mood pieces; he composed only six instrumental works in compound forms. Of those works, his single concerto for piano and orchestra best represents him in today's repertoire. The Concerto in A minor is typical of his style in that it avoids direct folk-song quotation but evokes moods that are recognized as Norwegian. In the majority of his works Grieg revealed an economical and restrained style; the Concerto, on the other hand, is robust, vigorous, and brilliantly virtuosic in the best Romantic tradition. The warm, lyric expression that animates its quieter moments shows Grieg at his best.

Russian Nationalist Composers

The movement toward Russian nationalistic music had its beginnings in the work of Michael Glinka (1804–57), a composer who studied in Italy and Germany, who imitated the Italian style in his early works, and who later consciously turned his back on Western musical styles in order to work with national musical materials. Glinka's second opera, *Russlan and Ludmilla,* made use of the non-European aspects of Russian music. It contains elements that suggest Persia, the region of the Caucasus, and similar exotic places, and it makes use of the irregular quintuple meter found in much Russian folk music.

In about 1860, a group of younger composers, inspired by the enthusiasm of Mili Balakirev in St. Petersburg, devoted themselves to building a Russian national music upon the foundations laid by Glinka almost a generation earlier. The group, later known as the "Russian Five," included César Cui, Alexander Borodin, Modest Mussorgsky, and Nikolai Rimsky-Korsakov, in addition to Balakirev himself. Only the latter was professionally trained; the others were musical amateurs whose livelihoods were gained in other fields (except that Rimsky-Korsakov eventually became a professional musician). Cui was a lieutenant general in the Russian Army and an expert on military fortifications; Borodin was primarily a chemist; Mussorgsky occupied a minor post in the government; and Rimsky-Korsakov spent many years as an officer in the Russian Imperial Navy. Yet the varied talents of these amateur musicians were sufficient to assure them honored places in music history, and with the exception of Balakirev and Cui, they are well represented on the concert stage today.

BORODIN

Alexander Borodin (1833–87) was kept busy by his work in the sciences; he was therefore the least prolific member of the "Five"—and also the one least interested in program music. His two completed symphonies and his two string quartets are not descriptive, but they are purely Romantic works written in an individual style. Nationalistic program elements are expressed only in his single symphonic poem, and his unfinished opera, *Prince Igor,* is also nationalistic in subject matter and coloring.

Borodin's Symphony No. 2, in B minor (1872–76) reveals the full extent of his musical qualities. Rich in color throughout, it is a work whose first movement is based largely upon repetitions of a single motive. The motive is seldom modified upon successive appearances; it serves rather as a static element that unifies the entire movement. Monotony is avoided, however, by Borodin's skillful use of the orchestral instruments. The remaining movements are a lively scherzo, a melancholy slow movement, and a brilliant and episodic finale. The whole is characterized by rapid alternations of intimate and barbaric moods: this feature gives the work what national character it possesses.

The thematic economy revealed by Borodin's Symphony No. 2 is found again in his symphonic poem, *In the Steppes of Central Asia* (1880). The work is a musical picture of treeless plains that are disturbed only by the passing of a caravan. The endless, empty landscape is symbolized by a long-held tone high in the violins; the Oriental caravan and its Russian escort are suggested by two quiet melodies of appropriate character, first heard separately and then together (see Example 80). In brief compass, and with the fewest of musical materials, Borodin created here a sensitive and imaginative musical sketch. In similar manner, the well-known "Polovtsian Dances" from the opera *Prince Igor* are vigorous and rhythmically compelling; they too make use of a few melodies that undergo no development as such but are only repeated with changed orchestration.

Example 80

MUSSORGSKY

Modest Mussorgsky, born in 1839, was trained in a military academy and spent several years in the Russian Army. When he met Balakirev, in about 1858, he left the army to devote himself to music. He became Balakirev's student in composition and continued with the piano study he had begun at an early age. Five years later, when he had not achieved the success he had hoped for, he was forced to take a minor clerical position in the government. Between 1863 and 1868 he began two operas but finished neither of them; between 1868 and 1872 he composed his operatic masterpiece, *Boris Godunov.* Several versions of the opera exist; it was first given in 1874 in a shortened form and later revised by Rimsky-Korsakov.

The first performance of *Boris Godunov* marked the highest point that Mussorgsky attained in his career. For several years thereafter he worked periodically on another opera, *Khovanshchina;* that work, like his earlier operas, remained unfinished (it was completed and produced by Rimsky-Korsakov in 1885). Then, becoming addicted to alcohol, he lost whatever sense of self-discipline he had; he died in 1881, a week after his forty-second birthday. Mussorgsky's life has been compared to Schubert's. Both men possessed musical talent of a high order, and both depended upon their friends for financial support at times; similarly, neither one achieved material success, and neither one completed a normal life span.

Mussorgsky's *Boris Godunov* ranks high among the operas of any nation. Laid near the end of the sixteenth century, it is concerned with actual happenings in Russian history. Boris, a nobleman acting as regent for the young Czar Feodor after the death of Ivan the Terrible, soon usurps power. He causes the brother and heir of Feodor to be killed, and after Feodor's death he assumes the throne, only to be driven out by another usurper, Dmitri. In the opera the historical facts are altered: Feodor lives to claim the throne. Mussorgsky shows keen insight into the varied characters in the opera—the Czar, various noblemen and priests, and an idiot among them—and his skill in painting revealing musical portraits is masterful. The music is sensitive and brutal in turn, but always imaginative and colorful. A melodic line that is often recitativelike and angular, a harmonic scheme that is dissonant when the action demands, and sharp contrasts of color and rhythm—such elements give *Boris Godunov* its great dramatic appeal.

Mussorgsky's principal orchestral work is a fantasy called *A Night on Bald Mountain.* Written in about 1860, it was at first designed to serve as incidental music in a drama called *The Witches.* It was later revised several times by the composer and was put into its present form largely by Rimsky-Korsakov, who was Mussorgsky's musical executor. The program has to do with supernatural voices, the spirits of darkness, and the glorification of Satan—all of which manifestations of evil are dispelled by the sounds of the church bell at daybreak. The grisly moods suggested by

The first presentation of the original version of Mussorgsky's *Boris Godunov,* St. Petersburg, February 16, 1928.

the program are realized in the music. Impulsive contrasts and an air of suppressed excitement add greatly to the fantastic impression made by this colorful and brilliant work.

RIMSKY-KORSAKOV

Nikolai Rimsky-Korsakov (1844–1908) began the study of the piano in his sixth year and of composition in his ninth. He was enrolled in the Naval Academy at St. Petersburg when he was twelve, and upon completing his studies there in 1862, he was ordered on a three-year world cruise. He had met Balakirev in 1861 and had begun a symphony; on his return to Russia the symphony was completed and performed. Other compositions were written in the years that followed, and in about 1871 he was appointed to a professorship at the St. Petersburg Conservatory, where he taught composition and orchestration.

Rimsky-Korsakov realized his technical shortcomings and set about on a course of self-training in theoretical matters. He resigned from the Imperial Navy in 1874 but retained a post as inspector of marine bands. He spent many years as a professional orchestra conductor and traveled in Belgium and France. His last appearance in Paris was in 1907, a year before his death.

The three orchestral works that best represent Rimsky-Korsakov on the concert stage today were written in the period between 1887 and 1888. The first, the *Capriccio Espagnol,* was originally designed as a fantasy on Spanish themes for violin and orchestra; it was later recast as a set of five movements for orchestra alone. Its brilliance is derived from the orchestration of the work itself; orchestral color is the essence of the composition, and the themes have little musical quality aside from the instrumental colors they present. This treatment, it may be said, was the composer's purpose and is not to be looked upon as a defect.

The first movement, in A major, is a lively piece in dance rhythm, with virtuosic passages for the violins and the first clarinet; the second movement is a quiet set of variations in which the wind instruments are featured. The third section is simply a reorchestration of the first movement, but now in B flat major. The fourth movement, entitled "Scene and Gypsy Song," begins with a series of cadenzas scored for brass instruments, solo violin, flute, clarinet, and harp, respectively. The various cadenzas are followed by a few melodic fragments set in a variety of rhythmic figures; in the fifth movement, these rise to great climaxes. The variety of its orchestration makes the *Capriccio Espagnol* one of the most colorful and exciting works in the orchestral literature.

Rimsky-Korsakov's skillful and imaginative use of instruments is revealed again in *Scheherazade,* a symphonic suite in four movements. The composer described the work as "a kaleidoscope of fairy tales and designs of Oriental character." The first edition of the score carried a descriptive title for each of the movements, but in the second edition the titles were withdrawn and a short descriptive note, derived from *The Arabian Nights,* was printed with the score. The program may be summarized as follows: the sultan Schahriar, distrusting all women, has formed the practice of killing each of his wives after their first night of marriage. Scheherazade, however, tells him tales of adventure and miracles, and so effective is her narrative ability that Schahriar is diverted and gives up his murderous practice.

To illustrate this program, Rimsky-Korsakov composed four descriptive sketches and unified them by means of two themes representing the sultan and Scheherazade, respectively; the result was a long work of unfailing interest characterized by great variety of color. The sultan's theme is a harsh and imperious phrase carried by the full orchestra (see Example 81*a*); Scheherazade's (see Example 81*b*) is a brief cadenza for solo violin and harp. These themes are heard, in the manner of Berlioz' *idée fixe,* at appropriate places in the various movements; but they also undergo considerable transformation from time to time and appear in different shapes and tempos. In the course of the four movements the sultan's theme gradually loses its harsh character; this may be considered to express the weakening of the sultan's murderous resolve.

Example 81

The third of Rimsky-Korsakov's orchestral works of this period is a one-movement fantasy on Russian liturgical themes. Called variously the *Russian Easter* and the *Easter Overture,* it expresses the contrasting moods of gloom and joy associated with the events of Holy Week. The overture begins with a slow, impressive introduction in which the plainsong chanting of Russian priests is imitated. A brilliant violin cadenza then leads directly into an allegro movement in which many quasi-liturgical themes are heard in a variety of instrumental colors. In the final portion of the work a festive mood is achieved by the composer's inspired use of the large orchestra, to which bells and other percussion instruments are added. The rejoicing at Easter is wonderfully depicted, and the entire work is one of Rimsky-Korsakov's finest.

The Russian nationalist composers were not greatly interested in manipulating themes in the manner of the German Classical composers; nor were they concerned with logical and well-organized forms. Rimsky-Korsakov was typical in this respect. In his works, particularly in *Scheherazade,* thematic reiteration is much in evidence, and the forms of the several movements are sectional rather than tightly organized. Yet his great mastery of orchestration allowed him to present the repeated themes in ever-new colors; the outstanding characteristic of *Scheherazade* is the variety of instrumental effects, which range from delicate to overwhelming. His orchestral virtuosity sometimes led him to consider variety of color as an end in itself—as he had done in the *Capriccio Espagnol.* His gift for writing lyrically and his ability to express warm sentiment are often overlooked because of the exciting and compelling nature of the orchestral sound in which his melodies are dressed.

Tchaikovsky

The composers of program music—and here we include the nationalist composers discussed in this chapter—were strongly convinced of the rightness of their musical philosophy: namely, that music should be descriptive or should have external meaning. Other composers, whom we shall discuss in a later chapter, were equally sure that descriptive music represented a violation of aesthetic principles, and that only the methods of the Classicists were legitimate in the field of composition. The two points of view are symbolized most strikingly by the descriptive symphonic poem and by the abstract symphony, and Liszt and Brahms represent the leaders of the two schools of thought.

Other composers embraced both points of view with equal ease; one senses a lack of conviction in their approach to the problem that faced musicians of the late nineteenth century. Tchaikovsky was the most outstanding of the men who adhered to neither camp but who visited both. He moved from one field to the other with no difficulty. Among his works, half a dozen nonrepresentational symphonies are balanced by about as many programmatic pieces; the latter are often nationalistic in spirit even though Tchaikovsky was not interested in the tenets of the "Russian Five." No essential structural or expressive differences are apparent between his works of the two dissimilar types. While outwardly Tchaikovsky represents a bridge between the two opposing aesthetic opinions of the time, he is truly representative of neither. He expressed only his unique individuality, one in which emotionalism, pessimism, and a tendency toward neurotic utterance were uppermost.

Peter Ilich Tchaikovsky (1840–93), whose music represents a bridge between two nineteenth-century aesthetic opinions.

Peter Ilich Tchaikovsky was born in Russia in 1840 and began to compose and play the piano at an early age. He attended the School of Jurisprudence in Moscow from about 1850 to 1859; then he took a clerical position with the Ministry of Justice, at the same time continuing his private study of music. In 1862, having determined upon a musical career, he entered the St. Petersburg Conservatory. A year later he resigned his government position and supported himself by giving piano lessons. In 1866 he joined the faculty of the Moscow Conservatory and remained there as a teacher of harmony for twelve years. He also visited often in Germany, Austria, and Italy.

After a visit to Germany in 1876, he entered upon a strange friendship with a wealthy and elderly widow. Nadezhda von Meck first had revealed her liking for Tchaikovsky's music by commissioning several works, for which she paid large fees. This contact resulted in an emotional attachment that lasted until 1889. But the friendship was carried on entirely by correspondence: Tchaikovsky and Mme. von Meck met only once, and then by accident.

In his other relationships with women, Tchaikovsky was less fortunate. His emotional nature made a normal relationship impossible for him, and his marriage in 1876, to a young student who had forced herself upon him, ended in disaster after a few weeks—almost at the cost of the composer's sanity. In this crisis Mme. von Meck came to his aid; she offered him an annuity that would allow him to travel and write without restraint. Tchaikovsky accepted the offer, resigned from the Conservatory in 1879, and devoted himself entirely to composition.

His professional debut as a conductor was not made until 1887, when he was forty-seven years old. In the years following that debut in St. Petersburg, he conducted his works in Germany, Paris, and London, and in 1891 he visited New York (conducting at Carnegie Hall) and other cities in the eastern United States, where he performed his works with great success. In 1893 he conducted again in London and received an honorary degree as Doctor of Music from Cambridge University; in that year he also composed his Symphony No. 6 ("Pathétique"). He conducted the first performance of that work in St. Petersburg on October 28 of the same year. On November 6 he died, a victim of the cholera epidemic that was raging at the time.

The earliest of the works on which Tchaikovsky's fame rests today is the overture-fantasy *Romeo and Juliet,* written in about 1869 and revised in 1880. The characters and situations of Shakespeare's play are pictured here: the love of Romeo and Juliet, the feud between the Montagues and the Capulets, the kindly Friar Laurence —all are symbolized by appropriate themes. The form of the work is Tchaikovsky's own version of the sonata-form. It contains a slow and somber introduction; a fast exposition section containing two themes, each of which is worked over after its first appearance; a development section proper; a recapitulation; and a coda that summarizes the earlier developments. That form became almost standardized in Tchaikovsky's works; it appears in such other descriptive pieces as *The Tempest, Francesca da Rimini,* and *Hamlet,* as well as in the first and last movements of his later symphonies.

Symphony No. 4, F minor, Op. 36, by Peter Ilich Tchaikovsky

FIRST MOVEMENT, Andante sostenuto; Moderato con anima

Meas.	*Theme*	
1	Intro.	Based on two short motives (Ex. 1)

Example 1

EXPOSITION

Meas.	*Theme*	
27	1st	First part (Ex. 2), F minor, repeated and extended

Example 2

Meas.	*Theme*	
53		Second part. Extension of motive from first measure, followed by development of meas. 27 and transition
116	2nd	A flat minor, small aba form (Ex. 3)

Example 3

Meas.	*Theme*	
134		Second part, B major, combined with rhythm of meas. 27
161	Codetta	B major; rhythmic figure derived from meas. 3
177		Second part; development of same rhythmic figure

DEVELOPMENT

Meas.	*Theme*	
193		Based on Ex. 1, meas. 1–4
201		Based on accompanying figure in meas. 161
218		Derived from Ex. 2, with new countermelody
253		Transition, based on introduction, Ex. 1 (meas. 1–3)

RECAPITULATION

Meas.	*Theme*	
284	1st	First part, Ex. 2; second part (meas. 53 ff) omitted
295	2nd	First part, Ex. 3 (meas. 116), in D minor
313		Second part (meas. 134), in F major
340	Codetta	Second part (meas. 177); first part (meas. 161 ff) omitted
355	Coda	First part, F minor; based on introduction, Ex. 1
365		Second part, new theme; figuration from meas. 48
381		Third part, new theme derived from meas. 3, but combined with meas. 1
404		Fourth part, derived from Ex. 2, meas. 27 ff. Movement ends in meas. 422

SECOND MOVEMENT, Andante in modo di canzona, B flat minor

Meas.	*Section*	
1	A	B flat minor. Theme in oboe (Ex. 4), repeated by cellos

Example 4

42	B	Theme in violins, 8 meas., plus extension and transition, 28 meas.
78	A	Theme of Ex. 4 in bassoon (first half) and violins (second half); no repetition
98	B	Theme in violins, 8 meas., plus extension, 20 meas.
126	C	F major. Series of eight-meas. phrases (Ex. 5), some extended; various keys

Example 5

200	A	Ex. 4, in B flat minor. No repetition, as in meas. 22–41
220	B	Theme, 8 meas., plus extension and transition
275	Coda	Based on theme A, Ex. 4. Movement ends in meas. 304

THIRD MOVEMENT, Scherzo, pizzicato ostinato, Allegro, F major

Meas.	*Part*	
1	A	Series of phrases, strings alone (Ex. 6)

Example 6

17	B	Key of D minor hinted at
33	C	Suggestion of A minor
49	B	Suggestion of B flat minor
57		Modulation
77	A	Return, Ex. 6, in F major
91		Modulation and transition

QUASI-TRIO

136	D	Woodwinds alone (Ex. 7), A major

Example 7

Tchaikovsky, Symphony No. 4 (cont.)

145		Second part; repetition of motives from meas. 137
163	D	Ex. 7, as in meas. 136 ff
170	E	New theme derived from A (Ex. 6); brasses alone
186	D	Return of woodwind theme D (Ex. 7), combined with theme E
194		Modulation and extension

DA CAPO

218–346		F major, strings alone. Exact repetition Ex. 6, meas. 1–130, then two-meas. extension
349	Coda	Based on first two meas. of part A (Ex. 6)
365		Combined with figure derived from Ex. 7
399		Return of part E as codetta. Movement ends in meas. 414

FOURTH MOVEMENT, Allegro con fuoco

Meas.	*Theme*	
EXPOSITION		
1	1st	First part (Ex. 8), F major

Example 8

10		Second part
30		Third part
47		Transition
60	2nd	Short phrases (Ex. 9) with many repetitions, B flat minor

Example 9

92		Development of 2nd theme (no true development section)

RECAPITULATION

119	1st	But begins with third part (meas. 30)
149	2nd	Ex. 9, short phrases with repetitions; modulations different from meas. 60–91
177		Development and transition
199	Coda	Introductory theme from first movement (Ex. 1)
223		Based on meas. 38–40 of 1st theme
249		Based on Ex. 8
269		Based on Ex. 9 (meas. 60). Movement ends in meas. 293

Romeo and Juliet brings to expression the full range of Tchaikovsky's style, a style compounded of somber and poignant melodies, considerable rhythmic animation, an imaginative use of the orchestral instruments, and exciting climaxes. Among other characteristics are a dramatic kind of writing, considerable reiteration of oratorical themes, and a variety of moods that range from sentimental to overwhelming. This combination of qualities is found also in Tchaikovsky's other single-movement descriptive pieces, of which the *Marche Slav, The Year 1812,* and the *Capriccio Italien* are well known.

Tchaikovsky's last three symphonies are not programmatic in that they do not carry descriptive titles. But in listening to them, one is constantly reminded of their composer's personality. Tchaikovsky was not among the composers who were interested in objectively manipulating their musical materials for purely musical reasons. In his music the expression of his own feelings predominates. His few happy moments are mirrored in graceful melodies; reflections of his melancholy states are found in the heavy, moody passages. There was little humor in his life; thus, there is little humor in his music. Few composers have been as subjective in their works as Tchaikovsky; few composers have so completely revealed their own moods and feelings.

The Symphony No. 4, in F minor, was described by Tchaikovsky as representing the workings of fate. It was begun in 1876, just at the time of his unfortunate and brief marriage; it was completed in Switzerland, where he had fled to regain his mental health. He had approached that marriage almost as though he were helpless, as though fate had taken him in hand, and at a later date he expressed his conviction that this had indeed been the case. To that extent the Symphony No. 4 is programmatic. A thematic outline of the symphony is given on pages 228–30.

The work begins with a forceful introduction; the somber first movement, based on a curious rhythmic figure that is halting and impelling at once (see Example 82*a*), is concentrated and powerful. Tchaikovsky's use of solo woodwinds, especially the clarinet and bassoon, is noteworthy throughout. The second movement, with a melancholy theme for the oboe (see Example 82*b*), also expresses the darker moods,

A scene from Tchaikovsky's ballet *Swan Lake,* performed by the National Ballet of Canada.

Example 82

even though the textures are more transparent and the expression more relaxed than in the first movement.

In the scherzo the gloom is lifted momentarily. Its first section is entirely for strings played pizzicato (see Example 82*c*); the trio is scored for woodwind and brass groups, first heard separately and then together; and the recapitulation of the first section again presents the pizzicato strings. This movement is deft, imaginative, and altogether charming. The last movement, a fast allegro, is relentlessly animated; the quiet melancholy of the andante and the charm of the scherzo are quite forgotten. This music is no longer merely gloomy; relentless and oppressive force is expressed here, and the overwhelming, powerful sonorities of the coda are among the loudest and most effective passages in the orchestral repertoire.

The Symphony No. 5, in E minor, is no less powerful than the fourth. It also contains one of Tchaikovsky's most graceful movements, a waltz on the theme shown in Example 83*a*. In the slow movement, with its lyrically inspired melody for solo horn (see Example 83*b*), Tchaikovsky reached a high level of warm and eloquent expression. Wherever one turns in the Symphony No. 5, one encounters the original, imaginative orchestral effects that give Tchaikovsky's music its rich, typically Romantic sound (this is also true of virtually all his larger works). Solo wind instruments are prominently featured (we have mentioned only a few of the outstanding passages

Example 83

A scene from *The Nutcracker,* performed by the New York City Ballet.

here); high and low ranges of all the instruments are utilized; and exciting climaxes abound. Tchaikovsky was above all a master of orchestral sound, and although his music very often reflects his confused emotional life, it never fails to be effective from the standpoint of orchestral color.

The Suite from Tchaikovsky's ballet *The Nutcracker* is especially rich in orchestral effects, even though here they are kept on a smaller, more intimate level. The set of episodes drawn from the ballet of that name begins with an "Overture Miniature," in which no cellos or basses are used. Then follows a set of "Characteristic Dances": a "March" alternates string and wind phrases; the "Dance of the Sugarplum Fairy" features the celesta; a "Trepak" (Russian dance) is for full orchestra; the "Arabian Dance" brings the clarinets and English horn forward; a "Chinese Dance" has the flutes and bassoons as principal performers; flutes, and later horns and trumpets, predominate in the "Dance of the Toy Flutes"; and the "Waltz of the Flowers" presents a harp cadenza, after which the full orchestra brings the Suite to a rousing conclusion.

With comparable instrumental variety everywhere in Tchaikovsky's larger works, the music cannot fail to be colorful. Subtlety is not among his outstanding characteristics, but in straightforward expression of mood and feeling he has few equals.

Listening Suggestions

BORODIN
In the Steppes of Central Asia (symphonic poem)
"Polovtsian Dances" from *Prince Igor* (opera)

GRIEG
Concerto for Piano, A minor, Op. 16
Norwegian Dances, Op. 35 (dances for orchestra)
Peer Gynt, Suites Nos. 1 and 2, Op. 46 and Op. 55

LISZT
Concerto No. 1 for Piano, E flat
Les Préludes (symphonic poem)
Sonata in B minor

MUSSORGSKY
A Night on Bald Mountain (symphonic poem)
Pictures at an Exhibition (orchestral version)

RIMSKY-KORSAKOV
Capriccio Espagnol, Op. 34 (orchestral suite)
Russian Easter, Op. 36 (concert overture)
Scheherazade, Op. 35 (symphonic suite)

SMETANA
The Bartered Bride (opera)
The Moldau (symphonic poem)

TCHAIKOVSKY
Concerto for Piano, B flat minor, Op. 23
The Nutcracker, Suite
Romeo and Juliet (symphonic poem, called "overture-fantasy" by composer)
Symphony No. 5, E minor, Op. 64
Symphony No. 6, B minor, Op. 74 ("Pathétique")

Chapter 12

OPERA

A theater-goer is exposed to a variety of aesthetic stimuli. The stage set orients him to the period and location of the play, the stage lighting helps him to enter into the moods the play evokes, and the costumes provide him with some insight into the nature of the people portrayed on the stage. Perhaps his strongest aesthetic response, however, results from observing the interactions between the characters themselves, from seeing how they succumb to psychological tensions or rise above them. A well-wrought play on a significant theme enables the theater-goer to project himself into the minds of the characters, to enter into their lives vicariously. Across the centuries this fact has without doubt contributed largely to the universal popularity of dramatic presentations.

The opera provides a means of going even beyond the drama in its portrayal of dramatic tensions, and since its inception in the early seventeenth century has been one of the most popular art forms. About 1585 a group of Italian poets, musicians, and patrons of the art experimented to develop a new kind of music. One of their first experiments was to set dramatic texts to music in order to strengthen the aesthetic responses to the drama by the addition of musical responses. At first they provided accompanied melodies for the actors who had previously spoken their lines. Within a few years their experiments had reached such a point that entire plays were adapted to the new method, and a new art form was born—the opera.

Early in its career opera began its conquest of the musical world; composers in other countries first imitated the Italian style, then developed their own national styles, and many types of opera ranging from the lightly comic to the profoundly serious emerged. Opera has been spectacular, symbolic, and sometimes religious, but most often it has been concerned with the dramatic values found in the text, thus making it possible for the opera-goer to achieve even more of the vicarious experience than a dramatic presentation can provide. Opera today is found in all parts of the world in a great variety of professional and nonprofessional performances.

In setting a play to music, the composer must adjust both the structure of the

Example 84

Gounod, *Faust*, Act IV

play and the forms of the music to a new set of dramatic requirements. Early composers in the field did in fact develop new forms: the *recitative,* a series of phrases set in free prose rhythms with a rather static melodic line and supported by chords at textual turning points (see Example 84 for a nineteenth-century recitative), and the *aria*, an extended series of expressive lyric melodies, sometimes in an ABA form. Lines of text that were distributed among several actors were set for vocal trio, quartet, or even chorus. And to round off the musical structure, purely instrumental portions were often written for the beginnings of acts (there called "overture" or "prelude"), between scenes and elsewhere, or in many instances to accompany the ballet that often became an element of the performance. This musical setting of a dramatic text was acted and sung with costumes, lights, and scenery, and an orchestra provided the accompaniment for all the participants.

A composition of this kind, with recitatives, arias, duets, larger ensemble numbers, chorus, and orchestral movements, is essentially a set of pieces or musical works tied together by a dramatic text. The name of the form is derived from this structure; the Latin term *opus* means a "work," and the word *opera* is its plural. Thus an opera is a compound form consisting of a series of works of the kinds mentioned above, musical works that are set to a dramatic text and augmented by staged effects.

One cannot generalize about the number of parts, forms, or inner relationships that result from the composition of an opera. At times a dramatic text may fall naturally into sections, scenes, or acts. The composer's intentions in setting the various sections (as two-part forms, as ABA structures, and so on) influence the total form. The composer may wish to raise one character to a position of greater importance than other characters by giving him a large proportion of the arias. These and other considerations determine the inner structure of an opera. The internal plan of one opera may be given here, nevertheless, if only to show how the various numbers and scenes are combined into acts. The opera chosen for illustration is Verdi's *Aïda,* produced in Cairo in 1871 and designed to be part of the ceremonies celebrating the opening of the Suez Canal. *Aïda* is firmly fixed in the repertoire as one of the finest examples of the form (see p. 237).

The *scene* (often given in its Italian form, *scena*), as the term is used in *Aïda* and many other operas, is related to the recitative-aria pair spoken of above. In the

The Paris Opera in 1875, its inaugural year.

Aïda, an Opera by Giuseppe Verdi

Prelude

Act I

Introduction
Romanza
Duet
Terzetto
Scene and Ensemble
Battle Hymn
Scene
Chorus
Dance
Prayer

Act II

Chorus
Dance
Scene and Duet
Finale and Chorus
March
Chorus
Scene, Ensemble, and Chorus

Act III

Prayer
Romanza
Scene and Duet
Duet
Terzetto

Act IV

Scene
Duet
Scene
Scene and Duet
Finale

scena, however, the recitative and aria are often intertwined, passages of one type being interpolated between those of another, while in the conventional recitative and aria the two are treated as separate short movements. Further, the *scena* often tends toward a dramatic type of expression, while the aria inclines toward lyricism.

Vast differences in content, expressive style, and required personnel exist between the earliest opera (the first composition that can be called an opera is *Dafne,* by Jacopo Peri, written about 1597) and operas such as *Aïda.* Yet the three basic elements of this compound form have changed but little in almost four centuries. These elements are the dramatic or literary, including the plot and the text; the theatrical, contained in the costumes, stage settings, and special stage effects; and the musical, embracing the vocal, choral, and orchestral material. In several periods of music history, different elements have been stressed at the cost of the others. At one time vocal virtuosity lay uppermost in the composer's mind, for example, and dramatic values took second place. At another time the amount of sheer spectacle overwhelmed both dramatic truth and dramatic music. With changes of taste on the part of the opera-going public, the operas that stressed one element out of all proportion to the others eventually fell from favor and were dropped from the repertoire.

The majority of the operas performed with any degree of regularity today were composed in the nineteenth and early twentieth centuries—notable exceptions being the later operas of Mozart. Those operas achieved the particular relationship between dramatic, theatrical, and musical elements that their first audiences found most satisfying—and that still appeal to present-day opera-goers. Yet even those works are of several types and reflect different operatic traditions.

There are two principal types of opera, which are differentiated first of all by subject matter. One type is concerned with dramatic or "dark" subjects—with matters that build to high levels of emotional tension and reveal people under great emotional stress. This type is called *serious opera* (*opera seria* in Italian and *opéra sérieux* in French). The other type has to do with light or humorous matters; it contains gay and lighthearted music and brings everyday people on the stage. This type is the *comic opera* (*opera buffa* and *opéra comique* in Italian and French, respectively).

The *opéra comique,* unlike its Italian relative and unlike the serious opera of either nation, traditionally employed spoken dialogue in place of sung recitative; a similar use of such dialogue is seen in operettas and musical comedies of the present day. This tradition became so firmly fixed that in nineteenth-century France any opera that contained spoken portions was called an *opéra comique,* regardless of its subject matter. For example, Gounod's *Faust* and Bizet's *Carmen,* both on tragic subjects, originally contained spoken dialogue (those sections were set to music in recitative style only later); hence technically they were *opéras comiques.*

The Italian version of the comic opera (*opera buffa*) was developed largely at Naples near the middle of the eighteenth century. Its subject matter was usually drawn from everyday life and it dealt with common people instead of exalted personages. Written in a pleasant, tuneful, and homophonic style and filled with humor and liveliness, *opera buffa* was enormously successful in Italy in the later 1700's. Composers such as Niccolò Piccini, Giovanni Paisiello, and Domenico Cimarosa contributed many masterworks to the form. Cimarosa's *Il matrimonio segreto* (*The Secret Marriage*) may still be heard today.

The Italian serious opera (*opera seria*) is also closely identified with Naples in the eighteenth century. It flourished there in spite of the competition provided by the *opera buffa* but it often made use of stylistic devices that served to minimize the dramatic action in favor of musical virtuosity. The recitative, for example, which earlier had been used to carry the plot forward, was often reduced to a chain of narrative phrases that did little to enhance the drama or to supply motivations for the actions of the singers, and the latter were permitted to embellish the vocal lines at will, further impeding the dramatic tension. Operas often became little more than vehicles for the display of vocal acrobatics, and by the middle of the century a need for reform was felt.

A number of composers shared in the reform of serious opera in the years after about 1750, among them Niccolò Jomelli (1714–74) and Tomaso Traëtta (1727–79). It remained for Christoph Willibald von Gluck (1714–87), a German composer trained in Italy but long a resident of Vienna and Paris, to make a reformed operatic style effective. In Gluck's operas (among them the famous *Alceste* and *Iphigénie en Tauride*) dramatic values were given precedence over musical values, vocal displays were avoided, and the chorus and ballet played important parts in furthering the dramatic action. Forms were treated with greater freedom, and the stylized *da capo* aria (in ABA form) was virtually abandoned.

We have seen earlier (p. 151) how Mozart, as the foremost operatic composer of the Classical period, made his characters come alive on the stage. Through the music he composed for them he revealed his insights into human behavior as no composer before him had done. Carl Maria von Weber (1786–1826), working later in the period, helped to usher in the developments that culminated in Romantic opera. Weber brought into his operas (*Der Freischütz* or *The Freeshooter,* 1821; *Euryanthe,* 1823; and *Oberon,* 1826) a remarkable blend of supernatural subject matter, glowing orchestral colors, and freer harmonic treatment that led the way to the works of Richard Wagner near the end of the century.

Grand Opera

In the first half of the nineteenth century Paris became the operatic capital of Europe. Regardless of the success a composer might have had elsewhere, he had not "arrived" until his work had been produced in Paris. The lavish standards of production, the enthusiastic audiences, and the number of capable singers available there made operatic performances brilliant spectacles. In order to partake as fully as possible in the rewards that Parisian performances held out to them, French composers concerned themselves largely with opera and paid little attention to composing instrumental music. Berlioz was the major exception, but he, too, wrote operas. And just as had happened in Germany with Weber and his successors, composers in France turned to Romantic subjects for their operas. Sir Walter Scott's novels provided several standard operatic plots (*The Monastery, Guy Mannering,* and *Ivanhoe* are examples), as did fairy tales such as *Cinderella* and others. But those French operas of the period from about 1810 to 1828 have long since lapsed into oblivion.

The year 1828 saw the emergence of a new type of French serious opera. A work of this type was likely to be concerned with a subject drawn from history. It portrayed violent action, extreme emotions, and sharp contrasts of mood. It was longer than operas of earlier decades had been and filled with much detail, some of which had little to do with the plot and served only to provide added moments of excitement. Elaborate ballets, crowd scenes, colorful and complex orchestration, and a great variety of vocal styles and effects contributed to the novelty of the new type. It well deserves the name given to it—*grand opera.*

Among the first of the grand operas was *The Deaf-Mute of Portici* (also known as *Masaniello,* the name of its hero), by Daniel Auber (1782–1871) and produced in 1828. Dealing with a revolution at Naples in 1647, it gave so realistic a picture of an enraged and aroused populace that it provoked riots in Brussels when it was produced there in 1830. Those riots eventually led to Belgium's separation from the Dutch Netherlands in 1831. The power of music to influence behavior had probably never before been revealed so clearly. The opera contained, in what came to be typical grand-opera style, the staging of an eruption of Mount Vesuvius. This elaborate detail was brought in for reasons of spectacle only, since the historic eruption of 1631 took place sixteen years before the revolution with which the opera is mainly concerned.

Gioacchino Rossini (1792–1868), after having written about three dozen comic operas, mostly in Italy, turned in 1829 to the field of the grand opera and composed *William Tell.* The work was extremely popular for many decades, but then disappeared from the standard operatic repertoire. The lightness, charm, and ironic humor that distinguished Rossini's comic operas (see below, p. 245ff) had no place in *William Tell,* and the composer was not always able to maintain the dramatic tension called for by the plot. Only the overture and a few arias have survived.

The most dazzling of grand-opera composers was Giacomo Meyerbeer (1791–1864). Meyerbeer, born in Berlin, was trained primarily as a pianist, but dramatic composition became his major interest. He wrote two German operas, neither of which enjoyed much success. He then went to Italy in order to master the popular style of which Rossini was the greatest exponent. Here he composed six Italian operas of which the last, *The Crusade in Egypt* (1824), became enormously successful. Following that experience he went to Paris, studied the grand-opera style, and mastered it as he had the Italian.

Meyerbeer's first work in the new style was *Robert le Diable* (1831); five years later *Les Huguenots* was produced. Then at longer intervals came productions of *Le Prophète* (1849), *Dinorah* (1859), and *L'Africaine* (1865), all of which had been composed in the years between 1842 and about 1864.

The earliest of those works were largely responsible for establishing the conventions according to which grand opera came to be written. Five acts were standard, and the ballet, which had formerly appeared near the end of an act or between acts, now took a prominent place within the act. The main arias were carefully distributed among the leading singers, and under no circumstances might a minor singer receive a more imposing aria than a principal one. Characters were typed: there were usually a tragic pair of lovers (dramatic soprano and tenor) and a secondary pair (coloratura soprano and bass), and so on. The chorus, made up of people who took part in the action (soldiers, villagers, or whatever was called for), became less of an ornament and more of a significant element in the unfolding of the spectacular plot.

In spite of the brilliance of Meyerbeer's works, they have almost disappeared from the operatic repertoire. Only one or two grand operas of this period have survived to the present day, and those works are not by Meyerbeer but by Jacques-François Halévy (1799–1862). Halévy's most successful work was *La Juive* (*The Jewess,* 1835). Its appeal now, just as a century ago, lies in the fact that its melodies are somewhat more attractive than the melodies of other grand operas, and that its orchestral writing is more colorful. But portions of the forgotten works of Meyerbeer are still heard occasionally. The "Coronation March" from *Le Prophète* is a favorite at festival occasions, commencement exercises, and the like; and the "Shadow Song" from *Dinorah,* the aria "Ah, mon fils" from *Le Prophète,* as well as other tuneful or brilliant pieces, still form part of singers' concert repertoires.

It should be pointed out in passing that the majority of the grand operas of the period between 1828 and 1860 catered to the popular taste of the time instead of leading it to higher levels. When musical standards changed for the better, those operas quickly passed out of favor. Grand operas in general were not written out of inner conviction or out of sheer emotional necessity. They were "occasional" pieces, and when the occasion passed, they lost the power to appeal to their audiences.

Lyric Opera

In the second quarter of the nineteenth century the *opéra comique* existed as a separate musical line parallel to that of the grand opera. Among the most enjoyable works of the time were *Fra Diavolo* (1830), by the same Daniel Auber who had introduced grand opera to Paris, and *Zampa* (1831) by Ferdinand Hérold. Those works may still be listened to with pleasure and amusement today.

A loosely defined form that contained a broad variety of subject matter, the *opéra comique* soon began to develop along two diverging lines. One line became even more amusing, witty, and satiric; this line of development led to the *operetta,* of which Offenbach's *Orpheus in the Underworld* is a well-known French example. The operetta in this form was soon exported to other countries. Johann Strauss's *Die Fledermaus* (*The Bat*) represents the Viennese type, while the works of Gilbert and Sullivan (*The Mikado, The Pirates of Penzance, H.M.S. Pinafore,* etc.) are English examples. And later, in the United States, many composers from Victor Herbert (*The Fortune Teller, Babes in Toyland,* etc.) to more recent figures such as Sigmund Romberg (*The Student Prince*) and Jerome Kern (*Show Boat*) continued the line of development begun almost a century earlier. In all these cases the distinguishing mark of the *opéra comique* was retained—namely, spoken dialogue interspersed with singing.

The other line of development followed by the *opéra comique* concentrated upon sentimental or mildly serious plots and kept humor to a minimum. Musically it rose high above the merely entertaining operetta. It employed a larger orchestra, and the expressive arias and dramatic climaxes it contained were foreign to the operetta. The lyric, purely singable elements were stressed, and the pretentiousness and spectacular events that characterized grand opera were avoided. Even though this type of opera often included a ballet and employed colorful and exotic settings, the vocal element remained uppermost. To this type the name *lyric opera* is given.

The most widely performed of all operas belongs to this type. The lyric opera *Faust,* by Charles Gounod (1818–93), was first produced in 1859; it received two thousand performances in Paris alone in the first seventy-five years of its existence. In addition, it has been performed in over two dozen languages in countries around the world.

Many qualities combine to make *Faust* so universally beloved. First of all, Gounod achieved an excellent balance between musical, dramatic, and theatrical elements. He revealed a sense of refinement in all matters of melody and harmony, for he was a composer of elegant music and seldom wrote crudely or with faulty proportions (see Example 85). Then too, the fine contrasts drawn between the main characters lend an

Example 85

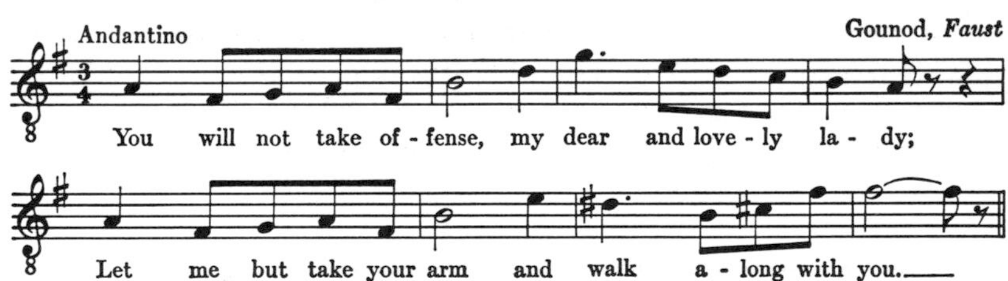

air of vitality to the opera. Faust himself (after his transformation, in the Prologue, from an elderly scholar to a virile, handsome, young man) makes an appeal both as a dashing character and through the warmth of the melodies given to him. The spectator is led to feel pity for Marguerite after her abandonment by Faust. And the figure of Mephistopheles provides touches of both humor and black magic. Colorful scenes, attractive arias and ensemble numbers, and delightful ballet music combine to make *Faust* worthy of the affection it has enjoyed for more than a century.

Close behind Gounod's masterpiece in international fame, and even exceeding it in musical quality, is *Carmen,* written by Georges Bizet (1838–75). After a boyhood spent in Paris, Bizet won the *Prix de Rome* in 1857. Between 1858 and 1872 he wrote a number of operas of various types (Italian and French, grand and comic), all of which remained unsuccessful. The incidental music he wrote for Daudet's play *L'Arlésienne,* in 1872, brought Bizet to public notice; the two orchestral suites arranged from that music are still widely performed. Bizet's masterpiece, *Carmen,* which was produced in March 1875, three months before the composer's death, made no real impression on its first auditors. Yet later in the same year it received over thirty performances in Paris alone, and by 1878 it had been presented successfully in Germany, Austria, Italy, and in countries as far afield as Russia and the United States. Since that time it has held its place as one of the finest and most beloved of all French operas.

It should be emphasized that *Carmen* is a French opera in spite of its Spanish setting. Bizet was among the first of the Romantic composers to bring Spanish idioms and rhythms to the musical stage. In this respect he was followed closely by another Frenchman, Édouard Lalo, who wrote a violin concerto called the *Symphonie Espagnole* and who employed Spanish folk songs in his Cello Concerto in D minor. Rimsky-Korsakov's *Capriccio Espagnol* came into being some ten years later. While it is true that those composers sought to capture something of musical Spain, they worked not as nationalists but as Romantic composers eager to find new or exotic means of expression. True Spanish nationalism in music was a late arrival on the European scene: still another decade was to pass before authentic Spanish composers made their presence felt.

Carmen contains little of the refined, rather sweet melodic style that is found in *Faust.* Its melodies are tense and concentrated or vigorously rhythmical (see Example 86), and they build up to dramatic climaxes. Bizet's harmonies are imaginative and wide-ranging; they seem perfectly chosen to suggest the moods of excitement, suspense, and tragedy that mark *Carmen.* The work also possesses a full-sounding texture that opera music seldom achieves; this richness of the musical sound results from the carefully worked out contrapuntal details in the accompaniments and from the colorful orchestration.

Several excerpts have long been familiar as concert pieces: in addition to the famous "Habanera" there are Micaela's well-known aria (see Example 86), Carmen's "Card Scene," Don José's "Flower Song," and Escamillo's "Toreador Song." The opera contains many other arias, as well as a number of delightful ensemble numbers. Its

Example 86

melodic charm, dramatic tension, orchestral color, and sheer excitement together make *Carmen* one of the operatic masterpieces of the late nineteenth century.

A few other lyric operas may be mentioned here; in spite of their individual differences, they all reflect the melodiousness that is basic to the type. Camille Saint-Saëns (1835–1921), although primarily a composer of instrumental music, is remembered in the operatic field for his *Samson and Delilah.* A prolific and facile writer, he inclined toward an ingratiating, superficially brilliant kind of music. He was greatly interested in the external effectiveness of what he wrote; consequently he was not averse to mixing various styles. *Samson and Delilah,* for example, is predominantly lyric (its best-known aria is "My Heart at Thy Sweet Voice"), but it also contains touches of grand opera, notably in the scene where the blinded Samson is chained to a treadmill and in the last scene where he causes the temple to collapse and crush his enemies. Choruses in *Samson and Delilah* take on something of the majesty and dignity of eighteenth-century opera. Yet the prevailing lyric quality is able to overcome the stylistic inconsistencies, and the total effect of the opera is one of brilliance and color.

Jules Massenet (1842–1912) avoided the mixture of styles that is often a disturbing element in the music of Saint-Saëns. His works are refined, even delicate throughout; and his somewhat melancholy melodies are combined with subtle orchestral effects to produce operas of unfailing charm. His masterpieces, *Manon* and *Thaïs,* have held their favored places in the repertoire to the present day.

Italian Opera

Italian opera composers of the early Romantic period, like their French contemporaries, cultivated both the comic and the serious types of opera. Of the many musicians of the time, three rose to positions of greatest eminence: Gioacchino Rossini (already mentioned in the account of grand opera), Vincenzo Bellini, and Gaetano Donizetti.

The Barber of Seville, illustration in Beautés de l'Opéra, Paris, 1845.

Rossini (1792–1868) began his career as a composer of comic operas in his native Italy in 1810. In spite of the failure of some of his works, he received many commissions from opera houses in Italy and elsewhere. He traveled widely to oversee the production of his operas, and in about 1825 he accepted the managership of an Italian theater in Paris. It was there that *William Tell* was written. Then, at the age of thirty-seven, Rossini abruptly gave up operatic composition for a reason that has never been satisfactorily explained. He lived for almost forty years past that point, dividing his time between Paris and various Italian cities; in that time he wrote only a few sacred compositions.

Rossini's famous comic opera *The Barber of Seville* (1816) is virtually the only one of his more than thirty operas that has retained a place in the repertoire today, although the overtures to several of them (*The Thieving Magpie, Il Signor Bruschino,* and *Semiramide,* among others) are still favorite orchestra pieces. *The Barber of Seville* is a masterpiece of the *opera buffa* type. It resembles eighteenth-century examples in its clarity of form, its musical charm, and its general sparkle and vitality. As a composer of graceful and attractive opera melodies Rossini was unsurpassed. His humor was broad, sly, and occasionally ironic, but never coarse, and it was often connected with particular situations in the action of the operas rather than with any comic elements in the music itself. As an example, the scene in the finale of Act I may be mentioned. The Count Almaviva, disguised as a soldier and pretending drunkenness, seeks entrance to the home of Dr. Bartolo with whose ward he is in love (see Example 87). The Count's en-

Example 87

trance and his deliberate mispronouncing of Bartolo's name ("Balordo," "Bertoldo," "Barbaro") provide one of the most delightful episodes in this comic gem. Furthermore, the music given to Rossini's characters in the opera cleverly underlines the motives for their behavior. And in his understanding of the human voice, its capabilities and its various colors, Rossini has seldom been equaled. The orchestra, lightly and clearly scored, is always kept subordinate to the voices, and the rhythms are clear and compelling. The end result is a "singer's opera" that is as fresh and charming today as it was in 1816.

Donizetti (1797–1848) composed over sixty operas in the twenty-six years between 1818 and 1844, when a paralytic stroke ended his creative activities. Many of those works were pale imitations of Rossini's and did not live past a few performances. Others, however, became enormously popular and remained so during much of the second half of the nineteenth century. A comic opera, *Don Pasquale* (1843), and a serious opera, *Lucia di Lammermoor* (1835), are still staples in the repertoire today.

The principal reason for Donizetti's success in his own time may lie in the fact that his music was what is generally called "popular." A prime example is found in *Lucia di Lammermoor.* There Donizetti met the audience on its own level; he supplied catchy tunes and an array of blood-curdling situations as sensational as they are improbable. The heroine is forced by her brother into a loveless marriage; she murders her husband in the bridal chamber and subsequently loses her sanity and dies. Incongruously enough, these events are carried by a set of naïve, simple tunes, crudely or ineptly

Example 88

Donizetti, *Lucia di Lammermoor*

harmonized and accompanied by a thin-sounding orchestra that does little more than outline the chord structures (see Example 88). Brilliant vocalizing and loud climaxes cannot overcome the almost complete lack of musical profundity.

Bellini (1801–35), with a mastery of melody that approached Rossini's, brought a greater range of feeling into his music than did Donizetti. His masterwork, *Norma* (1831), is especially rich in the expression of nostalgic and melancholy moods, and the routine harmonies that characterize much of Donizetti's music are seldom present in Bellini's. He possessed a refined, almost aristocratic taste; many commentators have compared him to Chopin because of the grace and perfection of his melodic line. Not as prolific a composer as his contemporaries, Bellini revealed in his short life a self-discipline and a standard of workmanship that others often lack. He strove for perfection of utterance—a quality that is extremely rare among operatic composers generally—and took great pains to ensure that his music was appropriate to the sentiment of his texts.

Verdi

In the second half of the nineteenth century, the Italian operatic tradition was upheld primarily by one man. Giuseppe Verdi, in a long creative period that extended across more than fifty years, remained faithful to the ideal of the "singer's opera." He refused to accept the revolutionary musical idiom of Wagner (see below, pp. 251–56). in whose works the orchestra takes on more importance than the singers. Verdi, achieving a balance of vocal, dramatic, and theatrical elements, composed a succession of operas that are unsurpassed for poignancy, deep feeling, and general effectiveness.

Verdi, the son of an innkeeper, was born in 1813 near Busseto, Italy. He studied with a number of obscure teachers, served as conductor and organist in Busseto for a few years beginning in 1836, and composed his first opera in 1839. The success of that work led to several commissions, and he was at once established as a professional composer. His career was marked by personal tragedy; before his twenty-seventh birthday he had lost two children and his wife, and in a despondent state he gave up all composition for a two-year period.

Verdi aligned himself with the nationalists who were working for a united Italian kingdom; for a time he played an active part in politics. He was elected to the first National Parliament in 1860 but resigned five years later when his political interest waned. His name became an acronym for the rallying cry of the patriots: "Vittorio Emanuele, Re d'Italia!" ("Victor Emmanuel, King of Italy!"), and the enthusiastic shouting of "Verdi!" at performances of his operas served a double purpose. It honored the composer and made his name known throughout Italy, and it provided the patriots with a means of circumventing the police, who had forbidden all revolutionary activity.

When *Aïda* was produced in 1871, Verdi was fifty-eight years old and had been Italy's outstanding composer for over thirty years. At this time he retired from the operatic scene for sixteen years. Then came two more masterpieces; *Otello* in 1887 and *Falstaff* in 1893, when he was in his eightieth year. Rather than showing signs of de-

Opening scene of *Aïda,* by Giuseppe Verdi (1813–1901).

clining power, Verdi's two late works reveal that he had grown greatly in musical and psychological insight. He died in 1901, at the age of eighty-eight.

The works that have remained most firmly established in the operatic repertoire are *Rigoletto* (1851), *Il Trovatore* (1853), *La Traviata* (1853), and *Aïda* (1871). Among other operas that are still performed occasionally are *Simone Boccanegra* (1857), *The Masked Ball* (1859), and *The Force of Destiny* (1862). All those works adhere to the essential ideals of the Italian operatic tradition. The human voice takes precedence over orchestral sonority, the simple melodic structures provide little room for involved contrapuntal textures, and the music serves to express human emotion.

Verdi also observed the conventions of Italian opera. He followed tradition in the number of acts included in each opera (usually four) and the location of principal arias, ensembles, and choruses within those acts. He retained also the conventions of the "number opera": that is, his works contain separate numbers—arias, ensembles, choruses, etc.—each of which is likely to be a closed form with a definite beginning and ending.

Verdi, like his predecessors, wrote for the opera-going public of his time, but it is evident that he held a higher opinion of that public than did Donizetti. Subtleties of characterization and of musical structure were largely missing from his early works, it is true, but as Verdi grew to artistic maturity he made increasing demands upon his audiences—and the audiences rose to the level he expected of them. Verdi took his art seriously at all times, revealing none of the glibness or superficiality that often marred the work of his predecessors.

The plots of all the operas mentioned above (except for the comic opera *Falstaff*) are tragic and grim. There is little humor in the situations in which his characters are placed, and a passionate or melancholy mood is the most usual. Except in a few cases, the settings are immaterial to the action. *The Masked Ball,* for example, was originally set in Sweden and had King Gustavus Adolphus for its principal figure. When the political authorities objected to this setting, Verdi transferred it to Puritan New England with no loss of dramatic effect. This was possible because in Verdi's operas the characters and their emotional problems are most important. These characters come alive, and it is the purpose of the operas to express musically the dramatic experiences they undergo.

Aïda is in a separate category from Verdi's other operas. It was commissioned by the Khedive of Egypt for festivities that celebrated the opening of the Suez Canal in 1869. (However, it was not produced until two years after the Canal had been placed in operation.) For this reason it is scenically more elaborate than Verdi's other works. In fact, it is not far removed from the idea of grand opera and contains some of the features that made French grand opera so spectacular: colorful processions, a massive ballet, and exotic color in the orchestra. But Verdi's essential sincerity did not desert him; the human aspects of his characters remained his principal interest. Aïda's famous aria "O Patria mia" is more than a formal gesture of nostalgia, for example: it represents the cry of an anguished heart (see Example 89).

Verdi, *Aïda* *Example 89*

In the years after *Aïda* was produced, Verdi felt that even his countrymen were being affected by what he considered the blight of Wagnerism. He thought that the Italian operatic tradition was weakening and that a false operatic philosophy (false for Italy, at least) was invading the form to which he had devoted his life. His greatest tragic work, *Otello* (1887), served to demonstrate that Italian opera could still be written.

Like all Verdi's operas, *Otello* is concerned with people; Verdi scorned the gods and mythical characters who moved across Wagner's stage. The musical numbers are more closely linked to each other than they were in his earlier operas, but this is achieved by means of transitional passages between them and not by the use of anything resembling Wagner's continuous web of melodies. Moreover, the melodies themselves depart from the pure lyricism of earlier works and are more plastic and freer in phrase structure.

Falstaff (1893), finally, reverses Verdi's tendency to concern himself with tragedy, for this gem among comic operas is filled with vitality and laughter throughout. The libretto, based on Shakespeare's *The Merry Wives of Windsor,* was skillfully adapted by Arrigo Boito, the composer and writer who had also prepared the libretto for *Otello.* A masterpiece resulted from this collaboration. The imaginative use of free forms, the suitability of music to text, and the warmth and optimism that pervade the opera belie Verdi's age—almost eighty. *Falstaff* is one of the great operas of the nineteenth century.

Both *Otello* and *Falstaff* illustrate many departures from Verdi's earlier style—departures that had been hinted at in *Aïda* some twenty years before. Nevertheless, Verdi remained true to what he had practiced for half a century: a way of composing in which human problems are presented in a straightforward manner and are surrounded by moving, sincere music that comes from the heart.

Richard Wagner (1813–83), one of the most influential musicians of all time.

Richard Wagner was born in Leipzig in 1813. His interests as a boy were directed more to literature than to music. The few lessons he took on the piano and the violin led to no satisfactory achievement, nor did his early attempts to teach himself composition enable him to write acceptably. In 1831, when he was eighteen, he studied for about a year with the cantor of the St. Thomas School in Leipzig. Two years later he began his professional career as chorus master in the Opera at Würzburg. Then followed six years as conductor in several German provincial opera houses. In that interval he wrote two operas (the text as well as the music) and began working on what was to become his first successful opera: *Rienzi.*

In 1839 Wagner set out for Paris, determined to conquer that city in the field of opera, as Meyerbeer had done a few years before. But after three years he had made no impression on the influential musicians there; he did, however, complete *Rienzi* and another opera *Der fliegende Holländer* (*The Flying Dutchman*). In 1842, *Rienzi* having been accepted by the Dresden Opera, Wagner moved to that city; both of the above-named operas were produced there within a few months of each other, and Wagner was appointed musical director to the court of Saxony. He proved himself an excellent conductor of opera there, and also found leisure to compose *Tannhäuser* (1844) and *Lohengrin* (1848), as well as to begin the long dramatic poem which eventually became the text for his opera cycle *Der Ring des Nibelungen.*

Wagner was revolutionary in his political beliefs as he was later to become in the field of music. He joined a radical political group and took an active part in the disturbances that led to a brief and unsuccessful uprising in Saxony in 1849. In order to escape arrest, he left Saxony secretly, was sheltered for a while by Liszt at Weimar, and eventually took refuge in Zurich. There, in the years between 1849 and 1852, he expanded his musical philosophy in a number of essays and completed the poem of *Der Ring des Nibelungen.* The latter work now consisted of four related sections, and Wagner immediately set about composing the music to which the poems were to be set. By 1857 the first two sections (*Das Rheingold* and *Die Walküre*) and part of the third (*Siegfried*) were completed. In that year one of Wagner's many love affairs put an end to work on the *Ring* cycle for almost a decade.

He had fallen in love with Mathilde Wesendonck, the wife of a wealthy merchant. Under the influence of that love he began to compose *Tristan and Isolde* (he had written the text a few years earlier). But the consequent crisis in the Wesendonck family resulted in Wagner's leaving for Venice, where *Tristan* was completed in 1859. A political amnesty was granted in 1860, and Wagner was permitted to return to Germany (and to Saxony in 1862). Free to travel again, he conducted in Paris, Moscow, and St. Petersburg and heard his first performance of *Lohengrin* in Vienna. Returning to Germany, he began to compose *Die Meistersinger* (1862–67). His self-incurred personal problems, however, had not been solved. Always borrowing money on the strength of his prospects for the future, Wagner contracted huge debts wherever he lived, and he seldom bothered to pay them back. By 1864 his creditors were making threatening gestures, and Wagner again had to run from them.

Ludwig II, the eccentric and extravagant King of Bavaria, came to his rescue at this point. With the support and financial help given by the King, Wagner was able to have *Tristan and Isolde* produced at Munich in 1865 (the Vienna Opera had given that work up after some seventy rehearsals). At about this time, Wagner entered into a love affair with Cosima von Bülow, Liszt's daughter and the wife of Hans von Bülow, the conductor of the Munich performance of *Tristan and Isolde.* In 1870, after her divorce from Bülow, Cosima married Wagner. She eventually became the leading spirit of the Bayreuth Wagner Festivals, which continue to the present day.

The King's extravagance on Wagner's behalf in addition to the composer's own flagrant disregard of moral standards combined to make Wagner unwelcome in Munich. By the end of 1865 he was forced to leave that city (with Cosima) and the couple settled in Switzerland. He returned to the compostion of *Siegfried,* which he had abandoned eight years before, and began the last work of the *Ring* cycle, *Die Götterdämmerung* (*The Twilight of the Gods*) and completed *Die Meistersinger.* The prospect of seeing the *Ring* cycle performed seemed impossibly remote in those years, for Wagner had no funds and had alienated many of the influential musicians of Europe.

Wagner's grandiose plans, however, included the building of an opera house designed according to his exacting specifications for the production of the *Ring* cycle and his other works. In 1872 the city of Bayreuth, in Bavaria, offered Wagner a site for such a theater, and the composer moved his family to that city. The *Festspielhaus* ("Festival Playhouse") was completed in 1876 and the first complete *Ring* cycle was performed in the same year. Between 1877 and 1882 Wagner composed *Parsifal* and lived to see its first performance in July, 1882. In the autumn of 1882 he went to Venice for his health, and he died there suddenly in February 1883. He was in his seventieth year.

Wagner's mature works differ from Italian and French operas in almost every important detail; yet he began his operatic career by writing conventionally. For example, the two minor operas that preceded *Rienzi* are based on German Romantic and Italian types, respectively. *Rienzi* itself is a grand opera in the French style with

A scene from a student production of Wagner's *Die Miestersinger,* Indiana University Opera Theatre.

which Wagner had hoped to conquer Paris—and thus the operatic world. *The Flying Dutchman* is again of the German Romantic type, as are *Tannhäuser* and *Lohengrin.* In *Tannhäuser,* however, Wagner introduced the first of a series of innovations that were to be of tremendous influence upon later composers.

The first major innovation took the form of *continuous narrative.* The distinction between recitative and aria was completely broken down. In place of the traditional type of melody came a fluid, sometimes declamatory type that followed the text closely and that seldom was cast in balanced phrases of regular length (see Example 90). To this new type Wagner gave the name *Sprechgesang* ("speech-song"). The continuous onward motion of the melodic line was achieved by avoiding strong internal cadences; thus a division between numbers was rarely apparent. The consistent use of this device eventually led to a breakdown of the concept of the "number opera"; *Tann-*

Example 90

häuser, at the beginning of this line of development, however, still contains a few separate numbers.

The next step, foreshadowed in *Lohengrin,* has to do with short musical entities that serve as symbols of ideas, objects, or characters. Such a musical symbol in Wagner's system is called *leitmotiv* ("leading motive"). The leading motive appears, usually in the orchestra, whenever the factor it symbolizes is referred to in the text or action. For example, in *Lohengrin,* Elsa is forbidden by Lohengrin to question his origin; in its original form, the prohibition is set in the form of an eight-measure melody (see Example 91). Whenever the matter of Lohengrin's origin is touched upon, or Elsa's faith is questioned, the motive returns.

Example 91

In the years of his exile in Zurich, beginning in 1849, Wagner expanded and systematized the new ideas that had begun to appear in *Tannhäuser* and *Lohengrin,* and published them in a series of essays in the 1850's. The third of his innovations, having to do with the relationship between text and music, was outlined in those essays; it may be paraphrased as follows: Drama is concerned with ideas, situations, objects, and persons, while music expresses the feelings that are aroused by such factors. Music, however, cannot describe or identify the particular factor that arouses the feeling being expressed. To provide a firm connection between drama and music, the factors of the drama (ideas, objects, and so on) are given musical symbols; those symbols are the leading motives described above. The motives may take the shape of fragments of melody, chord sequences, or rhythmic patterns; they are presented, transformed, and developed in accordance with the drama taking place on the stage. The action on the stage is *outer action;* that expressed by the music is *inner action.* The words of the drama, along with the gestures and inflections that accompany them, do no more than define the factors of the outer action. The essence of the drama—the expression of feelings—is contained in the music, and thus the music *is* the drama.

By this circuitous route Wagner arrived at the concept of a *Gesamtkunstwerk* ("composite work of art"), in which the arts of drama, music, the theater, and other areas are blended and fused. In his philosophy it follows that since the life of feeling (the inner action) is continuous, the music must also be continuous. In Wagner's later works all semblance of separate musical numbers disappears. Strong cadences are avoided, thematic transitions connect one section with the next, and the music (by which Wagner meant that of the orchestra, not that of the singers) becomes a thick contrapuntal web of leitmotivs and musical ideas derived from those motives. An unbroken, kaleidoscopic, luminous texture made up of motives and their developments constitutes the music of a Wagnerian work.

Wagner's theories, of which only the essentials are paraphrased here, came to fullest expression in the massive cycle of four works, *Der Ring des Nibelungen.* The four works

A scene from the opera *Lohengrin,* by Richard Wagner, in which the device of leitmotiv is foreshadowed.

of that cycle—*Das Rheingold, Die Walküre, Siegfried,* and *Die Götterdämmerung*—deal with a complex series of connected episodes freely adapted from the *Nibelungenlied,* the great medieval German poem that is based on Germanic myths. Characters, objects, and ideas that appear in one work often reappear in the others, and the four works are connected by means of the many leading motives that symbolize those factors. Some commentators have identified over two hundred such motives, of which a few are shown in Example 92.

Example 92

The leading-motive principle is employed also in *Tristan and Isolde* and to a lesser extent in *Die Meistersinger,* neither of which is thematically related to the *Ring* cycle. In employing that principle Wagner welded drama and music into a unity—a unity that he claimed was missing in the works of traditional opera composers. This quality was also absent in Wagner's works from *Rienzi* to *Lohengrin;* those works are consequenty called operas. But the works Wagner wrote after *Lohengrin* are not "operas"; for them Wagner invented the term *music drama.* And *Parsifal,* his last work, was called a *Bühnenweihfestpiel* ("stage-consecrating festival play") because of its religious content.

Costume sketches for *La Boheme.*

Wagner's music dramas differ from conventional operas in one other important respect. Wagner was more interested in expressing the interaction of universal forces than in working out individual human emotional problems musically. The conflict between divine love and insufficient faith is the basic element in *Lohengrin;* the conflict between creativity and the dead hand of tradition is expressed in *Die Meistersinger;* the forces of nature and the qualities symbolized by the hierarchy of Germanic gods are dealt with in *Der Ring des Nibelungen.* The people who carry on the outer action in Wagner's works are only incidental to the main drama; in a sense they too become symbols rather than flesh-and-blood human beings. The contrast between Verdi's purposes and Wagner's stands most clearly revealed here.

Perhaps the greatest cause for wonderment in regard to Wagner's genius arises from his incredible ability to suggest specific moods or entire states of feeling in his music. Virtually every emotion of which a human being is capable is called forth at one time or another. Awe, wonder, exaltation, humor, sympathy, love, and many other mood-complexes—including boredom—are expressed; the leading motives with their transformations and developments are the instruments that make these miracles possible. Largely self-taught beset with personal difficulties, and surmounting great obstacles in having his works performed and accepted, Wagner in spite of all this became one of the most influential musicians of all time.

Post-Romantic Opera

The revolutionary methods of Wagner in the field of opera resulted in a sharp division of opinion among the composers who followed him. On the one hand German composers carried forward the leitmotiv technique and continued to place great emphasis on the role of the orchestra: Richard Strauss, with his operas *Salome* (1905), *Elektra* (1909), and *Der Rosenkavalier* (1911), was the most successful of Wagner's followers. On the other hand, the composers who reacted unfavorably to Wagner's methods and to his choice of mythological and legendary subjects developed a style known as *verismo* ("realism"), which resulted in the production of a large number of post-Romantic operas that are stylistically related to those of Verdi.

The school of *verismo* brought to the operatic stage a variety of common people with everyday emotional problems. A group of Sicilian villagers in Mascagni's *Cavalleria Rusticana* (1890), a circus troupe in Leoncavallo's *I Pagliacci* (1892), a lower-class

Parisian family in Charpentier's *Louise* (1900)—such humble figures provided a notable contrast to the mythical and legendary figures in Wagner's compositions. In addition, a dramatic, recitativelike style became typical of operas of the realistic school (the well-known Prologue from *I Pagliacci* is an example); and symbolic leading motives were abolished in favor of direct, if sensational, musical expression. The singers were restored to positions of first importance. They sang about jealousy, faithlessness, passion, and other violent emotions with which everyone in the audience had a vicarious familiarity.

The world-famous operas of Giacomo Puccini (1858–1924) grew out of the school of realism, although Puccini's gift as a melodist impelled him to write more lyrically and romantically than did other composers of the time. Such works as *Manon Lescaut* (1893), *La Bohème* (1896), *Tosca* (1900), and *Madama Butterfly* (1904) are firmly fixed in the repertoire today; their lyric charm and warm sentiment never fail to appeal to audiences.

Fragment of Puccini's manuscript for *La Boheme.*

Puccini's choice of dramatic plots and his skill in appealing directly to his hearers' emotions may have contributed to his lasting success. Shock, tragedy, suspense, and sentiment are ingredients of his operas, and in each case he composed music appropriate to the scene. An appealing episode in the lives of French bohemians provides *La Bohème* with its plot, political intrigue with sordid overtones forms the story of *Tosca,* and a sentimental love story in an exotic setting is the basis for *Madama Butterfly.*

Writing in the tradition of Verdi, but on a smaller and more intimate scale, Puccini took into account the characteristics of the human voice and adapted his melodies accordingly. As a consequence, all the music he wrote sounds natural and unforced, but also eloquent and varied. His real sense of the theater caused him to write effectively at all times; the details of each libretto are set in such a way that they are believable, even if they are often melodramatic. One has but to hear some of his best-known melodies to realize how thoroughly Puccini knew his craft. The famous duet of Rodolfo and Mimi in Act I of *La Bohème,* Colline's farewell to his overcoat in Act IV of the same opera, Tosca's moving aria "Vissi d'arte," and Butterfly's "Un bel di" are typical of the many melodic gems that abound in Puccini's operas.

Listening Suggestions

AUBER
Fra Diavolo

BELLINI
Norma

BIZET
Carmen

DONIZETTI
Don Pasquale
Lucia di Lammermoor

GLUCK
Alceste

GOUNOD
Faust

HALÉVY
La Juive

LEONCAVALLO
I Pagliacci

MASSENET
Manon

PUCCINI
La Bohème
Tosca

ROSSINI
The Barber of Seville
Semiramide, Overture

SAINT-SAËNS
Samson and Delilah

STRAUSS, JOHANN, JR.
Die Fledermaus (*The Bat*)

STRAUSS, RICHARD
Der Rosenkavalier

VERDI
Aïda
Falstaff
Rigoletto
La Traviata

WAGNER
Die Götterdämmerung (excerpts)
Lohengrin
Die Meistersinger
Tristan and Isolde

Chapter 13

THE LATE ROMANTIC PERIOD

In Chapter 11 we were concerned with those composers whose interests lay primarily in the fields of musical nationalism or of programmatic music. In that chapter we discussed only a few of the large number of Czech, Russian, and other nationalistic works and a few of the many descriptive compositions written between the 1860's and about 1900. But an interest in abstract music, in nonrepresentational works, was by no means abandoned. We have seen that a number of composers worked in the abstract field part of the time—Tchaikovsky and Saint-Saëns among them. And we shall see in this chapter that abstract music became the principal concern of other equally representative nineteenth-century composers.

To review briefly, an abstract composition contains musical material that is chosen primarily for its musical characteristics—chosen because the composer is concerned, for purely musical reasons, with its particular melodic, rhythmic, or harmonic components. This material is manipulated and developed in accordance with musical laws and practices, and the forms in which it is cast are most often the traditional forms that served earlier composers. The emotional reaction to abstract music arises out of the music itself; there are neither descriptive titles nor extramusical content to influence the direction of that reaction. The titles of such works are likely to offer only numerical and type identification, thus: "Sonata No. 3," "Symphony in B flat," "Concerto, Op. 35," and so on.

A programmatic composition or a nationalistic work is necessarily related to something external to the music. Its form is likely to be free and it often bears only a casual relationship to the traditional forms. A programmatic work is likely to be even less closely related to the abstract form than a nationalistic one. These works are filled with special effects such as specific kinds of melody, distinctive chord progressions, national idioms, and unusual coloring, in order to illustrate the program or to suggest the national element. The emotional reaction to this music is influenced by the events, objects, or ideas that are "described" in it. And the title calls attention to the extramusical events or objects or ideas that inspired the composer to write as he did. Titles such as *Les Préludes, The Moldau, Capriccio Espagnol* and *The Year 1812* are typical.

Johannes Brahms (1833–97). His works reach high levels of warmth, inspired eloquence, and technical mastery.

Brahms

The composer who best represents the field of abstract music in the late nineteenth century is Johannes Brahms. Programmatic elements may occasionally appear in his vocal and choral works; this can scarcely be avoided if the music is to carry out the implications of the texts. Nationalistic elements likewise appear in a few compositions; for Brahms remained close to the spirit of German folk song, and sometimes employed Hungarian Gypsy idioms as well for their coloristic values. With those exceptions, however, Brahms was not in the least attracted by exotic or descriptive elements in music.

Brahms was born in Hamburg in 1833; his father was a bass player of no great professional renown. The boy's musical talent revealed itself at an early age, and he began to study with Eduard Marxsen, an esteemed local musician. At the age of fourteen Brahms had already distinguished himself as a pianist. When he was twenty he became the accompanist for an excellent Hungarian violinist named Reményi, with whom he undertook a concert tour. He became acquainted with Liszt and Schumann during the course of that tour and played his own compositions for the latter.

Schumann subsequently eulogized him in an article published in 1853 in his *Neue Zeitschrift für Musik.* Brahms was thereby brought to public notice before he felt himself to be ready. Schumann assumed that the young musician would align himself with the group of composers, headed by Liszt and Wagner, who called themselves the "neo-German party" and whose purpose was to further "music of the future"—that is, program music. In this assumption he was to be very much mistaken.

The composers of the neo-German party took it for granted that they spoke for all composers, and this position irritated Brahms. In 1860 he helped to draw up a petition protesting against their principles and also circulated it for signatures. Its premature publication, when it carried only four names, caused the young composer great embarrassment and provoked a vicious attack against him. Thereupon Brahms withdrew into his shell, became an avowed if conservative champion of Classical ideals, and turned his back upon merely colorful music. The restoration of abstract music, the practice of austerity and economy in the choice of materials, and an objective attitude toward all composition—those became Brahms' principles. And in carrying out those principles he was aided by a sense of self-criticism and a capacity for self-discipline scarcely matched by any other composer.

Brahms' friendship with Schumann coincided with the time of the older composer's mental collapse in 1854. An acquaintance with Schumann's wife, fourteen years older than the youthful Brahms, developed into a romantic infatuation. Schumann's death in 1856 abruptly terminated the one-sided love affair. Other emotional involvements ended similarly; Brahms was at the point of marriage several times but always stopped short fearing that domestic responsibilities would interfere with his composing. He adopted a mask of gruffness in later years and kept his emotions under tight control.

His professional activities from 1864 to about 1878 included a few positions as a conductor and many concert tours as a pianist. Beginning in 1878, when Vienna became his permanent home, he devoted himself largely to composition. His fame spread across the continent and he was in demand as a conductor of his own works in all the German-speaking parts of Europe. He refused invitations to visit England, however, out of fear of crossing the Channel. Festivals devoted entirely to his compositions became features of the musical scene in Germany and elsewhere.

Brahms' friendship with Clara Schumann, which had replaced the youthful infatuation as far back as in 1856, remained steadfast. The death of his old friend in 1896 marked the beginning of his own decline. He died in 1897, a month before his sixty-fourth birthday. Foreign countries sent representatives to his funeral, and thousands of people marched in the cortege to honor one of the greatest masters of all time. His life had been a lonely one, and he had often been misunderstood by his closest friends. He had been attacked by the champions of Wagner and had seen his ideals ridiculed. Yet he had remained true to those ideals. Under their influence he wrote a large number of compositions that revealed a keen imagination, profound musical insight, a warm heart, and a noble character.

The key to an understanding of Brahms lies in his relationship to the past. In his early years, until about 1865, his music was exuberant in mood and was melodically eloquent in the manner of Schubert. The works of those years are primarily for piano, for voice, or for chorus; they include the famous *German Requiem,* many of his incomparable art songs, and about a third of his chamber music compositions. Enthusiasm, Romantic color, and richness of sound are typical of them. But Brahms' veneration for Beethoven and Mozart impelled him to balance heart and mind, and even the early works reveal a controlled and disciplined composer.

Brahms' relationship to the past is seen especially in his fondness for four-movement instrumental forms. For example, chamber music played a major part in his creative career, and only two or three of his twenty-four chamber music works depart from Classical forms. Brahms restored the objectively written symphony in four movements to its high place in musical literature, and in his four works in that form he revealed that the development of themes somewhat in the style of Beethoven was still a valid, powerful musical principle. But also in the manner of Beethoven, he showed his willingness to depart from tradition when his musical material made a departure necessary. There are, for example, no scherzos in Brahms' symphonies; instead, there are moderate or fast movements that have little relationship to the minuet-scherzo type but that fit perfectly into the compound forms of which he was so great a master.

Brahms' deliberate and conscious espousal of Classical practices, however, did not result in his becoming merely a copyist of earlier composers' music. Employing the same principles and techniques as they did, he went further in the direction of a thick, detailed texture, and he exploited rhythmic elements to a greater degree than any composer since the Renaissance. He was abreast of his time in harmonic matters also and had a keen ear for Romantic instrumental color effects. Thus his music represents a new flowering of Classical elements, not merely a reworking of old ideas.

The four symphonies have demonstrated their lasting qualities and their right to be technically and emotionally linked with Beethoven's. They were not written lightheartedly by a youthful composer puffed up by early successes, but are the works of a mature man who took his musical responsibilities seriously. For example, the Symphony No. 1, in C minor, was completed in 1876 after twenty years of intermittent work. It is intense, profound, and concentrated; it reflects moods of morbidity or gloom in its early movements and expresses optimism and sheer power in its finale. Its technical excellence and weighty emotional content allow it to stand beside similar works of Beethoven.

At the same time, however, the depth and quality of that work may prove overwhelming for a listener who is not prepared for the majesty and force of Brahms' music. The Symphony No. 2, in D major, composed in 1877, offers a better approach to his orchestral works. It is a clear and melodious work; it avoids the darker emotions that were so eloquently expressed in its predecessor, and it contains more variety of orchestral color than perhaps any other of his works.

The Symphony No. 2 is an economically written composition, as the thematic outline given on pages 264–66 will show. One three-note motive, heard at the outset of the first movement, dominates that movement's themes and transitional material (see Example 93). The motive is expanded, inverted, and otherwise manipulated.

Brahms, Symphony No. 2

Example 93

And a melody given to the horn near the beginning of the coda (see Example 93*g*)—a melody that is filled with eloquence and charm—is like a chain, each link of which consists of that same motive in inverted position. The entire movement is a miracle of lyric beauty and vigorous expression, achieved with the simplest of melodic means.

The second movement is a serene and beautiful adagio. Rich harmonies accompany melodic fragments that come and go in a contrapuntal texture. The movement as a whole illustrates one aspect of Brahms' treatment of rhythm and meter: many of its phrases are written across the bar lines in a way that negates the strong beat at each measure's beginning (see the two versions of the phrase in Example 94, each of which does this differently).

The third movement, like the first, makes use of a minimum of melodic materials. It consists of a quiet folk-song-like allegretto in triple meter, the sedate motion of which is twice interrupted—once by a fast duple-meter "trio" that is thematically

Brahms, Symphony No. 2

Example 94

Symphony No. 2, D major, Op. 73, by Johannes Brahms

FIRST MOVEMENT, D major, Allegro non troppo

Meas.	*Theme*	
EXPOSITION		
1	1st	First part, D major (Ex. 1)
	Example 1	
44		Second part, D major
59		Transition
82	2nd	First part, F sharp minor (Ex. 2)
	Example 2	
102		First part repeated and extended
127		Second part, A major (Ex. 3)
	Example 3	
136		Third part, on dominant of A
156		First part (Ex. 2), but now in A major and serving as codetta
DEVELOPMENT		
183		Based on Ex. 1 (meas. 2)
204		Based on 1st theme (meas. 6–8)
224		Based on Ex. 1 (meas. 1)
264		Based on meas. 1 and 2 together, plus meas. 44
RECAPITULATION		
302	1st	First part (Ex. 1) combined with elements of second part (meas. 44); hence second part is not recapitulated
350	2nd	First part (Ex. 2), now in D major
370		Repeated and developed
395		Second part, D major
404		Third part, on dominant with modulations
424	Codetta	Based on 2nd theme (Ex. 2), now in D major
447	Coda	Further development of meas. 4
477		Further development based on meas. 1 and 66. Movement ends in meas. 523

SECOND MOVEMENT, Adagio non troppo, B major

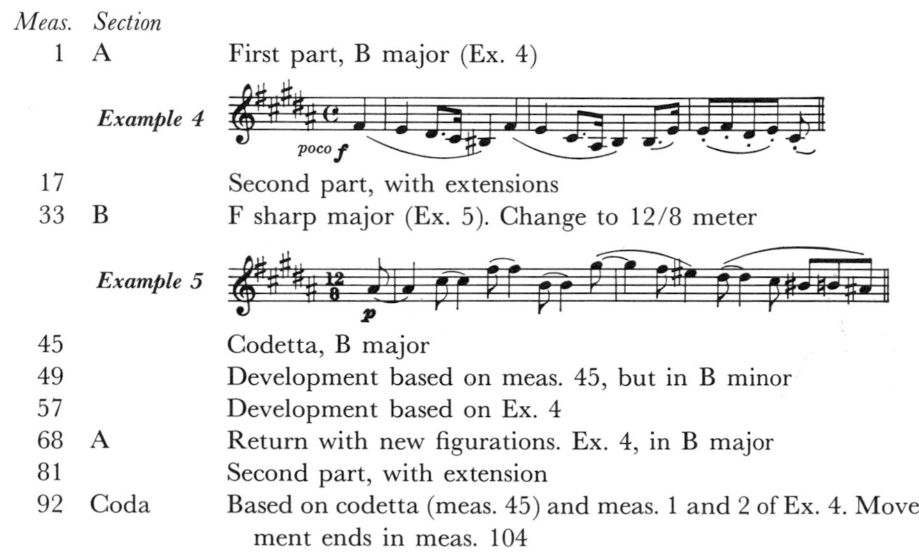

Meas.	Section	
1	A	First part, B major (Ex. 4)
	Example 4	*poco f*
17		Second part, with extensions
33	B	F sharp major (Ex. 5). Change to 12/8 meter
	Example 5	*p*
45		Codetta, B major
49		Development based on meas. 45, but in B minor
57		Development based on Ex. 4
68	A	Return with new figurations. Ex. 4, in B major
81		Second part, with extension
92	Coda	Based on codetta (meas. 45) and meas. 1 and 2 of Ex. 4. Movement ends in meas. 104

THIRD MOVEMENT, Allegretto grazioso, G major

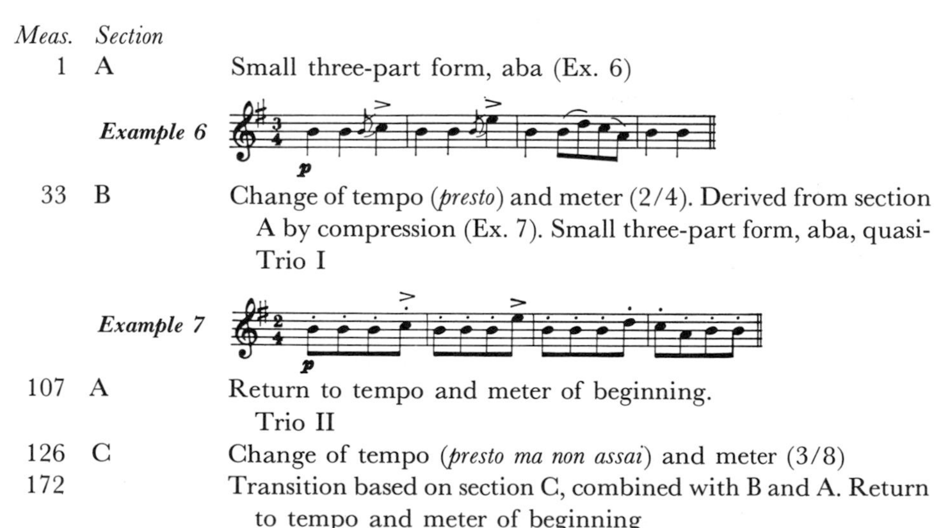

Meas.	Section	
1	A	Small three-part form, aba (Ex. 6)
	Example 6	*p*
33	B	Change of tempo (*presto*) and meter (2/4). Derived from section A by compression (Ex. 7). Small three-part form, aba, quasi-Trio I
	Example 7	*p*
107	A	Return to tempo and meter of beginning. Trio II
126	C	Change of tempo (*presto ma non assai*) and meter (3/8)
172		Transition based on section C, combined with B and A. Return to tempo and meter of beginning

Brahms, Symphony No. 2 (cont.)

194	A	Begins in F sharp major, thence to G major as expected
225	Coda	Movement ends in meas. 240

FOURTH MOVEMENT, Allegro con spirito, D major

Meas.	*Theme*	
EXPOSITION		
1	1st	In D major (Ex. 8)
	Example 8	
24		Repeated with extension
44		Development of fragments of theme
78	2nd	First part, A major (Ex. 9)
	Example 9	
98		Second part, derived from first part by extension
114		Transition
142	Codetta	In A major
DEVELOPMENT		
155		Based on Ex. 8, meas. 1–4
184		Based on meas. 9–11
206		Derived from meas. 1 by compression
234		Transition derived from meas. 9–11
RECAPITULATION		
244	1st	In D major
265		Repeated with extension; development (meas. 44 ff) is omitted here
283	2nd	First part, Ex. 9, in D major
301		Second part, as in meas. 98 ff
345	Codetta	In D major
353	Coda	Based on Ex. 8
375		From Ex. 9 (meas. 78) combined with meas. 206
387		From Ex. 8, meas. 1 and 2
417		From Ex. 9 (meas. 78). Movement ends in meas. 429

related to the first part (see Examples 6 and 7 in the thematic outline), and once by a fast section in triple meter that provides a moment of contrast but that then flows smoothly and easily back into the mood of the beginning.

Contemporary sketch of Brahms.

The fourth movement is more brilliant than the others. The movement is in sonata-form, but since Brahms made the exposition sufficiently long to permit himself to manipulate his themes in that section, he found no need for an extended development. The recapitulation also is shortened, and the listener's attention is thus directed to the powerful coda of the movement. Forceful writing for the entire orchestra, moods of triumph and vigor, and sonorous masses of orchestral tone make the movement one of the most effective and colorful in all Brahms' works.

The foregoing brief discussion of Brahms' Symphony No. 2 has stressed the thematic relationships and rhythmic complexities that abound in that work. What has been said here applies in greater or lesser degree to virtually all his mature compositions in extended forms. Brahms was always conscious of what he was doing; his craftsmanship in all technical matters depended not a whit upon momentary inspiration but rather upon the activity of a keen musical intellect. Brahms' music is "contrived" in the best sense of that word: his musical effects are the result of thematic elaboration and manipulation.

Usually his workmanship was carefully concealed. To give only a single example, the third movement of the Symphony No. 1 begins with a pair of five-measure phrases; that ten-measure fragment (see Example 95) at first glance seems to contain nothing more than limpid beauty carried by an undulating melodic line. Closer inspection, however, reveals that the second phrase is an exact inversion of the first phrase: the contours of the first five measures have been reversed to form the second five. This is a small detail, it is true, yet it discloses the direction of Brahms' imagination and the fact that he was able to combine technical subtlety and musical beauty.

Example 95

Brahms' rhythmic subtlety is further revealed by an example taken from the second movement of the Symphony No. 1. A freely moving oboe solo is accompanied by syncopated figures in the strings, resulting in an effect that seems to negate the bar lines entirely. This means that background and foreground rhythms come into sharp conflict (see Example 96). The resolution of that conflict, then, enhances the effect of the rhythmic details, and the musical effect of the passage is greatly strengthened.

In the manipulation of rhythms Brahms developed what might be called *rhythmic counterpoint.* Repeatedly in his works one rhythm is set against another. Passages such

Example 96

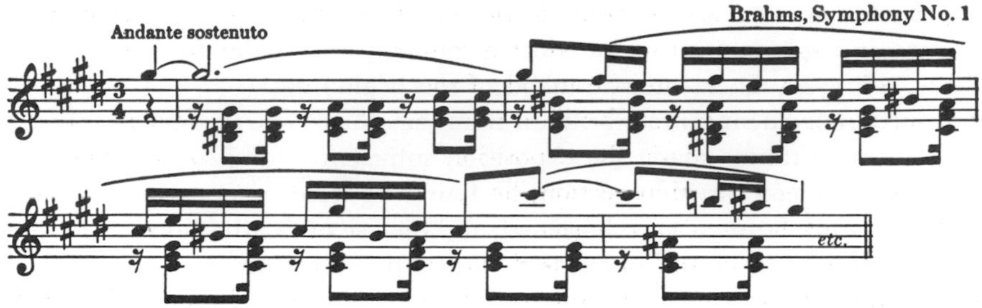
Brahms, Symphony No. 1
Andante sostenuto
etc.

Example 97

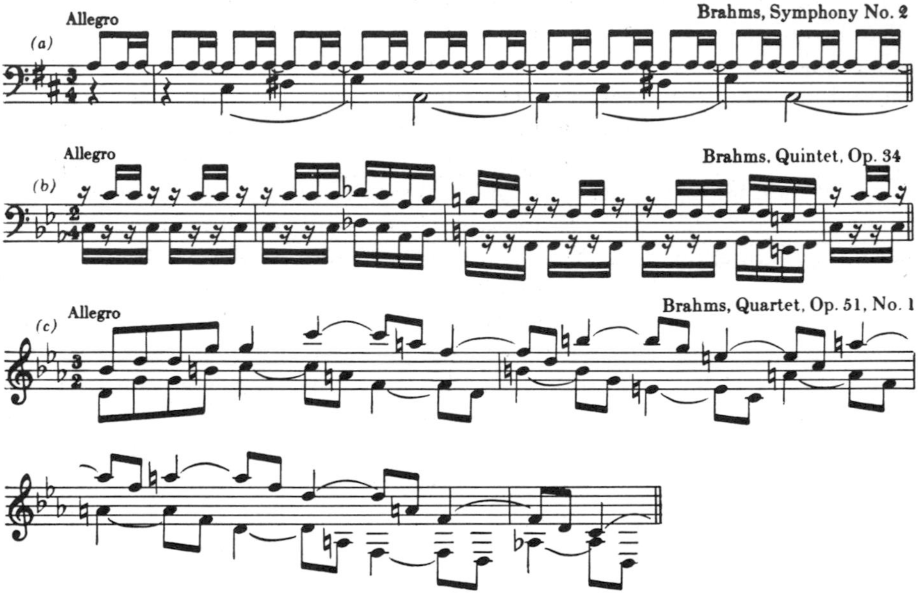
Brahms, Symphony No. 2
Allegro
(a)
Allegro
Brahms, Quintet, Op. 34
(b)
Allegro
Brahms, Quartet, Op. 51, No. 1
(c)

as those shown in Example 97 are typical. In other passages the imaginative treatment of phrase structure of the type seen in the first two symphonies (see Example 94, p. 263, and Example 96) leads to momentary abandonment of metrical rhythm within a context that is notated metrically. Perhaps the most extreme example of this is found in the Quartet in C minor, Op. 51, No. 1. In the third movement of that work, notated in 4/8 meter, an undulating melody is written so that a series of measures of irregular length is implied (see Example 98).

In addition to the two style characteristics discussed here—namely, the "contrived" nature of his music and its rhythmic complexity—Brahms' work was also affected by his tremendous self-critical sense. Brahms revised his compositions many times before

Example 98

Allegretto
Brahms, Quartet, Op. 51, No. 1
IMPLIED:

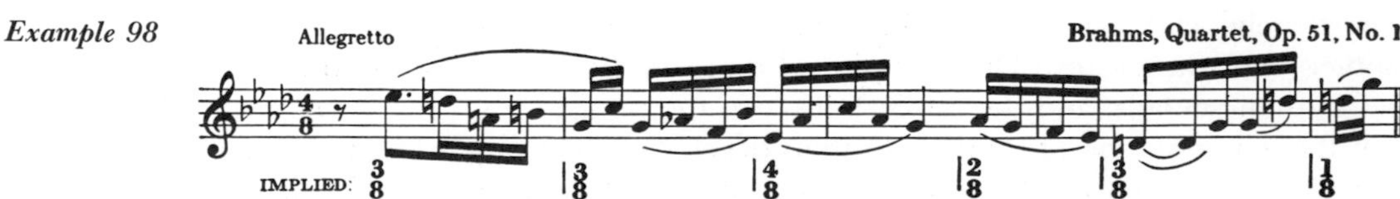

he allowed them to be heard; he did not hesitate to put aside or destroy any work that did not meet his exacting standards. For example, the Symphony No. 1 was begun in 1856; but not until 1876, when Brahms felt himself ready to be judged by the highest musical standards, did he announce the work as finished. He composed and destroyed almost two dozen string quartets before he published the two quartets of Op. 51 in 1873. And one of his earliest works, the Piano Trio in B major, Op. 8, written in 1854, was largely rewritten and republished as a "new version" in 1890, near the close of Brahms' career—probably because he considered the first version to be unduly Romantic.

With self-criticism so strong an element in his personality, it is not to be wondered at that Brahms produced so great a proportion of masterpieces. His chamber music, his songs, his piano pieces, and his orchestral compositions are all on a high level and reveal a fine balance of musical beauty and technical excellence. Particularly in the chamber music, which was composed between 1854 and 1894, is the uniformly high level of excellence maintained. That series of twenty-four works includes compositions for strings alone, for strings and piano, for strings and clarinet, and also a few miscellaneous works.

The Piano Quintet, Op. 34, has remained one of the most universally esteemed of those works. It was first composed as a string quintet (with two cellos) in about 1860. But Brahms was dissatisfied with the work in that form and rewrote it as a sonata for two pianos in about 1862. That version lacked the sustained quality that only string instruments can supply; Brahms therefore did not hesitate to rewrite it again. In 1864 the work appeared in its final form—for piano and string quartet.

In size and in its exuberant mood this quintet is typical of the works Brahms wrote before 1865. The first movement contains two first themes and two second themes, and the transitions that link the thematic sections are themselves melodically distinctive enough to give the impression of unbroken melodic flow. The slow second movement reveals, in its first part, the rhythmic subtlety that is Brahms' trademark (see Example 99); the reserved, eloquent mood that animates the entire movement is equally typical of Brahms' finest works.

The third movement is a scherzo with trio and recapitulation, but is in 6/8 meter instead of the usual 3/4. It is a vigorous movement whose rhythmic themes develop tremendous energy as they move toward the climaxes (see Example 100). The last thirty-odd measures of the scherzo proper constitute an example of controlled fury that is scarcely matched elsewhere (see Example 97*b* for a portion of the treatment to

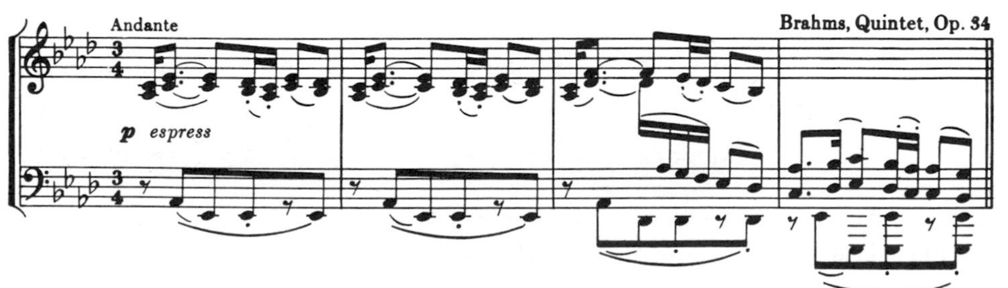

Example 99

A German Requiem, by Johannes Brahms

Soprano and baritone solos, mixed chorus, and orchestra

FIRST MOVEMENT, Poco andante

Meas.	*Section*	
1	Intro.	Orchestra
19	A	Chorus on text *Blessed are they that mourn* (Ex. 1)

Example 1

Poco Andante

Bless - ed, bless - ed are they that mourn,

Meas.	*Section*	
47	B	Chorus on text *They that sow in tears*
65	Episode	Chorus, derived from meas. 1–19, but on text *Who goeth forth and weepeth*
79	B′	Chorus, variant of meas. 47–63, but on text *Who goeth forth and weepeth*
96	Transition	Orchestra, derived from meas. 1–19
106	A	Chorus, recapitulation of meas. 19–45, on text *Blessed are they that mourn*
140	Coda	Chorus, development of motives in meas. 27–28, on text *They shall have comfort.* End in meas. 158

SECOND MOVEMENT, Moderato in modo d'un marcia

Meas.	*Section*	
1	A	Orchestra, first setting of principal melodic material
23		Chorus, repeat of meas. 3–22 on text *Behold all flesh is as the grass*
43		Orchestra, extension of motive from meas. 3–4
55		Chorus, return of meas. 23–42, harmonically modified
75	B	*Piu animato.* Chorus on text *Now therefore be patient, O my brethren* (Ex. 2)

Example 2

127	A	Recapitulation of meas. 3–73
198	Transition	Chorus on text *Albeit the Lord's word endureth*

207	C	Change to *Allegro* 4/4. Chorus on text *The redeemed of the Lord shall return again*
303	Coda	Chorus on text *Joy everlasting upon their heads.* End in meas. 337

THIRD MOVEMENT, Andante moderato

Meas.	*Section*	
1	A	Baritone solo on text *Lord, make me to know the measure of my days on earth*
17		Chorus, repetition of meas. 1–16
33	B	Baritone solo on text *Surely all my days are as a handbreadth to Thee*
48		Chorus, modified repetition of meas. 33–47
67	A′	Baritone solo, recapitulation of meas. 2–15, then extended and supported by chorus
93	Transition	Orchestra
105	C	Change to 3/4. Baritone solo on text *Verily, mankind walketh in a vain show*
129		Chorus, transposed repetition of meas. 105–14
143	D	Baritone solo and chorus on text *Now, Lord, what do I wait for?*
164	Transition	Chorus on text *My hope is in Thee*
173	E	Change to 4/2. Choral fugue on text *But the righteous souls are in the hands of God* (Ex. 3). End in meas. 208

Example 3

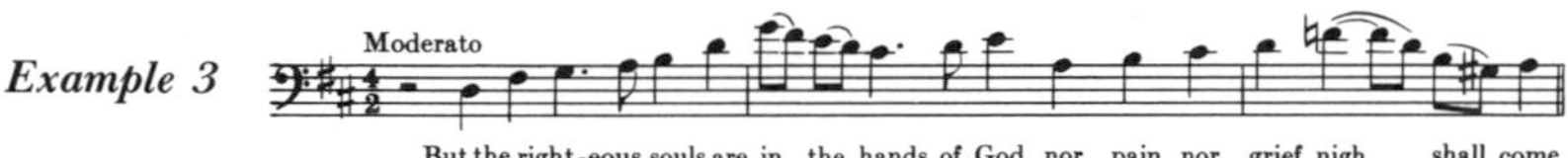

FOURTH MOVEMENT, Con moto moderato

Meas.	*Section*	
1	Intro.	Orchestra
5	A	Chorus on text *How lovely is Thy dwelling place*
47	B	Chorus on text *For my soul and body crieth out*
66		Chorus on text *My soul and body crieth out*
85	Transition	Orchestra
90	A′	Chorus, recapitulation of meas. 5–13, then developed
111	C	Chorus on text *O blest are they that dwell within Thy house*
123		Chorus on text *They praise Thy name for evermore*
155	Coda	Chorus, return of text *How lovely is Thy dwelling place* but with music derived from motives in meas. 1–4. End in meas. 179

FIFTH MOVEMENT, Andante

Meas.	*Section*	
1	Intro.	Orchestra

Brahms, *A German Requiem* (cont.)

Meas.	Section	
4	A	Soprano solo on text *Ye now are sorrowful*
19		Choral commentary on text *Yea, I will comfort you*
28	B	Soprano solo on text *Ye know that for a little time*
35		Choral commentary on text *Yea, I will comfort you*
49	A′	Soprano solo, modified recapitulation of meas. 4–19
65		Choral commentary, transposed version of meas. 19–27
72	Coda	Soprano solo and chorus on text *Yea, I will comfort you.* End in meas. 82

SIXTH MOVEMENT, Andante

Meas.	*Section*		
1			Orchestra
3	A		Chorus on text *Here we have no continuing place*
28	B		Baritone solo on text *Lo, I unfold to you a mystery.* Chorus accompanying the solo from meas. 40 in quasi-chorale style on text *We shall not all sleep when He cometh*
82	C	(a)	Change to *Vivace* 3/4. Chorus on text *For the trumpet shall sound and the dead shall be raised*
105		(b)	Baritone solo, commentary on text *Then what of old was written*
105		(a)	Chorus, recapitulation of meas. 82–104 on text *For death shall be swallowed in victory*
150		(c)	Chorus on text *Grave, where is thy triumph?*
208	D		Change to *Allegro* 4/2. Choral fugue on text *Worthy art Thou to be praised* (Ex. 4). End in meas. 349

Example 4

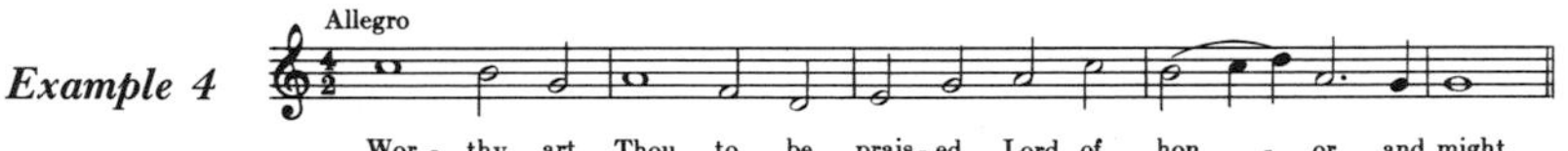

SEVENTH MOVEMENT, Maestoso

Meas.	*Section*		
1	A		Chorus on text *Blessed are the dead which die in the Lord*
34			Orchestra, interlude
40	B		Chorus on text *Saith the spirit, they that rest from their labors*
102	A′		Chorus, recapitulation of meas. 2–10, then development
127	Coda	(a)	Continuation of the text *Blessed are the dead*
147		(b)	Chorus, based on meas. 19–22 of First Movement
153		(c)	Recapitulation of meas. 144–58 of First Movement, but on text *Blessed are the dead.* End in meas. 166

Example 100

which the theme in Example 100*b* is subjected), and the broadly lyrical trio that follows provides the appropriate calming mood. The finale consists of a slow introduction and a sonata-form movement; the latter, virtually dispensing with a development section, is in effect a continuous development from start to finish. The coda of the movement reveals Brahms at his best, for here both of the movement's main themes are developed simultaneously in passages of the greatest emotional intensity.

The majority of Brahms' larger works reach the same high level of warmth, inspired eloquence, and technical mastery. In another category, and differing completely in mood, is his famous choral work *A German Requiem.* Unlike Catholic Requiem Masses—such as the well-known settings by Mozart, Berlioz, Verdi, and Fauré, which are based on liturgical texts—Brahms' work is a setting of scriptural verses of his own selection. Its aim is to console the living rather than to commemorate the souls of the dead, and in this aim it succeeds wonderfully. Particularly in the chorus "How Lovely Is Thy Dwelling Place" does Brahms reveal the depth of his feeling and the warmth of his imagination. An outline of *A German Requiem* is given on pages 270–72; it reveals how subtly Brahms chose forms that would enhance the dominant sentiments of the texts.

All of his compositions, in fact, disclose a composer whose heart and intellect were in balance and whose self-restraint never failed. This is particularly true of the more than 250 songs for voice and piano. With those works Brahms took his high place as one of the half-dozen great masters of the form. About 60 are arrangements of German folk songs; the remainder are of the art song or *Lied* type. Taking Schubert as his model, Brahms composed many songs on a strophic plan—that is, on a plan in which all verses of the text are set to the same music. The majority of the songs, however, are of the "through-composed" type, in which each verse is given its own characteristic music. The integration of melody and piano accompaniment results in textures that vary from song to song and that are wonderfully suited to express the moods of the texts. Songs such as *To the Nightingale, True Love, Ever Softer Is My Slumber, If I But Knew the Pathway,* and similar gems provide satisfying introductions to this rich and varied literature.

In the songs, in the piano music, in the concertos, and elsewhere, Brahms appears as a sincere, strongly masculine individual. He makes great demands upon his audience; there is little place for daydreaming when listening to his music. Anyone who will listen for the tiniest of details as well as to the over-all musical conception, who will listen with a fraction of the care that Brahms exercised in composing, will be richly rewarded. Only to the superficial listener is Brahms a "difficult" composer.

Dvořák

The color, eloquence, and dramatic power of Wagner's music overwhelmed the world in the years after about 1865, and the majority of the minor composers followed along the path that Wagner had marked out. In the German-speaking countries only one major instrumental composer other than Brahms wrote abstract, nonrepresentational music. Anton Bruckner (1824–96) in nine massive symphonies composed between 1865 and 1896, outwardly adhered to the form inherited from Beethoven: the characteristic four movements and the use of sonata-forms and fast scherzos. But the use of chromatic harmony, an oratorical style, great length, and lavish orchestral effects are also characteristic—and in these respects Bruckner, too, is allied to Wagner.

It remained for a Czech composer, Antonin Dvořák, to become the foremost exponent of Brahms' abstract style. Dvořák was born in Mülhausen, Bohemia, in 1841. After an unhappy childhood, during which he had some training in music, he became a viola player in a theater orchestra in Prague. His compositions attracted little attention until about 1877, when Brahms interested himself in them and aided in having them published. Subsequently, Dvořák became a successful teacher of composition and gradually became known as an outstanding composer. This reputation led to his being appointed director of the National Conservatory in New York for three years, beginning in 1892. In 1895 he returned to Prague and resumed his teaching career at the Conservatory in that city. He died in 1904, and was mourned as Bohemia's greatest composer.

Dvořák's approach to the style of Brahms was not made directly. At first greatly influenced by the music of Schubert, he later was attracted to the Wagnerian ideal of sound and to program music. Still later, at about the time his friendship with Brahms began, he became a nationalist; his *Slavonic Rhapsodies* and *Slavonic Dances* are typical works of this phase. The rhythms of Czech folk dances, with their abrupt contrast of mood, are expressed in these works, along with the melodiousness that is one of Dvořák's most appealing characteristics.

In the works for which he is best known, however, nationalistic elements generally give way to an abstract kind of expression, and to a style that often resembles that of Brahms. A mastery of thematic development is evident in all his larger compositions; rhythmic vitality and considerable use of polyrhythms are equally characteristic. Dvořák's sense of form, too, was highly developed, and his works are uniformly well proportioned.

But nationalistic elements do not disappear from his compositions entirely. For example, Dvořák remained fond of the *dumka,* a Czech elegiac form that is slow in tempo and melancholy in spirit, but that has a middle section in fast tempo and in a lively mood. Many of the slow movements in Dvořák's symphonies and chamber music are written in the national *dumka* form. One of his best-known chamber music works, the Piano Trio in E minor, Op. 90 (1890), is called the "Dumky" Trio (*dumky* is the plural of *dumka*); it consists of six such elegies with contrasting middle sections. Likewise, many of his scherzos are cast in the form of the *furiant,* an energetic Slavonic dance in triple meter.

The first performance of Dvořák's most famous symphony, Symphony No. 5, "From the New World," at Carnegie Hall, New York, December 1893. The work was inspired by Dvořák's visit to America.

Among Dvořák's more than a dozen orchestral works and about thirty chamber music compositions, several are outstanding. The Symphony No. 2, in D minor (1884–85), reveals Dvořák at his most universally appealing. The tense first movement, the lilting scherzo, the sentimental slow movement, and the exciting finale are among the most skillfully organized of his compositions. The work as a whole is a monument to Dvořák's imagination, mastery of compositional techniques, and expressive warmth. Equally delightful and brighter in tone is the Piano Quintet, in A major, Op. 81 (1887). This work contains both a *dumka* and a *furiant;* thus it is related to the nationalistic compositions of Dvořák's middle period.

Dvořák composed several major works during his stay in New York. The Symphony No. 5, in E minor, with its subtitle "From the New World," has become one of the most beloved of all symphonic works. Dvořák here expressed the spirit of the American people, but without actually quoting folk songs. He departed somewhat from his usual rigorous style of thematic development in this work, for its themes are repeated rather than developed. But he also employed the cyclical principle here (see p. 213): the first movement's themes reappear in the second and third movements, and in the coda of the fourth movement themes from the three preceding movements are quoted.

A string quartet in F major, Op. 96, and a string quintet in E flat, Op. 97, followed directly upon the "New World" Symphony; the first of these works is often called the "American Quartet." As in the symphony, Dvořák again expressed the spirit of America without alluding to or quoting specific American tunes. Passages written in the pentatonic scale (F–G–A–C–D) and rhythmic figures based on American Indian dances give these works an exotic flavor in part. In other respects they are models of traditional form and texture, and they represent Dvořák at his best. Finally, the Cello Concerto in B minor, also written while Dvořák was in New York, is not "American" in the least. It is a romantic and melancholy work in which the solo instrument is given ample opportunity to display its capabilities; it is dramatic and colorful in the best concerto tradition.

The above works are typical of Dvořák's late style in general. They express wide contrasts of mood, they are characterized by abrupt changes from joy to deepest gloom, and they are unfailingly melodious, even in their most concentrated passages. They reveal a sense of appropriate expression and a musical imagination that few nineteenth-century composers could equal. And they are among the most immediately approachable of late Romantic works in their clarity of form, richness of color, and honesty of sentiment.

Franck

In the period roughly between 1800 and 1875, French composers had concerned themselves primarily with opera or choral music; even Berlioz is represented by works set to a text as often as he is by purely instrumental compositions. From about 1875, and continuing into the twentieth century, however, the balance shifted to such an extent that many French composers devoted themselves largely to writing

César Franck (1822–90), Belgian composer responsible for the resurgence of French instrumental music, shown at the organ of the Church of Ste. Clotilde in Paris.

instrumental music. French symphonies, symphonic poems, chamber music, and allied forms took on an importance they had not had in earlier decades. Responsibility for this shift of interest may to a great extent be attributed to César Franck, who inspired a number of his pupils to work in the field that French musicians had so long neglected. Vincent d'Indy, Ernest Chausson, and Gabriel Pierné are among the more prominent of later composers who profited by the years they spent as Franck's pupils.

César Franck was born in Liége, Belgium, in 1822. He was trained both in Belgium and at the Paris Conservatory for a career as a piano virtuoso, but against his father's wishes he embraced the fields of composition and teaching. A resident of Paris from 1844 onward, he became a church organist and, later, a teacher of the organ at the Conservatory. His organ lessons, however, became in effect lessons in composition, and Franck's organ classes supplanted the regular composition classes as a training ground for the Conservatory students. In this respect Franck's influence on the future course of French music was enormous.

His life was spent in obscurity for the most part, and his music received virtually no public recognition until he was in his sixties. Even today his reputation as a composer is based on less than a dozen works written in the last ten years of his life. One symphony, a set of variations for piano and orchestra, a violin sonata, a string quartet, a few organ compositions, and two or three choral works—those are the compositions that are still performed with a degree of frequency. Franck died in 1890, when he was sixty-eight.

Franck's larger works are distinguished first of all by the use they make of the cyclical-form principle. It was characteristic of Franck to employ his themes in more than one movement of his larger works, to transform them appropriately, and thus to give those works a high degree of thematic unity.

The well-known Symphony in D minor, written in 1888, provides an example. The first movement, an allegro in sonata-form, begins with a short section in slow tempo. That section serves as an introduction, but it reappears in other positions in the main movement as well. The short motive that appears in various parts of the movement is transformed on occasion. An echo of Liszt's practice in his symphonic poems is seen here; indeed, the motive itself is very similar to the one employed by

Example 101

Liszt in *Les Préludes* (compare Examples 101*a* and 101*b* with the motive seen in Example 76*a*, p. 216).

The second movement of the symphony, containing a famous solo for English horn (see Example 101*c*), is an allegretto that includes a more animated middle section (see Example 101*d*); it is as though a slow movement and a scherzo were combined here. The finale has themes of its own, but it also quotes liberally from the second movement and contains further development of the first movement's main theme. Since the three movements have themes in common and the themes are appropriately modified when they reappear, one can speak of a cyclical principle.

A modification of the cyclical principle is seen in Franck's *Symphonic Variations* for piano and orchestra. This is a one-movement work with three thematically connected sections. The first section, a fantasy, contains two themes; the second section is a set of variations on the second of those themes; and the third section is a brief sonata-form whose main theme is derived from the first of the fantasy's themes.

SECTION	I	II	III
CONTENT	fantasy	variations	sonata-form
THEME	a, b	b	a

Parallel to Franck's use of the cyclical principle is the improvisatory nature of his music. His themes are short, in general, and usually come to a distinct close after a few measures. The manipulation of those themes proceeds harmonically rather than melodically: that is, the harmonies are altered continually, the tonality shifts freely, and a thick, chromatic texture results. Melodic motion is subordinated to harmonic variety, and long connected melodies seldom appear. Such techniques of composition would occur naturally to an organist-improviser, and Franck's reputation in that field was great. However, the cumulative, sustained, and emotionally concentrated type of writing that other nineteenth-century composers had employed so effectively is not a major ingredient of his style.

Even though this discussion of Franck's music has been placed in a chapter devoted in great part to Brahms, there is almost no point of contact between those men. It is only because Franck generally remained aloof from the concept of program music that he finds a place here. He composed two or three programmatic works, it is true, but only one—the symphonic poem *Le Chasseur maudit (The Accursed Hunter)*—is occasionally performed.

In all other respects, Franck was a man of his time. He was strongly influenced by Liszt; thematic transformation, the cyclical principle and chromatically inflected harmony as employed by Franck are elements that Liszt had exploited a generation earlier. The emotional tone of Franck's music, however—a tone called "mystical" or "religious" by some and "vague" or "naïve" by others—was not derived from Liszt. It represents a unique contribution, one that is said to be typically French. And in spite of the harmonic sweetness of some of his passages and the lack of rhythmic vitality in others, Franck's late compositions have continued to occupy a high place in the repertoire.

Listening Suggestions

BRAHMS

Academic Festival Overture, Op. 80 (concert overture)
Concerto for Violin, D major, Op. 77
A German Requiem, Op. 45 (choral work)
Piano Quintet, F minor, Op. 34
Piano Trio, E flat, Op. 40 ("Horn Trio")
Piano Works:
  Intermezzos, Op. 76 and Op. 116
  Rhapsodies, Op. 79
Songs
String Quartet, C minor, Op. 51, No. 1
Symphony No. 2, D major, Op. 73
Symphony No. 4, E minor, Op. 98
Variations on a Theme by Handel, Op. 24 (for piano)
Variations on a Theme by Haydn, Op. 56*a* (for orchestra)

DVOŘÁK

Symphony No. 2, D minor, Op. 70
Symphony No. 5, E minor, Op. 95 ("New World")
String Quartet in F major, Op. 96 ("American")
Concerto for Cello, B minor, Op. 104

FRANCK

Symphonic Variations
Symphony in D minor
Sonata for Violin and Piano, A major

Chapter 14

AT THE TURN OF THE CENTURY

During the course of the past several chapters we have seen that the changes in musical style from one period to the next have come about gradually rather than abruptly. The Classical style was transformed into the early Romantic almost imperceptibly, for example, and the two styles shared the same harmonic system, similar forms, and virtually identical instrumental media. In historical perspective one may see that the similarities between those styles are greater than the differences.

The musical events accompanying the change from the late Romantic style to that of the twentieth century, however, were of quite a different order, for the decades just before and after 1900 mark one of the major turning points in music history. The new century witnessed the decline of subjective expression, the apparent abandonment of the tonal system, a new approach to rhythm, and a new enthronement of the musical intellect. These were accompanied by the end of German musical domination and the development of individual styles in many parts of the musical world to a degree unmatched in earlier periods of music history.

The new technical approaches and aesthetic attitudes that ushered in the twentieth century signified the end of the Romantic period and the beginning of a period that has not yet received a satisfactory, all-embracing name. As in all similar instances in cultural history, creative activity in the old style did not cease abruptly on all fronts, nor did a new style come into being overnight. With decades of stubborn adherence to the old on the part of some composers, and years of experiment leading toward the new on the part of others, the transitional period from about 1890 to 1920 was a time of contradictions and confusions—for musicians and listeners alike.

The transitional years were marked first of all by a last flowering of Romantic elements. Romantic subjectivity, program music, and nationalism came to vital and sonorous expression at the hands of Mahler, Strauss, Sibelius, Rachmaninoff, and many others. Simultaneously, a new style called *Impressionism* appeared. This style, developed by Debussy, became internationally influential; it sought to provide an antidote to German-dominated Romanticism, but Impressionism nevertheless had its roots in Romantic thinking and feeling. And in the years immediately after 1900, various composers in several European countries began experiments that were to lead to a truly non-Romantic music. We shall in the present chapter discuss the representative composers and trace the principal events of the two musical streams that eventually dried up: the post-Romantic and the Impressionistic. Later, in Chapter 18, we will take up the new music of the twentieth century.

Post-Romantic Music

MAHLER

Gustav Mahler (1860–1911), born in Bohemia and educated mainly in Vienna, became one of the great conductors of his time. As the director of operatic establishments in Budapest, Hamburg, and Vienna, and as a guest conductor of the Metropolitan Opera and the New York Philharmonic Society, he disclosed great musical insight and skill, and tremendous energy. Under his direction from 1897 to 1907 the Vienna Court Opera became one of the foremost musical organizations in the world. His reputation as a composer rests primarily upon nine massive symphonies and a symphonic song-cycle, *The Song of the Earth.*

Mahler's symphonies represent a structural type that had become common in the late nineteenth century. (Brahms' four symphonies, however, are not of this type.) Older symphonies had been based on the contrast between themes, on contrasts between dramatic and lyric, pungent and suave, spectacular and intimate. In the works of minor composers after about 1870, and to a lesser extent in the enormous works of Anton Bruckner (1824–96), the symphony became a loosely constructed composition made up of an endless stream of motives or melodic fragments. A clear distinction between first and second themes, or between thematic and transitional material, or even between one section and the next was not always discernible. A fluid, amorphous texture, similar in its effect to that of Wagner's "endless melody," became usual. Moreover, harmonic distinctions between the keys of one thematic group and another were lost sight of as a result of the thickened, chromatically inflected writing that followed the methods of Liszt and Wagner.

Mahler, in typical late-Romantic fashion, sought to compose works that reflected the whole world—that is, works that expressed every facet of life and environment. So grandiose a conception allowed him to introduce the most varied kinds of music into his symphonies; for cosmic experience is reflected in the tawdry as well as in

Contemporary cartoon of Mahler.

the sublime, in the intimate as well as in the bombastic, in the sentimental as well as in the unfeeling. Folk songs and elaborate musical symbolism, chorale-like passages and involved contrapuntal textures—and all shades between these extremes—may be found in Mahler's works. Several of the symphonies include parts for singers, either as soloists or in chorus, and his texts are drawn from varied sources. Folk songs are used in his second, third, and fourth symphonies; a portion of Goethe's *Faust* and a Latin hymn appear in the eighth; and a cycle of Chinese poems is employed in *The Song of the Earth.*

Listening to any of Mahler's works provides an unusual musical experience. The quality of his orchestral sound is unique; instruments are used as individuals and a rich texture alternating between the utmost transparency and the utmost sonority results. His harmonies are often strikingly dissonant, pointing the way to the polytonality of the twentieth century. The great variety of thematic content produces a wide range of emotional responses, and the listener is led from the most vulgar expression to the most exalted. Mahler's symphonies are among the longest that have ever been written; the Symphony No. 3, for example, contains six movements, the first of which is forty-five minutes in duration. Several of the symphonies also require a larger orchestra than other composers of the time employed; additional brass instruments, complete families of clarinets, and enlarged percussion sections are often called for. Thus in size, color, and variety of expressive content, the symphonies of Mahler are unlike any other works of the period.

WOLF

Hugo Wolf (1860–1903), born in Austria, made a precarious living as a teacher and music critic. He antagonized Brahms, Mahler, and others who sought to help him gain recognition as a composer; he was long unsuccessful in having his orchestral works performed, and he died in a state of complete mental collapse. Yet he composed about 300 art songs, many of which are among the finest examples of the type. Wolf stands next to Brahms among the few great masters of the art song; his songs contain some of the most eloquent and sensitive music written in the late nineteenth century.

Wolf was greatly influenced by Wagner. He adopted some of the devices of chromatic harmony that Wagner had introduced in *Tristan and Isolde,* and his melodic lines often approach a declamatory style. In other respects, however, his style is individual. It reveals a great sensitivity to the moods of the texts; the piano accompaniments enhance those moods, and a fine balance between the voice and piano is achieved.

Wolf usually composed his songs in sets, each set devoted to the work of one poet. The poems of Eichendorf, Mörike, and Goethe occupied him from 1886 to 1889, and the resulting sets are among his most significant and attractive works. Later he turned to translations of Spanish and Italian poems and in addition composed three songs on sonnets by Michelangelo; this phase occupied him from 1889 to 1898. The style of each song is admirably suited to its text, and although the full resources of late Romantic harmony lay open to Wolf, he revealed great harmonic control and subtlety. The purely diatonic *Now Wander, Mary* is a masterpiece of restraint; the chromatically inflected *Anacreon's Tomb* conveys moods of veneration and hope; and *E'en Little Things* represents miniaturization at its best.

Wolf's songs are in general through-composed; strophic settings are rare. Subtleties of phrase structure, declamatory writing in the melodies, and contrapuntal textures in the accompaniments are set to rhythms that are often syncopated and relatively free of the measure lines. The end result is a flexible, marvellously expressive idiom, well suited to the lyric or passionate or profound texts that Wolf favored.

STRAUSS

Richard Strauss (1864–1949), a native of Munich, rose through several opera conductorships (Munich, Weimar, Berlin, and Vienna) to a position as the most eminent German musician of his generation. As a guest conductor of his own works he traveled far afield, and he visited the United States in 1904 and 1922. His mature style is reflected in his early symphonic poem *Don Juan,* written about 1888; he continued writing in that style with relatively little change for more than fifty years. At the beginning of his career he was regarded as the foremost innovator of his time, but at its end he was considered quite old-fashioned. This single fact reveals how basically musical thought changed its direction in the years with which this chapter is concerned. While Strauss was a contemporary of the musical revolutionaries of the early twentieth century, his music belongs to the late nineteenth; he was in effect the last of the German Romanticists.

Three or four of Strauss's nine symphonic poems, written between 1887 and 1915, are important items in the standard orchestral repertoire, and two or three of his more than a dozen operas are widely known. Of the latter, *Der Rosenkavalier* (*The Cavalier of the Rose*) still enjoys great popularity. The symphonic poems embrace various forms, but their musical content is invariably rich, fluent, detailed, and exciting. *Macbeth, Don Juan, Thus Spake Zarathustra,* and *Ein Heldenleben* (*A Hero's Life*) are built in sections, as are the symphonic poems of Liszt. *Till Eulenspiegel's Merry Pranks* carries the phrase "in old-fashioned rondo form" as part of its title, and *Don Quixote* is a set of variations for cello and orchestra. *Death and Transfiguration* is essentially a single movement in sonata-form with a slow introduction and an epilogue. The remaining two works are cast in movements but are symphonic poems in spite of their external form and their titles: *Sinfonia Domestica* and *An Alpine Symphony.*

The thematic outline of *Ein Heldenleben,* given on pages 284–86, serves to illustrate Strauss's method of organizing his larger symphonic poems. Almost a dozen themes or motives appear in the six sections that constitute the work. Virtually all of them appear in more than one section, and thus a high degree of formal cohesiveness is assured. Yet the contexts in which the themes reappear are always different, so that the elements of variety and fluidity are provided for. A Strauss symphonic poem is a masterpiece of organization. The copious material is skillfully manipulated both to serve the program (stated or implied) and to meet the requirements of musical logic.

Ein Heldenleben (A Hero's Life), by Richard Strauss

Meas. *Theme*

SECTION I, Moving with Animation

1 A — Contains several motives that often appear separately (Ex. 1)

Example 1

21 B — Group of contrasting motives and phrases (meas. 25–28 given in Ex. 2)

Example 2

45 A, B — Developed together in contrapuntal texture

94 A — Recapitulation of first phrase

102 Codetta — Derived from meas. 3

SECTION II, Somewhat Slower

118 C — Consists of three independent counterpoints

137 A — New version of Ex. 1, rhythmically modified and extended

169 C, A — Developed simultaneously

SECTION III, Moving with Animation

188 B, D — Based on meas. 27 of Theme B (Ex. 2) in orchestra and Theme D (Ex. 3) in solo violin

Example 3

210 E — A group of phrases with similar beginnings (Ex. 4) interspersed with expanded figurations and new themes in solo violin (see below); continues to meas. 288

Example 4

218	F	In solo violin (Ex. 5)

229	G	New theme (Ex. 6) on which coda will be based is introduced here and in meas. 256

276	D	Returns in solo violin, with extensions
288	E	Tempo changes to *Moderately Slow.* Development of phrase from Theme E (Ex. 4*c*) in orchestra
296	D	Extended and developed (Ex. 3)
309	F	Developed (Ex. 5)
323	E, F	Themes developed simultaneously
336	Codetta	Based on new Theme H, together with counterpoint derived from Theme D (Ex. 3) and Theme A (Ex. 1); brief return of Theme C

SECTION IV, Lively

369	I, A	New Theme I, together with development of Ex. 1, meas. 1–2; countermelodies derived from meas. 27
410	I, D	Development of two themes simultaneously, with countermelodies derived from meas. 27 still present
434	J	Tempo changes to *Very Lively.* New Theme J (Ex. 7)

449		Further development of Theme A, together with Themes J, I, and D and countermelodies derived from meas. 25 (Ex. 2)
556		Development continues; new counterpoint derived from meas. 68–71. The complex mixture of themes and theme fragments continues to meas. 615
616		Transition based on meas. 27 (Ex. 2) and Theme D (Ex. 3)

Strauss, *Ein Heldenleben* (cont.)

SECTION V, Quasi-Tempo I, Moving with Animation

631	A	Recapitulation of first eight meas. (Ex. 1); then a brief development
654		Portions of Themes D and B
660	K	New theme (Ex. 8)

Example 8

686		Quotation of theme from Strauss's *Don Juan,* together with a portion of Theme A
699	C	Tempo changes to *Moderately Slow.* Portion of Theme C, leading to a transition
711		Tempo changes to *Very Quietly.* Development of meas. 25 (Ex. 2), then a series of quotations of themes from Strauss's other symphonic poems: meas. 723, *Death and Transfiguration;* meas. 725, *Don Quixote;* meas. 729, *Don Juan;* meas. 731, *Till Eulenspiegel;* meas. 744, *Thus Spake Zarathustra,* etc. In addition, countermelodies derived from Themes B (meas. 733), E (meas. 737), D (meas. 764), and A (meas. 774)
781		Tempo changes to *Moderately Slow.* Transition based on meas. 705
790		Tempo changes to *Vigorously Moving.* Derived from meas. 13 and 1
828		Tempo now *Twice as Slowly.* Transition derived from Ex. 1, meas. 1

SECTION VI, Coda, Slowly

852	G	An expansion of phrase heard in solo violin, meas. 229 (Ex. 6)
878	E	Derived from meas. 240 (Ex. 4*b*)
883	D	Derived from meas. 193 (Ex. 3)
898	K	Derived from meas. 660 (Ex. 8) The work ends in meas. 927

Richard Strauss (1864–1949), the last of the German Romanticists, conducting the Vienna State Opera orchestra in 1937. (From a painting by Wilhelm K. Kraus.)

Strauss is generally held to be the foremost exponent of program music, and there is no doubt about his ability to describe extramusical elements musically. The broken breathing of a dying man is depicted in suitably broken rhythms at the beginning of *Death and Transfiguration* (see Example 102). In *Don Quixote,* the hero's

Example 102

DEATH AND TRANSFIGURATION: Reproduced with the permission of C. F. Peters Corporation, New York, owners of world rights in this composition.

encounter with a flock of sheep is described by orchestral bleatings (produced by the so-called "flutter-tongue" effect in the flutes and the brass instruments), and his flight through the air is accompanied by a wind machine that whistles and roars appropriately. Martial effects with drums and trumpets usher in the battle scene in *Ein Heldenleben*, and the shriek of Till Eulenspiegel on the gallows is depicted realistically in *Till Eulenspiegel's Merry Pranks.*

Yet the fact remains that the programs of many of Strauss's works were written after the music had been composed and performed. His audiences expressed a need to have the strange works explained to them, and Strauss then reluctantly permitted bits of poetry, explanatory subtitles, and the like to be included in the scores and the printed programs. In other words, his works become descriptive only if one reads the programs into them, as it were. Strauss insisted on many occasions that his compositions were to be listened to as music and not as musical description, and the listener may indeed derive great pleasure from doing so. A knowledge of the several programs may reveal the direction of Strauss's imagination, but except in a few cases where realistic description cannot be denied, his music requires no props.

Strauss, like many other nineteenth-century composers, employed the devices of the leitmotiv and of theme transformation. His skill in musical invention was akin to Wagner's in that his melodic fragments and his harmonies have the power to suggest specific emotions or specific character traits. The texture of Strauss's works, too, is similar to Wagner's; it is composed of a succession of melodic details that take on the function of leading motives. Those motives are altered, combined, and heard in many different contexts, and they are dressed in glowing orchestral colors. Strauss's orchestra is brilliant or somber, discreet or bombastic, as the music requires; the varieties of sound he draws forth are scarcely duplicated in any other works in the literature. Few composers have been able to write as excitingly as he; the rhythmic sweep of his music is enormous, and it rises to heights of sonority unequaled by anyone of his generation.

SIBELIUS

Jan Sibelius (1865–1957), born in Finland, is generally grouped with the nationalist composers. It is true that he was the first Finnish composer to gain an international reputation and that among his early works written between 1893 and about 1900 are a few that contain nationalistic overtones. Four legends for orchestra, of which *The Swan of Tuonela* and *Lemminkäinen's Homecoming* are well known, were originally designed to be parts of an opera based on the *Kalevala,* Finland's national epic poem. Those works may consequently be considered nationalistic in intention. A few other works, notably the short symphonic poem *Finlandia* (1899), also breathe the national spirit.

The compositions upon which Sibelius' reputation is founded, however, are abstract symphonies that contain neither programmatic nor nationalistic elements. Seven works of that type were written between 1899 and 1924, after which no major compositions emerged. The symphonies differ widely in form and mood content. Four of them contain the standard four movements; in the third and fifth symphonies the scherzo is combined with one of the other movements, so that each of these works is in three movements; and in the seventh, the movements or sections are connected to form a large, one-movement piece.

In spite of those formal differences, the seven works reveal similar style characteristics. Sibelius was given to abrupt, almost impulsive contrasts. A quiet passage may be followed by a sudden outburst of tone, as in the finale of the Symphony No. 2; or a slow-moving section may give way to rapid explosive motion, as in the Symphony No. 7. Sibelius revealed a fondness for blocks of tone, in which one entire family of instruments—the woodwinds, say—is heard as a unit and then is followed by another family. Almost every one of his works contains an extended passage in which the entire string section plays in pizzicato fashion. The prevailing orchestral colors of his compositions are dark; this is caused in part by his consistent employment of the lower ranges of the instruments.

Sibelius' method of manipulating themes gives his music a virtually unique texture and character. Themes grow out of motives, as they do in many nineteenth-century compositions, but with Sibelius the motive is not always placed in a prominent position at the beginning of a work or a movement, nor is the relation of a theme to a motive always immediately apparent. In the Symphony No. 2, for example, various thematic fragments (motives) do not attain the status of themes until the middle portion of the first movement, after which, in the recapitulation, the themes dissolve into their respective components.

With his unique methods of construction, and with his distinctive manner of handling instruments and providing mood contrasts, Sibelius developed an individual style. Almost entirely devoid of humor, serious rather than profound, and forbidding in their melodic outlines, his symphonies may well reflect the harsh northland in which they originated. Perhaps it is this characteristic that causes many commentators to consider Sibelius a representative of the nationalistic school of composers.

VAUGHAN WILLIAMS

For more than two hundred years after the death of Henry Purcell (*circa* 1659–95) British-born composers seldom achieved more than local renown. The musical life of the country was stimulated in large part by foreign-born musicians. The most active periods of that life coincided with Handel's residence in England (from about 1712 to 1759), the visits of Haydn (from 1790 to 1793), and the many tours of Mendelssohn (between 1829 and 1847). The work of Sir Edward Elgar (1857–1934), however, restored England to a place on the international scene and led to the formation of a twentieth-century English school of composition.

The leading figure of the school was Ralph Vaughan Williams (1872–1958), whose works spanned a period from 1901 (Serenade for Orchestra) to 1958 (Symphony No. 9). Vaughan Williams does not fit easily into the usual categories; his work remained individual and his style was somewhat eclectic. Certain of his compositions are in the tradition of program music. Typical of this style are his first symphony, called *A Sea Symphony* (1910), for soloists, chorus, and orchestra on texts by Walt Whitman; his second, *A London Symphony* (1914, revised 1920); and his

Ralph Vaughan Williams (1872–1958), eminent English composer whose works spanned a period of almost sixty years.

seventh, *Sinfonia Antarctica* (1952), containing material composed for a film, "Scott of the Antarctic."

In other works the influence of the Elizabethan period is to be seen. Such works include the well-known *Fantasia on a Theme by Tallis* (1910), for string orchestra; *Five Tudor Portraits* (1936), for chorus, soloists, and orchestra; and the Mass in G minor (1923), which employs a neomodal idiom. Another group includes abstract works in post-Romantic or contemporary idioms. Four symphonies (No. 3, 1922; No. 4, 1935; No. 5, 1943, No. 6, 1948) vary considerably in style and expressive content. The quiet No. 3, subtitled "The Pastoral," contrasts greatly with the harsh and dissonant No. 4, in F minor. The consonant, serene No. 5, in D major, is quite different from the strong, even tempestuous No. 6, in E minor. Similar contrasts are found among Vaughan Williams' many choral works and smaller pieces.

Apparently unmoved by the experiments of Schoenberg and Bartók in the 1920's and unafraid to remain within the system of tonality, Vaughan Williams expressed his strong musical individuality in a masterful and expressive style. There are few quotations of folk songs in his works, but the spirit of folk song is never far away. Vaughan Williams' melodic lines are direct and clear, and reserved in emotional tone. In spite of employing a harmonic scheme that had its roots in the late Romantic period, he seldom permitted excess sentiment to stand in the way of forthright, humorous, or straightforward expression.

OTHER ENGLISH COMPOSERS

In the works of Gustav Holst (1874–1934), exotic and mystical elements came to expression. Holst's best-known composition is an orchestral suite, *The Planets* (1914–16). Here, in exciting fashion, the several movements convey the astrological or mystical characteristics of Mars, Venus, and the other planets. An interest in Hindu literature led to the *Choral Hymns from the Rig-Veda* (1910) and other works based on Hindu legends. And in another category, his two Suites for Military Band (1909 and 1911) have remained favorite items in the concert band repertoire.

William Walton (b. 1902) and Benjamin Britten (b. 1913) have continued the tradition of the modern English school with a variety of outstanding works. Walton is known primarily for an overture, *Portsmouth Point* (1926), several sets of film music, and an oratorio, *Belshazzar's Feast* (1931). The latter is one of the most successful and striking choral works of the twentieth century. Compounded of strong tonal harmonies, unaccompanied recitatives for baritone solo, rhythmic vitality akin to Stravinsky's, and choral writing that is chordal and contrapuntal in turn, *Belshazzar's Feast* presents the Old Testament text in a highly dramatic idiom (see the outline on p. 292).

OTHER POST-ROMANTIC COMPOSERS

The subjective, melancholy strains found in the music of Tchaikovsky were carried into the twentieth century by the Russian composer Sergei Rachmaninoff (1873–1943), who was also one of the greatest pianists of all time. Rachmaninoff's Prelude in C sharp minor, known to every piano student, is by no means an adequate example of his considerable skill and talent as a composer. One must turn to his Piano Concerto No. 2, in C minor (1901), and to his Symphony No. 2, in E minor (1907), for a full revelation of the technical excellence and rich emotional content of his music.

The symphony is a long but concentrated work in standard four-movement form. A three-note motive, similar to the motive used by Brahms in his Symphony No. 2 (see Example 93*a*, p. 263), is the seed out of which many of the symphony's themes grow. The moods of the work range from deep pessimism to fiery energy, and the consistency of the technical method reveals a composer second to none of his post-Romantic contemporaries in skill and imagination. Those qualities are likewise apparent in the piano concerto, and there a virtuoso piano part adds a brilliance and a spectacular quality that make the work a favorite of performers and audiences everywhere.

Reinhold Glière (1875–1956), a contemporary and countryman of Rachmaninoff's, is best known in the United States for his monumental symphony in B minor, *Ilya Mourometz,* written between 1909 and 1911. The work is long, varied in content, and programmatic in intention. It describes events in the life of Mourometz, a legendary

Belshazzar's Feast, by William Walton

Oratorio for baritone solo, chorus, and orchestra

Orch. score page		*Text*
1	Chorus (men)	Thus spake Isaiah
2	Chorus (8-voice)	By the waters of Babylon
6	Chorus (4-voice)	For they that wasted us required of us mirth
9	Chorus (6-voice)	How shall we sing in a strange land
12	Baritone solo and semi-chorus	If I forget thee, O Jerusalem
17	Chorus I and II	O Jerusalem
20	Chorus I and II	By the waters of Babylon
22	Chorus (6-voice)	O daughter of Babylon
28	Baritone recit.	Babylon was a great city
29	Chorus (4-voice)	In Babylon Belshazzar the King
39	Chorus I and II	Then the King commanded
41	Chorus (4-voice)	And all kinds of music
43	Chorus (4-voice)	They drank wine again
46	Chorus (4-voice)	And then spake the King
49	Baritone solo (p. 49, 5-voice chorus; p. 51, 8-voice chorus)	Praise ye the god of gold
75	Orchestra	Interlude
77	Chorus (4-voice)	Thus in Babylon the mighty city
85	Chorus (8-voice)	After they had praised their strange gods
90	Chorus (4-voice)	Then they pledged the King
97	Baritone recit. with 4-voice chorus	And in that same hour as they feasted
99	Orchestra	Interlude
103	Chorus (4-voice)	Then sing aloud to God
111	Chorus (8-voice)	For Babylon is fallen, alleluia
118	Semi-chorus (p. 128, 4-voice chorus; p. 130, semi-chorus I and II)	While the kings of the earth lament
133	Chorus (4-voice)	Then sing aloud to God our strength
136	Chorus (4-voice; p. 138, chorus I and II)	For Babylon is fallen, alleluia
149	Chorus (4-voice)	Then sing aloud
157	Chorus (4-voice; p. 159, chorus I and II)	For great Babylon is fallen, alleluia
163	Orchestra	Coda. Ends on page 165

Serge Prokofiev (1891–1953), who led the return to a warm and appealing style in the 1940's. (From a painting by Konchalovsky.)

Russian hero, and contains passages that are sentimental, some that are descriptive, others that are boisterous, and still others that are tense and dramatic. With so great a variety in mood content, the symphony rises to sonorous and exciting climaxes. Its sheer richness of orchestral color and its melodic attractiveness make it one of the most enjoyable of all post-Romantic compositions. The composer's skillful artistry and fertile imagination are apparent throughout the entire symphony.

Other prominent Russian composers followed the Romantic tradition in part only. Sergei Prokofiev (1891–1953) developed a warm, expressive style late in his career. He began with an interest in the work of the experimentalists, and at first composed in a dissonant, percussive, and abstract style, of which the *Scythian Suite* (1914) is a notable example. His *Classical Symphony* (1917) is less extreme harmonically; written for small orchestra, it is brief, to the point, and witty. Prokofiev implied that if Mozart had been alive in the twentieth century he might have written such a work. Toward the 1930's he introduced lyric elements and intense feeling into his works; the Concerto No. 2, in G minor, for violin and orchestra (1935) is typical of this change of direction. Prokofiev was capable of charm, humor, and consonance also; these qualities are amply demonstrated in *Peter and the Wolf* (1936), a work for narrator and orchestra.

Prokofiev's works of the 1940's became even more direct and appealing. His fifth and sixth symphonies are the finest representatives of that period. Whatever harmonic changes took place in his style, his music never lost its rhythmic vitality and its clearly defined expressive purpose; its technical excellence, too, increased from work to work. Prokofiev's sense of humor also remained in evidence, and contributed greatly to the charm of his music.

Dimitri Shostakovich, considerably younger than the men discussed above (b. 1906), has long seemed uncertain of his artistic direction. His Symphony No. 1, written in 1926, revealed a witty composer who was able to write a gay tune in a conservative harmonic idiom. Later works (three symphonies and several operas among them) gave evidence of his willingness to write music that was politically acceptable; sentiment and old-fashioned harmonies became typical. His Symphony No. 7 (1941), written during the siege of Leningrad, is sonorous in the best late Romantic tradition. However, in his Symphony No. 9 (1945), he returned to an effervescent, humorous style that is filled with sentimental expression and transparent textures. His most recent works, up to the middle 1960's, have been mostly in the field of chamber music, and reveal considerable use of the cyclical form principle.

Impressionism

The subjective, grandiose, and sentimental aspects of music had reached new heights in the 1890's. The Romantic period was coming to an end, and many composers consciously or unconsciously sought new means of expression in order to restore an element of balance and proportion to music. Their efforts had been preceded in France by reactions against existing methods and styles in painting and literature. In the 1860's, a group of painters led by Claude Monet had developed a new style that came to be called *Impressionism.* The purpose of Monet and his followers—Manet, Degas, and Renoir among them—was not to copy nature in their paintings, but to recall the impression an object made upon the viewer and to capture the exact shade of light and the condition of the atmosphere that accompanied the impression.

At about the same time, a group of French poets reacted against the realism of the day and founded a movement that came to be known as *symbolism.* Such men as Baudelaire, Mallarmé, and Verlaine turned to a poetic style that sought to suggest rather than to state directly. Words were often chosen for their values as sounds instead of for their meanings, strict forms were loosened or abolished, and free verse (unmetrical and unrhymed) became typical.

DEBUSSY

Claude Debussy (1862–1918) became the foremost of the musicians who, influenced by the impressionist painters and the symbolist poets, attempted to find a musical counterpart of the new styles. And even though Debussy objected to the application of the term to the style he developed, that style, too, has become known as *Impres-*

Claude Monet, *Poplars,* a typical example of Impressionist painting.

sionism. Debussy, born in France, was educated at the Paris Conservatory and won the *Prix de Rome* in 1884. Returning to Paris in 1887, he devoted himself almost entirely to composition. Intermittently, in the years between 1901 and 1914, he wrote articles and criticisms for various musical periodicals, and he appeared on a few occasions as a pianist and conductor of his own works. The compositions for which he is best known and the works that influenced generations of later composers were written mainly in the years between 1890 and 1910.

The sources of Debussy's style are varied. His friendship with Mallarmé and other symbolists dates from about 1887. An encounter with Javanese music at the Paris Exposition of 1889 led to his interest in exotic expression. On the other hand, his second visit to the Bayreuth Festival in 1889 made him a strong anti-Wagnerian. Of these and other unrelated influences, that of the symbolists was perhaps the strongest. Debussy's music attempts to recapture the emotion aroused by events, objects, or thoughts in forms that are free of traditional shackles. The music does not actually describe the subject; although it is subjective, it is not always to be construed as program music.

His first important works in the new style were the well known *Prelude to the Afternoon of a Faun* (1892), based on a poem by Mallarmé, and his single string quartet, in G minor (1893). In about 1899 he completed a set of three Nocturnes for orchestra, the titles of which are *Nuages, Fêtes,* and *Sirènes* ("Clouds," "Festivals," and "Sirens," respectively); the last-named includes a chorus of women's voices that vocalize or hum wordlessly. The Nocturnes are among the most imaginative of Debussy's works, and they reflect all the elements of Impressionistic style.

The first of the Nocturnes, *Nuages,* suggests cloud formations drifting across the sky; the clouds change texture and form as they drift, and the music is appropriately vague, changeable, and quiet in mood. *Fêtes* has to do with an imaginary procession that passes by gaily in the restless, dancing, and scintillating light of the atmosphere itself. *Sirènes* shows a picture of the sea, with its changing rhythms, under a silvery moon; the mysterious song of the Sirens is heard, and the sea remains undisturbed. The elusiveness of this programmatic description, a paraphrase of that given by Debussy himself, is carried out in the music.

The new approach to musical form, the shifting quality of the harmonies, and the instrumental effects employed all contribute to the vague qualities of his music. Debussy's purpose was to suggest rather than state; he concerned himself more with the momentary effect of sound and color than with balanced phrases or integrated structure. A free, rhapsodic type of music best served his purpose. Melodic fragments take the place of themes; particular harmonic combinations are dwelt upon, and

Example 103

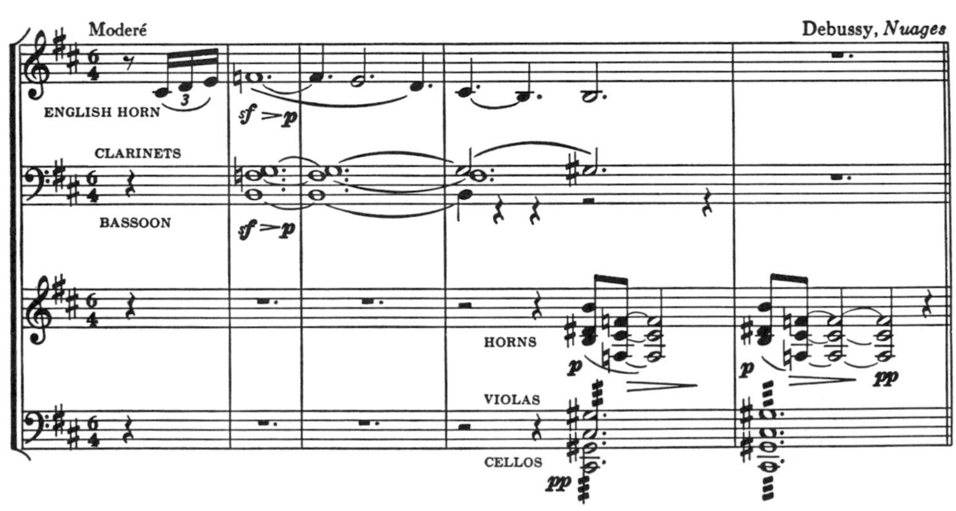

NUAGES: From Nocturnes for Orchestra (Hampton Scores, Vol. 7). Copyright Edward B. Marks Music Corporation. Used by permission.

Example 104

these may be unrelated in the traditional sense to the chords that surround them (see Example 103). Many tremolos, harp glissandos, and rapidly alternating pairs of tones give a shimmering, elusive quality to the whole (see Example 104).

A number of harmonic innovations also contributed to the new sound of Debussy's music. For example, dissonant chords were treated as entities not in need

Claude Debussy (1862–1918), founder of the Impressionistic style.

of resolution; seventh and ninth chords moved in parallel motion; consonant triads had foreign tones incorporated into their structure. A considerable amount of chromaticism in the melodies became typical also; scales that were made up of whole steps as well as progressions of elusive chromatic chords added their share to the new sound of the music. All those innovations were carried out with taste and discrimination, and a vital, colorful, and animated kind of music resulted. In other compositions, notably the opera *Pelléas et Mélisande* (1902), the set of three symphonic sketches called *La Mer* (1903–05), the three-movement orchestral work known as *Ibéria* (1906–12), and in many piano pieces, Debussy's style was crystallized and further refined; the result was music even more atmospheric and colorful than the earlier works.

INTERNATIONAL IMPRESSIONISM

In the first decades of the twentieth century Impressionism became an international style. Maurice Ravel (1875–1937) was the principal French follower of Debussy. Among the composers from other countries who adopted the Impressionistic style were Ottorino Respighi (1879–1936) in Italy, Cyril Scott (b. 1879) in England, Manuel de Falla (1876–1946) in Spain, and Charles Martin Loeffler (1861–1935) and Charles Griffes (1884–1920) in the United States. Vaughan Williams, too, in at least one work, *On Wenlock Edge,* for tenor and piano quintet, made use of Impressionistic style elements. In the case of each of these composers the Impressionistic elements were suitably modified, and the above composers were by no means mere imitators of Debussy.

In Ravel's music, for example, the subjective element was replaced by an objective, almost impersonal tone. A regard for formal clarity and for traditional methods of thematic development distinguish his early compositions from other Impressionists. The two series of "symphonic fragments" (as they were called by Ravel) from the ballet *Daphnis and Chloé* (1909–11), and the "choreographic poem" *La Valse* (1920) are among the works of Ravel in which Impressionistic elements are forcefully and brilliantly expressed. The brilliance is in large part a reflection of Ravel's genius as an orchestrator. Great variety of instrumental color, flexibility of expression, and sensous tone are present throughout these works.

Ravel's later compositions are relatively free of Impressionism and mark a turn to a style that came to be called *neo-Classical.* His Piano Concerto in G major, written in about 1930, his *Concerto for the Left Hand* of about the same time, and a few smaller works (including the world-famous *Bolero,* written in 1928) have none of the vagueness, the shimmering quality, or the elusive atmosphere that marked Impressionistic works. They substitute a regularity of phrase structure, a propulsive rhythmic quality, and a general clarity of mood that are related to the music of the eighteenth century (hence the neo-Classical label). The turn taken by Ravel was taken by many other composers also. From the early 1930's Impressionism became dated; several new styles, the results of experiments begun in the earlier 1900's, came to dominate the musical scene. Those styles will be discussed in Chapter 18.

Listening Suggestions

DEBUSSY

Prelude to the Afternoon of a Faun
Nocturnes for Orchestra

MAHLER

Symphony No. 4, G major

PROKOFIEV

Classical Symphony, Op. 25
Concerto No. 3 (for piano), Op. 26
Symphony No. 5, Op. 100

RACHMANINOFF

Concerto No. 2 (for piano), C minor

RAVEL

Daphnis and Chloé, Suite No. 2
La Valse ("choreographic poem")

RESPIGHI

The Pines of Rome (symphonic poem)

SHOSTAKOVICH

Symphony No. 5, Op. 47

SIBELIUS

Symphony No. 2, D major

STRAUSS

Don Juan (symphonic poem)
Der Rosenkavalier (opera)
Till Eulenspiegel's Merry Pranks (symphonic poem)

VAUGHAN WILLIAMS

Fantasia on a Theme by Tallis
Symphony No. 6, E minor

H·B

PART THREE The Older Music

Chapter 15

THE RENAISSANCE PERIOD

In the foregoing chapters of Part II we were concerned with music composed between about 1740 and 1940. The discussion in Chapter 8 centered upon the forms and technical practices that existed just before the Classical period; the accounts through Chapter 14 then dealt with the more significant musical changes in the two centuries after the 1740's. Music has obviously been in a state of flux during those centuries; the sound, shape, and content of a composition written at one time differed considerably from those written at another.

In Part III we will be concerned with still earlier music that again illustrates the constantly changing state of the art—music written in other forms and styles than those we have considered above. Much of that music is finding a new place in today's repertoires after having remained virtually unknown to all but historians for several centuries. Its expressive values and attractiveness are being discovered anew by performers and listeners throughout the musical world, and many contemporary composers have adopted technical procedures derived from it. We will deal with that music here not only because of its general musical interest to the present generation, but also because it leads to a clearer understanding of the music discussed up to this point.

The Renaissance

The term "Renaissance" as applied to the late fifteenth and all of the sixteenth centuries is in a sense misleading. It implies a rebirth—of culture, learning, and indeed of civilization itself—after the period that is often called the Dark Ages. The name gives the impression of a gap in cultural continuity; it leads to the feeling that the period that began about 1450 represents a new beginning. And to that extent the term "Renaissance" is unfortunate, even though it is universally employed. In other respects, however, the term is apt.

History teaches us that the Renaissance received a rich cultural heritage from the Medieval period that preceded it, and that began, musically speaking, about the year 1300. The men of the Renaissance reworked that heritage according to their own needs. They built upon a solid foundation in music and in the other arts, as well as in other areas of human activity. In so building, they created the institutions, cultural patterns, and habits of thought we associate with modern Europe. And if evidence were needed to show that music occupied a place of great importance in that culture, we have but to point to the countless references to music in the literary and art works of the period.

The Renaissance represents what might be called the adolescence of our civilization, with all the strengths, contradictions, and upheavals characteristic of that stage of life. One of the period's most significant events, for example, was the Protestant Reformation, motivated by Martin Luther in the 1520's. Many men turned away from the writings of the early Church philosophers and reached far back into the past to rediscover the literature and art works of the classic Greeks and Romans. One consequence was a growing interest in worldly matters. In the field of music, this interest is reflected in the considerable growth of secular music—both instrumental and vocal.

To the extent that they became familiar with the past, Renaissance men experienced a widening of their own horizons. The spreading of the cultural impulse called *humanism* resulted in the feeling that "natural" human concerns—satisfaction, self-gratification, love of family, and personal development, for example—were as worthy of attention as self-denial, sacrifice, and preoccupation with the afterlife.

This feeling led many of the laity, as opposed to the clergy, to express themselves creatively to a degree unknown earlier. Writers, soldiers, statesmen, artists, and composers emerged from the great anonymity that had marked earlier periods of history. Laymen whose names, biographies, and lists of accomplishments are known began to become active in increasing numbers. They expressed themselves as individuals; their characteristics and feelings were mirrored in the work they did. In the field of music, personal styles of composition became more pronounced; we can differentiate between the work of one man and another to a much greater degree than ever before.

It goes without saying that the rise of individualism was not accomplished without turmoil and conflict. The Renaissance, in addition to disclosing much that was noble

Left: A page of Gregorian chant, from a fifteenth-century antiphonarium, illustrating monophonic texture.

Below: A chanson by Antoine Busnois (*c.* 1440–92), "J'ay pris amours." In the first publication of this piece (in 1501, in one of the earliest music collections ever printed), the soprano and tenor parts, shown here, occupied the left-hand page, the alto and bass parts the right.

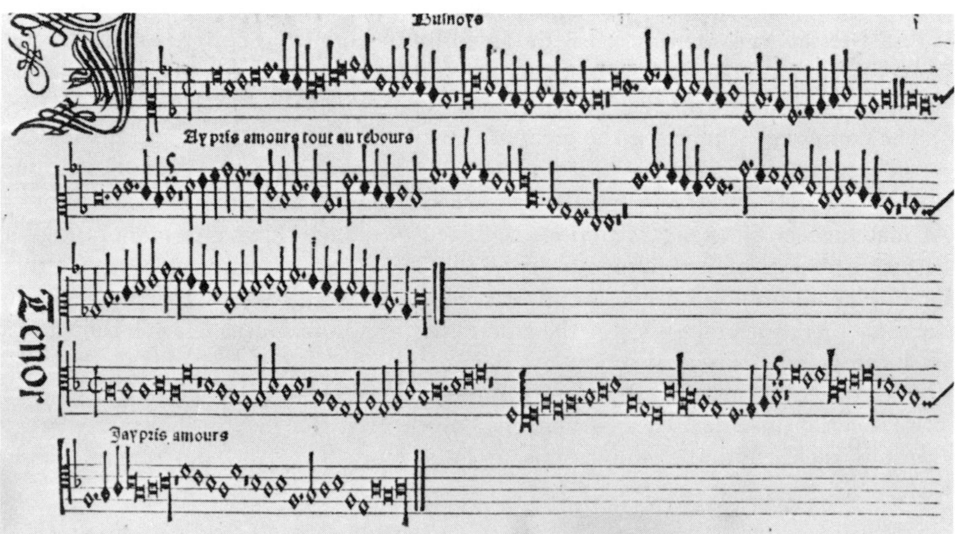

in the human spirit, disclosed also a great degree of egotism, license, and lack of self-discipline. It is perhaps here that one is most justified in speaking of the period as the adolescent phase of our civilization. Inner and outer struggle, a resistance to established things, but also a new sense of stability and beauty—such contradictions are typical of the Renaissance.

For almost three centuries after the end of the Renaissance period, its musical works were all but forgotten, its composers unknown or ignored, and its musical accomplishments misunderstood. Only in recent decades has a thorough study of Renaissance music been undertaken; only recently have large amounts of that music been heard by the public. Performances and recordings have revealed its musical beauties and have introduced it to today's listeners in an enjoyable and historically authentic fashion. Renaissance music exists today as a rich source of significant musical experiences and as a reflection of the work of some of the greatest composers of all time.

The Medieval Heritage (1300–1450)

Many of the forms, stylistic elements, and theoretical details that came to full development in the Renaissance period had their origins in the Medieval period, which included roughly the fourteenth and the early fifteenth centuries; others even antedate the Medieval. They were associated primarily with the part of Europe that now includes the countries of France and Belgium. (This generalization is valid in spite of the work of an important group of fourteenth-century Italian composers headed by Francesco Landini.)

Much of the music that has come down to us from the Medieval period is sacred music. Secular songs and a number of polyphonic forms employing all manner of worldly texts were also composed, and instrumental music was cultivated as well, although major developments in that field did not occur until the seventeenth century. On the basis of such Medieval manuscripts as have been preserved, however, it is safe to say that the concern with sacred music equalled or exceeded the interest in secular music. The two streams existed side by side, but apparently the sacred stream flowed more swiftly.

The composers who made the greatest contributions to the evolution of Medieval music were priests or monks, or were associated in some other way with the Roman Catholic church, and they naturally concerned themselves largely with sacred music. At first their chief musical activities consisted of embellishing and elaborating the vast store of Gregorian plainsong melodies that were used in the liturgy of the Church; later they began to concern themselves with composing works based on or embodying those melodies. Out of these activities grew the musical forms that served later composers for several centuries.

The concept of metrical rhythm is another Medieval contribution to music; composers of the time devised a system of notation that made it possible for them to transmit their rhythmic innovations to later musicians. And polyphonic texture itself, the unique possession of music of the Western world, was developed by Medieval musicians and their predecessors, many of whom are unknown to music history. Working quietly in monasteries for the most part, these composers evolved various techniques for employing two or three melodies (seldom more) simultaneously, techniques that are still in use today.

Medieval musicians employed a system of scales or tonal formulas that are unlike the major and minor scales that underlie music from the seventeenth century onward. The term "modal system" (as opposed to the tonal system of our own time) is applied to these scale formulas, and individual scales are called *church modes* or *Medieval modes.* The archaic or other-worldly effect of much Medieval (as well as Renaissance) music, felt especially at phrase ends and cadences, results largely from the use of these modes rather than the major or minor scales familiar to us today.

Thus in the areas of polyphony, rhythmic notation, musical form, and the modal system itself, Medieval musicians made direct and important contributions to the Renaissance. In the pages to follow we shall examine those contributions in some detail and describe some of the sixteenth-century music that is so greatly indebted to the composers and theorists of the Medieval period.

Modes in the Renaissance Period

It seems likely that much of the early development of the church modes took place in Rome or under direct Roman influence for the first thousand years of the Christian era. Gradually, however, the chief centers of composition moved northward. From about the twelfth century they appeared in southern and northern France, and in the Medieval period they reached high levels of accomplishment in Burgundy, Flanders, and elsewhere in the Netherlands. Each of the centers had its period of glory, after which it declined; but each center made notable contributions to the art of composition while it remained active. And each one came closer to the formulation of the definitive form of the modes in the Renaissance period.

The speculations of the philosophers in the field of music theory were accompanied—and often preceded—by the activities of the composers who carried the art forward. One of the principal modifications occurring early in the Renaissance was a concern with four-part writing as opposed to the three-part writing that had characterized much of the Medieval period. The vocal quartet (soprano, alto, tenor, bass) introduced by early Renaissance masters such as Johannes Okeghem (*circa* 1430–95) and Jacob Obrecht (1452–1505) has remained a mainstay of choral music to the present day. Further, the equality of all the voices in a polyphonic texture was established, especially in the works of Okeghem. The old domination of one voice over the others was abolished, and all voices took equal part in forming the web of melodies. Cadence forms and melodic inflections approached such a degree of standardization that one may speak of a Renaissance style. All these developments took place within the framework of the modal system and gradually brought about changes in the system itself. In 1547 a Swiss theorist, Henricus Glareanus, published a treatise, the *Dodecachordon,* that summarized the modal developments of the past and established a theoretical basis for recognizing twelve modes. Glareanus' theory was modified by an Italian, Gioseffe Zarlino, a few years later, at which time the modes reached their final form.

One mode is differentiated from another by its formula of half steps and whole steps, its range, and its *finalis,* which is the last (or first) tone of the mode. Example 105 contains a few typical Renaissance melodies together with the series of tones

Example 105

on which they are based. The tones are arranged in ascending order with the half steps indicated by brackets. In each example a different formula of half and whole steps results. The series of tones in Example 105*a*, with its half-steps between 2–3 and 6–7 and its *finalis* on D, constitutes one mode; that in Example 105*b*, with half steps between 3–4 and 6–7 and *finalis* on G, is another; and Example 105*c*, with half steps between 2–3 and 5–6 and *finalis* on A, yet another. Other modes beginning on C, E, and F, each with its individual formula, are also parts of the system.

Theoretically each mode embraced the range of an octave; but an extension of that range by one or two tones beyond the *finalis* is often found. The *finalis* itself took on greater importance than the other tones. (This is analogous to the place of the tonic in a major or minor scale.) A melody written in a particular mode made use of the mode in one of two forms: either the melody was confined to the octave range (plus a tone or two) between the lower and upper finals, as are the melodies in Example 105; or the melody descended to a fourth below and ascended to a fifth above the final (again plus a tone or two). The two forms of the mode were called the *authentic* and the *plagal,* respectively. (The plagal modes have names using the prefix *hypo,* which is Greek for "below.") The six authentic and six plagal modes, together with their respective names, are shown in Example 106. They represent the forms arrived at by Glareanus in the mid-sixteenth century.

A glance at Example 106 reveals that any mode may be reproduced at the piano by selecting the proper final and playing only the white keys. Further, it shows that the Ionian mode is identical with what we know as the C major scale, and that the Aeolian mode is identical with the descending form of the A minor scale. It happens

that the Ionian and Aeolian modes were among those used as prototypes for the twelve major and twelve minor scales in the seventeenth century, at which time the other modes fell victims to historical evolution and declined in usefulness.

Let us again refer to the differences in sound and effect between modal music (which is based on the modes) and tonal music (which employs the major and minor scales). A composition written in the strict Lydian mode (on F), for example, will normally employ B naturals; whereas a work in F major will contain B flats. Similarly, a composition in the Mixolydian mode (based on G and with a whole step between G and F) will usually lack the distinctive half step between G and F sharp that is characteristic of a composition in G major (see Example 105). The same is true for all the other modes. The melodic cadences, the succession of implied chords, the very shape of the melodies—such elements will have qualities in modal music unlike those in tonal music; the different arrangements of half and whole steps in the two kinds of musical formulas are responsible. If the listener becomes aware of details seemingly as insignificant as the location of the half steps in a modal work, he will understand the source of many of the musical effects he experiences, and his enjoyment of each work will be increased accordingly.[1]

[1] In the sixteenth century a technique called *musica ficta* did much to affect the integrity of the various modes. See Willi Apel, *Harvard Dictionary of Music,* for an account of this development.

Renaissance Forms and Practices

The early Renaissance composers were greatly indebted to their Medieval predecessors in three ways: for the modal system (as we have seen), for a number of techniques for manipulating two or more melodies simultaneously, and for several of the forms that remained current to the end of the period and beyond—notably the motet and the Mass.

THE MOTET

The motet is the form in which much of the sacred music of the Medieval and Renaissance periods was written. A motet text is usually drawn from the Book of Psalms and is set in polyphonic style for three to six or more voices. The requirements of the text itself determine the form of the music, in the sense that the brevity or length of the prose passage being set determines whether the motet is to be short or long. Since the accompanying texts are seldom symmetrical, musical symmetry is rare in this type of composition.

The device of melodic imitation most often characterizes the motet. Example 107*a* gives the beginning of a motet by Orlando di Lasso, one of the greatest of late Renaissance composers. This brief excerpt shows that the first measures of the

The National Gallery, London

"A Concert," by Ercole de Roberti (1430–96), illustrating the Renaissance lute. In the foreground, a pochette, a dancing-master's pocket violin.

Example 107

soprano melody are imitated by the other voices in turn; the melodic contour and rhythmic pattern of the one are imitated by the other voices, but after the first few tones each melody is free to take its own course. This procedure of freely imitating the beginning of the principal melody is typical of the great majority of sixteenth-century motets. (But see Example 11*c*, p. 21, for a motet that does not employ imitation.)

Occasionally, at the point where a new sentence or paragraph of the text begins, a new melody is introduced; the other voices then imitate that new melody instead of continuing with the old. At the ends of textual sections or at climactic points in the motet, the imitative writing often gives way to a chordal texture, as Example 107*b* illustrates. This free mixture of musical textures results in expressive variety, richness, and flexibility of form. Moods ranging from divine joy to deepest melancholy are found in Renaissance motets, and the motet literature contains some of the most dignified as well as some of the most exuberant music in the entire choral repertoire.

THE MASS

The Mass is the solemn service of the Roman Catholic church that commemorates the sacrifice of Christ on the Cross. As such, and considered only in its liturgical function, the Mass would have little place in a book devoted to the needs of the concert-goer. However, selected musical portions of the Mass are often separated from the liturgical actions they are designed to accompany and are performed as concert pieces. For this reason, then, a consideration of the Mass as a musical form, quite apart from its religious significance, is appropriate.

During its long history, which began perhaps in the second century, the Mass has undergone many changes in style. For several centuries it was chanted by priest and choir to plainsong melodies that reach back to the beginning of the Christian era. From the mid-fourteenth century through the sixteenth—namely, the period with which we are concerned here—it was usually composed as a polyphonic work for choir with or without instrumental support. Many different kinds of musical treatment were applied to it, resulting in several different types of Masses. Yet through all these changes of style, the liturgical text was unaltered.

In its complete form, the Mass consists of a number of Latin prayers and psalms in addition to eighteen textual parts mentioned below. Some of the eighteen parts are spoken, others are chanted or sung. They are divided into two classes: those with variable texts and those whose texts are invariable. The variable texts are reserved for or are proper to specific days of the Church year, hence are called the *Proper of the Mass.* The invariable texts are appropriate throughout the year, regardless of the season; they constitute the *Ordinary of the Mass.* On the basis of this fourfold division (spoken or sung, Proper or Ordinary), the classification shown in the table on the facing page may be made.

The phrase that may be chanted at the end of the service, *"Ite, missa est,"* signifies "Go, (the congregation) is dismissed." From this word of dismissal comes the term that is applied to the entire service: *missa, messe, Messe,* and *Mass* in Latin or Italian, French, German, and English respectively.

In a musical context, however, the term "Mass" usually refers only to the five sung sections of the Ordinary that appear within the rectangle in column 4 of the table. Those sections have especially interested composers from the fourteenth century onward; for since the five texts were invariable throughout the Church year, a musical setting of the texts would receive a considerable number of performances. Conversely, a musical setting of a text of the Proper would be performed only on the day for which that text was set aside.

It is those sung sections or movements of the Ordinary, then, that we have in mind whenever the Mass is referred to in this book. The *Sanctus* and *Benedictus* were long considered to be one unit and are found as such in the liturgical books of the

PATROCINIVM MVSICES.

LAVDATE DOMINVM OMNES GENTES

ORLANDI DE LASSO,
Illuſtriſs: Ducis Bauariæ, Chori Magiſtri,
MISSÆ ALIQVOT
Quinque vocum.
SECVNDA PARS.
Illuſtriſs: Principis D. GVILHELMI Comitis Palatini Rheni, vtriusq; Bauariæ Ducis, liberalitate in lucem editum.
Monachij excudebat Adamus Berg.
M. D. LXXIIII.

Title page of a Mass by Orlando di Lasso.

Structure of the Mass

Spoken		Chanted or Sung	
PROPER	ORDINARY	PROPER	ORDINARY
		1. Introit	
			2. *Kyrie*
			3. *Gloria*
4. Collect			
5. Epistle			
		6. Gradual	
		7. *Alleluia* or Tract	
8. Gospel			
			9. *Credo*
		10. Offertory	
11. Secret			
12. Preface			
			13. *Sanctus* (with *Benedictus*)
	14. Canon		
			15. *Agnus Dei*
		16. Communion	
17. Post-Communion			
			18. *Ite, Missa est* or *Benedicamus Domino*

Church. For almost four centuries, however, in choral settings of the Mass text, the *Sanctus* and *Benedictus* have usually been treated as separate movements; and the five numbered sections shown in column 4 become six in the majority of the musical settings. The texts of the six sung parts of the Ordinary are given on pages 314–15 (the Kyrie is Greek, the others are Latin).

Even though the text of the Mass remained unaltered through many changes of musical style, the forms in which the texts were set changed considerably from time to time. At the high point in the history of Mass composition, namely in the late Renaissance period, the Mass was most often set in motet forms—that is, the various movements were composed in a polyphonic, imitative style. Three, four, or five voice parts usually sufficed the composers of the time, and the polyphonic texture

1. KYRIE

Kyrie eleison. Christe eleison. Kyrie eleison.

Lord, have mercy upon us. Christ, have mercy upon us. Lord, have mercy upon us.

2. GLORIA

Gloria in excelsis Deo. Et in terra pax hominibus bonæ voluntatis. Laudamus te. Benedicimus te. Adoramus te. Glorificamus te. Gratias agimus tibi propter magnam gloriam tuam. Domine Deus, Rex cœlestis, Deus Pater omnipotens. Domine Fili unigenite, Jesu Christe. Domine Deus, Agnus Dei, Filius Patris. Qui tollis peccata mundi, miserere nobis. Qui tollis peccata mundi, suscipe deprecationem nostram. Qui sedes ad dexteram Patris, miserere nobis. Quoniam tu solus Sanctus. Tu solus Dominus. Tu solus altissimus, Jesu Christe. Cum Sancto Spiritu, in gloria Dei Patris. Amen.

Glory be to God in the highest. And on earth peace to men of good will. We praise Thee. We bless Thee. We adore Thee. We glorify Thee. We give Thee thanks for Thy great glory. O Lord God, heavenly King, God the Father almighty. O Lord Jesus Christ, the only-begotten Son. Lord God, Lamb of God, Son of the Father. Who taketh away the sins of the world, have mercy on us. Who taketh away the sins of the world, receive our prayer. Who sitteth at the right hand of the Father, have mercy on us. For Thou alone art holy. Thou alone art Lord. Thou alone, O Jesus Christ, art most high. Together with the Holy Ghost, in the glory of God the Father. Amen.

3. CREDO

Credo in unum Deum, Patrem omnipotentem, factorem cœli et terræ, visibilium omnium, et invisibilium. Et in unum Dominum Jesum Christum, Filium Dei unigenitum. Et ex Patre natum ante omnia sæcula. Deum de Deo, lumen de lumine. Deum verum de Deo vero. Genitum, non factum, consubstantialem Patri: per quem omnia facta sunt. Qui propter nos homines, et

I believe in one God, the Father almighty, maker of heaven and earth, and of all things visible and invisible. And in one Lord Jesus Christ, the only-begotten Son of God. Born of the Father before all ages. God of God, light of light, true God of true God. Begotten, not made; of one substance with the Father: by whom all things were made. Who for us men, and for propter nostram salutem descendit de cœlis. Et incarnatus est de Spiritu Sancto ex Maria Virgine; et homo factus est. Crucifixus etiam pro nobis; sub Pontio Pilato passus, et sepultus est. Et resurrexit tertia die, secundum Scripturas. Et ascendit in cœlum: sedet ad dexteram Patris. Ex iterum venturus est cum gloria judicare vivos, et mortuos: cujus regni non erit finis. Et in Spiritum Sanctum, Dominum et vivificantem: qui ex Patre Filioque procedit. Qui cum Patre, et Filio simul adoratur, et conglorificatur: qui locutus est per prophetas. Et unam, sanctam, catholicam et apostolicam Ecclesiam. Confiteor unum baptisma in remissionem peccatorum. Et expecto resurrectionem mortuorum. Et vitam venturi sæculi. Amen.

our salvation, came down from heaven. And was made flesh by the Holy Ghost of the Virgin Mary: and was made man. He was also crucified for us, suffered under Pontius Pilate, and was buried. And on the third day He rose again, according to the Scriptures. And ascended into heaven: He sitteth at the right hand of the Father. And He shall come again with glory to judge the living and the dead; and of His Kingdom there shall be no end. And in the Holy Ghost, the Lord and Giver of life, who proceedeth from the Father and the Son. Who together with the Father and the Son is adored and glorified: who spoke by the prophets. And in one, holy, catholic and apostolic Church. I confess one baptism for the remission of sins. And I expect the resurrection of the dead. And the life of the world to come. Amen.

4. SANCTUS

Sanctus, Sanctus, Sanctus, Dominus Deus Sabaoth. Pleni sunt cœli et terra gloria tua. Osanna in excelsis.

Holy, Holy, Holy, Lord God of hosts. Heaven and earth are filled with Thy glory. Hosanna in the highest.

5. BENEDICTUS

Benedictus qui venit in nomine Domini. Osanna in excelsis.

Blessed is He that cometh in the name of the Lord. Hosanna in the highest.

6. AGNUS DEI

Agnus Dei, qui tollis peccata mundi, miserere nobis. Agnus Dei, qui tollis peccata mundi, dona nobis pacem.

Lamb of God, who taketh away the sins of the world, have mercy on us. Lamb of God, who taketh away the sins of the world, grant us peace.

that resulted from the manipulation of the several melodies became a wonderfully flexible and expressive medium for such masters as Palestrina, Lasso, and Vittoria. In short setting of the Mass, each of the six movements was continous in the manner of a motet. In longer or more elaborate settings, cadences at the ends of sentences or paragraphs of the text interrupted the forward motion and made each movement essentially a series of connected motets.

THE CANTUS FIRMUS

One of the contrapuntal techniques inherited by Renaissance composers involved the use of the *cantus firmus,* which may be translated as "fixed melody." In its earliest form as used in the Medieval period, the *cantus firmus* was a fragment of Gregorian plainsong, itself centuries old. In a typical case the melodic fragment was stretched out into a series of long sustained tones; around and above this elongated version of the melody, other newly composed melodies in normal tonal lengths were woven. The *cantus firmus* was usually given to the voice that later came to be called the tenor. This fact, incidentally, throws light on the original meaning of "tenor"—namely, the voice part that contained the "held" tones. (Compare the Latin *tenere,* "to hold," and our own English words "tenant," "tenable," and "tenacious.")

Celebration of the Mass, from *Encomium Musices* (1590). A Latin text accompanies the original engraving; the translation reads in part: "The church nourishes divine worship with musical arts and adorns the mysteries with sacred songs. The horn sounds the *Sacris Dulce* . . . the pipes harmonize with the Etruscan bronze (trumpet) . . ."

Example 108

An early example of the *cantus firmus* technique, applied to a motet by an anonymous Parisian composer of the mid-thirteenth century, is shown in Example 108. The beginning of the original plainsong is given in Example 108*a*, with the fragment that serves as a *cantus firmus* marked by the bracket. Example 108*b* shows the beginning of the Medieval motet that is based on that fragment.

At later stages in the evolution of the technique, melodies other than Gregorian plainsong were employed and the practice of elongating the original melody was often abandoned. In the latter case the borrowed melody appeared in a rhythmic shape close to that of the original and in voices other than the tenor. Secular tunes, folk songs, and other melodies found their way into contrapuntal compositions in this manner. Also, a melody from a work by one composer was often used in a Mass written by another. An outline of a *cantus firmus* Mass employing a Gregorian plainsong fragment, by the Renaissance composer Josquin des Prez, is given on pages 322–24.

In other Renaissance Masses, not only a *cantus firmus* but all the voices of a preexisting composition were used. The resulting form is called a *parody Mass,* for the reason that the earlier work (a motet or a secular song, for example) is freely elaborated, paraphrased, or parodied in the new work. (In spite of the usual meaning of parody, there is no satirical or humorous connotation involved in this form.) Often, as a result of this practice, Renaissance compositions are known by the name of the *cantus firmus* or other work on which they are based. Outstanding examples are Okeghem's *Missa L'Homme Armé* (Mass on the popular song *The Armed Man*); Cavazzoni's organ piece *Canzona super Falte d'Argens* (Chanson on Lack of Money, itself a song by Josquin des Prez); and Monte's *Missa super Cara la Vita* (Mass on *My Dear Life,* a madrigal by Jacob van Wert). The relationship between the *cantus firmus* technique illustrated in many Renaissance works and the *basso ostinato* technique as used by composers from Bach to Brahms is relatively close (see Examples 119 and 120, pp. 360–61).

RHYTHMIC PRACTICES

The manner in which the melodies in Example 105 (p. 308) were notated (that is, without bar lines or measures) calls attention to another characteristic of Renaissance and earlier music, one that is obscured in modern editions and performances alike. When compared to the familiar metrical rhythms of music from the seventeenth century to the present day, the rhythms of Renaissance music may often seem unclear and the prevailing polyphonic texture may seem cloudy. These qualities are not native to the music, but result from faulty performances or from a misunderstanding of the nature of Renaissance rhythm.

An overwhelming majority of the sacred works of the Renaissance are choral compositions set to prose texts. The vocal polyphonic texture and the technique of contranpuntal imitation (see Example 107, p. 311) make textual overlapping almost inevitable. One voice frequently enters with a phrase of the text at a moment when each of the other voices is singing a different word of the same phrase (see Example 112, p. 321, in the last beat of the second measure, where *-te, -mus,* and *Lau-* are sung together). In Renaissance music the normal textual accents usually determine the musical accents as well. For example, in a five-voice motet by the English composer William Byrd (*circa* 1543–1623), the following phrase occurs: *Justorum animae*

Example 109

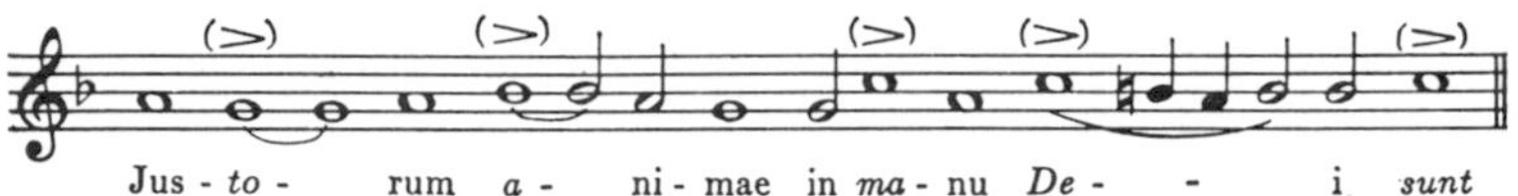

in manu Dei sunt ("The souls of the righteous are in the hands of God"). In the first soprano part Byrd has set that phrase as seen in Example 109. The normal word accents, shown by Italic type in the text and by musical accents in the melody, are mirrored in the melodic line itself, for the tones carrying the accented syllables are either longer or higher than the tones surrounding them and thus attract more attention to themselves. Other voices set to the same text have different melodic lines and enter at different moments, so that the accents in the various parts do not always coincide.

The melodies shown in Example 105 (p. 308) and Example 109 may offer some difficulty to today's singers because they are not divided into the familiar measures: the bar lines are missing. Renaissance choral composers seldom made use of bar lines until late in the period. The conditions under which their singers performed made the indication of measures unnecessary. Each singer read from a portion of a page that contained only the music for his part, and full scores were a late arrival on the Renaissance scene. In modern editions, however, bar lines are often supplied to mark out measures—and the whole concept of metrical rhythm implies an accent on the first beat of every measure. Difficulty arises in the process of forcing unmetrical (prose) phrases into a metrical notational scheme.

To return to Byrd's motet: the first phrase is shown with modern barring in Example 110, and the note picture that results is one in which a metrical rhythm is seemingly appropriate. As a consequence, however, a group of singers trained only in Classical or Romantic music will place accents at the beginning of each full measure. First sopranos and altos will accent *in* (measure 8) because it is on a strong beat, but will fail to accent the following syllable *ma-* (which according to the prose

Byrd, *Justorum animae* *Example 110*

meter should have a strong accent) because it is on a weak beat of the music. Similar rhythmic distortions will occur in the other parts as well.

If Example 110 is rescored in a way that allows the proper rhythmic values to appear, the notation shown in Example 111 results. In each voice part the bar lines have been placed before the word accents only. Each part now contains its own free

Byrd, *Justorum animae* *Example 111*

rhythmic scheme; accents coincide in all five parts only on the word *animae* and *sunt.* In its entirety, the passage embodies what might be called a polyrhythmic texture; one prose rhythm is set against another, just as one melody is set against another in a polyphonic texture. The expressive subtleties of the music are mirrored in the notation, and thus the singers are able to reflect those subtleties in performance and comply with the composer's intent.

Hearing such a correct performance, the listener becomes aware of a unique characteristic of Renaissance and earlier music: what formerly seemed stiff or unclear is now seen to be marvelously organized and fascinating in its effect. The momentary conflicts between the rhythmic background (the even succession of beats) and the foreground (the musical accents that coincide with the word accents in the several parts), as well as the conflicts between one foreground rhythm and another, can be experienced fully. And the resolution of those conflicts at climactic points or at phrase ends (as on the word *sunt*) provides a feeling of musical satisfaction.

This rhythmic aspect of Renaissance music is one of its greatest charms, and it proves rewarding to the perceptive listener. Many composers, from Okeghem in the 1450's to the Elizabethan madrigalists in the early 1600's (see below, p. 328ff) are plentifully represented on today's concert stage and in recordings. With the concept of polyrhythm in mind the listener can profit from all these performances—even when the performers themselves are not clear on this point.

Josquin des Prez

One of the characteristics of the Flemish composers at the beginning of the Renaissance period was a willingness to leave their homeland. Because of their artistry and skill they were greatly sought after by the noblemen and church officials of the time, and were able to find employment in all corners of Europe. Okeghem, for example, worked in various parts of France and visited Spain for a two-year period; Obrecht traveled to Italy after having worked at Antwerp and Bruges. Others moved farther afield and remained longer: Heinrich Isaak, after some years at Florence, lived in Vienna for twenty years; Weerbecke spent much of his professional lifetime in Rome and Milan; and so it was with many others. This diffusion of Franco-Flemish composers to various parts of Europe continued to the end of the Renaissance period. The end result was the enrichment of all European music and the formulation of a highly distinctive Renaissance style—which was, of course, subject to regional variations.

The most influential of the Franco-Flemish composers near the beginning of the Renaissance was Josquin des Prez (*circa* 1450–1521), born in the Belgian province of Hainaut. As a young man in Milan in the 1470's, Josquin (as he is usually called) was in the employ of Cardinal Ascanio Sforza, the brother of the Duke Ludovico Sforza at whose court Leonardo da Vinci spent sixteen years; the musician and the painter may have been colleagues for part of that time. About 1486 Josquin became a singer in the Papal Choir; later he traveled about Italy and France and became chapel master to Louis XII of France. After the king's death in 1515, Josquin returned to what is now Belgium, where he died in 1521.

Josquin was one of the most highly esteemed composers of his time, and his fame endured. His music was in great demand; the evidence is afforded by the fact that Petrucci, who published the very earliest collections of part music, printed three books of Josquin's Masses and later found it necessary to reprint the first two. Few other Renaissance composers were so honored during their lifetimes. Fifty years after Josquin's death many of his secular polyphonic songs (called *chansons*) were included in the popular French collections of the time, and consequently were widely circulated.

The qualities that set Josquin apart from his contemporaries are the sweep of his musical imagination, his technical virtuosity, and his sense of proportion and balance. His works, secular and sacred alike, are filled with canons (see p. 362), a form that in the hands of an ordinary craftsman is likely to sound mechanical and contrived. But in Josquin's hands canonic writing reached heights of expressive power not attained even by Okeghem, Josquin's teacher. Josquin achieved equalization of all voices in the polyphonic texture by virtue of his complete mastery of the technique of imitation, in which the beginning of each voice in a motet or a Mass is related melodically to the other voices (see Example 112). An outline of Josquin's

Josquin, *Missa de Beata Virgine,* "Gloria" ***Example 112***

Missa Da Pacem, based on the old Medieval technique of *cantus firmus,* is given on pages 322–24. A study of the outline will reveal how consistently Josquin employed the techniques of canon and imitation. Yet in spite of the severity of the techniques he employed, Josquin seldom failed to write expressively, warmly, and with clearly delineated forms.

For generations, Flemish music had been distinguished by contrapuntal dexterity but not by expressiveness and emotional warmth; the latter had been the special province of Italian composers. It was Josquin's great accomplishment to weld the

Missa Da Pacem, by Josquin des Prez

Soprano (S), *Alto* (A), *Tenor* (T), and *Bass* (B)

Based on the Gregorian chant, *Da pacem, Domine* (in *Liber Usualis,* page 1867)

Example 1

KYRIE ELEISON

Meas.	*Voice*	
1	S,A,B	*Kyrie eleison.* Imitative passage based on first four notes of *cantus firmus* (Ex. 1)

Example 2

Meas.	*Voice*	
5	T	*Cantus firmus,* Phrase A. Other voices in imitative counterpoint which Tenor joins in meas. 13
21	S,A,B	*Christe eleison.* Imitations based on various motives, continuing to meas. 41
23	T	*Cantus firmus,* Phrase B, with extension
43	S,A,B	*Kyrie eleison.* Imitations of various motives, continuing to meas. 64
46	T	*Cantus firmus,* Phrase C, freely extended; at meas. 49, Phrase D. At meas. 58 Tenor joins other voices in imitations. Movement ends in meas. 64

GLORIA IN EXCELSIS DEO

Meas.	*Voice*	
1	S,A,B	*Et in terra pax.* Vocal parts identical with meas. 1–4 of *Kyrie* (Ex. 2)
5	T	*Cantus firmus,* Phrase A. Other voices in imitative counterpoint which Tenor joins in meas. 18
24	T	*Cantus firmus,* Phrase B. Other voices in imitations based on various motives
52	T	*Qui tollis. Cantus firmus,* first half of Phrase A with extension. In other voices, imitations based on various motives; passage continues to meas. 79
67	T	*Cantus firmus,* second half of Phrase A
80	S,A,T,B	*Qui sedes.* Various motives, imitated in four voices
95	T	*Cantus firmus;* Phrase C with extension. In other voices, imitations of various motives. Movement ends in meas. 122

CREDO IN UNUM DEUM

Meas.	*Voice*	
1	S,A,B	*Patrem omnipotentem.* Vocal parts identical with meas. 1–4 of *Kyrie* (Ex. 2), but extended
8	T	*Cantus firmus,* Phrase A (not in meas. 5 where expected). Other voices in imitative counterpoint which Tenor joins in meas. 29
35	T	*Cantus firmus,* Phrases B and C, elaborated and extended to meas. 53. Other voices in imitative counterpoint
54	S,A,T,B	*Et incarnatus.* Chordal texture in four voices; but Tenor is based on *cantus firmus,* Phrase A and first half of Phrase B
78	A,B	*Crucifixus.* Imitative passage derived from *cantus firmus,* second half of Phrase B. Alto and Bass replaced by Soprano and Tenor in meas. 98
118	T	*Et iterum. Cantus firmus,* Phrase A. In other voices, various motives in imitative texture which Tenor joins in meas. 136. Passage continues to meas. 168
158	T	Freely derived from *cantus firmus,* Phrases C and D
169	S,A,B	Free counterpoints, imitative texture. Movement ends in meas. 203

Josquin, *Missa Da Pacem* (cont.)

SANCTUS

Meas.	*Voice*	
1	S,A,B	*Sanctus,* the vocal parts identical with meas. 1–4 of *Kyrie* (Ex. 2)
5	T	*Cantus firmus,* Phrases A, B, C, D, somewhat modified, extending to meas. 32
10	S,A	Based on *cantus firmus,* Phrase B, alternating with phrases set for Tenor and Bass. Full quartet at meas. 18
34	T,B	*Pleni sunt cœli.* Canon based on *cantus firmus,* Phrase A; alternates with Soprano and Alto (meas. 45, Phrase B); return of Tenor and Bass (meas. 54, Phrase C), etc. Full quartet at meas. 72
87	S,A,T,B	*Osanna.* Quasi-chordal passage; but Tenor is based on *cantus firmus,* Phrase A
99	S,A	*In excelsis.* Series of two-voice phrases, alternating with Tenor and Bass. Tenor at meas. 111 based on *cantus firmus,* Phrase C
146		*Benedictus qui venit.* Series of phrases, mainly two-voiced, imitations freely derived from *cantus firmus,* first half of Phrase A. The passage extends to meas. 199; then *Osanna* (meas. 87–145) is recapitulated

AGNUS DEI

Meas.	*Voice*	
PART I		
1	S,A,B	*Agnus Dei.* Vocal parts similar to meas. 1–4 of *Kyrie* (Ex. 2); but now Tenor enters in meas. 3, Bass in meas. 6, and the passage is extended to meas. 13
13	S,A,T,B	Series of motives, imitated in full quartet; but Tenor is based mainly on elaborations of *cantus firmus,* Phrase B
PART II		
31	B,T	Canon between Bass and Tenor, based on entire *cantus firmus.* Soprano and Alto in part imitate, in part introduce free counterpoints
PART III		
83		Now set for six voices. Three-voice canon, based on entire *cantus firmus,* between Soprano II, Bass II, and Soprano I. Other voices (Soprano III, Alto, Bass I) present various motives in imitation, but in part are freely contrapuntal. Movement ends in meas. 129

technical excellence and self-discipline of the North to the melodiousness and sentiment of the South. He marks a fusion of two opposing styles, to the great advantage of both. And in composing large quantities of music in his new personal style, music that was sung enthusiastically and reverently in many parts of western Europe, Josquin greatly influenced the composers who followed him.

An additional feature of Josquin's music is its characteristic variety of sound and vocal color. The earlier practice in writing, say, a four-voice composition had been to keep all four voices fully occupied throughout all or most of its length. The result was a solid and resonant work, true, but also one that presented a certain monotony of vocal color; the effect was similar to that of a composition for orchestra or band in which all instruments are required to play continuously. In Josquin's music such monotony is avoided by his practice of varying the number of vocal parts. Even in a Mass composed basically of four voices, extended sections for two voices or three voices appear in various passages; this contrast in the weight of the vocal texture is one of its most attractive features (see Example 112). Occasionally, too, the colors of individual voices are exploited: low soprano parts are written against high tenor parts, for example.

The end result is a body of music that has few equals in expressive power, variety of means, balanced form, and technical excellence. Relatively few works by Josquin have appeared so far in recordings, but even those few will serve as excellent examples of his style. Increased familiarity with the recorded works now available can only strengthen our conviction that he was one of the truly great figures of the Renaissance, one who deserves a place beside Lasso and Palestrina, the two composers who until recently have been held to be the most accomplished musicians of that period.

Palestrina

In the nineteenth century, when musical scholarship had not yet revealed the full glory of Renaissance music, Giovanni Pierluigi da Palestrina was looked upon as a lone figure who stood at the peak of musical accomplishment and who was approached only by Orlando di Lasso. Palestrina's music was felt to reflect the perfect linking of polyphonic art to religious expression; his technical mastery of counterpoint was legendary, and he was seen as a composer without a flaw. Since the middle of the eighteenth century the study of the branch of music theory called *strict counterpoint* has been based on an interpretation of Palestrina's technical practices. Generations of music students have written what purports to be "Palestrina counterpoint" in an effort to approach the self-discipline, lucidity, and expressive power of that master's music.

Recent advances in musical knowledge have uncovered many other great composers of the sixteenth century and have brought about a truer understanding of the time in which they lived. Palestrina is today no longer the isolated figure he once was held to be, but the quality of his music has not suffered by comparison with that of other Renaissance composers who were little more than names to nineteenth-century music historians.

Giovanni Pierluigi (*circa* 1526–94) was born in Palestrina, a town near Rome; later he adopted the name of his birthplace, and he is most generally referred to by that name. In his early teens he was a choirboy in Rome, and he presumably continued his musical studies there for some years. In any event, when he was about twenty he was engaged as organist and singer in the cathedral of his birthplace. The bishop whose jurisdiction included the town of Palestrina later became Pope Julius III. He must have been favorably impressed by the young man's ability, for about 1550 he (as Pope) engaged Palestrina as choirmaster in the Julian Chapel in St. Peter's at Rome. Then followed a succession of other positions in various Roman churches (interrupted by a short term as a teacher in a seminary and a longer term as musical director at the estate of Cardinal d'Este) including finally the position of composer to the Papal Chapel. With the exception of the five years between about 1566 and 1571, Palestrina's professional career from about 1544 to his death in 1594 was spent in the service of the Roman Catholic church.

His personal life was marred by deep tragedy; his two brothers, his wife, and two of his three sons died in epidemics, and his creative output all but ceased for a six-year period beginning in 1575. In 1581 he married the widow of a furrier and became, incongruously enough, the owner of a fur shop. But this and other successful business ventures apparently did not stand in the way of his profession; more than half of the forty-eight Masses Palestrina published during his lifetime (out of the 104 he is known to have composed) appeared in the years of his second marriage.

The majority of Renaissance composers wrote with equal facility in both the secular and sacred fields. Madrigals or chansons as well as motets and Masses appear in considerable numbers in the works of such men as Josquin, Monte, Lasso, and many others. Palestrina, however, devoted himself almost entirely to sacred music; the few madrigals that he composed are scarcely distinguishable from his motets and have virtually the same musical idiom and the same subdued mood. The 104 Masses mentioned above represent the most important body of Palestrina's work, but some 250 motets and over 200 other sacred choral compositions are equally representative of the controlled, balanced style that was peculiarly his own.

Restraint, consistency, economy—these words characterize Palestrina's technical style. The dramatic fervor and involved polyphonic writing found in other Renaissance music are missing from Palestrina's. He spent a lifetime pursing one ideal: to set the sacred texts so that they could be understood both intellectually and emotionally—to express with musical materials the meanings of the texts in forms that would allow the spiritual light of the words to shine through. In pursuit of this ideal Palestrina exercised the greatest of technical skill, but the musical results he achieved seem effortless and direct. He revealed his boundless imagination but kept it under firm control through his sense of proportion and appropriateness.

The almost perfect proportion shown by Palestrina's music is as much a result of his concern with small details as with over-all scope. For example, his melodies undulate gently in well-rounded curves; the motion is mainly stepwise, and a balance

Example 113

between long and short tones is usually present. Leaps within a phrase are used discreetly, on the principle that many such leaps become unduly noticeable, destroy the smoothness of the melodic line, and even call attention to themselves and away from the text. And long florid melodic fragments set to a single textual syllable (such a fragment is called a *melisma:* see Example 105*c*, p. 308, on the syllables *Ag-* and *De-*) are not as prominent in Palestrina as they are in other composers of the time—very likely because they too exert the attention-attracting force that he took pains to subdue (see Example 113).

Another of Palestrina's principles, and an example of his consistency in the application of small details, is seen in his treatment of dissonances. In Chapter 3 we defined a dissonance as a tonal combination that suggests a degree of unrest or motion and that requires resolution to a point of stability—namely, to a consonance. If dissonance is employed indiscriminately or excessively, the relative proportion between motion and rest is affected. The listener receives a restless or nervous impression from music that employs excessive dissonance. (It is understood that "excessive" is to be interpreted with the standards of the sixteenth century in mind, not with those of the twentieth.)

Giovanni Pierluigi da Palestrina (*c.* 1526–94), whose imagination and skill were dedicated to the highest ideals of church music.

Palestrina's musical idiom is controlled and reposeful; excitement and unrest have no place in his musical scheme. Within the system of modes in which he worked, dissonances are virtually unavoidable if the music is to have any life. Yet Palestrina rarely employed dissonance to intensify the emotional effect of his texts, as did composers before and after him; rather he employed it primarily for its musical value. He established a system in which the amount and type of dissonance are related to the length of the tones concerned. So consistently was that system employed that one may make this statement: In a given rhythmic situation Palestrina leads his melodies one way or another. If the tones are short, the amount of allowable dissonance is greater than if the tones are long. If the tones are accented (thus in a position to attract attention in their own right), dissonance is not used.

Taken as a whole, Palestrina's Masses, motets, and other sacred works illustrate a careful balance between a consistent polyphonic style and what may be called a chordal style. In the first style, the texts of the various voices may so overlap that no words can be understood; in the second, all voices carry the same text simultaneously, as in a hymn, and the words can be understood easily. In achieving this balance, Palestrina achieved also a texture that was well adapted to the principles established by the Council of Trent (1545–63) in respect to the purification of church music in general and to the intelligibility of the texts in particular. Thus his Masses became virtual models for Roman Catholic church music. They were reverent and unsensational in mood, they emphasized the text rather than the purely musical effect, and they aided the worshipper instead of distracting him.

The works of Palestrina may be heard at the present time in Roman Catholic churches, in recordings, and in concert performances. Today, as 400 years ago, they reflect the creative expression of a devout musician whose imagination, technical skill, and taste were dedicated to the highest ideals of sacred music.

The Elizabethan School

During the last third of the sixteenth century, English musicians apparently were suddenly attracted to the richness and variety of Italian music. Quantities of that music were imported; large numbers of Italian compositions circulated among the singers and singing societies that were typical of English culture of the time. This interest in the musical products of Italy was paralleled by an interest in continental poetry. Italian and other poems were translated, adapted, and imitated enthusiastically, and not even the greatest of Elizabethan poets remained immune to the wave of Italian culture. And of the musical forms that were most assiduously imported, the *madrigal* led the list.

The madrigal originated in Italy early in the sixteenth century (an earlier fourteenth-century form with the same name does not come into account here). It resulted from attempts by Cardinal Pietro Bembo and others to raise literary standards and to give to the Italian language the same prestige that Latin enjoyed among cultivated people. A large number of madrigals were composed to secular texts by

Petrarch. Lyric poems by Michelangelo, Tasso, and Aristo appeared in musical settings also. The madrigal enjoyed an enormous vogue in sixteenth-century Italy; it engaged the attention of Flemish as well as Italian composers (Orlando di Lasso and Philippe de Monte, for example), and became perhaps the most important and influential secular form of the time.

In a sense, the madrigal is the worldly counterpart of the motet. Unlike the sacred text of the motet, that of the madrigal is usually jovial, sentimental, or tender. The madrigal, like the motet, often is written in imitative style, but in general a more chordal, rhythmically varied treatment is typical. The length of the text determines the form of the madrigal, as it does of the motet, and madrigals are seldom over a few minutes in duration. The great variety of moods reflects the varied sentiments of the texts employed.

The English madrigal is associated primarily with the reign of Queen Elizabeth, who ruled England from 1558 to 1603; her reign is marked by the tremendous growth of England as a world power and a cultural force. In 1588, the year of the Spanish Armada, there was published an anthology of Italian madrigals with texts translated into English—the first of five similar publications. With Italian models at hand, English interest in the form was stimulated. Within a few years after 1588, sets of English madrigals were published also—some of them set to the same poems that had been translated from the Italian, and some even borrowing and adapting the Italian melodies. But the English madrigal became far more than an imitation of the Italian. Instead of setting the poems written by the great literary figures of their day, English madrigalists turned to the smaller lyric poets and writers of popular verse, achieving a lightness of mood and variety of subject matter that was often lacking in the serious Italian madrigal.

Thomas Morley (*circa* 1557–1603), a pupil of the great William Byrd, was among the first and the most influential of English madrigal composers. He was active as organist, publisher, author, composer, and "Gentleman of the Chapel Royal." Two of the five sets of translated Italian madrigals mentioned above were published by him, and he composed quantities of madrigals modeled in part upon the Italian type. Several of Morley's works are frequently found in the repertoires of singing groups today—notably *Sing We and Chant It, Now Is the Month of Maying,* and *My Bonny Lass.*

Even more successful than Morley were two of his younger contemporaries, John Wilbye (*circa* 1574–1638) and Thomas Weelkes (*circa* 1575–1623). Wilbye spent his professional life in the service of a noble English family. Although he wrote comparatively few madrigals, his two sets, published in 1597 and 1609, reveal him to have been extremely sensitive to the poetic implications of his texts. Unfortunately for the field of music, he became a wealthy farmer in middle life and stopped composing. Weelkes became the organist at Chichester Cathedral in about 1602, after which time he devoted himself almost entirely to church music. His four sets of madrigals, three of which appeared before his move to Chichester, disclose a rhythmic charm and an unbounded imagination scarcely equaled by other composers of the time.

Example 114 Morley, *Now Is the Month of Maying*

In accord with the English practice, madrigals appeared under a number of different names: *madrigal, ayre* (air), *sonet* (sonnet), and *canzonet* all refer essentially to the same form. A related form bears the name *ballet,* from the Italian *balletto,* and is a light dancelike madrigal in simple style, characterized by a repetition of the syllables "fa la" in the refrain (see Example 114). In the madrigal and ballet as cultivated by Morley, Wilbye, Weelkes, and a host of other Elizabethans, we find typically English moods of lightheartedness and merriment. Other works express melancholy or deep sentiment of the lovesick kind, as well as moods between the gay and somber extremes. The merry moods are often reflected in buoyant rhythms, in unexpected changes of meter from duple to triple across short-time spans, and in a lightly moving melodic line (see Example 115).

The Elizabethan composers exhibit another characteristic in which they differ from their Italian predecessors—namely, their approach to the concept of the tonal

Weelkes, *Hark, All Ye Lovely Saints* *Example 115*

system with its major and minor scale patterns. Their Italian contemporaries, notably Marenzio and Gesualdo, had greatly exploited chromaticism but had remained largely within the framework of the church modes even in their secular music. The English composers worked differently; passages that can be explained only in eighteenth-century harmonic terms abound in their music. And it is this "modern" touch that contributes to the appeal these late-Renaissance English works have for today's listeners.

A few decades after the beginning of the seventeenth century, however, the Elizabethan madrigal became virtually obsolete. The Baroque style, imported from Italy, came into vogue: the madrigal declined as quickly as it had emerged.

Listening Suggestions

Recordings of Renaissance and earlier music are most generally available in anthologies or sets. Selections from two such anthologies, among the most valuable in the field, are listed below. Other pre-1600 compositions are often difficult to locate in general record catalogues; for that reason the following list of recordings includes the manufacturer's name and the record number.

ANTHOLOGIE SONORE

Vol. 1, Gregorian Chant to the Sixteenth Century (Anth. Son., AS-A)
Vol. 2, Vocal Music of the 15th, 16th, and 17th Centuries (Anth. Son., AS-B)

ARCHIVE PRODUCTION

Early Renaissance: Florentine and Netherlands Composers (Decca, ARC-3003)
High Renaissance: Campion, Dowland, Morley (Decca, ARC-3004)

Byrd, Mass for Five Voices (London, 5725)
Gabrieli, *Sacrae Symphoniae* (Bach Guild, 611)
Josquin, *Missa Pange Lingua* (Decca, 9410)
Lasso, *Lamentations of Jeremiah* (Concert Hall, CHC-47)
Morley, Elizabethan Madrigals (Esoteric, 520)
Palestrina, *Missa Papae Marcelli* (Westminster, 9605)
Weelkes, Madrigals (Westminster, 1006)
Wilbye, Madrigals (Bach Guild, 578)

Chapter 16

THE BAROQUE PERIOD

Late in the eighteenth century, art historians looked back at the period of about a century and a half that began in the late 1500's. They examined the art and architecture of the seventeenth century from a critical point of view influenced both by the Renaissance and by their own Classical tastes, and what they saw struck them as being grotesque, unduly massive, and excessively elaborate. To those works they consequently gave a derogatory name—"baroque." This word, of Portuguese origin, is often used to describe pearls and means "irregular" or "misshapen." The same derogatory adjective was later applied to the music of that period also.

Now, almost two centuries later, we are in a better position to evaluate the period, and we find it anything but grotesque. We can see the Baroque era as a time of experiment and refinement, of bold imagination, of search and accomplishment, of problem and solution. In short, the accomplishments of the Baroque period were very much like those of any other; only its materials and means of achievement were different, even unique.

The Baroque period marked another step forward in man's eternal quest for freedom of spirit and intellect. It was a time in which the struggle between Protestant and Catholic rose to its last great climax and then subsided: the Thirty Years' War (1618–48) had begun as a religious conflict. It was a time, too, in which scientists, under the promptings of Francis Bacon, seized upon the experimental method and applied inductive reasoning to known facts. The seventeenth century began to place its reliance upon independent inquiry, and turned away from the writings of the ancient authorities such as Aristotle. Great names—Kepler, Galileo, and Newton, for example—loom large in the history of astronomy and mathematics, and their work is based upon their own observations and reflections.

The new philosophers Descartes, Locke, and Spinoza, each in his own way, spoke out for freedom of thought and against the continued enshrinement of outworn tradition. The poet John Milton was a strong advocate of intellectual as well as political freedom. The lives and actions of men such as these make it clear that the Baroque period was an age in which the dead hand of the past was loosened, in which men rebelled against the old order and became more free. If the Renaissance was the adolescence of our civilization, the Baroque era was its first maturity.

In music, too, the Baroque period began with a revolt against the practices of the sixteenth century. The influence of the Netherlanders had given way to that of the Italians at the beginning of the Baroque period, but toward its end German composers became supreme. Almost two centuries of German musical domination followed. The period encompassed the rise of independent instrumental music, the formation of national musical styles, the decline of the church modes, and the full victory of the tonal system. It was one of the most turbulent and complex periods in music history. Several strands of musical development existed side by side. Musical forms, textures, and performing groups were in a state of flux for many decades. Thus the year 1600, the approximate beginning of the Baroque period, marks one of the great turning points in the history of musical thought.

The several parallel stands of Baroque music are tied together by one common technical device, the *basso continuo,* or "continuous bass." In opera, instrumental music, and choral music alike, the *continuo,* as it is usually called, provided one of the most useful and distinctive tools a Baroque composer possessed, although considerable changes took place within those areas of music during this period. In this chapter we shall discuss the *continuo* in relation to the opera, where it first found regular employment, and follow the opera into the early eighteenth century. Returning to the beginning of the period, we shall then discuss instrumental and choral music in this century of growth, up to about 1720. The foundation will then be laid for a discussion of Handel and Bach, the two great composers with whose work the period ended.

Basso Continuo and the Opera

At the very end of the Renaissance period, a group of poets and musicians meeting in Florence took steps to correct what they considered a serious fault in the music of the time. Thereby they precipitated a series of events that was to change radically the forms, textures, and the very sound of all music.

Their criticism was directed to the treatment of the text in polyphonic compositions. We have seen (Example 11*c*, p. 21, and Example 112, p. 321) that several different words are likely to be sung simultaneously in such a work, and the men of the Florentine *Camerata,* as the group was named, objected strongly to this "laceration of the poetry." They strove to subordinate the music to the text, so that the individual words and the sense of the entire passage could be clearly understood.

To establish their point they turned away from polyphony entirely and experimented with a texture in which a single line of tones carried the text. To provide a musical center of gravity, they permitted the melodic line to be supported by chords. Further, the rhythm of the line mirrored the rhythm of the words themselves; in effect, the line became a kind of "speech song." And what we have called the background rhythm (the even succession of beats that creates a rhythmic pulse) was vir-

Peri, *Eurydice*, Recitative *Example 116*

tually abolished, even though the symbols of rhythmical notation were retained. Thus arose the *recitative* (see Example 116*a*), and when the recitative style was applied to a dramatic work throughout its entire length, the opera was born.

The men of the *Camerata* favored the more intense emotions in music. The expression of passion, pathos, grief, and anger had not been stressed by Renaissance composers, but it is precisely these emotions that were most often expressed in the works of the *Camerata* and of other composers who quickly adopted the new style. The recitatives were performed with gestures and grimaces; the singers gave way to emotional excesses —even to the extent of crying or sobbing—in their efforts to convey the meanings of the words.

The emotional range expressed in these works required a new treatment of dissonance. Instead of resulting from a momentary clash between two melodies, as had been normal in the Renaissance, dissonance now became a purposeful expressive element carried by or within the chords that supported the "reciting" melody. As a consequence, the bass line upon which the chords were built became an important structural factor of the musical texture.

There arose, as a result of this new function, a kind of polarity between the melody and bass, and a form of musical shorthand was developed to express it. By employing this shorthand, the composer could indicate the nature of the chord over each of the bass tones—whether major or minor, whether triad or seventh, whether in root position or inverted, and so on. It became unnecessary, consequently, to write out the inner parts; when the composer wrote melody and bass lines, including the figures and other symbols that specified the desired chords, his work was done. The system of shorthand utilizing such symbols is called *figured bass* (see Example 116*a*). Used by virtually all the Baroque composers until about 1750, it was occasionally employed by nineteenth-century musicians and is still used in the study of harmony today.

There remains to be explained the manner in which the figured bass was performed. Harmony instruments such as the organ, harpsichord, lute, and guitar were available for playing the indicated chords; but the bass tones of those instruments (except for the organ) often vanished in the moment of playing, so short-lived was their period of resonance. A player of an instrument capable of sustained tones, such as the bass, and later the cello, the bassoon, or even the trombone, was assigned the task of playing the line of written-out bass tones along with the keyboard or lute player. The latter then filled out or "realized" the required chord structures at his instrument, improvising, as it were, upon the harmonic structure outlined by the composer (see Example 116*b*).

It is this continuous bass line with chords built upon it, performed by two or more instruments, that is meant by the term *basso continuo.* Thus the term implies both a method of writing and a manner of performing. The use of the *continuo* became so universal that its presence is taken for granted in virtually all music of the Baroque period; in fact it is one of the most important distinguishing marks of that music. If for some reason a composer did not wish his music to be performed in *continuo* fashion, he found it necessary to specify this fact.

Early Italian Opera

The recitatives with *continuo* as composed by members of the Florentine *Camerata* were first used in connection with pastoral dramas. Soon they were applied to dramatized versions of popular mythological subjects—and it is with these works that the history of opera begins. A musical presentation called *Dafne,* with text by Rinuccini and music by Jacopo Peri, was performed in about 1597 at Florence; that work, since lost, is the first that can be called an opera. Another opera, *Eurydice,* by the same two men, was presented in 1600, and from that date onward the production of operas has continued without interruption.

The earliest operas were little more than strings of formless recitatives tied together by a dramatic text. There were a few choruses at the ends of scenes, but lyric melody was absent. The orchestra, consisting of a few players, was confined largely to playing the *continuo,* and the homophonic texture of the recitatives was seldom relieved by passages in counterpoint. The novelty of the new style attracted attention for a while, but monotony was inevitable.

It remained for Claudio Monteverdi (1567–1643), one of the great composers of the early Baroque period, to make opera something more than a sung imitation of speech and to invest it with qualities of drama, intensity, and eloquence. Monteverdi spent about twenty years as violist, singer, and later chapelmaster to the Duke of Mantua. After that he served for thirty years as choirmaster of St. Mark's in Venice—a position that was perhaps the most important in the musical world of that time. His compositions include many sacred works in the old style, but his interest in secular music—particularly in the madrigal and the opera—was maintained even during his service as a church musician. And he is chiefly remembered today for his secular works.

Monteverdi's opera of 1607, *Orpheus,* showed the way to a richer expression. A large orchestra of about forty players provided varied instrumental colors; the recita-

Claudio Monteverdi (1567–1643)

tive became more expressive and dramatic. Monteverdi's keen sense of harmony and his bold use of dissonance provided a high degree of emotional tension. Well-organized forms tied the music and text together in satisfactory fashion. Elaborate instrumental interludes, vocal sections repeated to heighten the dramatic effect, settings of strophic texts with each stanza having a different orchestral accompaniment—such devices added considerably to the over-all unity of the form as well as to its effectiveness.

The early operas had been spectacles devised for the entertainment of the nobility. When the first public opera house was opened in Venice in 1637, opera became a spectacle for the people as well. And again Monteverdi's works set standards for other composers to follow. His *Return of Ulysses* (1641) and *The Coronation of Poppaea* (1642) mark the highest points reached in the recitative style. At the same time, both works depart from that style sufficiently to introduce the full resources of music—including counterpoint—to the opera.

Intensity of expression and concern with a wide range of emotions distinguish Monteverdi's late operas. Moods of drama, sentiment, deep tragedy, pathos, and comic relief follow each other in quick succession. Variation forms are introduced to reflect the complex natures of the principal characters. Unfortunately, those operas are seldom heard today. Nowadays, in order to receive an insight into the beauty, dramatic power, and human appeal of Monteverdi's style, one must turn to his dramatic madrigals. These works, supplied with *continuo* and often with orchestral accompaniment, contain all the harmonic resources of the early Baroque era. Such works as the *Madrigals of War and Love, The Combat of Tancred and Clorinda,* and the single madrigals Monteverdi included in his Books One and Four have all been recorded. They provide excellent examples of his dramatic, intense style and are among the finest of early Baroque works.

Early French Opera

French composers in the early seventeenth century held more closely to tradition than did the Italian. They took pride in their elaborately staged court ballets (*ballets de cour*) as well as in their well-developed classically inspired dramas—especially those of Corneille and, later, Racine. Consequently, the recitatives and emotionally rich operas of the Italians left them unmoved. They satisfied the need for staged musical works by concentrating on the court ballets, which often had sketchy plots set forth in a series of danced tableaux. Not until the 1650's did the *continuo* become much of a force in French music, and French opera did not appear until another twenty years after that date.

Jean Baptiste Lully (*circa* 1633–87) was the most successful composer of the time. His success was due not only to his musical talent but also to his political talent, his opportunism, and his driving will. Born in Florence, Lully came to France as a boy and in 1652 entered the service of young King Louis XIV, who was then fourteen years old. Under the protection of Louis he engaged in a series of shrewd maneuvers that made him successively composer of the royal chamber music, superintendent of all the King's music, and holder of the royal patent. The latter position gave him a virtual monopoly over French operatic composition and production. At his death he had accumulated a large fortune derived from his operatic ventures as well as from his real estate speculations.

Ballet dancers at the court of Louis XIV.

Lully's operas differ basically from those by Italian composers. His works emphasized choruses, huge ballets, and imposing and spectacularly staged scenes. The recitatives departed widely from those of the Italians in that Lully paid close attention to the accentual scheme of the French language and cast the recitative rhythms in well-defined patterns. Vocal and choral numbers were usually written in clear forms, mainly arias and rondos; and a distinctive form was developed for the overture. The Lully type of overture (or *French overture,* as it is usually called), with imposing dotted rhythms in the slow first part and fugal passages in the fast second section, was employed by Baroque composers for half a century after Lully's death; the type is still heard today. The opening sinfonia of Handel's *Messiah* is such an overture, for example. In composing his operas, Lully made use of a rich and varied orchestral accompaniment. He also exhibited a complete disregard for expense in the cost of staging and costuming his works. Those factors, combined with their musical qualities, made Lully's operatic productions suitable even for the exacting taste of Louis XIV, who was Lully's principal auditor.

Jean Baptiste Lully (*circa* 1633–87)

Individual works by Lully were performed until well into the eighteenth century—but with additions of melodic ornamentation to satisfy the taste of the time. For several decades they remained the models for other composers to follow. At the hands of Jean Philippe Rameau (1683–1764), Lully's style was revived, and some of the finest of all French operas were written by Rameau between 1733 and about 1740. Unfortunately, the operas of Lully and Rameau have long since disappeared from the stage. Their dramatic strength and rhythmic charm can be recaptured in recordings, but the visual impact they made can seldom be experienced today.

Neapolitan Opera

In the decades after Monteverdi's death in 1643, the Venetian opera spread to all parts of Europe and became enormously popular. Late in the seventeenth century another center of operatic activity arose at Naples, and through much of the following century the Neapolitan operatic style offered real competition to the Venetian. The Neapolitan opera developed certain stylistic mannerisms. A recitative, for example, was conventionally followed by an aria; the former carried forward the dramatic action, and the latter provided a moment of contemplation or a commentary on that action. The aria, in two parts, was usually designed so that the first part was repeated after the second; thus the important ABA form of aria, or *aria da capo,* arose.

Choruses played little part in these new operas, and orchestral accompaniment was kept to a minimum. The three-part *Italian overture* of this period, however, with its fast-slow-fast sections, became the prototype for the instrumental sinfonia, which in the hands of Austrian composers developed into the Classical symphony of the mid-eighteenth century.

In many of the operas written around the turn of the eighteenth century, Neapolitan and Venetian alike, the complete system of major and minor keys was fully established. In these works, a melody or a harmonic cadence that reminds one of the old church modes is a decided rarity. But at the same time, the polyphonic style which had been discarded by the earliest opera composers found its way back into the form. With the amorphous recitatives now confined to specific locations (before the respective arias) and to one specific function (to carry forward the dramatic action), the arias developed a considerable degree of inner organization and balance, both in phrase structure and in form. The melodic style was also influenced by developments in instrumental music. Often, however, the aria became a display piece for the egotistical, overbearing virtuoso singers of the time, who delighted in adding all manner of vocal embellishments and acrobatics to the melodic line. At this point, about 1710, the stage was set for the appearance of Handel (see pp. 349–53).

Instrumental Music

Probably few periods in music history present so bewildering an array of new musical forms as do the first decades of the seventeenth century. Musical instruments had been known and utilized for several centuries, but they had been employed primarily to provide accompaniments for singing or dancing or to substitute for voices. In the early years of the seventeenth century, they also began to attract the attention of the serious composers. Some of the resulting music carried forward the function and rhythmic patterns of Renaissance dance music. Other compositions were in all respects similar to choral forms such as the motet except that they dispensed with the text. Still others began their existence as organ arrangements of French chansons and developed into the instrumental ensemble pieces that provided the foundation for the important eighteenth-century chamber music literature. Some music was designed to be played in church services when no organist was available. Other works for keyboard instruments were used as preludes to the service or within the service, and still other served simply as secular display pieces. Works for brass ensemble, pieces for string-and-wind orchestra, and a variety of other large ensemble works appeared. Most of these developments took place in the first half of the Baroque period, mainly in Italy.

Neither the forms nor the names of these works were standardized, and a complex series of influences and cross-fertilizations further confuse the picture. Much of the new instrumental music adopted the *continuo* principle first used in the opera. Some of it was written in the old polyphonic style of the Renaissance—but employed the *continuo* also. As the decades passed, dance patterns began to creep into the instrumental pieces that were designed for church use, and the quiet melodies originally found in church music found their way into the dance forms. Some new forms had a life of a few decades only, after which they disappeared or merged with other forms. Still others had a longer life, persisting through the entire seventeenth century but

changing with each decade, until in the late Baroque period they were brought to the highest stage of development by such masters as Handel and Bach.

THE SUITE

The suite of dances is one such form, one that had its roots in the fifteenth century or earlier. During the Renaissance and Baroque periods its form was modified considerably before it culminated in the works of Bach. In the Baroque version the suite consisted of a set of dance tunes for harpsichord, lute, or instrumental ensemble, all in the same key and form, but each in a different tempo. Each of the dances had its own rhythmic character and mood, and each movement was traditionally set in a two-part form with both parts designed to be repeated. The minuet and trio, described in Chapter 8 and found in many sonatas, quartets, and symphonies of the eighteenth century, is actually a survivor of this earlier period, for it consists of two dances each in two-part form, the first minuet being one dance and the trio another. The term trio indicates that the second dance was formerly set for only three instruments.

Four contrasting dances formed the nucleus of the suite: the *allemande,* in moderate duple meter; the *courante,* in fast triple meter; the *sarabande,* in slow triple meter; and the *gigue,* in fast compound meter. Often other dances, such as the bourrée, gavotte, hornpipe, or minuet were added or substituted. It was quite usual for the set of dances to be supplied with an introductory movement not in dance character; that first movement was called variously an *overture, prelude,* or some similar name. Such a suite could contain as few as four or as many as a dozen movements.

The staging of a Baroque opera ballet. The sumptuousness of the set is in keeping with operatic standards of the late seventeenth century. (Scenery of Giuseppe Galli da Bibbiena, Vienna.)

In this form the suite is well represented in the works of many Baroque composers. To give only one example, Bach's keyboard works include six English suites, six French suites, and six *partitas* (an alternate name for suite), all of which conform to the type described above. Ranging from five to eight movements, and consisting largely of idealized dance tunes, the eighteen works represent the suite at its highest level of grace, charm, and masterful organization.

THE CONCERTO

Unlike the suite, the *concerto* had its roots entirely in the Baroque period and originated near the middle of the seventeenth century. It is an orchestral form, usually in three movements, but it may exist in three different versions: without soloists (then called orchestral concerto), with one soloist (solo concerto), or—most often—for a group of soloists, usually three (*concerto grosso*—literally a large or great concerto). In the fast first and third movements, thematic material is divided between the solo group (called the *concertino*) or the solo instrument and the accompaniment, and these two components play more or less alternately throughout the respective movements. The second movement, in slow tempo, presents a series of melodic phrases and is usually in no set pattern. The form of the fast movements is similar to that of a rondo (ABABA, for example), except that in the *concerto grosso* and the solo concerto the various thematic statements are generally led into a variety of keys by means of circle-of-fifth modulations, by series of seventh chords, and the like.

Arcangelo Corelli (1653–1713), of great importance in establishing standardized forms and idioms in the field of the ensemble sonata and in violin music generally,

The shop of a Baroque instrument-maker. Violins and lutes hang from the ceiling, a serpent is displayed on the back wall, and a hurdy-gurdy lies in the foreground.

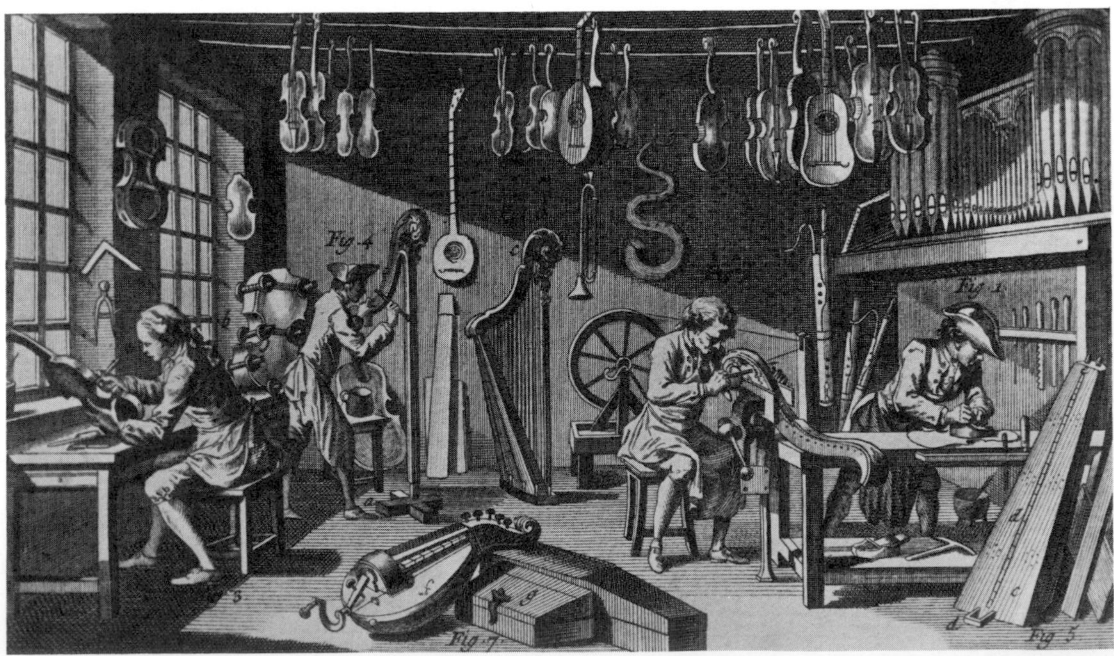

was also one of the earliest composers of the *concerto grosso* type. His work was paralleled by that of Giuseppe Torelli (1658–1709), who was active primarily in the fields of the solo concerto and the orchestral concerto. Hundreds of concertos of all three types were composed in the early eighteenth century, but the form attained its first maturity in the works of Antonio Vivaldi, whose concertos will be discussed below. The concerto of the later eighteenth century was based on different structural principles, as we saw in the discussion of Mozart's works (see pp. 146–47), but the idea of a competition—which is one of the original implications of "concerto"—between soloists and orchestra is common to both early and late types. That idea is still attractive to many composers.

Choral Music

The history of choral music in the first half of the seventeenth century is only slightly less complex than that of instrumental music. The Renaissance polyphonic style did not die out at once after the invention of opera but was cultivated by conservative composers in many parts of Europe. Many sacred works were written in imitation of the style made famous by Palestrina in Rome decades earlier. At the same time other composers of sacred works quickly adopted the device of the *continuo,* discarded all counterpoint, and produced short works called *monodies,* which were not essentially different from the operatic arias of the time.

Another group of composers at or associated with Venice had developed, in the sixteenth century, another style of sacred choral writing. Here, instruments and voices were used together—sometimes with the instruments merely accompanying the voices, as had happened in the Renaissance, but more often with one group opposing the other. This is called the *concertato* style, from *concertare,* "to compete." (It is interesting that other English words related to *concertare* have developed the opposite meaning: for example, "concert" implies "togetherness" and not "competition.")

In place of the long lines of melody that had characterized earlier music, short rhythmic motives with distinctive melodic contours were common, and the motives moved freely from one part to another. A large number of parts also characterized music written in the *concertato* style. Often eight different vocal parts were called for, sometimes combined into one chorus but more often divided into two, with four voice parts in each. From this practice grew the polychoral works that became a feature of the Venetian school and that are found especially in the compositions of Giovanni Gabrieli (1557–1612). Compositions exist for as many as four choruses, one or more of which were made up of instruments.

As in the field of instrumental music, elements of one style were soon applied to other styles. Monodies grew in length and in the number of voices used, and took on some of the vocal coloristic effects found in many Venetian works. Motets in the old conservative style often adopted the *continuo* and even included recitativelike passages. Composers associated with Venice often abandoned the massive polychoral style and wrote more economically; at the same time, many Roman-style composers adopted the polychoral effects that the Venetians no longer employed. Perhaps the largest choral work on record is the famous Mass by Orazio Benevoli (1602–72), written for the consecration of the cathedral at Salzburg. This is a work for fifty-three parts; two eight-voice choruses compete with six separate instrumental groups, and the whole is tied together by a *continuo.*

This array of styles and stylistic mixtures gives only a part of the picture. For in addition to the foregoing, all developed by Catholic composers, a variety of forms and styles was introduced by Protestant musicians, especially in Germany. We see Protestant composers such as Heinrich Schütz (1585–1672), who worked in Italy with Gabrieli, bringing back the operatic *continuo* and employing it widely in Protestant sacred compositions. We see Lutheran composers turning their backs upon the hymn melodies (*chorales*) introduced by Luther himself and writing primarily in free forms—that is, forms not based upon *cantus firmus* techniques and not employing pre-existing melodies. Yet later Lutheran composers championed those very elements that their earlier colleagues had avoided. Many other Protestant composers employed the chorale as a *cantus firmus* in polyphonic works, quite in the conservative Roman manner. Other stylistic mixtures also occurred.

Out of this complex and often baffling situation, one musical form was to rise to a position of eminence—namely the oratorio, particularly as developed by Handel. And another, the Lutheran chorale, was to become an important ingredient of the transformed Catholic church cantata and was to find wide employment in the eighteenth century, especially at the hands of the Lutheran Bach.

Vivaldi

One of the most noteworthy musical trends of recent decades has been the awakening of interest in the music of the Baroque period. Many composers of the seventeenth and early eighteenth centuries, virtually forgotten by performers and concert-goers alike for two centuries or more, have recently been restored to public attention. Their works have been republished (or newly published, in many instances) and recorded, and have taken honored places in today's concert repertoires. Perhaps the most dramatic rise from obscurity to popularity has been that of Antonio Vivaldi.

Vivaldi (*circa* 1675–1741) was associated primarily with Venice, although he composed and conducted in many other European cities during his career. For almost forty years he was director of the conservatory attached to the Ospitale della Pietà, where his charges included hundreds of orphans and foundlings. He composed many oratorios, a large amount of church music, and hundreds of instrumental compositions for the students (mostly girls) of the conservatory, who performed in regular series of public concerts. Most of Vivaldi's choral music has remained in relative obscurity, but the instrumental works have been rediscovered by performers and listeners in what may be called a Vivaldi revival.

Vivaldi composed over four hundred concertos, the majority for a solo instrument (most often the violin) and orchestra. His works are in general similar to the concerto forms that were introduced by Corelli and Torelli, but Vivaldi frequently de-

Antonio Vivaldi (*circa* 1675–1741), who composed more than four hundred concertos and whose music is being heard again after a lapse of two centuries.

parted widely from the standard practice, and in doing so he revealed himself to be a masterful and imaginative composer. In addition to the traditional harmonic devices, he employed chromaticism in a subtle manner, and he did not hesitate to mix major and minor modes in the same passage. The rhythmic energy engendered in the fast movements is enormous; conversely, the slow movements are models of repose. In place of the somewhat mechanical alternation of *soli* and *tutti* passages, Vivaldi introduced a varied and flexible relationship between the opposing elements. The relationships between the solo instruments themselves, too, changed freely from section to section so that tonal and textural variety become an outstanding element. The thematic outline of Vivaldi's Concerto Grosso in A minor, Op. 3, No. 8, given on pages 346–47, reveals something of this flexibility.

In respect to emotional content or mood, Vivaldi's works have much in common with other music of the time. This music is so designed that one mood (or "affection," as it was called) prevails throughout a movement. Usually one rhythmic figure or motive, repeated exactly or modified appropriately, serves as a seed out of which the various melodies grow (see Example 12*b*, p. 22), and that figure provides the unity of mood. The sharp contrasts of mood characteristic of late eighteenth- and nineteenth-century music are largely missing from Baroque concertos, dances, and the like. As a consequence, a typical Baroque movement in fast tempo develops a high degree of momentum, an onward-driving force that is one of its most compelling features. Similarly, a slow piece is likely to suggest a feeling of respose or relaxation throughout its entire length.

But rather than producing a feeling of monotony, such sustained moods give a sense of intensity and of long architectural line. The singleness of expressive purpose found in any typical movement of Baroque music evokes a response that brings new

Concerto Grosso, Op. 3, No. 8, A minor, by Antonio Vivaldi

Two violins, string orchestra, and harpsichord

FIRST MOVEMENT, Allegro

Meas.	*Part*	
1	A(A^1)	Tutti, full orchestra, A minor. Last three measures (14–16) constitute a ritornello, A^1
17	B	Soli, two violins, A minor (Ex. 1)

Example 1

23	A^1	Tutti, ritornello, as in meas. 14–16, A minor
26	B	Soli, two violins, on Ex. 1; but now parts are reversed
30	C	Solo, Violin I, figuration, A minor
37	C	Tutti and soli alternate at short intervals, C major
43	A	Tutti, derived from meas. 1; begins C major, ends D minor
48	D	Soli, two violins, D minor (Ex. 2)

Example 2

52	A	Tutti, as in meas. 1–3, but in D minor
55	D	Soli, two violins, D minor on Ex. 2; but now parts are reversed
63	A	Tutti, derived from meas. 9–13, A minor
66	B	Soli, two violins, on Ex. 1, A minor
68	A	Tutti, as in meas. 1–3, A minor
72	D	Soli, two violins, on Ex. 2, D minor
79	D,A^1	Tutti on Ex. 2, in A minor, followed by ritornello (as in meas. 14–16) in meas. 84–86
86	D	Soli, two violins, on Ex. 2, but in A minor
90	A^1	Tutti, ritornello, as in meas. 14–16, A minor. Movement ends in meas. 93

SECOND MOVEMENT, Larghetto e spiritoso

Meas.	*Part*	
1	A	Tutti, 4 meas. D minor, quasi-introduction
5	B	Solo, Violin I, D minor (Ex. 3); phrase repeated by Violin II, meas. 8

Example 3

13	C	Soli, D minor, in Violin I; Violin II plays in imitation (meas. 13 ff) and in thirds (meas. 30 ff)
41	A	Tutti, D minor, like meas. 1–4. Movement ends in meas. 45

THIRD MOVEMENT, Allegro

Meas.	*Part*	
1	A	Tutti, A minor
14	B	Soli, two violins, A minor (Ex. 4)

26	A	Tutti, A minor, as in meas. 1–14
37	C	Soli, rhythmic pattern (Violin II), and arpeggiated figure (Violin I)
51	D	Tutti, new figuration in orchestra, with short passages for a
69		solo violin in meas. 69 and 72, A minor
75	E	Soli, rhythmic pattern in thirds beginning in C major but ending in A minor
82	A	Tutti, derived from meas. 1–4, A minor
86	F	Soli, new melody (Ex. 5) in Violin II, with figuration in Violin I, A minor, ending in C major

Example 5

114	A	Tutti (meas. 1–4, modified), as in meas. 82–85, C major
118	E	Soli, as in meas. 75, but in A minor
128	G	Tutti, new figure, A minor
132	C	Soli, as in meas. 37–50, A minor
142	A	Tutti, as in meas. 8–13, A minor. Movement ends in meas. 148

insight into the age in which it was written. Vivaldi and other late Baroque composers are seen as poised individuals who felt no need to shift continually from one emotional effect to another within a single movement.

This does not mean that contrast is missing in Baroque music. It is closer to the truth to say that this music is actually based on contrast—of every kind except mood. The organizing principle of the *concerto grosso,* for example, is that of the alternation of two dissimilar instrumental groups: the *concertino,* of usually three solo instruments, and the *ripieno,* or *tutti,* made up of the entire accompanying forces. Furthermore, contrasting harmonies are introduced in a well-defined order; in general, the recurring sections played by the *tutti* group are in one set of closely related keys, while the interspersed *concertino* passages move further afield in a harmonic sense. Contrasts of harmony are thus assured.

Contrasts in dynamics also play a large part in Baroque music. It is customary in all ensemble works of the time to employ levels of loud and soft alternately. In the *concerto grosso,* the sheer difference in size between the two groups makes such a dynamic alternation inevitable; the term *terrace dynamics* is thus especially appropriate when used in connection with this form. Contrasts in texture are also common; a four-voice texture, for example, may give way to extended two- or three-voice passages on occasion, or homophonic and polyphonic sections may alternate.

These contrasts of instrumental medium, harmony, dynamic level, and texture result in a rich and varied musical sound, to which rhythmic momentum and sustained mood supply stabilizing and unifying elements. Vivaldi's instrumental works, his concertos in particular, eloquently illustrate these aspects of Baroque music. Thus they hold a deservedly high place in the music of the period.

Listening Suggestions

ARCHIVE PRODUCTION

The Italian 17th Century: Monteverdi, Carissimi (Decca, ARC-3005)
The German Baroque: Schütz (Decca, ARC-3006)
Western Europe, 1650-1750: Purcell (Decca, ARC-3007)
The Italian 18th Century: A. Scarlatti, Corelli (Decca, ARC-3008)

Corelli, Trio Sonatas, Op. 3 and 4 (Vox, 163)
Lully, Operatic Arias (Lyric, 16)
Monteverdi, *The Combat of Tancred and Clorinda* (Vox, 8560)
——, Madrigals, Book 4 (Period, 551)
Purcell, *Dido and Aeneas* (Period, 546)
——, Fantasies in Four and Five Parts (Vanguard, 420)
Rameau, Excerpts from the Operas *Dardanus, Castor et Pollux, Les Indes galantes,* etc. (Decca, 9683)
Vivaldi, Concertos, Op. 4 (Vox, 103)

Chapter 17

HANDEL AND BACH

Many outstanding composers were active in the second half of the Baroque period. Antonio Vivaldi serves as one representative; to his name may be added those of Johann Joseph Fux (1660–1741), François Couperin (1668–1733), Antonio Caldara (1670–1736), Georg Philipp Telemann (1681–1767), Johann Adolf Hasse (1699–1783), and Karl Heinrich Graun (1701–59). These composers were highly esteemed in their day; their works were widely performed, and many were published. But with the changes in musical taste that followed upon the emergence of the Classical style, they lost their positions of eminence. The general growth of interest in Baroque music, as exemplified by the many performances of Vivaldi's music today, has begun to make some of them—Couperin and Telemann, for example—better known. The great representatives of late Baroque music, however, are still Handel and Bach, both born in Germany less than a month apart.

Handel

Few composers are more honored today than Handel, an Italianized German who spent almost fifty years in England. His reputation as one of the world's great musicians is secure. But that reputation is not founded upon intimate knowledge of all his major works, as is the case with Beethoven and Brahms, or even upon familiarity with a well-chosen selection of his later ones, as happens with Haydn and Mozart. It is founded, rather, upon three or four major works, a dozen smaller ones, and a few isolated fragments—only a minute portion of Handel's enormous output. The *Messiah* and one or two other oratorios, a few instrumental compositions, and an opera or two are the compositions for which Handel is generally known today.

George Frideric Handel (1685–1759) was born in Halle, in central Germany. His musical talent revealed itself early; even in his middle teens he enjoyed a reputation as an excellent performer. After a thorough course of instruction on the violin, oboe, and organ, as well as in counterpoint, Handel was ready at the age of seven-

George Frideric Handel (1685–1759), German-born representative of Italian music, honored by the English people as one of their greatest musicians. (From a painting by Hudson.)

teen to undertake his first musical position–that of organist at the cathedral in Halle. He had also entered the University of Halle as a law student. But within a year he abandoned the study of law, into which his father had forced him, and left his home to find employment in the opera orchestra at Hamburg. By 1705 he had composed his first opera, and a brilliant career as an operatic composer opened before him, though even as a youth of twenty he realized he had much to learn. Soon Italy drew him, as it had drawn other composers for centuries.

In about 1706 Handel undertook a long visit to Italy, one which was to last almost four years and which brought him into contact with many of the famous composers of the time. Arcangelo Corelli, Alessandro and Domenico Scarlatti, and other eminent musicians, as well as many noblemen, welcomed the young German warmly and admired his skill as a performer and improviser. But Handel's purpose in coming to Italy was to compose; he poured forth a stream of compositions in a variety of forms. Energy and enthusiasm, which were to mark the composer throughout his lifetime, were greatly in evidence during his Italian stay, and the particular melodic style that he made entirely his own took form in this period.

During the few years in Italy, Handel rose from the position of a talented newcomer to that of a master of international reputation. He had written operas, oratorios, chamber cantatas, and a variety of other works. He had quickly mastered the Italian style, and he had brought elements of the *concerto grosso* into his vocal works. Even at this time, his music was invested with rhythmic drive, melodic charm, and an emotional richness that few of his contemporaries could equal. His writing for voice and *continuo* alike made great demands upon the performers. The technical difficulty of these works, along with their brilliance and effectiveness, may be taken as a reflection of the virtuosity Handel had developed on the organ and harpsichord.

In 1710 Handel returned to Germany as musical director at the court of the Elector of Hanover. His stay there was relatively brief, however, for he took a leave of absence in 1711 to produce his opera *Rinaldo* in London and traveled to London again the following year. He remained a resident of England for the rest of his life, ignoring the fact that he was technically on leave of absence from Hanover. Legend has it that Handel suffered severe embarrassment in 1714 when his erstwhile employer came to England in his new role as George I, but this legend is not founded on fact.

In London Handel became a producer of operas on a grand scale. Composing, engaging singers, rehearsing, conducting, and often looking after the financial matters connected with the productions kept him working at top speed. Yet in the thirty years between 1711 and 1741 he wrote about forty operas, among them some of his finest works. During this time, periods in which financial returns were great alternated with periods of failure: Handel was on the verge of bankruptcy several times, and the possessor of a considerable fortune at others.

Political chicanery, as a result of which he found himself caught between the German and anti-German factions at the English court, contributed to the uncertainty of his position. The competition furnished by his opera-composer rivals, Ariosti and Bononcini, along with difficulties created by his temperamental leading singers, made Handel's life anything but calm and meditative. In 1737 he suffered a paralytic stroke and for a time was physically and mentally incapacitated. His tremendous vitality made a complete recovery possible, but when he returned to composing he found that his situation in regard to opera-writing was precarious.

The opera of Handel's time was created largely for the entertainment of the nobility, to whom it looked for its support; the large and active middle class in England was not opera-minded. When aristocratic support was withheld (as it was with increasing frequency in the period 1730–37), Handel sensed that his career as a composer of operas was nearing its end. He turned then to the oratorio, a form that commanded the interest of the middle class. He had written oratorios from time to time since his Italian trip; now, from about 1738, the composition of oratorios became his principal concern, and the stream of operas ceased. The fifteen oratorios, beginning with *Saul* and *Israel in Egypt* (1738–39) and ending with *The Triumph of Time and Truth,* were of a new type and represent Handel's great contribution to music.

Handel became blind in 1753, but his creative energy was scarcely affected. He dictated large portions of his last works, conducted from the harpsichord in the traditional manner, and engaged with unabated zeal in all the work of a musical producer. In 1759 he conducted ten oratorios in little more than a month; the last one of the series was *Messiah.* A few days later he died. He was buried in Westminster Abbey, honored by the English people as one of their greatest musicians. He had come to London half a century before as a German-born representative of Italian music, but he died secure in the affections of his adopted nation.

OPERAS

During his more than thirty years as an opera composer, Handel incorporated many stylistic elements of the Italian opera into his works, especially those characteristic of the Venetian and Neapolitan schools. All the excitement, drama, passion, and exuberance found in the Italian operas generally are also found in those by Handel. But so notable were his personal contributions to the style, and so individual were certain melodic traits, that Handel's forty-odd works in this form constitute a unique chapter in the history of opera.

Handel was an enthusiastic borrower—of his own as well as other men's music. A particular rhythmic pattern, a stylistic effect found in a *concerto grosso,* or an entire section of a pre-existing composition might find its way into one of his works. Yet in virtually every case Handel transformed the borrowed portions, recast them to meet his own musical or dramatic needs, and welded the whole into a higher unity.

This borrowing was quite in keeping with Baroque practice; copyright laws did not exist, "ownership" of a musical idea had scarcely occurred to musicians of the time, and the idea of musical plagiarism had not been born. Borrowing was expected and condoned—only with the proviso that the borrower "pay back with interest"; in other words, he was expected to improve upon the original. Certainly those from whom Handel borrowed could feel that they had received full interest.

Of several melodic types to which Handel turned again and again in his operatic arias, two are especially noteworthy. One type is a sustained melody in slow tempo, moving with a graceful rise and fall to the cadences. Whether its sentiment is intense or languid, whether bright or mournful, such an aria represents the famous *bel canto* type, the development of which was one of Italy's great contributions to music. The essence of *bel canto* is that the melody is no longer subordinate to the text; it exists in its own right and is not dependent upon the rhythm or accentual scheme of the words. The harmony is uncomplicated and direct, the rhythmic flow is not broken up by all manner of vocal embroidery, and the simple structure conceals deep feeling. The best known, perhaps, of all Handel's melodies is of the *bel canto* type: the aria "Ombra mai fu" (usually referred to as the *Largo*), from his opera *Xerxes* (see Example 117). Religious significance has often been erroneously attributed to this melody.

Handel's other characteristic melodic type is so common in his works that it might almost serve as his trademark; it occurs in all tempos, and in works of all categories. It contains a melodic or rhythmic motive that is repeated many times, always with pauses between. Much of the time an animated or pulsating accompaniment is

Example 117

Handel, *Rinaldo*, "Lascia ch'io pianga" *Example 118*

provided to bridge the gap between pauses and to tie the parts into a whole. The well-known "Lascia ch'io pianga," from Handel's opera *Rinaldo* (1711) is an illustration (see Example 118). In the field of the oratorio the same melodic type exists; a well-known example is the beginning of the "Hallelujah" chorus from his *Messiah.*

ORATORIOS

The compound form called the oratorio is in many respects similar to the opera. It too may contain a variety of recitatives, arias, small ensembles, choruses, and purely instrumental pieces. It also makes use of solo singers, chorus, and orchestra, and it may be divided into parts that correspond to the acts of an opera. But here the similarity ends. In many cases the oratorio is based on a Biblical text and has a definite religious background. It makes no use of scenery, costumes, or any other element of theatrical staging, and the chorus takes a position of greater importance than in opera.

The oratorio originated in Italy early in the seventeenth century. It was a result of attempts by members of the Jesuit order to combat the rise of secularism that came in the wake of the newly introduced opera. The Jesuits encouraged the development of a form externally similar to the opera but concerned with religious subjects. Since it was designed for popular consumption, the new form employed the simplest of harmonies based on the use of the *continuo.* Giacomo Carissimi (*circa* 1604–74), the most important of the early oratorio composers, made considerable use of the chorus, whose usual function was to carry the dramatic action forward. An important feature of the oratorio was the part of the narrator or *testo,* who introduced the episodes or events dramatized in the other musical portions of the work.

When Handel abandoned the opera and returned to the composition of oratorios, he made increasing use of elements he had first seen in the oratorios of Carissimi—notably the chorus. But while the function of the chorus remained what it had been in the earlier composer's works, its scope was now greatly increased. Pomp, vocal color, polyphonic texture, and monumental size distinguish the choruses of Handel's oratorios from those of all previous works.

Three types of oratorio, based on differences in subject matter, can be distinguished throughout the history of the form, and all are represented in Handel's works. In one type, the events in the life of one character (often drawn from the Old Testament) are dramatized and set to music. Titles such as *Saul, Samson, Esther,* and *Belshazzar* reveal the subject matter of many of Handel's works of this type. Inner struggle and outer action are expressed, hence drama is seldom missing; indeed, Handel's oratorios are often called choral dramas. In another type the text is based on a great Biblical event or concept; Handel's *Messiah* is among the best-known examples (as is *The Creation* by Haydn, discussed in Chapter 8). Oratorios of the third type draw their textual material from mythology, secular epic poems, or other literary sources rather than from the Scriptures. Handel's *Hercules, L'Allegro,* and *Semele* are examples. And no matter what the type, Handel's musical imagination was always equal to the great task of providing proper settings for the characters represented in his oratorios.

The most beloved of Handel's works in this form is of course *Messiah;* it is an exceptional work and stands apart from the other oratorios in both text and treatment. (An outline is given on the facing page.) *Messiah* is concerned with the concept of redemption as expressed in the Christian philosophy. Its text is drawn from both the Old and the New Testaments. Unlike the majority of oratorios—including Handel's other works—*Messiah* is a contemplative rather than a dramatic oratorio. Its religious expression contributes to its universal appeal, yet that expression is not derived from any particular denomination of Christianity. *Messiah* transcends doctrinaire religion and has no liturgical function.

INSTRUMENTAL COMPOSITIONS

Handel's instrumental works include several sets of sonatas for one or more instruments and *continuo,* and over four dozen orchestral works, mainly concertos. Of the latter, the twelve *concerti grossi* of Op. 6 (*circa* 1738–39) are outstanding. They are

A manuscript page from Handel's Messiah.

Messiah, an Oratorio by George Frideric Handel

Orchestra. Sinfonia

PART I

Arioso. Comfort ye, my people
Air. Every valley shall be exalted
Chorus. And the glory of the Lord
Recitative. Thus saith the Lord
Air. But who may abide
Chorus. And He shall purify
Recitative. Behold, a Virgin shall conceive
Air and Chorus. O thou that tellest good tidings
Arioso. For behold
Air. The people that walked in darkness
Chorus. For unto us a child is born
Orchestra. Pastoral Symphony
Recitative. There were shepherds abiding in the fields
Arioso. And lo, the angel of the Lord
Recitative. And the angel said
Arioso. And suddenly there was with the angel
Chorus. Glory to God in the Highest
Air. Rejoice greatly
Recitative. Then shall the eyes of the blind be opened
Air. He shall feed his flock
Chorus. His yoke is easy

PART II

Chorus. Behold the Lamb of God
Air. He was despised
Chorus. Surely He hath borne our griefs
Chorus. And with His stripes we are healed
Chorus. All we like sheep have gone astray
Arioso. All they that see him laugh him to scorn
Chorus. He trusted in God
Recitative. Thy rebuke hath broken his heart
Arioso. Behold and see
Recitative. He was cut off out of the land
Air. But thou didst not leave his soul in hell
Chorus. Lift up your heads
Recitative. Unto which of the angels
Chorus. Let all the angels of God worship him
Air. Thou art gone up on high
Chorus. The Lord gave the word
Air and Chorus. How beautiful are the feet of them
Air. Why do the nations so furiously rage
Chorus. Let us break their bonds
Recitative. He that dwelleth in heaven
Air. Thou shalt break them
Chorus. Hallelujah

PART III

Air. I know that my Redeemer liveth
Chorus. Since by man came death
Recitative. Behold, I tell you a mystery
Air. The trumpet shall sound
Recitative. Then shall be brought to pass
Duet. O death, where is thy sting
Chorus. But thanks be to God
Air. If God be for us
Chorus. Worthy is the Lamb
Chorus. Blessing and honor
Chorus. Amen

externally modeled upon the concertos of Corelli, who, some forty years earlier, had set the standard for other instrumental composers to follow. But the works of Handel are considerably more varied in texture and expressive content. Two solo violins constitute the solo group of the *concertino,* with the occasional help of a solo cello, and a string orchestra with *continuo* constitutes the *tutti.*

Variety is the keynote of Handel's Op. 6, along with an improvisatory tone that suggests that the composer was greatly pressed for time while he was writing these concertos. Enormous fugues, marchlike slow movements, passages in which the *bel canto* style is transferred to the orchestra, and passages of serious or somber intent are all present. The bustling, rhythmically animated figures characteristic of the majority of Baroque orchestral works are found here in abundance. And while the concertos of Op. 6 are not always on the same level as Handel's inspired oratorios, they are among the relatively few works of the enormous eighteenth-century concerto repertoire that have survived.

Quite different is another, earlier orchestral composition of Handel's—the famous *Water Music.* Its name is derived from the nature of its inception. King George wished to have music for a barge party on a July evening in 1717; Handel was engaged to provide the music, and he arranged to have it played from a second boat that accompanied the King's barge down the river. He composed a suite of twenty movements for an orchestra of strings and half a dozen wind instruments. The suite begins with a massive French overture on the model made famous by Lully in his operas, and it continues with a number of dances, airs, and polyphonic pieces in a variety of styles and forms.

Heard in its entirety as a concert suite, the *Water Music* makes an impression of diffuseness. But thought of in its original setting, as outdoor music composed for a festive occasion, it is delightful. One can imagine long pauses for refreshments and conversation between movements: the lack of unity is then not felt to be a flaw. Most often today the *Water Music* is heard in an arrangement by Sir Hamilton Harty. The eminent Irish conductor and composer selected six of the movements, expanded the orchestra in keeping with present-day orchestral practice, and in this form succeeded in rescuing the charming work from the oblivion that has befallen so many of Handel's masterpieces.

Bach

Bach's music is among the earliest that is heard regularly on the concert stage today. That fact has probably contributed to the widely held belief that Bach is the first of the "modern" composers, that he stands at the head of the line that includes Haydn, Mozart, and all the other familiar masters. The historical facts point to another conclusion, however. Probably no composer had his roots embedded so deeply in the past. Rather than being the first in a series of great musicians, Bach represents the culmination of the musical developments that began in the early 1600's. He had no musical heirs.

Johann Sebastian Bach (1685–1750) was born in Eisenach, in central Germany. He was an exact contemporary of Handel–yet the two greatest musicians of the late Baroque period never met. On the outskirts of Eisenach is a famous eleventh-century castle, the Wartburg, where Martin Luther found refuge from his enemies in the sixteenth century and where he completed his translation of the Bible. Bach remained faithful to the spirit of Luther and to the Lutheran liturgy throughout his lifetime.

Bach came from a family of musicians; for about six generations its members had supplied the towns of Thuringia with music. His earliest teachers were his father and an elder brother, and even as a boy he was an accomplished violinist and organist. But Bach's formal instruction was the least significant part of his training. To the end of his life he was his own teacher, studying and copying the music of Italian, French, and German composers of the time, imitating their styles, and learning thereby the techniques of composition. The result was a fabulous technical skill scarcely matched by any composer before or after him. In addition to being an accomplished violinist, he was also one of the two greatest organists of his time; only Handel was his equal. And from the very beginning, his music was dedicated to the service of God.

After positions as organist in the towns of Arnstadt in 1703 and Mühlhausen in 1707, Bach entered upon the first of the three important musical posts he was to occupy in his lifetime: he became organist and later concertmaster to the Duke of Weimar. Always a practical musician who wrote according to the requirements of his position, Bach at this time concerned himself primarily with organ compositions. Most of his great works for that instrument were composed during his nine years in the service of the Duke. At Weimar he also obtained his first important contact with

Johann Sebastian Bach (1685–1750), whose music is the greatest monument of the Baroque period, playing for Frederick the Great at Potsdam in 1741. (From a painting by Kaulbach.)

Italian music, and he proceeded to master the elements of Italian style. Brilliance, warmth of expression, and solidity were combined with his native German aptitude for polyphony in these works. Enthusiastically adopting the style of the Italian concerto, Bach infused it with contrapuntal textures and applied it in fugal compositions.

When Bach was called to the court of the Prince of Anhalt-Cöthen in 1717 as chapelmaster and director of music, he attained the highest social position he was ever to hold. He found himself at a court whose interests were more secular than religious. He had virtually no vocal resources at his command, and the Reformed church services at Cöthen made little demand upon him. With characteristic energy, Bach turned away from the organ and voice and devoted himself to composing for keyboard, string, and wind instruments.

The majority of his works for keyboard (harpsichord and clavichord) and for orchestra were written at Cöthen, and many of them served a pedagogical purpose. Bach was concerned with teaching his sons and with providing guides and models for his pupils. The Two- and Three-part Inventions, familiar to generations of piano students, belong to this period, as does the first volume of the *Well-Tempered Clavier.* The six "Brandenburg" Concertos are among the most important of the orchestral works of this time. At Cöthen Bach renewed his contact with French music, and as he had done at Weimar with the Italian, he now made the French style completely his own. He combined the gracefulness, ornamental melodic line, and stylized dance forms typical of French music into a unity that utilized polyphonic textures and expressed deep feeling.

In 1723 Bach changed employers for the last time: he was appointed cantor at St. Thomas' Church in Leipzig—a position he was to hold until his death in 1750. His duties were considerable: at the choir school attached to the church he trained singers for the two principal churches of the city and instructed the boys in Latin; he supervised the music at the church of St. Nicholas; and he served as organist, choirmaster, and resident composer for St. Thomas'. Among his assignments was the writing of a cantata for each Sunday and feast day of the church year—some sixty occasions annually. In carrying out this assignment Bach composed five complete sets (about three hundred cantatas), of which almost two hundred have been preserved.

The position at Leipzig gave Bach ample opportunity to return to his compelling purpose—that of providing music to serve the needs of the Lutheran service. But it also exposed him to the petty tyranny of the municipal council that employed him. Annoyances such as interference with his rights as a creative musician, bickering about fees withheld, and complaints about the freedom of his playing embittered the composer's later years.

But regardless of the unpleasantness of his professional associations, Bach enjoyed a rich life, secure in the affections of his large family. He had twenty children, of whom about half did not survive infancy; of the survivors, three became important composers in their own rights. He was honored as an outstanding organist and was often called upon to evaluate and perform on new instruments. He advanced continually in his mastery of musical art, and his inner purpose and creative zeal never faltered. Devoting himself largely to choral composition at Leipzig, he wrote some of the most profound and heartfelt works in the entire literature—notably the Mass in B minor and the *Passion According to St. Matthew.*

Near the end of his life, Bach turned to the composition of works that summed up all the resources of the polyphonic art—works that in their profundity and musical insight stand at the creative peak of the Baroque period. They include a set of canonic variations for the organ, on a chorale theme; *The Musical Offering,* a work composed of canons, fugues, and a trio sonata, all built upon a theme given to Bach by Frederick the Great, King of Prussia; and the mystical, abstract *Art of the Fugue,* a series of fugues all based upon a single theme that is presented in a different form in each of its movements (see Example 12*b*, p. 22). The last fugue of this work remained unfinished.

Shortly before his death in 1750, Bach's eyes failed. He dictated his last composition to his son-in-law; it is a setting of the chorale, "I stand before thy throne, my God." To the very end his strong religious faith endured.

FORMS AND PRACTICES

In the course of the Baroque period, several new musical forms and practices had been introduced and were employed by many composers of the time, and certain others, originating in the Renaissance, had been revived and brought to new levels of expressiveness. In the music of Bach, a number of those forms and practices culminated their development and became essential elements of Bach's style. They may therefore be considered in connection with his music, even though they appeared in the works of other composers, a century or more before Bach's time. Among them are the *basso ostinato,* the *canon,* and the *fugue.*

In discussing the variation principle (see Chapter 5, pp. 78–79, and Chapter 9, pp. 160–63) we considered the melody of a composition as generally being in the topmost voice. Let us imagine now a musical form in which the melody is transferred to the lowest voice, where it serves as the theme of the work and where it is repeated many times without significant change. Imagine further that in a higher voice above each of the bass repetitions a suitable new melody or accompaniment is introduced, different for each repetition. We thus have variations *above* a recurring bass theme, not variations of the theme itself. This is the plan of one of the finest of Bach's organ works, the Passacaglia in C minor, a piece that occupies a high place in the concert repertoire. The work also exists in orchestral transcriptions and has been widely recorded in that form.

The term "passacaglia" is supposedly derived from the Spanish words *pasear,* to stroll or amble, and *calle,* a street; the spelling *passacaile* is also found. The term originally referred to a kind of street dance in which one phrase was repeated many times, with variations built above and around it. Bach's famous Passacaglia is perhaps the best-known example of the form. It consists of an eight-measure phrase, presented first in the bass without accompaniment, and some twenty variations built above it. Example 119 shows the phrase and portions of several of the variations. Each variation is concerned with its own melodic or rhythmic figure, and the whole set of variations is held together by the recurring phrase in the bass.

This type of treatment is called "variations on a ground" or, more picturesquely, *basso ostinato* (literally, "obstinate bass"). It is one of the oldest types of variation and has been used by composers for almost four centuries. Example 120 illustrates the bass phrases of several other compositions in which the *basso ostinato* treatment is used. All are outstanding examples of the use of this device. In the Brahms work

Example 119

Bach, Passacaglia in C minor

THEME

VAR. 1

VAR. 3

VAR. 4

Example 119 (cont.)

(Example 120*d*) mentioned on page 160 as an example of the theme and variations form, the *basso ostinato* section forms the closing portion and brings the whole to a stirring conclusion.

Another method, and one of the very oldest, of manipulating a melody to create a polyphonic texture results in a form that is well known under the name *round.* In *Three Blind Mice, Scotland's Burning, Sumer Is Icumen In,* and other familiar rounds, the following occurs (see Example 121): (1) One voice sings a melody that may run on

Example 120

(a) Purcell, *Dido and Aeneas*

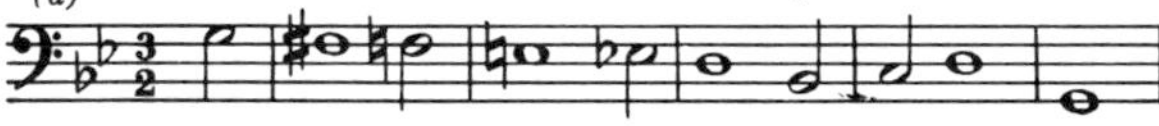

(b) Beethoven, Quartet, No. 16, Op. 135

(c) Bach, Mass in B minor, "Crucifixus"

(d) Brahms, *Variations on a Theme by Haydn,* Finale

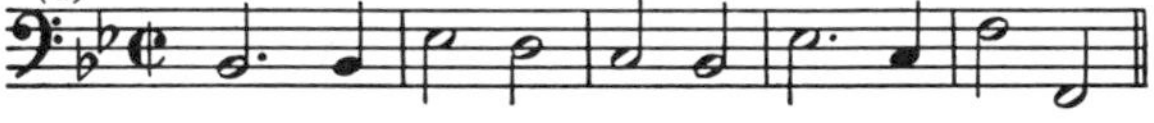

Example 121

Round, *Scotland's Burning*

I etc.

II etc.

III etc.

to considerable length. (2) A second voice, beginning at a specified distance behind the first, performs exactly what the first voice had done a moment before. (3) A third voice, beginning at the same distance behind the second one, again repeats the melody exactly. (4) The process is repeated as long as desired, after which the voices drop out one by one or end together.

The organizing principle involved here is that of repetition by imitation—but repetition after a specified time interval. Specifying the time interval thus establishes the rule or law governing the construction of the piece. In Example 121, for instance, the rule is: The melody is to be repeated on the same pitch after one measure.

In a more formal context, this procedure is called *canon*, since canon itself means "rule" or "law." But the imitating voice in a canon need not always enter on the same pitch, as is usual in a round. A canon "at the interval of a fifth after two measures," or "at the octave after three measures," or at any other interval after any time lapse—these are all technically possible. Many canons have been composed by master craftsmen from the late thirteenth century onward. For example, the opening of Bach's "Brandenburg" Concerto No. 6, several movements of Bach's *Musical Offering*, and the scherzo of Schubert's Piano Trio in E flat, Op. 100, are canons. To write an expressive canon is one of the great tests of a composer's competence and disciplined imagination.

A less consistent application of the principle upon which rounds and canons are based results in a related form and procedure called, respectively, *fugue* and fugal treatment, both of which reached their highest point of usefulness in the Baroque period. The essence of the fugue as a form is this: one melody called the *theme* or *subject* runs through large sections of the composition; in fact, the term "fugue" is derived from this fugitive or fleeing behavior. Fugues are written for voices or instruments or both; in every case, however, each of the single lines of melody employed in the form is called a *voice*. Four-voice fugues are perhaps more common than fugues requiring a larger or smaller number of voices.

A typical fugue begins with a theme presented without accompaniment; the theme is likely to be two to four measures in length. When the theme has been presented once on the tonic, it is imitated by another voice on the dominant, and then alternately on tonic and dominant by the remaining voices. After its statement of the theme, each voice may then present a contrasting melody called a *countertheme*, or it may drop out of the texture temporarily. The countertheme may be composed of fragments or motives taken from the theme itself.

The section in which the theme is thus announced by the various voices is called the *exposition*. Several expositions, often containing fewer than the full number of voices, are usual in a fugue. Each one after the first is usually (but not necessarily) in a key other than the tonic, and each one is separated from the next by a section called the *episode*. The episodes are often lighter in mood than the expositions, and usually contain short developments of motives taken from the theme. The series of expositions and episodes, increasing in tension and expressive power during the course of the work, culminate in a climax called a *stretto;* here the theme or theme fragments enter closer together, usually overlapping, and build in sonority.

Example 122

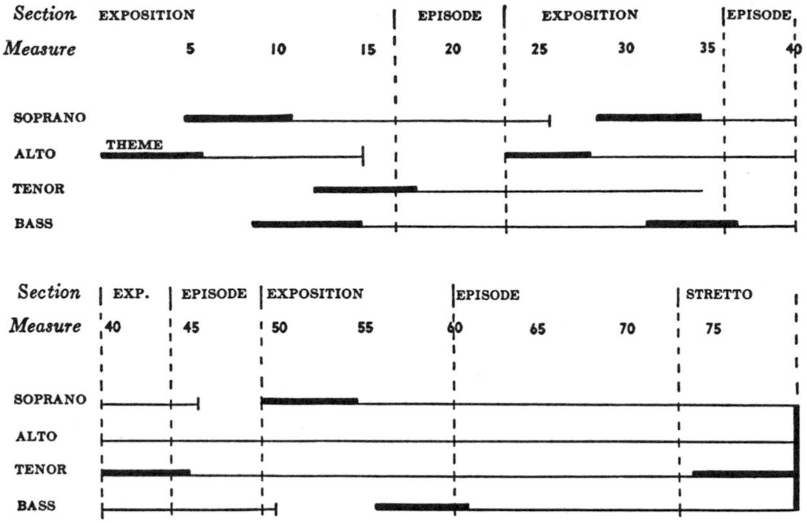

Section EXPOSITION | EPISODE | EXPOSITION | EPISODE
Measure 5 10 15 20 25 30 35 40
SOPRANO
ALTO THEME
TENOR
BASS

Section EXP. | EPISODE | EXPOSITION | EPISODE | STRETTO
Measure 40 45 50 55 60 65 70 75
SOPRANO
ALTO
TENOR
BASS

As an example of the structure of a fugue, the first movement of Bach's *Art of the Fugue* is given in Example 122. At that master's hands the fugue developed an extraordinary variety of ground plans; each fugue has its own inner arrangement of details. Inexhaustible invention in the creation of themes, variety in the shape and number of the expositions, melodic sweep and power in the episodes, and great skill in working out the contrapuntal combinations—these combine to make a Bach fugue an outstanding musical achievement.

INSTRUMENTAL WORKS

Bach's position was not that of a revolutionary or a pathfinder; he worked almost entirely with forms that had been in use before his time. However, every form he touched—whether fugue, concerto, Mass, cantata, or any other—rose so far above his models in technical detail and expressive content that it became in effect a new form. The six concertos he wrote for the Margrave of Brandenburg provide ample evidence of his mastery of composition.

The "Brandenburg" Concertos, composed about 1721, are Bach's earliest works in the orchestral field and are among his finest accomplishments. No two are alike, either in form or instrumentation, as is shown on page 367.

The outstanding characteristic of the "Brandenburg" Concertos is their exuberant mood. All the rhythmic drive and brilliance found in concertos by Italian masters are recaptured in these works. In addition, there is a solidity of sound brought about by Bach's typical fusion of polyphonic and homophonic textures (see Example 123). Short rhythmic motives intertwine with running figures, imitate each other in different voices, and unify the texture in a masterful manner. Yet Bach's enthusiasm is under perfect control; the forms are proportioned with mathematical exactness despite their apparent spontaneity.

"Brandenburg" Concerto No. 2, F major, by J. S. Bach

Trumpet, flute, oboe, and violin in concertino

FIRST MOVEMENT, Allegro, F major

Meas.	*Section*	
1	A	Tutti, entire phrase, 8 meas. (Ex. 1)

Example 1

9	B	Soli and tutti; series of two-meas. solo phrases (Ex. 2), alternating with first two meas. of Ex. 1. As an exception, at meas. 23–28, last six meas. (instead of first two) of Ex. 1

Example 2

31	A	Tutti; Ex. 1 modified in meas. 3–4; D minor
40		Soli; meas. 1 and 2 of Ex. 1 in various keys
50		Soli; meas. 5 of Ex. 1 repeated six times in modulatory passage
56		Tutti; meas. 5–8 as a codetta, ending in B flat
60	B	Soli; two-meas. phrase (Ex. 2) repeated four times in various keys
68	A	Tutti; various sections of Ex. 1 in various keys
84		Soli; meas. 1 and 2 of Ex. 1 in modulatory phrase, ending in A minor with meas. 5–8
103	A	Tutti; entire phrase (Ex. 1) beginning and ending in F major, but with fifth meas. repeated eight times in modulatory passage (meas. 107 ff). Movement ends in meas. 118

SECOND MOVEMENT, Andante, D minor

Flute, oboe, and violin solos with basso continuo; *tutti not present*

Meas.	*Section*	
1		Introductory meas.

2	A	Series of thematic statements (Ex. 3) in canon at two-meas. intervals, mainly in D minor; passage ends in A minor

15		Episode based on parts of Ex. 3, beginning in A minor
24	A	As in Ex. 3, meas. 2–14, but beginning in C major and ending in B flat
33		Episode based on parts of Ex. 3, beginning in B flat and ending on dominant of F
40	A	Isolated statement of Ex. 3, in G minor
43		Episode based on parts of Ex. 3, beginning in G minor
58	A	Two final statements of Ex. 3, in D minor, leading to coda. Movement ends in meas. 65

THIRD MOVEMENT, Allegro assai, F major

Meas.	*Section*	
1	A	Soli; five statements of Ex. 4 (in meas. 1, 7, 21, 27, and 41)

separated by two episodes (in meas. 13 and 33)

47	B	Tutti, based on Ex. 5, in C major

57	A	Soli; two returns of Ex. 4, C major and D minor
72		Tutti; Ex. 4 in bass, A minor, with return of Ex. 5 in D minor at meas. 79
87	C	Soli; modulatory passage from D minor to B flat by circle of fifths, based on Ex. 6.

97	B	Tutti; based on Ex. 5, in B flat
107	A	Soli; return of Ex. 4, beginning in B flat
119	A	Tutti; Ex. 4 beginning in C and ending in F, with Ex. 5 inserted at meas. 127 ff. Movement ends in meas. 139

Example 123

As an example of the mathematical relationships that Bach could infuse into even the most buoyant of his works, the second concerto of the set may be examined in greater detail (see the outline on pp. 364–65). In the first movement, measures 23–28 contain the last 6 measures of the principal *tutti* phrase; measures 31–60 are also concerned with that phrase, but in a series of modulations. Later in the movement, measures 68–103 contain the same material, but now the modulations are somewhat more remote.

Three sections, each one building in rhythmic intensity and harmonic interest, are involved here; they are 6, 29, and 35 measures long respectively. Cumulative growth toward the final cadence is thus assured. But at the same time, the first two sections (6 and 29 measures) are exactly balanced by the last (35). Perfect balance is thus achieved in a context that leads the listener inexorably from the beginning to the final climax. This single example may suffice to demonstrate how thoughtfully Bach worked, and how he brought the smallest details into proper relationship with each other.

KEYBOARD WORKS

Bach's organ works do not truly reflect his position as one of the greatest organ virtuosos of the Baroque period. They are neither as numerous as his works in other cate-

The "Brandenburg" Concertos

	SOLO GROUP (*concertino*)	ACCOMPANIMENT (*tutti*)	MOVEMENTS
No. 1 F major	two horns three oboes *violino piccolo*	two violins viola *continuo* (with bassoon)	Allegro Adagio Allegro Menuetto
No. 2 F major	trumpet oboe violin flute	two violins viola *continuo*	Allegro Andante Allegro assai
No. 3 G major	concerto for orchestra, with no solo group as such; scored for three violins three violas three cellos *continuo*		Allegro Allegro
No. 4 G major	violin	two flutes two violins viola *continuo*	Allegro Andante Presto
No. 5 D major	violin flute harpsichord	violin viola *continuo*	Allegro Affetuoso Allegro
No. 6 B flat major	concerto for orchestra, with no solo group as such; scored for two *viole da braccio* two *viole da gamba* cello *continuo*		Allegro Adagio ma non troppo Allegro

gories, nor are they display pieces designed to reveal the astounding technical mastery he achieved on his favorite instrument. Rather they are profound and sincere works of art that bring to expression Bach's intense religious feeling and his consummate skill as a composer. They include some of his most intimate works as well as some that are scarcely equaled for drama and massiveness. Many of them have been transcribed for orchestra; in that form they have become standard works in today's concert repertoire.

Among Bach's organ compositions two forms are the most numerous: the *fugue* and the *chorale prelude.* As we have seen, the fugue in Bach's hands became an individual work of art and not an example of a type. This is especially true of the organ fugues. The resources of that instrument, even in Bach's day, were considerable, for they regularly included three keyboards (two manuals and the pedals). These resources provided Bach with the means to vary textures, expand episodes, and overlap thematic entrances in exciting fashion. The solid sonority, the skillful manipulation of the polyphony, and the variety of moods they contain make Bach's organ fugues rich in emotional and intellectual appeal.

In Bach's works, the fugue is most often paired with a contrasting movement. One type of movement in this category has an improvisatory character and is called a *fantasia,* or *fantasy;* another is a more reflective or dramatic piece called a *prelude;* and a third is a brilliant display piece called a *toccata.* Notable examples of such pairings include the Fantasy and Fugue in G minor, often heard in its transcribed form for orchestra, and the Prelude and Fugue in E flat, called "St. Anne's" because of the similarity of the fugue theme with the hymn tune of that name. ("St. Anne's" is also used in the well-known hymn "O God Our Help in Ages Past.") The Passacaglia and Fugue in C minor, described above, are related to these works in majesty and power as well as in the great climaxes.

The *chorale prelude* is essentially a short movement for organ and is cast in the form of an improvisation on, or a variation of, a chorale melody. In the eighteenth-century Lutheran service, the chorale prelude was played before the chorale itself; the latter was sung by the congregation. Bach composed almost 150 chorale preludes of this type. They include an astounding variety of expressive content. Intimate, poignant, lively, brooding, and monumental expression is found, establishing the mood of the chorale text that traditionally ends the work.

Sometimes, however, they range far beyond the chorale melody upon which they are based. Indeed, Bach was occasionally reprimanded by his superiors for introducing too much variety and displaying too much creative imagination in the chorale preludes. For Bach was not averse to confusing his congregation, who could not always distinguish the familiar chorale melody in the midst of polyphonic and harmonic complexity. He was concerned above all with the proper expression of his musical ideas; in comprehension of those ideas, the congregation and the Leipzig officials who employed Bach were often left far behind.

Among the important keyboard works of Bach, the *Well-Tempered Clavier* takes a high place. The term "well-tempered" refers to a system of tuning that tended to equalize all the half steps in the octave. This system, which came into prominence early in the eighteenth century, made it possible to play in tune in all keys. Other systems had provided satisfactory tuning in the key of C and in other keys related to it (G and F, for example), but became progressively more unsatisfactory in more remote keys. The term "Clavier" in the title of the work is the German generic term for keyboard instruments such as the harpsichord, clavichord, and spinet.

The *Well-Tempered Clavier* consists of two parts: each part contains a prelude and fugue in each of the twelve major and twelve minor keys, arranged in chromatic order. Thus, in the first book, the Prelude and Fugue in C major are followed by those in C minor, C sharp major, C sharp minor, D major, and so on through the entire series of twenty-four keys. The second book, beginning again with C major, follows the same order.

The 48 preludes and fugues were probably designed to serve as teaching pieces, or, as Bach's title states, ". . . for the use of those musical youth eager to learn, as well as to provide entertainment for those already skilled." Nevertheless, their musical content ranges far beyond the usual content of pedagogical material. The variety of expressive types seems inexhaustible. The preludes are gay, eloquent, somber, or profound (the well-known *Ave Maria* by Bach-Gounod is nothing more than the first Prelude of Book I to which Gounod added a melody of his own contriving; see Example 29*b*, p. 44). Many of the fugues resemble idealized dance forms; others are abstract works, at once serious and melodious. The fact that the *Well-Tempered Clavier* has often been called "the pianist's Old Testament" testifies to the revered place it has held for generations. (Beethoven's 32 piano sonatas are "the pianist's New Testament.")

CHORAL WORKS

The *cantata* in the late 1600's was related to the oratorio, but usually it was shorter and required smaller musical forces than the older form. And rather than dramatic, it was generally narrative or contemplative. About 1700, a new type of cantata grew out of a reform movement in the Lutheran church. The authors of the new cantata texts paraphrased the sacred words instead of employing them directly, and often poetic commentaries on the meaning of the texts were introduced. The cantatas of this type often contained recitatives and arias that were not unlike those in the operas of the time.

Unlike the oratorio, the cantata was used in the Lutheran service and was written to be performed on a specific day in the church year. In the course of his official duties at Leipzig, Bach composed several cycles of cantatas, one for every Sunday and feast day of the year; of these, about two hundred have been preserved. In those works he turned away from the sentimental content of the reform cantatas and established a close connection between his music and the Lutheran chorale. Most often he reverted to the chorale texts themselves, setting the several stanzas in a variety of musical forms. Usually the first stanza was composed for a large chorus. Intermediate stanzas

From a caricature by Gustave Dore.

were set as recitatives, arias, or ensemble numbers, and the last stanza appeared in simple four-part harmonization and in a quiet mood.

Within this framework, Bach again demonstrated his ability to transform diverse stylistic elements and adjust them to his own expressive requirements. Those requirements and the requirements of the Lutheran liturgy came closer and closer to being identical. A bewildering array of interpenetrated forms and styles is found among those of his cantatas that employ the chorale. The well-known Cantata No. 80, *A Mighty Fortress Is Our God* (about 1730), is an example.

The cantata contains eight movements, as follows:

1. *Chorus.* A mighty fortress is our God
2. *Duet* (soprano and bass). Standing alone are we undone
3. *Recitative* (bass). Thou child of God
4. *Aria* (soprano). Come, dwell within my heart
5. *Unison chorus.* Though fields appear on every hand
6. *Recitative* (tenor). So take thy stand
7. *Duet* (alto and tenor). Blest he who praises God
8. *Chorale.* The word of God will firm abide

The first chorus is set in fugal style, with the themes of the various expositions derived from the several lines of the chorale, and with a trumpet intoning the chorale melody independently over the sonorous texture. The soprano and bass duet (No. 2) presents a highly ornamented version of the chorale melody in the soprano, while the bass is concerned with a rapidly moving countermelody (see Example 124). The recitative and aria that follow (Nos. 3 and 4) are contemplative in mood, as are the recitative and duet (Nos. 6 and 7). The chorus that intervenes (No. 5) again presents the chorale melody, but this time in unison against a brilliant orchestral accompaniment, and in strongly rhythmic fashion. The closing chorale (No. 8) is in simple harmony and is unaccompanied except for the *continuo.*

Example 124

Bach, Cantata No. 80, *A Mighty Fortress Is Our God*

The entire cantata recaptures the spirit of Luther's text in its several verses, and each verse is composed so that the innermost meaning of the words shines through. Moods of tenderness and strength, of faith and praise are contained here; the whole is one of Bach's masterpieces.

Bach's Mass in B minor, composed about 1732–37, grew out of his desire to be named court composer to the Elector of Saxony in Dresden. The court being Catholic, Bach composed the *Kyrie* and *Gloria* of the Mass and sent them to the Elector as evidence of his competence. Later he wrote the remaining movements, some of them containing sections he had first used in his cantatas. The complete work, among the most expressive of all Masses, has taken its place as one of the great monuments of Western culture.

The transition from the style of the Renaissance Mass to that of the Baroque brought with it a breakdown of the previously accepted form. Single movements of the Mass were sometimes written as fugues or arias; often the forms were closely akin to those being used in the contemporaneous opera and oratorio. In the early eighteenth century the Mass was often given an organ or orchestral accompaniment, which in turn made it possible to insert instrumental passages between the vocal sections. The whole often became so elaborate that the liturgical significance of the Mass was virtually obscured.

In Bach's massive setting, the operatic extravagances are avoided, yet the work contains its full share of dramatic contrasts. The usual six parts of the Mass are set as twenty-five separate numbers; the table on page 372 gives the beginning of the text of each. This division of a movement of the Mass into several numbers may have been made necessary by the aesthetic philosophy, prevalent in the Baroque period, that a single composition or movment should embody only a single mood (or "affection," as it was then called). A real contrast of mood within a single piece violated the aesthetic feeling of the time. Yet certain consecutive sections of the text of the Mass differ so widely in mood that the composer was virtually compelled to separate a paragraph or sentence of the text into two or more contrasting pieces if the moods were to be respected.

For example, the middle section of the *Credo* contains the following: ". . . He was also crucified for us, suffered under Pontius Pilate, and was buried. And on the third day He rose again . . ." (see the full text on pp. 314–15). The contrast of moods suggested here is the same as that between Good Friday and Easter, and no single treatment could do justice to two such dissimilar moods. Thus Bach and other Baroque composers divided the text of the Mass into shorter sections, each set to appropriate music.

Although the B minor Mass is entirely too massive to serve the needs of the Catholic liturgy and is not suited to the Protestant service, it stands as a testimony to Bach's musical and religious ideals. Its sheer size and length make it inappropriate for any church service, and it is too lofty in conception for routine concert-hall performance. But its grandeur, scope, and symbolism lift it far beyond any other choral setting of the Mass text.

Mass in B Minor, by Johann Sebastian Bach

KYRIE

Chorus. Kyrie eleison
Duet. Christe eleison
Chorus. Kyrie eleison

GLORIA

Chorus. Gloria in excelsis Deo
Aria. Laudamus te
Chorus. Gratias agimus
Duet. Domine Deus
Chorus. Qui tollis
Aria. Qui sedes
Aria. Quoniam tu solus sanctus
Chorus. Cum sancto spiritu

CREDO

Chorus. Credo in unum Deum
Chorus. Patrem omnipotentem
Duet. Et in unum Dominum
Chorus. Et incarnatus est
Chorus. Crucifixus
Chorus. Et resurrexit
Aria. Et in spiritum sanctum
Chorus. Confiteor unum baptisma

SANCTUS

Chorus. Sanctus, dominus Deus
Chorus. Osanna in excelsis

BENEDICTUS

Aria. Benedictus qui venit
Chorus. Osanna in excelsis

AGNUS DEI

Aria. Agnus Dei, qui tollis
Chorus. Dona nobis pacem

From the first anguished cry of the full chorus in the opening "Kyrie eleison" to the quiet and confident mood of the closing "Dona nobis pacem," the Mass in B minor is unique. Bach's fondness for symbolism is copiously revealed. In the *Credo,* for example, on the words "I believe in one God," the combination of Gregorian plainsong with what may be called German Protestant counterpoint suggests the unity of all Christian belief. Later in the *Credo,* to the text "And in one Lord Jesus Christ," Bach provides a duet for soprano and alto, with the melodic lines set in close imitation (see Example 125*a*). And the motive that symbolizes the spirit of the Holy Ghost in the "Et incarnatus est" hovers in the middle and high ranges of the orchestra until the moment of incarnation, when it descends into the bass (see Example 125*b*).

The magical sequence of moods presented in the three consecutive numbers in the *Credo* that deal with the incarnation, crucifixion, and resurrection of the Savior has no parallel in the literature. Elsewhere, various solos and ensemble numbers are written in a style externally similar to that of operatic arias. Yet so profound is Bach's conception of the liturgical text that his music transcends style and becomes a universal expression of religious faith.

Similar in profundity and even more dramatic in its effect is Bach's *Passion According to St. Matthew,* written in 1729. The Passion as a musical form is a type of oratorio; its text is concerned with the betrayal, suffering, and resurrection of Jesus. Like the spoken Passion Play (the famous one performed every decade at Oberammergau is a modern example), it had its origin as far back as perhaps the fifth century, but

Bach, Mass in B minor, *Credo* *Example 125*

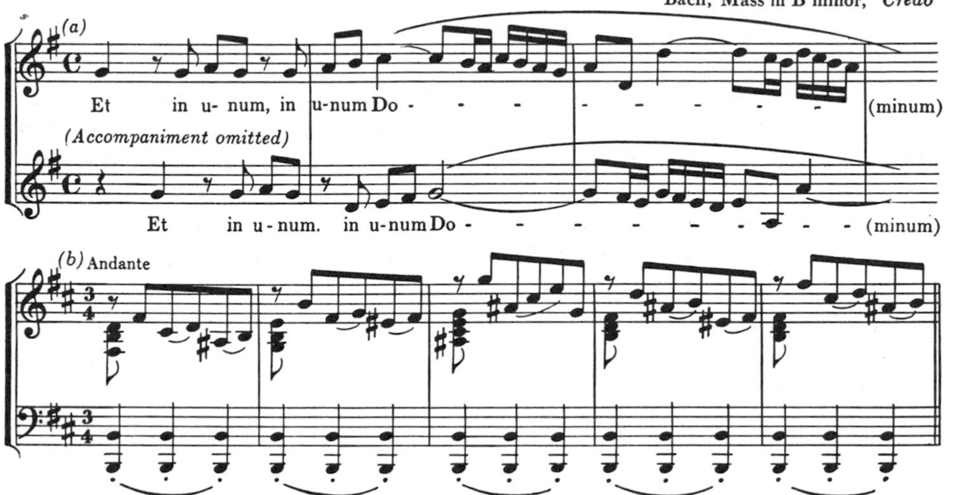

it was then sung in plainsong. Its text is taken from, or is a paraphrase of, the appropriate passages in the Gospel from which it takes its name. Musical settings of the Passion are numerous from the sixteenth century onward, but none of them approaches the eloquent, reverent, and soul-stirring tone of Bach's setting.

In the seventeenth century, contact with the opera had cheapened the Passion text; the Biblical story was often sentimentalized in a crude manner, and many liberties were taken with it. In Bach's setting the Biblical text is restored and, in the manner of the oratorio, is given to a narrator. The words spoken by the various characters in the sacred drama (Jesus, the Apostles, the priests, Pontius Pilate, and the others) are given mainly to soloists. These sections are set in recitative style, and are accompanied by a harpsichord and *continuo*—except that the words of Jesus are always lifted to a higher, more mystical level and are accompanied by a string orchestra. In general, the choruses and the majority of the arias provide commentaries or reflections on the action, and the chorales, chosen in accordance with the appropriateness of the several texts, are interspersed throughout the *Passion.* The much-beloved chorale melody "O Sacred Head Now Wounded" occurs several times with different texts and harmonies (see Example 126). The melody always seems appropriate to its texts, in spite of the fact that it was originally a Medieval secular song.

Bach, "O Sacred Head" *Example 126*

Recitatives, arias, chorales, dramatic choruses, and ensemble numbers follow each other closely, as the text requires. Dramatic outcries, such as the chorus's single word "Barabbas!"; poignant melodies, such as the aria setting of the text "Have pity, Lord"; moods of reconciliation, such as permeate the closing chorus, "Here yet a while"; passages filled with sadness and remorse, such as the elaborate chorale setting "O man, bewail thy grievous sin"—all this variety of expressive content is found in the *St. Matthew Passion.*

The mood of the entire *Passion* is set by the opening double chorus with chorale and double orchestra—one of the noblest, most concentrated, and most inspired of all musical passages. The gigantic scope of the entire work, the depth of its religious feeling, and its absence of external effect require that an air of vastness, fervor, and simplicity be established, and Bach accomplished all this in the opening chorus. The mood of the whole rises from this profound beginning, so that the *St. Matthew Passion* in its entirety stands as one of the most moving expressions of religious faith in all of our culture.

In summary, we may say that Bach's historical position is unique. Ever since the *Camerata* reform became effective in the period 1590–1610 (see pp. 334–35), composers were faced with the conflict between polyphony and homophony, between melodic and harmonic elements. The abandonment of counterpoint laid bare the melodic skeleton of music, which had then been given the sketchiest kind of harmonic support. The resultant texture was adequte for the vocal music of the time, but it provided no foundation upon which new vocal and instrumental forms could be built. And a return to modal counterpoint was unthinkable.

Bach found a solution. He arranged chordal progressions so that they created real melodic parts, and he composed melodies in a contrapuntal context that was firmly tied to a functional harmonic scheme. Harmonic inner parts became independent melodies; the polyphonic texture was harmonically conceived. Thus a fusion of vertical and horizontal elements resulted. (See Example 126 for an example of this fusion in a chorale.)

During the course of the seventeenth century, various style elements became nationalized. The concerto forms, with their extremes of mood, became identified with Italy; the suite, characterized by dance patterns and facile ornamentation, represented France. Bach, with the graceful dance rhythms of his concertos and with the opposition of solo and *tutti* in his choral works, resolved these national differences and superimposed upon the resulting product the logical harmonies and contrapuntal textures that stood for Germany. And upon this Italian-French-German fusion he impressed the power and universality of his own creative genius. A new style emerged, one that contained national elements and yet was surcharged with religious feeling—a style that was uniquely Bach's own. After Bach there could be no progress along these lines; there could only be a new beginning in yet another style.

Listening Suggestions

HANDEL

Concerti Grossi, Op. 3, Nos. 1–6
Messiah (oratorio)
Sonatas, Violin and Harpsichord, Op. 1, Nos. 1–6
Water Music (suite for orchestra)

BACH

"Brandenburg" Concertos, Nos. 1–6
Cantata No. 80, *A Mighty Fortress Is Our God*
"Italian" Concerto (concerto for harpsichord solo)
Mass in B Minor
Organ Works:
  Fantasia and Fugue, G minor ("The Great")
  Prelude and Fugue, E flat ("St. Anne's")
Passion According to St. Matthew (a type of oratorio)
Suite in B minor for Strings and Flute

PART FOUR The Twentieth Century

Chapter 18

CONTEMPORARY MUSIC

Chapter 14 was concerned with a number of composers who lived well into the twentieth century. The most widely known of those composers—notably Mahler, Strauss, and Sibelius—had their roots firmly embedded in the nineteenth century; they carried forward the aesthetic and technical elements of the earlier period and remained essentially post-Romantic in their general outlook. Others among them, principally Debussy and his followers, reacted against the tenets of Romanticism and brought forth a new style, Impressionism; yet that style too was subjective in intent and was derived from the technical approaches and the harmonic system of the nineteenth century.

Still other composers, beginning their careers even while the post-Romanticists and Impressionists were active, departed from existing practices, developed individual styles, and gave rise to radically new kinds of music. Composers such as Schoenberg, Bartók, and Stravinsky, making enormous contributions to twentieth-century repertoires, also laid the bases upon which a truly contemporary music could be built. Those composers will be discussed in the present chapter.

The New Music

We have seen that Impressionism began as a movement among painters and took the form of a protest against the methods of Romanticism, and that Debussy and other musicians created a musical counterpart to the new style in painting. In the early years of the twentieth century another group of painters opposed themselves to the tenets of Impressionism and emerged with a radically new style that was called *expressionism.* A parallel development among composers, who worked a decade or so after the painters and who reacted similarly against musical Impressionism, was given the same name. Picasso, Kandinsky, and Klee best represent the expressionist painters; Arnold Schoenberg and his pupils, Anton von Webern and Alban Berg, are the principal exponents of musical expressionism.

Whereas Impressionism, in both the arts, reflects the impressions derived from the outer world, expressionism seeks to reveal the world of the inner self—that is, the subconscious. The latter world, according to the teachings of the psychoanalysts, reveals itself in abstract forms that do not necessarily reflect beauty. Expressionistic music, therefore, casts out the traditional elements of musical composition. Melodies that are angular and stark, harmonies that are completely independent of the tonal system, and forms that reveal new relationships between their parts—such elements are common.

SCHOENBERG

Arnold Schoenberg (1874–1950), born in Vienna, began as a typical post-Romanticist. In his powerful, impassioned string sextet, *Verklärte Nacht* (*Transfigured Night*), written in 1899, he carried the form of the descriptive symphonic poem into the field of chamber music. That work is intense, dramatic, and full of a rich Wagnerianism: it is one of the most moving of post-Romantic compositions. But it also marks the highest point reached in subjective, emotion-laden music; a continuation of that style could have led only to anticlimax in Schoenberg's career. He therefore abandoned the principles of Romanticism, experimented to find new means of expression, and eventually, in the 1920's, invented the *twelve-tone system.* Schoenberg himself referred to it as "the system of composing with the twelve tones"; and today it is sometimes pretentiously called the "dodecaphonic system."

Sketch of Schoenberg.

In this system the twelve tones of the chromatic scale may be arranged arbitrarily in any desired manner. No one of the tones is different in function from any of the others; thus there can be no tonic or keynote. The series of tones is called a *tone row,* and a particular row becomes the basic structural unit of a composition. The tone row may be used in its original form (O); it may be inverted (I), which is to say that each descending interval is replaced by the same interval ascending, and vice versa. Further, the row may be used from end to beginning, in retrograde form (R), and the retrograde form may be inverted (RI). Finally, each of these four forms of the row may be transposed as a whole to any of the twelve positions within the chromatic scale. Forty-eight versions of the row are thus possible; they provide the sequences of tones out of which the composition's melodies are formed, and they also provide the basis for the chords used in the work. One chord, for example, may be made out of the first three tones of the row, another chord out of the next three, and so on.

Schoenberg's String Quartet No. 3, Op. 30, published in 1927, was one of several works in which the principles of the twelve-tone system were first formulated. The thematic outline of that work, given on pages 382–84, indicates how the tone row was used in composition. Two practices are noteworthy: one is *octave displacement,* in which a given tone may be shifted an octave or two higher or lower than its original position within the row. A comparison between the inverted form (I) of the row and Example 2 of the outline will show how great a degree of melodic angularity can result from the use of this device. The other is the practice of *perpetual variation,* in which no repetition or recapitulation is exact. This can be verified by comparing measures 5–12 of the first movement with the parallel passage in measures 174–80. Even when the recapitulation is apparently exact, as it is when measures 239–45 recapitulate measures 62–68 (both passages are based on Row I, 1–12), octave displacement, new counterpoints, or new rhythms serve to make every thematic statement virtually a fresh one.

Since music constructed according to the principles of the twelve-tone system has no tonal center, and since its chords do not have dominant-tonic or similar relationships (see p. 46) to one another, twelve-tone music is said to be *atonal,* that is, without tonality. Schoenberg objected vigorously to the term, but atonality has long since taken a place in the technical vocabulary that has developed around the new music of the twentieth century.

Music written in this abstract and "arbitrary" way (so called by those who disapproved of the musical results of this systematic approach to musical composition) became a controversial subject about 1925. Several of Schoenberg's chamber music works, some short pieces for the piano, and a few of his miscellaneous compositions are dissonant in the extreme and full of unrelieved harmonic tensions; their melodies are angular and contain intervals that do not lie easily in the human ear. They contain no "tunes" in the accepted sense, nor do they appeal to the emotions in the ways that earlier music does. They are the products of intellectuality carried to a high level, and they must be listened to with concepts other than nineteenth-century ideas of musical beauty in mind. Schoenberg's purpose was to lead to a new kind of music, and he succeeded admirably.

WEBERN

Many other composers adopted the principles of the twelve-tone system and wrote according to those principles, notably two of Schoenberg's pupils, Alban Berg (1885–1935) and Anton von Webern (1883–1945). In the music of Berg one senses an interest in relating Schoenberg's discoveries to the past. This is seen in Berg's creation of tone rows that definitely suggest major or minor tonalities, and in his interest in the forms of the eighteenth century. His Violin Concerto (1935), which contains strong references to B flat major and G minor, also contains a quotation from a Bach chorale, "It is enough, Lord."

Anton von Webern, on the other hand, carried the implications of the twelve-tone system into the future. Suggestions and ideas that Schoenberg had only hinted at were developed and expanded by Webern to create a virtually new world of music. One such suggestion had to do with the creation of a melodic type depending largely on changes in tone color for its musical content. The idea of a "tone-color melody" appealed strongly to Webern; many of his works show the most meticulous concern with the sound of single tones.

For example, the first of his Five Orchestral Pieces, Op. 10, begins with a single tone, B natural, played by trumpet and harp at the dynamic level of *pianississimo* (*ppp*). The following tone, C, is played by harp and celesta, still *pianississimo* (*ppp*),

Quartet No. 3, by Arnold Schoenberg

FIRST MOVEMENT, Moderato

Meas.	*Theme*	
EXPOSITION		
1	Intro.	Based on Row O, 1–5
5	1st	Row O, 8–12, and Row RI, 1–3, 7, 9 (Ex. 1)

Example 1

(O) 8 9 10 11 12 (RI) 1 2 3 7 9

13		Row O, 1–5, and Row RI, 8–12
20		Modified repetition of meas. 13–18
43		Modified repetition of meas. 5–12
50		Transition based on meas. 43
62	2nd	Row I, 1–12 (Ex. 2), and Row R, 1–12

Example 2

76		Transition based on Row R, 8–12
DEVELOPMENT		
95		Based on Row O, 1–12
130		Based on Row O, 1–5, with transpositions
150		Based on Row R, 1–6
161		Based on Row I, 6–12, transposed
RECAPITULATION		
174	1st	Row O, 1–12
181		Row RI, 1–12
193		Row RI, 8–12, and Row O, 1–5 and 6–12 freely
207		Transition based on meas. 1–5
231		Based on Row I, 1–12, used freely
239	2nd	Row I, 1–12
263		Development based on Row I, 1–12

278	Coda	Based on Row O, 1–12, and Row I, 1–12
315		Derived from Row I, 1–12, and Row O, 1–12. Movement ends in meas. 341

SECOND MOVEMENT, Adagio

Meas.	*Part*	
1	A	Theme. Row O, 1–12, and Row RI, 1–12, used freely (Ex. 3)

Example 3

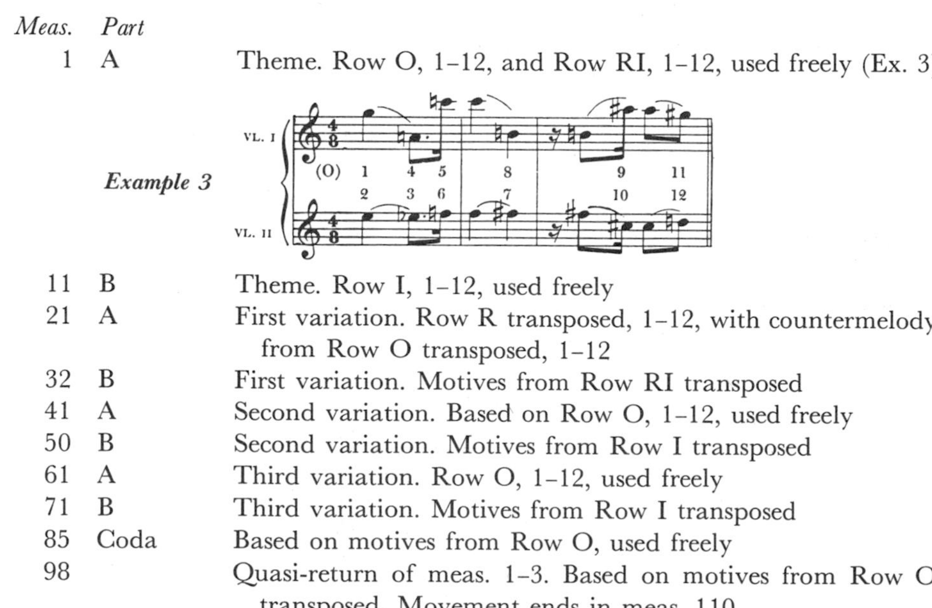

11	B	Theme. Row I, 1–12, used freely
21	A	First variation. Row R transposed, 1–12, with countermelody from Row O transposed, 1–12
32	B	First variation. Motives from Row RI transposed
41	A	Second variation. Based on Row O, 1–12, used freely
50	B	Second variation. Motives from Row I transposed
61	A	Third variation. Row O, 1–12, used freely
71	B	Third variation. Motives from Row I transposed
85	Coda	Based on motives from Row O, used freely
98		Quasi-return of meas. 1–3. Based on motives from Row O transposed. Movement ends in meas. 110

THIRD MOVEMENT, Intermezzo, Allegro moderato

Meas.	*Section*	
FIRST PART		
1	A	Row O, 1–12 (Ex. 4), and Row RI, 1–12

Example 4

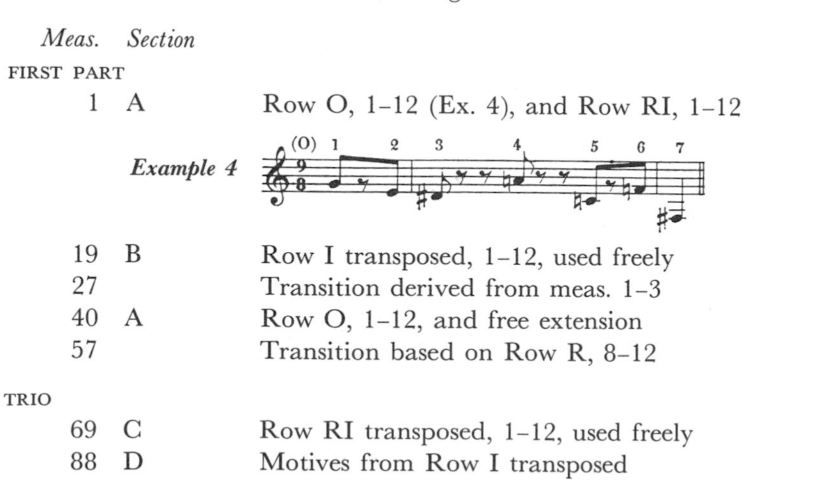

19	B	Row I transposed, 1–12, used freely
27		Transition derived from meas. 1–3
40	A	Row O, 1–12, and free extension
57		Transition based on Row R, 8–12
TRIO		
69	C	Row RI transposed, 1–12, used freely
88	D	Motives from Row I transposed

Schoenberg, Quartet No. 3 (cont.)

107	C	Free recapitulation of meas. 69–87
128		Transition

FIRST PART DA CAPO

133	A	Row O, 1–12, and Row RI, 1–12
145	B	Row O, 1–12, used freely
149		Transition
156	A	Row RI, 1–12, used freely
167	Coda	Row O, 1–12. Movement ends in meas. 183

FOURTH MOVEMENT, Molto moderato

Meas.	*Section*	
1	A	Row O, 1–12, used freely (Ex. 5)

Example 5

14		Transition based on Row O transposed, 6–12
23	B	Motives from Row R transposed, used freely
33		Second part, based on Row I transposed, used freely
44	A	Row O, 1–12, used freely
53		Transition based on Row I, used freely
62	B	Motives from Row O transposed, used freely
73		Development based on Row I transposed
99	A	Row O, 1–12, used freely
119		Transition based on Row I transposed, used freely
128	B	Motives from Row R
144		Second part, based on Row I, 1–12, used freely
151	A	Row O, 1–12, used freely
163		Development based on motives from Row O
186	Coda	Based on Row O, 1–12, used freely. Movement ends in meas. 209

Example 127

but now a solo viola is added on the same pitch, at the dynamic level of *pianissimo* (*pp*). The third tone, again B, is played by harp and flute. Here then is a three-tone melody with a characteristic and different tone color for each tone.

The brevity, clarity of texture, and consistency of style introduced by Schoenberg were carried to the utmost limits by Webern. The latter's Symphony, Op. 21, provides a case in point. The work is for a chamber orchestra consisting of clarinet, bass clarinet, two horns, harp, and strings (without basses), and is about ten minutes in length. The second movement of the symphony consists of a theme and seven variations. The theme, given to the clarinet, is based on the tone row of the work. It is accompanied by harp and two horns, and the accompaniment is based on the retrograde form of the same row (see Example 127); this is but one illustration of Webern's economy of resource.

Anton von Webern (1883–1945), whose use of the twelve-tone system has influenced contemporary American composers.

Another illustration of economy is seen in the structure of the row itself, for the second half of the row is actually the retrograde form (transposed) of the first half. Example 127*a* illustrates this point. It will be seen that the row proceeds from 1 to 6 and is then transposed down an augmented fourth and made to turn back upon itself. This economy permits Webern to produce a highly complex contrapuntal structure. The first variation, for example, is a canon in four parts (see p. 362), but each new part is rhythmically modified in keeping with the principle of perpetual variation. The variation progresses to its midpoint, after which all four voices are led from the middle backwards to the beginning.

BARTÓK

A different approach to the problem of creating a new type of music was made by Béla Bartók (1881–1945), the most important Hungarian composer of the twentieth century. Bartók's early interest in nationalism turned him toward the study of folk song; he began with Hungarian popular tunes. Soon his studies were expanded to include the folk songs of neighboring countries as well; he became an authority on the scales, rhythms, and melodic idioms of much eastern European folk music. And in that music are to be found the sources of his style as a composer.

Unlike most other nationalists, Bartók concerned himself scarcely at all with program music. Between about 1912 and 1930 he wrote a number of abstract compositions in an uncompromising atonal idiom, but there is no relationship between the atonality of Bartók in those works and the atonality of the twelve-tone system.

Béla Bartók (1881–1945), eminent Hungarian composer, photographed shortly before his death.

Bartók makes use of the following devices: chords built out of fourths or fifths instead of thirds (see pp. 40 ff.); chords that are both major and minor at once (F, A flat, A and C, for example); groups of nearly consecutive tones called *tone clusters;* series of unresolved ninth and eleventh chords; chromaticism in the melody and chromatic alteration within the harmony; and other types of dissonance as well. Rarely were Bartók's dissonances relieved by consonances.

Title page of an early piano work.

Even more important than his harmonic innovations were his innovations in the field of rhythm. We have spoken in an earlier chapter of unmetrical rhythm (see p. 26) and of Stravinsky's characteristic use of the device. Bartók too became an exponent of unmetrical rhythm in the period after 1910, and he continued, in later works, to exploit to the utmost other aspects of rhythm as well. Syncopations, percussive chord complexes at irregular intervals within the measure, metrical patterns of unusual nature, and passages in which several different rhythms occur simultaneously—such devices became typical. For example, in the scherzo of Bartók's Quartet No. 5 (1936), the first part is metrically noted as $\frac{4+2+3}{8}$; that is to say, within each measure nine eighth notes are grouped in four's, two's, and three's, or the respective equivalents of these combinations. And in the trio of the movement the metrical signature of $\frac{3+2+2+3}{8}$ is employed.

The instrumental effects in Bartók's music are distinctive enough to constitute yet another element of style. The string parts, for example, are full of various kinds of pizzicato chords: chords strummed up and down in what may be called "pizzicato tremolo," and chords or single notes plucked so violently that the string rebounds against the fingerboard. A peculiar howling effect is often employed, in which the string player slides a finger along the string from one note to another, sounding all possible pitches between; this effect is called *glissando* (see Example 128). These ele-

Example 128

Concerto No. 3 for Piano and Orchestra, by Béla Bartók

FIRST MOVEMENT, Allegretto

Meas.	*Theme*	
EXPOSITION		
1		Introductory meas.
2	1st	First part, in E (Ex. 1)

Example 1

17		Modified repetition and development
27		Second part, in D flat
44	2nd	In C (Ex. 2)

Example 2

54	3rd	In G (Ex. 3)

Example 3

68		Transition
DEVELOPMENT		
76		Derived from meas. 2 (Ex. 1)
94		Derived from meas. 54 (Ex. 3), with portions of first theme
107		Derived from meas. 64
RECAPITULATION		
118	1st	First part, in E (Ex. 1)
137		Modified repetition and extension. Second part of theme (meas. 27) is omitted
154	2nd	In A (Ex. 2)
162	3rd	In E (Ex. 3)
175		Transition to coda
180	Coda	Derived from meas. 54. Movement ends in meas. 187

SECOND MOVEMENT, Adagio religioso

Meas.	*Part*	
1	A	Orchestra alone (Ex. 4)

Example 4

16	B	Piano alone, quasi-chorale (Ex. 5)

Example 5

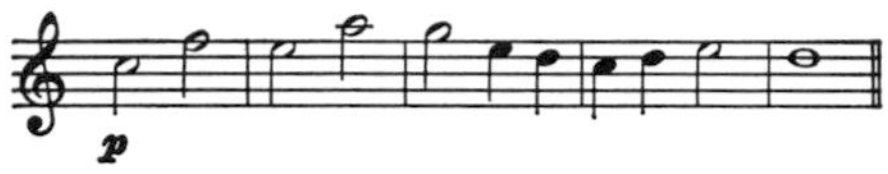

20	A	Orchestral interlude
24	B	Piano alone, second line of chorale
28	A	Orchestral interlude
31	B	Piano, third line of chorale
35	A	Orchestral interlude
38	B	Piano, fourth and fifth lines of chorale
46	A	Orchestral interlude
48	B	Piano, sixth line of chorale and extension
54	A	Orchestra, epilogue
58	C	Piano and orchestra, development of fragments of chorale melody
89	B	First line of chorale, as in Ex. 5, meas. 16, but now in orchestra. New counterpoint in piano
93	A	Piano, figure based on harmony of last meas. of chorale line
96	B	Orchestra, second line of chorale (meas. 24). New counterpoint in piano
100	A	Piano, figuration and extension of last meas. of chorale line
105	B	Orchestra, third line of chorale (meas. 31). Counterpoint continues in piano
109	A	Piano, figuration and extension of last meas. of chorale line
112	B	Orchestra, fourth and fifth lines of chorale (meas. 38), with figuration in piano
120	A	Piano. Continuation of contrapuntal embellishment
122	B	Orchestra. Modification of sixth line of chorale, then (meas. 128) continued in piano
134	A	Orchestra. Epilogue, as in meas. 54. At meas. 137, leads directly into third movement

Bartók, Concerto No. 3 for Piano and Orchestra (cont.)

THIRD MOVEMENT, Allegro vivace

Meas.	*Part*	
138	Intro.	
141	A	First part, in E (Ex. 6)

Example 6

161		Second part, in C
191		First part repeated and modified, in E
213		Transition
228	B	Fugue. First exposition in C sharp (Ex. 7)

Example 7

269		Episode
284		Second exposition, in F
306		Episode
322		Stretto
344	A	First part (Ex. 6, meas. 141), but modified
392	C	First part, in B flat
427		Second part, in A flat
473		First part modified, in B flat
497		Transition
527	A	First part (Ex. 6, meas. 141) in C sharp
543		Second part, in E
589		Third part, based on first part, in C
644	Coda	Movement ends in meas. 768

ments, along with a considerable use of dissonant counterpoint, combine to make Bartók's music varied in its texture, vital in its rhythms, and strong in its expressive content.

Bartók's six string quartets, written during the interval between about 1908 and 1936, are among the most successful of twentieth-century works. Impersonal, and barbaric in certain rhythmic aspects, the quartets reveal Bartók's sincerity of purpose, his far-reaching imagination, and his technical skill. Later works, notably the Violin Concerto (1938), the Concerto for Orchestra (1944), and the Piano Concerto No. 3 (1945), show a lessening of the savage dissonance and a partial restoration of consonant, lyric elements. A thematic outline of the third piano concerto, given on pages 388–90, reveals the extent to which Bartók employed conventional forms in first and last movements. The slow movement of the work, based on lines of a chorale separated by interludes, has many points in common with the corresponding movement of Beethoven's String Quartet in A minor, Op. 132. In general, after about 1935 Bartók composed music that had many points of contact with music of the eighteenth century. This turn to a milder and less acrid style was taken by many other composers also, as we shall see below.

STRAVINSKY

Igor Stravinsky, born near St. Petersburg in 1882, became one of the foremost exponents of the return to a modified eighteenth-century style, but his early works gave no hint of the direction his future path would take. He first came to public notice with three ballets, written between 1910 and 1913 for Diaghilev in Paris: *The Firebird* (1910), *Petrouchka* (1911), and *The Rite of Spring* (1913). The last of these, radically different in every respect from earlier music, provoked a riot at its first performance. Its violently dissonant harmony, its percussive quality, its extreme use of unmetrical rhythm, and its inclusion of a great variety of strange instrumental effects combined to make the work incomprehensible and vastly irritating to most listeners. It was called primitive by many, for Stravinsky appeared to have written in ignorance of all the rules, purposes, and traditions of music, but it was applauded by others. Only after the heat of controversy had died down did antagonistic critics realize that Stravinsky's work was a logical continuation of processes begun in the nineteenth century.

Sketches by Picasso for Stravinsky's ballet *Pulcinella.*

Unmetrical rhythm and polyrhythms had been present in Brahms' music, as we have seen, and Debussy's music had gone far to free rhythm from its metrical shackles. The kinds of dissonances Stravinsky employed were natural consequences of the move toward chromaticism and toward a broadened concept of tonality, both of which tendencies had become especially evident since the 1850's. Unusual instrumental effects date back to at least as early as the time of Berlioz and had appeared in much music composed since the 1830's. In his use of these devices Stravinsky had merely gone on more consistently and extensively than his predecessors.

In works of the following decades he refined and modified many of the elements that had been so radically presented in *The Rite of Spring.* For example, the ballet entitled *Pulcinella* (1919) is based on music attributed to the eighteenth-century Italian composer Pergolesi. The Octet for Wind Instruments and the Piano Concerto (both about 1924) are objective and relatively subdued. In the *Symphony of Psalms* (1940), for chorus and orchestra, Stravinsky recaptured some of the seriousness and austerity found in the best examples of Baroque music. The orchestra is reduced in size, in that violins, violas, and clarinets are not employed; the colorful writing and violent moods that had appeared in his earlier works are missing here.

Symphony of Psalms, by Igor Stravinsky

Mixed chorus and orchestra, without violins or violas

FIRST MOVEMENT, Quasi-allegro

Meas.	*Section*	
1	Intro.	Orchestra, broken chord motive
25	A	Altos on text *Exaudi orationem meam* ("Hear my prayer"), Ex. 1.

Example 1

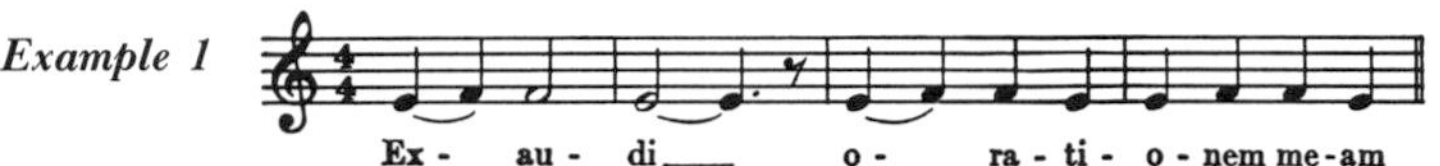

		Orchestral accompaniment derived from motive of meas. 2 by expansion. Phrase in full chorus, meas. 33
41		Ex. 1, meas. 25–32 repeated, with changed orchestration, on text *Auribus percipe lacrimas meas* ("Give ear to my cry")
49		Codetta
53	B	Chorus on text *Quoniam advena ego sum* ("For I am a passing guest"), Ex. 2

Example 2

66		Chorus on text *Remitte mihi* ("Look away from me"). Orchestral accompaniment is similar to meas. 49–52, expanded, and from meas. 68 is derived from meas. 25 (Ex. 1) and meas. 41. Movement ends in meas. 78

SECOND MOVEMENT, Quasi-andante

Meas.	*Section*	
1	Exposition	Fugal exposition; first oboe, theme on C (Ex. 3)

Example 3

6		First flute, theme on G
13		Second flute, theme on C
18		Second oboe, theme on G
23	Episode	
29	Exp.	Cellos and basses, theme on E flat (Ex. 3). But also a separate fugal exposition in chorus (Ex. 4), with orchestral accompani-

ment derived from orchestral fugue theme (Ex. 3). In meas. 29 sopranos on E flat

Example 4

33		Altos, theme on B flat
39		Tenors, theme on E flat
43		Basses, theme on B flat
47		Episode
52		Stretto
71	Exp.	Return of orchestral fugue theme (Ex. 3), rhythmically modified and combined with development of Ex. 3. New counterpoint and development of meas. 29–30 in chorus
81		Return of meas. 29 (Ex. 4) in chorus
84	Coda	Derived from meas. 2. Movement ends in meas. 88

THIRD MOVEMENT, Quasi-adagio; vivace

Meas.	*Section*	
1	Intro.	Chorus on text *Alleluia*
4		Chorus on text *Laudate Dominum,* based on one-meas. motive (Ex. 5) out of which two short phrases develop. Orchestra is static on C major harmony

Example 5

24	A	Tempo changes to quasi-*vivace.* Orchestra alone; series of phrases growing out of a rhythmic motive (Ex. 6) over a *basso ostinato*

Example 6

41		Part 2; arpeggio figuration in triplets
53	B	Chorus; series of chantlike phrases: meas. 53, soprano; meas. 72, alto; meas. 80, alto and tenor; meas. 87, full chorus. In orchestra, continued development of motives derived from Ex. 6, meas. 24 and 41

Stravinsky, *Symphony of Psalms* (cont.)

99		Transition
115	A	Return of meas. 24–51 with changed orchestration and greater extension. Now chorus assists in development of motive from meas. 24 on text *Laudate Dominum*
127		Part 2, as in meas. 41
150	C	New theme in chorus (Ex. 7) in imitative texture

Example 7

163		Part 2 (Ex. 8)

Example 8

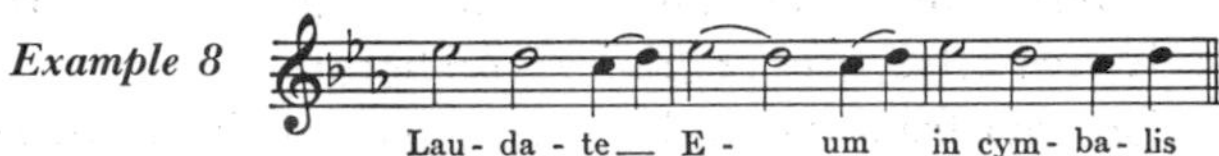

187		Repetition of meas. 163–174 (Ex. 8) on text *Omnis spiritus laudet Dominum*
205	Coda	Return of introductory phrase, meas. 3–8. Movement ends in meas. 212

In place of those elements are a reverent tone and a sustained line appropriate to the psalm texts that are sung by the chorus. The thematic outline of the *Symphony of Psalms* given on pages 392–94 shows how strongly the forms of this work are related to the forms of the eighteenth century; the fugal writing of the second movement is especially striking. It is as though Bach had been rediscovered; indeed, "back to Bach" had become a slogan of the years after about 1925, and the slogan remained in force for almost two decades.

It is such elements that caused critics of the time to call these and similar compositions *neo-Classical.* Actually, the term *neo-Baroque* would have been more accurate, for the counterpoint, forms, and other elements of these compositions have their closest parallels in the period before 1750 and not in the time of the Classical period. But the term has found worldwide acceptance. *Neo-Classical* became the rallying cry of the period from about 1925 to 1940.

In the neo-Classical phase of his career Stravinsky did not abandon the rhythmic vitality or the percussive, hard, and objective content of his earlier works. The shifting of accent and meter and a complete avoidance of sentimental expression have continued to distinguish his writing. However, in compositions written after 1940 he came closer to the spirit of the early nineteenth century. The Symphony in C (1940), the Symphony in Three Movements (1945), the Concerto in D (1946), and the *Ebony Concerto* (1946) show a lessening of the percussive quality and of the contrapuntal element. But the strong, incisive objectivity that has distinguished Stravinsky's music for almost fifty years has not been weakened.

The harmony of Stravinsky's works (of both his earlier and later periods) is often based on the use of two or more tonalities simultaneously. Polytonality, as the device is called, had sometimes been employed casually in earlier periods, but in the twentieth century it has become an outstanding stylistic device. Stravinsky's *Petrouchka* contains sections in which one part is in C major and another, played simultaneously, is in F sharp; a similar use of two or more tonalities together occurs in others of his compositions. Darius Milhaud (b. 1892), a French composer opposed to the tenets of Impressionism, consistently employed polytonality to combat the so-called vagueness of Debussy's style. The device is often found in the works of other composers who wrote after about 1920. In addition to the use of polytonal devices, Stravinsky's music is also characterized by chords containing both major and minor thirds at once—C, E flat, E natural, and G, for example. In his later works, those written after about 1954, he has not hesitated to adopt in modified form some of the principles of the twelve-tone system introduced by Schoenberg.

A scene from the ballet *Agon* (1957), an outstanding work of Stravinsky's later style period, performed by the New York City Ballet.

HINDEMITH

A fourth personal approach to the problem of creating a new music was made by Paul Hindemith (1895–1963), the most versatile and eminent of the German-born twentieth-century composers. In three string quartets written between 1921 and 1924 Hindemith revealed his interest in contrapuntal writing. In his counterpoint, however, the horizontal (melodic) element takes precedence over the vertical (harmonic) to an extreme degree. That is, each melodic line is led independently so that it develops its own tensions and releases, regardless of how the other lines progress. The preoccupation with the horizontal aspects of music results in extreme dissonance, for harsh tonal clashes are inevitable in music of this kind. But it is a kind of dissonance that differs from the chordally derived dissonance of Schoenberg, Bartók, and Stravinsky. To distinguish between this type of counterpoint and the eighteenth-century type, the term *linear counterpoint* was devised; it refers to the domination of the horizontal (linear) aspects over the vertical.

Linear counterpoint became one important aspect of the neo-Classical style; other elements of that style are also found in Hindemith's works. The three quartets mentioned above make use of Baroque formal devices: for example, the fugue, the passacaglia, and sections in canon are characteristic. Moreover, there is little thematic development of the nineteenth-century variety in his music. Hindemith showed a fondness for continually expanding his melodies in a way that is typical

Paul Hindemith (1895–1963) shown conducting in an informal setting.

of the late Baroque period and a fondness for writing a series of melodies of the same general type in the manner of composers of the Rococo period.

One other neo-Classical detail may be mentioned here. The so-called Symphony from *Mathis der Maler* ("Mathis the Painter") is not a symphony in the usual sense, but a set of three pieces drawn from Hindemith's opera of that name (1934). It will be recalled that in the Baroque period a sinfonia was an instrumental piece inserted into or preceding a stage work such as an opera or an oratorio.

In all of Hindemith's neo-Classical works the relationship to the past is modified by an astringent, dissonant texture, by cool and objective writing, and by energetic rhythms. Often, however, the rigorousness of the linear counterpoint is lessened and only a faint suggestion of its pungent dissonance remains (see Example 129). Later works, such as the String Quartet No. 5 (1943), the Symphony in E flat (1940), and the *Symphonia serena* (1946), show a further decline in the use of linear counterpoint, a relaxation of the strict objectivity, and an appearance of some measure of warm expressiveness.

Somewhat out of the main stream of Hindemith's work is the delightful *Symphonic Metamorphoses of Themes by Weber* (1943). Based on themes from Weber's in-

Hindemith, *Mathis der Maler* *Example 129*

Hindemith's own drawing on the title page of his Suite for Piano (1922).

cidental music for Schiller's play *Turandot,* this composition exploits the liveliness and sparkle of those themes in a rich and varied orchestral texture. The work is rhythmically alive throughout, and it is filled with humor; indeed, that ingredient has seldom been missing from Hindemith's music. The *Symphonic Metamorphoses* provides a charming introduction to Hindemith for those people who find the earlier works a bit forbidding and austere.

Hindemith's period of experimentation, a period in which intellect and a personally established system of composition dominated, ended in about 1940. Hindemith, like Schoenberg, Bartók, and Stravinsky, had led the way to a new style—a style embracing, first of all, a widened concept of tonality and a concern for objective expression, a style distinguished by great rhythmic vitality and harmonic freedom notable for its lack of sentimentality.

Music After the Second World War

We have seen that the music composed in the first half of the twentieth century did not represent a single style. Each of the leading composers developed his own manner of expressing his musical ideas, his own techniques for elaborating them, and virtually his own forms in which to present them. And each of these composers was of some influence on his lesser contemporaries, serving sometimes as a model and at other times as a point of departure. Subsequently, a host of composers emerged in all parts of the world—composers who reflected to a greater or lesser degree the accomplishments of the leaders even as they crossed stylistic lines and tended to merge elements of one major style with those of another. Many such composers, in the countries of Europe as in other regions, composed fluently and achieved local or national renown as they contributed to their regional repertoires, and a few have received international acclaim.

SERIAL MUSIC

By the 1950's, one style began to interest more and more composers, and a degree of stylistic unity could be sensed. The twelve-tone system of Schoenberg lay at the base of the new interest, but the special methods and transparent textures introduced by Webern constituted its structure. A decade of development brought many changes to the style, and even the term "twelve tone" was abandoned in favor of the term "serial." The serial technique makes use of some or all of the tones of the chromatic scale in a predetermined row or series (hence the term given to the technique), but it also extends that principle to other variables such as rhythmic components, phrase lengths, tone colors, and even dynamic levels. For example, the lengths of tones in a melody are derived from calculations similar to those employed in transformations of the melodic row itself. If a melodic series or tone row contains the numbers 6, 3, 8, 5, 1 (which are chosen arbitrarily here simply for purpose of illustration), one may expect the tones that carry those numbers to have lengths that correspond to the numbers—say, six sixteenths, three sixteenths, eight sixteenths, and so on.

The concept of a texture that is thin to the point of vanishing is often suggested in some music of the present day. A typical musical tapestry might consist of an isolated tone at one level, followed by a (louder or softer) tone at another level several octaves away; this may be followed by a chord in yet another range, after which another isolated tone continues the sequence. The tones, rhythms, and even the dynamic levels are carefully calculated in their relationships to each other, and are meticulously designed to produce specific emotional and intellectual effects. Many analyses of this music must be made in mathematical terms; indeed, the music is often composed with the aid of tables and formulas. The mathematical laws of permutation play a role in its construction, and mathematical competence has become an almost essential element of the composer's equipment. It seems obvious that the ideas and techniques that were barely introduced by Webern (see p. 381) have been systematized and developed to an advanced stage.

Rigorous serial technique, for all its attractiveness to many composers throughout the world, has not found total acceptance. Much of today's music blends serial and diatonic styles, some avoids serialism completely and relies upon new and imaginative uses of diatonic techniques, and other music brings primarily rhythmic components and nationalistic elements to expression. The range of styles is probably as wide as it has ever been, and no one style may be called dominant. As examples of the variety of contemporary music, three composers may be mentioned whose music is currently being performed in the United States.

DALLAPICCOLA

Luigi Dallapiccola (b. 1904) is among the composers who in the 1930's contributed to the revitalization of Italian instrumental music. At first interested in the neo-Classicism of Busoni, Dallapiccola later was influenced by Schoenberg and Webern. He has developed a warm and expressive blend of diatonic and serial techniques and has composed powerful and lucid works in that style. Among the compositions that first brought him to public notice was a choral work performed in 1946, *Songs of Imprisonment,* accompanied by two harps, several percussion instruments, and two pianos. An opera, *The Prisoner* (1948), a work for violin and orchestra (1951), and several later choral compositions and songs show an increasing closeness to the economical methods and textures of Webern.

GINASTERA

Alberto Ginastera (b. 1916), the most prominent Argentinian composer of the twentieth century, first espoused the nationalistic tradition in his country; several early works made use of folk idioms. And in a *Cantata para América Mágica* (1960) he set six texts from Mayan and Aztec sources for soprano and an orchestra consisting of fifty-three percussion instruments. In later works, notably two operas, *Bomarzo* (1963) and *Don Rodrigo* (1964), devices such as chance music (see p. 435) and *Sprechstimme* (speech-song, employed by Schoenberg in 1912) are used. Ginastera's mastery of rhythmic techniques and his vivid imagination in the use of complex rhythms gives his music extraordinary vitality and force.

PENDERECKI

Krzysztof Penderecki (b. 1933) has recently emerged as an outstanding Polish composer, although only a few of his compositions have become known to Western audiences. A performance of his work for string and percussion instruments, *Anaklasis,* at an international festival in Donaueschingen, Germany, in 1960 served to introduce him to the musical world at large. His orchestral *Threnody for the Victims of Hiroshima,* played at Amsterdam in 1963, heightened his reputation, and his dramatic and moving *Passion According to St. Luke* (1966) has been widely acclaimed. Based on a style that is derived from twelve-tone writing but having an individual touch, Penderecki's music exploits new instrumental sounds in the manner of Bartók. Glissandi, tappings on the bodies of string instruments, and streams of air blown through wind instruments are among the color components of his music. In such details Penderecki reveals himself to be one of the composers who are seeking to enlarge the means of musical expression.

A Change of Scene

In the years immediately after 1945 the major European countries exerted themselves to heal their wounds and restore their economies. They also found the energy

Luigi Dallapiccola (b. 1904), foremost Italian exponent of serial music.

to rebuild their musical establishments; only a short time elapsed before orchestras and opera companies attained their pre-war levels, composers found it gainful to practice their art, and the field of music again began flourishing. The world-renowned composers, however, were missing.

The deterioration of political conditions that began in the 1930's with the rise of Hitler in Germany resulted in the emigration of most of the continent's leading composers. Personal freedom was endangered, official pronouncements against "modern music" were circulated, and the musical climate became unbearable. Between 1933 and 1940 many of the leaders discussed earlier in this chapter took up residence in the United States. Schoenberg, for example, taught in Boston from 1933 to 1935 and after that at the University of California at Los Angeles; Hindemith taught at Yale from 1940 to 1953; Stravinsky came to Harvard in 1939 and later made his home in California; Milhaud lived in California from 1940 to 1947; and Bartók lived in New York from 1940 until his death in 1945.

The presence of most of the world's most eminent composers in the United States had a considerable bearing on the formation of an American version of contemporary music. The influence of Schoenberg, Milhaud, and Hindemith in particular on their American pupils was direct and wholesome, and their effect on the rank and file of American composers was no less vital. As the present generation of European composers has continued to experiment and develop, their American colleagues have kept pace, and in the past decade the United States has become one of the foremost centers of composition. The contributions of American composers to the contemporary scene will be taken up in Chapter 20.

Listening Suggestions

BARTÓK

Concerto No. 3 (for piano)
Music for Strings, Percussion, and Celesta
String Quartet No. 6

BERG

Wozzeck (opera), excerpts

HINDEMITH

Mathis der Maler (sinfonia from the opera of the same name)
String Quartet No. 3
Symphonic Metamorphoses of Themes by Weber

SCHOENBERG

String Quartet No. 3
Verklärte Nacht (*Transfigured Night,* sextet akin to symphonic poem)

STRAVINSKY

The Firebird, Suite (ballet)
Petrouchka, Suite (ballet)
The Rite of Spring (ballet)
Symphony in Three Movements

WEBERN

Five Orchestra Pieces, Op. 10
Symphony, Op. 21

Chapter 19

JAZZ AND ITS IDIOM

Shortly after the turn of the twentieth century there began in the United States a musical development that has influenced the music of the entire world. To many people, jazz represents America's greatest contribution to music. Although its status as an art has at times been widely debated, jazz has given lasting evidence of its vitality and has gained universal acceptance. The exact derivation of jazz is somewhat in doubt, since various origins have been suggested, but New Orleans is generally accepted as its birthplace, and the role of black musicians in its birth is universally acknowledged.

The Origins of Jazz

Jazz is probably the product of an African as well as an American heritage, but the widespread belief that jazz was introduced by slaves before the nineteenth century does not seem to be based in fact. Percussion instruments—drums for the most part—played a large part in African tribal cultures, as they do in jazz. But the earliest twentieth-century jazz drummers used only a basic duple beat in all their compositions, while African drummers employed compound meters, irregular rhythmic beats, and other related complexities. Syncopation is an important ingredient of jazz style, of course, but syncopation has been used in European music at least since the fifteenth century. Syncopation has a much wider application and broader definition in jazz than in European art music, however, and in that respect it resembles West African practices. Thus the exact extent of the formative influences on jazz cannot now be determined; it is sufficient to point out that individual black musicians developed the new style shortly after the 1900's.

The original version of this chapter was contributed by Bryce Jordan, now of the University of Texas.

The folk songs and folk dances of Latin America and the West Indies, notably the tango, rumba, and beguine, employ rhythms that can be traced back to West African sources and hence may have transmitted the African heritage indirectly to early jazz. It may be pointed out that two late types of jazz—the bop and cool styles—were in turn developed with the help of the bongo and conga drums of Latin America and its nearby islands.

The elements of West African music that appear in jazz are transmitted to that music principally through the Afro-American folk song. Of the three main types of such songs—*work songs, blues,* and *spirituals*—the work song seems to have been the earliest. It was sung by the slaves to relieve the monotony and to ease the burden of tasks that required repeated motions, and it frequently accented the text syllable that occurred where the stress of the work was greatest.

The blues, which developed extensively after the Civil War, probably stem from the work song. Actually, it is sometimes difficult to draw a dividing line between the work song and the blues, for the blues also often express the rhythms of labor. Other subjects treated in the blues run the whole gamut of unhappy human experience: living and dying, the problems of love and the loss of love, lack of life's necessities, fear, hatred, loneliness, and envy.

Blues did not spring only from New Orleans; they were sung all over the South since about the last quarter of the nineteenth century. And in addition to contributing stylistically to jazz, blues have remained an independent folk-song type to the present day. Singers such as Gertrude ("Ma") Rainey (1886–1939) and Bessie Smith (*circa* 1900–37) were responsible for perpetuating and spreading the authentic blues tradition. The earliest published blues was W. C. Handy's *Memphis Blues,* which appeared in 1909. A steadily increasing commercialization began with this publication, and by 1914 some popular songs of Tin Pan Alley began to reflect blues characteristics.

The third principal type of black folk song, the spiritual, is an admixture of certain blues characteristics (principally the rhythms) and Anglo-American psalmody and hymnody. The blacks, learning hymns and psalms from white northern missionaries, fused a style of religious folk music from these two elements. In addition to making its influence felt in jazz, as the blues have done, the spiritual has continued to the present as a type of black folk song. Unfortunately, most of the so-called spirituals one hears today are slickly arranged pieces for chorus or concert singer; little of the true black folk-song idiom remains. However, the present-day singing of Rosetta Tharpe (b. about 1910) and Mahalia Jackson (b. 1911), among others, would seem to be more in the authentic spiritual tradition.

A secondary influence on the development of jazz was the minstrel show. This type of entertainment, which enjoyed great popularity for years before the Civil War, featured white performers in blackface who sang and danced in supposed imitation of the black man. Some of the music was in the black idiom; much was not. Actually, they sang the songs of several traditions: British folk ballads, American and British popular songs, and plantation songs. The latter type of minstrel tune reflected the influence of the polka, of certain West Indian dances, and of the cakewalk, a black dance that found its way into the minstrel repertoire. *Old Zip Coon,* later known as *Turkey in the Straw,* is a typical plantation song. In most cases, such music was sung to the accompaniment of the banjo. The minstrel show had declined as a popular form of entertainment by 1900.

One of the principal predecessors of jazz was *ragtime,* a type of piano music that seems to have been derived from the cakewalks and banjo tunes of the minstrel show and from the European dance rhythms—polka, quadrille, and so forth—that were popular with the Creoles of Louisiana and elsewhere in the South. The jerking, dotted rhythms of the banjo are easily heard in a piano rag (see Example 130). As this example shows, an important element of ragtime is the imposition of triple meters at two levels upon the basic four-beat metrical background. This metrical device is reflected in jazz.

Example 130

The early development of ragtime centered around St. Louis, where Thomas M. Turpin (d. 1922), composer of the first published rag, and Scott Joplin (1868–1917), composer of *Maple Leaf Rag,* were active from the decade before 1900. Ragtime, which was spectacularly popular by 1910 and began to decline shortly after that, developed at the same time as the first important school of jazz, the classic New Orleans school, which will be discussed later. When the influence of ragtime spread to New Orleans, the fabulous Ferdinand ("Jelly Roll") Morton (1885–1941), an important figure in the history of both ragtime and jazz, and the composer of *Tiger Rag,* served as a transitional force between the two types of music. Ragtime also spread to New York where, among others, Thomas ("Fats") Waller (1904–43) revealed its influence in his hot piano style.

One other influence on jazz is of importance. After the Civil War, the brass bands of New Orleans grew in number and activity, probably as the result of military band instruments being sold or abandoned at the end of the war. These bands were heard at festive occasions such as parades and picnics, and in funeral processions. They were usually composed of brass and percussion instruments only—cornets, alto horns, tenor horns, baritone horns, trombones, tubas, bass drum, and snare drum. And their repertoire was one that might be expected from such groups: they played military marches, polkas, and quadrilles for the festive occasions, and hymns for the funerals.

Although there is no positive evidence, such as phonograph recordings, to furnish proof, it is likely that these brass bands, particularly those that included blacks, played their music not as it was written but with the improvised rhythmic subtleties (syncopations, and so on) and the pitch inflections of Afro-American folk songs. The accounts of those who heard these bands in the late nineteenth century seem to bear this out.

Gradually these bands, which had names like "Diamond Stone Band" and "Onward Brass Band," began to play for dancing. Their instrumentation changed in accordance with this new function, and the New Orleans type of jazz band (see p. 410) thus developed. In the period roughly from 1885 to 1910, the three black musical traditions of blues, ragtime, and the brass band came together. Thus it was that the New Orleans, or classic, style of jazz was born. However, despite the emphasis given to New Orleans in the pages that follow, it must be remembered that the early development of jazz was not confined to one city. Many other cities shared in this process.

The Characteristics of Jazz

Jazz has been examined from a number of viewpoints and has been variously defined. Some observers see it as an improvised black folk art that was taken over for commercial purposes by white publishers and thereby lost its identity. Others hold that jazz is essentially an art of improvisation, that it cannot gainfully be written down in notation because to do so destroys its spirit. Jazz has long been the predominant type of dance music, and certain commentators define it in the light of that function. It is also a unique method of performance, one that departs widely from the tones indicated by the notation and from conventional methods of producing instrumental sounds. Finally, to judge from the fact that the decade of the 1920's is still called the "jazz age," one may assume that jazz should be thought of as part of a sociological phenomenon.

All these definitions or descriptions have validity and provide partial characterizations. One other may be attempted here, one that will focus on the material and techniques employed to create vital jazz. It must be pointed out, however, that jazz has been undergoing a process of change ever since its inception. This process is of course responsible for the widely different sound of Louis Armstrong's "Hot Five" and Woody Herman's large band of the 1950's, for example, or between the latter and one of Dave Brubeck's "cool" ensembles of a decade later. Yet in spite of such basic differences of sound, certain principles and stylistic elements are as valid as they were at the turn of the century.

RHYTHM AND METER

All jazz is in duple meter—with either two beats per measure, or four. This two-beat or four-beat background is virtually always present and gives jazz a steady and regular rhythm. Superimposed on this background are the rhythms of the melodic, harmonic, and contrapuntal voices or parts. And whether written out or improvised, those rhythms make considerable use of normally unaccented beats and unaccented portions of beats. As we have seen (p. 28), these unaccented portions create the elements called "syncopation."

Yet jazz goes far beyond the normal and traditional meaning of syncopation. In a typical situation, combinations of long and short tones are heard in sequence, and every tone is accented; or a short triple-meter fragment may be inserted between three of the duple-meter beats, creating a brief cross-accent or cross-rhythm. While such devices are technically not syncopation (which in the strict sense is the shifting of the foreground rhythm to create a conflict with the background rhythm), they are generally referred to as such, and only the pedant is likely to object.

A much more characteristic problem in the consideration of jazz is the fact that metrical notation is only approximate and is not to be taken in the conventional sense; in other words, the approach to notes and tones is an improvisatory one. Many notational patterns can be written down, of course, but jazz performers go beyond such patterns and play them in stylized fashion. Example 131 illustrates only a few widely accepted conventions in respect to notation; various performers, however, have no hesitancy in placing their own stamp on such figures and playing them in a yet more individual manner.

Example 131

SCALE AND CONTOUR

Three principal influences on the contours of jazz melodies are: (1) art music in the Western tradition; (2) British and white American folk and popular songs of the nineteenth and twentieth centuries; (3) Afro-American folk songs, particularly the blues. It is from the third influence that the contours of jazz melody seem to inherit some of their most characteristic traits.

If one were to analyze the melodies of a large number of blues and jazz performances, one would find that several scales are basic to both of these related types of music. The most prevalent of these is the so-called *blues scale,* which has certain features in common with both the orthodox major and minor scales. It has eight basic tones, of which the first and fifth seem to be the most important. The third and seventh degrees of this scale often occur in flatted form. These flatted tones, called *blue third* and *blue seventh,* do not fit into any of our orthodox scale patterns, since performers of blues and jazz "worry" or "bend" these tones. In the scale of C this usually results in blue tones whose pitches are between E flat and E natural, and between B flat and B natural. The blues scale is shown in Example 132; the blue degrees are indicated by diamond-shaped notes.

Example 132

In an exhaustive study of jazz melody, the critic Winthrop Sargeant has found that the tones of the blues scale appear to be gathered into two groups of four tones each. One group centers around the first degree, and the other around the fifth degree. Sargeant has also discovered the principal tendencies of these scale tones in their musical contexts. The most significant tendencies are perhaps these: in the lower group of four, the first degree is usually preceded by the sixth degree below it or the blue third degree above it; and in the upper group, the fifth degree is often prefaced by the regular third degree below it or the blue seventh degree above it. All the principal tonal tendencies of this scale are summarized in Example 133. It can be seen that the tonal tendencies of the orthodox major and minor scales are for the most part not present.

Example 133

HARMONY

Jazz harmony is built on the harmonic concepts of orthodox music. Though its harmonic style has consistently advanced, jazz has in most instances done no more than follow harmonic trends that were fifty to two hundred years old at the time jazz performers and arrangers began to use them. It might be said as a broad generalization that since the early 1930's (the beginning of the era of arranged jazz), jazz harmonies have been those of the art music of the Romantic and Impressionist schools. All types of altered chords are frequent, and chords with an added sixth, seventh, ninth, eleventh, or thirteenth are the rule rather than the exception.

TEXTURE

The texture of jazz is primarily homophonic. Any well-wrought arrangement of written jazz will of course have a certain amount of contrapuntal interest; arrangers also have occasionally used such devices as the canon and the fugue. But it is in the completely improvised jazz of the New Orleans, Chicago, and Revival schools (see below) that the most interesting type of texture appears. Here the three or four "front line" instruments (that is, cornet or trumpet, clarinet, and trombone, with occasionally a second cornet or trumpet) weave improvised free counterpoints on a given melody or harmonic scheme.

Though these counterpoints are in no sense planned, the idiomatic tendencies of each instrument cause the instrument to be played in a somewhat similar way in each piece. The cornet or trumpet often essays a free version of the melody; the trombone provides an active lower counterpoint; and the clarinet plays an intricate decoration above the melody.

FORM

Jazz generally avoids complicated forms. It has taken over the regular four-measure phrase as its standard unit, and it combines such phrases into simple over-all structures. Though there is no design that could be called *the* jazz form, certain structures can be mentioned as occurring widely in jazz performances.

The unique twelve-measure form of the blues verse, for instance, is frequently heard in jazz. A number of slightly different harmonic schemes are common, but the structure usually is as shown in the diagram below. (The letters in parentheses in the line labeled "melodic phrase" show that, in some blues, the second phrase is similar to the first. The I^7 chord, which occurs in measures 3 and 4, is merely the I chord with the blue seventh of the scale added. A minor seventh is also sometimes added to the IV chord in measures 5 and 6.)

MEASURE NUMBER	1 2 3 4	5 6 7 8	9 10 11 12
TEXT PHRASE	a———	a———	b————
MELODIC PHRASE	a———	b (a′) —	c (b) —
HARMONY	I—I^7—	IV—I—	V^7—I—

Another structural feature of the blues should be noted here. The form of the blues is such that each melodic phrase usually ends on the first beat of the third measure of the basic four-measure phrase. If the blues-harmony pattern or a particular blues melody is being used as a basis for improvisation, the gap from the middle of the third to the fourth measure is often filled with an instrumental *break*. The break is a solo or ensemble cadenza which is played in rhythm. While the break is played, the rhythm section of the ensemble usually drops out; this creates a delightful sense of anticipation on the part of the listener, who waits for the return of the steady background rhythm.

The improvised jazz performance based on the blues form is simply a theme and variations design. The theme is the harmonic pattern of the blues, with a preexistent melody sometimes added. The variations are the "hot" solos played one after the other by the various instruments of the ensemble. And the other front line instruments often join the rhythm section in providing accompaniment for such solos. Breaks may occur in an ensemble presentation of the theme, or in an ensemble variation in which the gaps are filled by different solo instruments. An improvised theme and variations design such as this usually ends with an ensemble finale that features driving rhythm and the highest emotional level of the performance.

Also of great influence on jazz are the forms of the popular song. The form of most such songs is in two major sections, the verse and the chorus; these sections have a relationship to each other somewhat similar to that between the minuet and the trio. The jazz group, however, whether improvising or playing an intricate arrangement, seldom uses more than the chorus.

Tin Pan Alley uses the AABA design for the choruses of most of its songs. The chorus of the long-popular *Honeysuckle Rose,* for example, is such a form. Only very occasionally does one encounter other designs such as ABAB, ABCA, and so on. The same theme and variations structure that we encountered in improvised performances of the blues occurs in the jazz treatment of a popular song. The chorus of the song, usually in AABA form, is the theme, and the hot solos that follow are the variations.

Though the forms of written jazz vary widely with the tastes and abilities of the individual arrangers, there is a stock form of arrangement that is widely used. Such a form is indicated below. (Each large letter indicates a complete chorus, the form of which is, as indicated above, likely to be AABA.)

MEASURE NUMBER		1–32	33–64	65–96	97–128
CHORUS	introduction	A	A^1	A^2	A^3
INSTRUMENTATION (Rhythm section always present)	full orchestra	brass	saxophones	vocal or instrumental solo	full orchestra
KEY	tonic	tonic	tonic	another key—not always closely related to the tonic	tonic

INSTRUMENTATION

The instrumentation of jazz ensembles has changed greatly through the years. It is nevertheless possible to indicate three basic combinations of instruments that have been and are being used widely.

The fundamental type of ensemble consists basically of two sections—rhythm and front line (clarinet and two or three brasses). The rhythm section in this type of group consisted originally of tuba, banjo, and drums. Later the string bass and the guitar tended to replace the tuba and the banjo, and the piano was added to the rhythm section. Several of the more classically minded Revivalist groups (see pp. 415–17) have returned to the tuba and banjo in an attempt to produce a more authentic sound.

The large dance band, which came into prominence in the early 1930's, consists of three sections: rhythm, brass, and reed. The rhythm section contains string bass, guitar, piano, and drums. While the size of the brass section is not standardized, the most popular instrumentation has been three trumpets and two trombones. Some bands have had sections of up to five trumpets and four trombones, while others have had as small a brass group as two trumpets and one trombone. One or two French horns have also occasionally been used.

The reed section of the large dance band usually consists of four or five saxophones. If four players are used, two usually play alto saxophones; the other two may both play tenor saxophone, or one may play tenor and one baritone saxophone. All of the saxophone players usually play clarinet also, and some play flute, oboe, bass clarinet, and other woodwind instruments as well. Only the saxophone and the clarinet are basic to the jazz performance, however. In the case of a five-man reed section, the saxophones used are generally two altos, two tenors, and one baritone.

The instrumentation of the commercial, "sweet," and hotel-type dance bands, while still containing the three sections outlined above, sometimes varies considerably from what has been described. Such groups often use all tenor saxophones, and they sometimes include a section of three or four violins. This type of band, however, has little place in the discussion of jazz.

Jazz is sometimes played by groups called *combos* (combinations). A combo is a small ensemble, ranging in size from three to eight players. It sometimes consists of a partial or complete rhythm section only; the combination of piano, bass, and drums is common, for example. In other instances it comprises a three- or four-man rhythm section and a small group of wind instruments.

THE SPECIAL SOUNDS OF JAZZ

One often hears in jazz performances certain qualities of sound not heard in orthodox music. It is probable that most of these have originated in an attempt to imitate, with both voice and instrument, the highly idiomatic vocal quality and technique of Afro-American folk song.

Jazz singers and instrumentalists, for instance, produce a variety of tone qualities similar to those one hears in authentic black work songs, blues, and spirituals. These tone qualities range from coarse to smooth, from muffled to resonant, from harsh to mellow, from savage to tender. And the jazz performer sometimes contributes further to the characteristic sounds of his art by adding various nonmusical sounds—the growls, rasps, and groans that are found in the black folk song.

Beyond the matter of tone quality, certain types of pitch inflection (that is, pitch variation) that are characteristic ingredients of the jazz sound appear. These are again traceable to the folk songs of the Afro-American. Perhaps the most widely used is the *vibrato,* which involves change of intensity as well as of pitch of a single tone. The jazz performer's vibrato is changeable, varying from narrow to wide and from slow to fast; it is also expressive, contributing to the establishment of mood. One of the most characteristic uses of this device, occuring particularly in solo performances, is that where a single tone is intensified near its end by an increase in the width and speed of the vibrato. Such a procedure might be illustrated by the following figure:

Other uses of pitch inflection are on occasion apparent at the beginning and the end of the jazz player's or singer's individual tones. Most often, the inflected tones begin below the notated pitch and then slide up to it, and in certain instances the pitch slides downward at the end of the tone. These procedures occur in both improvised and arranged jazz. In the latter, a variety of diacritical markings indicate some of the inflections desired by the arranger. Other inflections, not notated, are the result of an understanding on the part of the performers that certain kinds of melodic or accompaniment figures are to be played with a particular type of pitch inflection.

It should be noted here that not all jazz performers or ensembles use the various tone qualities or pitch inflections in the same way or to the same extent. The peculiar use of these elements is, in fact, an important factor in the establishment of an individual style by a performer or a band. Also worthy of comment is the fact that, although these techniques have been presented as departures from the standards of orthodox musical performance, they are in reality special aspects of the jazz art. It is the rare singer or player of orthodox music who can also be successful at jazz, and the reason usually is that the orthodox performer cannot develop the particular musical concepts that would allow him to produce these special sounds of jazz.

Also contributing to the characteristic sounds of jazz are the various kinds of mutes used by the brass players in certain types of bands. (The mute is a device, usually made of fiber or metal, that the brass player uses to change his instrument's basic tone quality. In most cases the mute is inserted in the bell of the instrument.) The mutes used in jazz vary in shape and construction, and they produce a wide range of sounds.

IMPROVISATION AND ARRANGEMENT

Improvisation is the impelling force of jazz. Even in the performances of a band that features carefully conceived arrangements, the improvised solo is usually a principal element. As we have noted earlier, the improvising performer bases his efforts on a previously known melody and its harmonies, as in the improvised presentation of a popular song, or on a previously known harmonic scheme, as in the use of the blues chord progression (see p. 408). It is the individual performer's spontaneous creation of mood and musical logic, based upon the foundation of these previously known elements, that is the essence of jazz. This is in some cases as true of the singer as of the instrumentalist; jazz singers sometimes make only slight reference to the basic melody of the song that they are performing. In the case of written jazz, the arranger shares with the improvising soloist the responsibility for producing works of jazz art. And the arranger's success, like the soloist's, is in direct proportion to the spontaneity and musical logic of his work.

Jazz, then, is not a composer's art. The particular melody and harmonies that form the basis of a performance, improvised or arranged, are of secondary importance. Rather, jazz is the art of the performer, the performing ensemble, and the arranger. And the quality of the art is dependent upon their creative ideas.

Schools of Jazz

In the course of its relatively brief existence, jazz has undergone a considerable amount of development. Being largely an art of performers, it has varied in its sound and practice from one location to another. Three cities have been instrumental in bringing jazz to its present status, however; of these, New Orleans takes first place.

NEW ORLEANS JAZZ

In the decades after the Civil War, the New Orleans brass bands extended their activities to include dancing. The traditions of blues and ragtime came to join the bands' erstwhile repertory, and the instrumentation of the groups was altered accordingly. Perhaps just after the turn of the century, and perhaps imperceptibly, the jazz band was born.

The first New Orleans jazz performers continued performance activities very much like those of the bands. Their music, in fact, invariably tended to stress the background rhythm of two beats to a measure, as had long been done in the band. Soon they played for celebrations and funerals, and they served as an advertising medium.

Among the important bands of early New Orleans jazz were those of Charles ("Buddy") Bolden (1886–1931) and Charles ("Kid") Ory (b. 1886). Prominent players of this school included Joseph ("King") Oliver (1885–1938), a cornet player; Sidney Bechet (b. 1897–1959), clarinet and saxophone; and Louis ("Satchmo") Armstrong (b. 1900), cornet. Certain New Orleans performers later became well known in other schools of jazz.

In the years between 1915 and 1917, New Orleans jazz began to spread to other parts of the country. "The Original Dixieland Jazz Band," a group of white performers, was enthusiastically received in Chicago and New York. Many jazz musicians found employment on the river excursion boats that ran on the Mississippi. This spread jazz to cities along the river and its tributaries—to Memphis, St. Louis, Kansas City, Pittsburgh, and so on. But more than to any other city, jazz musicians moved to Chicago.

CHICAGO JAZZ

Some critics contend that a Chicago style of jazz developed after 1920. Careful analysis of recordings, however, will reveal that the style of jazz played in Chicago in the 1920's and the early 1930's was merely a modification of the New Orleans style. Among the modifications are these: the rhythm section in Chicago bands of this time sometimes contained guitar and string bass instead of banjo and tuba, and it almost always contained a piano; the rhythm section tended to stress four rather than two beats to a measure; the Chicago bands sometimes used one or even two saxophones; and a second trumpet or cornet also was sometimes added.

King Oliver moved from New Orleans to Chicago in 1917. The band he organized in the latter city, known as "King Oliver's Creole Jazz Band," became the most important jazz band in the country. Louis Armstrong joined the group as second cornetist in 1922, after having previously played in his native New Orleans and on the river boats. In 1923, Oliver's group made the first important recordings of black jazz. *Dippermouth Blues, Alligator Hop,* and *Zulu's Ball,* among others, are important documents in the history of jazz.

Louis Armstrong has been one of the important figures of jazz since his early Chicago days. After playing with Oliver's group for two years, he spent a short while in New York, returning to Chicago to organize his "Hot Five" and "Hot Seven," both important bands. A number of the recordings made by these groups in the years between 1925 and 1928 are considered classics. It is interesting to note that Armstrong, after taking part in the jazz movement known as *swing* (see p. 416), later, with his six-piece band, became a part of the movement to revive classic jazz.

The work of Oliver, Armstrong, and others influenced an important group of native Chicagoans. Of the native bands, one of the most significant was that organized in 1922 by five boys from Austin High School. This group has since become known to jazz historians as the "Austin High Gang." Among its members were the cornetist Jimmy McPartland (b. 1907) and the saxophonist Lawrence ("Bud") Freeman (b. 1906), both of whom are still active in jazz today. Another band, called the "Wolverines," featured the cornet playing of Leon Bismarck ("Bix") Beiderbecke (1903–31). Beiderbecke has been considered by some to be the most important single figure in the entire history of jazz. This reputation is probably exaggerated, for some writers are wont to make a legendary figure of the man. He possessed little technical skill, but the warmth and imagination of his improvisations were exceptional. His was an unusual natural talent, and his influence was great.

Two of the most important bandleaders and soloists of the swing era, Benny Goodman (b. 1909) and Tommy Dorsey (1904–57), often played with the two bands mentioned above—Goodman with the "Austin High Gang" and Dorsey with the "Wolverines." Other notable jazz musicians active in Chicago at various times up to the early 1930's included Eddie Condon (b. 1904), "Pee Wee" Russell (b. 1906), "Wild Bill" Davison (b. 1906), and Ernest L. ("Red") Nichols (b. 1905). Anyone familiar with the work of the Dixieland Revival movement will recognize these names. ("Dixieland" is the name that has been attached to improvised music played by a small band in the general New Orleans-Chicago style.)

After 1930, a definite trend toward the larger band developed in Chicago. (Louis Armstrong, however, had a ten-piece band as early as 1927.) As this trend developed, the center of jazz activity shifted from Chicago to New York. Dixieland jazz was forced into obscurity—and it was to remain in that state until the 1940's.

NEW YORK AND WRITTEN JAZZ

In the 1920's, one of the most important large bands in New York was that of Fletcher Henderson (1898–1952). Henderson, who came from Georgia, was a gifted pianist and arranger; his twelve-piece groups in the middle 1920's featured the style that was to make him Benny Goodman's chief arranger in the early swing era. The work of Edward Kennedy ("Duke") Ellington (b. 1899) is also important in the history of early and present-day written jazz. Although his groups have played a highly individualistic style of jazz and have remained on the periphery of swing, Ellington's influence on the swing movement is unmistakable.

The essence of swing, as the term was understood in the 1930's, was in its softening of the pounding rhythm, loudness, and direct expression characteristic of the "hot" period of the 1920's. Swing made use of rich and even subtle harmonies, a degree of chromaticism in employing them, and sharply contrasting tone colors. Impeccable performance of carefully worked-out arrangements, played primarily by large bands, further characterized the style.

The success of Benny Goodman's bands, from about 1935, ushered in the swing era. Between 1935 and 1941, the traveling swing band became a national institution. Hundreds of so-called "name" and "semi-name" bands toured the country. Among the important swing groups were those of Tommy Dorsey, Jimmy Lunceford (1902–47), William ("Count") Basie (b. 1904), and Harry James (b. 1916). One cannot always draw a line between swing and commercial dance music, hence a list of this kind must remain somewhat controversial. The band of Glenn Miller (1904–44), for example, played music mostly in the style of commercial dance music, but some of its arrangements and several of its soloists were in the best swing tradition.

The era of swing was also an era of great jazz singers. Performers such as Mildred Bailey and Ella Fitzgerald developed highly improvisatory styles of singing that contributed importantly to the history of jazz. In many instances their performances have rivaled in imagination and feeling the solo improvisations of the great instrumentalists.

The Second World War brought about a curtailment of the traveling activities of swing bands and also produced a severe shortage of musicians. Thus began the decline from which the swing movement has not recovered. Since the mid-1940's, however, Dixieland has made a comeback and two new trends have emerged.

THE DIXIELAND REVIVAL: BOP AND COOL JAZZ

During the Second World War, a renewed interest in improvised jazz of the Dixieland type took place. Veterans of the early New Orleans days reappeared. Louis Armstrong organized a new "Hot Five"; Kid Ory's "Creole Jazz Band" was reconstituted in 1943; and Lu Watters (b. 1915) organized the "Yerba Buena Jazz Band,"

Upper left: "King Oliver's Creole Jazz Band," which became the most important jazz band of the 1920's. Lower left: Erskine Tate's Little Symphony, with Louis Armstrong playing his "long horn" (trumpet). Right: Miles Davis, whose bop trumpet led the way to the "cool" jazz of the 1950's.

a group that attempted to revive the style of the earliest New Orleans bands. Rudi Blesh, the jazz critic and a principal force in the revival, lectured extensively on the subject. Further, musicians who had been prominent in Chicago in the 1920's—Condon, Russell, Davison—were again in great demand. The revival has continued to the present day.

The jazz movement called *bop* got its start in New York about 1942. It derived its name from the words with which its practitioners referred to the terse, disconnected melodic phrases that typify the style. Onomatopoetic combinations of syllables that imitated the first motive of typical phrases became a descriptive language for these musicians. Thus appeared such widely publicized terms as "be-bop," "re-bop," and "oo-bop-sha-bam." Bop almost always is played by small groups who feature "worked-out" (but not written) arrangements. Besides the short phrases, other main style characteristics include the harmonic and melodic use of chords with a diminished fifth, irregular accent patterns that produce a polymetric effect, and the use of Latin-American percussion instruments. Principal developers of bop have included the trumpeter John B. ("Dizzy") Gillespie (b. 1917), the alto saxophonist Charlie ("Yardbird") Parker (1920–55), and Miles Davis (b. 1926).

A type of jazz closely connected to bop, but more intimate in style, is that referred to as *cool.* This music, which might be described as jazz chamber music, is played by small ensembles of standard jazz instruments as well as by groups that contain flute, oboe, or French horn. Cool jazz draws on the forms and textures of traditional art music, being sometimes contrapuntal; it has been influenced by the contemporary techniques of polytonality and atonality. Cool jazz has become music for listening, for in most cases it is too introverted and too complex to serve as dance music. One of the best known performers in the cool tradition is the pianist Dave Brubeck (b. 1920), a pupil of Darius Milhaud. The "Modern Jazz Quartet," an ensemble founded by Brubeck, was a major force in making cool jazz and its sophisticated idiom well known.

ROCK

Cool jazz proved to be too objective and complex to serve the needs of the general public, and before long a number of folk-based styles developed. At first these styles were characterized by the reiteration of simple triadic harmonies, diatonic melodies sung to sentimental or earthy texts, and regular phrase structures. Accompaniments were provided by one or more electrically amplified guitars, sometimes augmented by percussion instruments. One type acquired the name "country music" because of its derivation from the music traditionally used at country dances and similar rural entertainments; it featured nasal singing and twanging sounds. Unsophisticated at first, country music quickly attracted the attention of commercial interests and has since become a carefully wrought product in which driving rhythms, unremitting loudness, and hypnotic fascination are essential elements.

Another style, at first called "rock 'n' roll," soon developed beyond its country cousin. The strong pulsating beat was retained, but phrases of uneven length (five, six, or more measures as opposed to the regular four measures in country music) became characteristic, and advanced harmony was often employed. The melodic line was sometimes highly ornamented with series of wails and slides and was filled with dissonant and unresolved tones; sometimes the structure in which it was cast was at variance with the regular pulsating accompaniment. The texts too went beyond the subjects common to country music. In addition to employing the themes found there and in the blues—life and death, love and hate, fear and joy, and all the rest—rock 'n' roll often expressed social satire and social protest, sometimes in an extreme form.

In the past decade, and under the influence of commercial interests, rock 'n' roll has undergone many transformations. The term itself has generally been shortened to "rock," and various subtypes known as "soul music" and "acid" have emerged. An ensemble of guitars of various sizes and shapes customarily accompany the rock singers; piano is sometimes added to the ubiquitous percussion, and electrical amplification of all the instruments is customary. More recent developments include the addition of colored, flashing, and rotating lights as a background for the type of

The New York Rock and Roll Ensemble explores the relationships between rock and the music of the Baroque. Here they tape a rock treatment of a Bach concerto for a television broadcast.

music called "psychedelic," experiments with electronically produced tones and sound effects, and an occasional use of free rhythms and other contemporary devices.

Through all this expanison of the several types of rock, the central field of jazz has maintained its place—although in a somewhat less elaborate style. Shorn of its later manifestations (mainly bop and cool), jazz upholds its integrity as an art. Under the general term "mainstream jazz," it has approached concert music in its search for new instrumental colors as well as in its use of serial techniques, polyphonic writing (including fugal devices), and sometimes larger forms. Mainstream jazz, still in the process of development, continues to be a vital force in contemporary music.

Listening Suggestions

Anthology of Jazz (Ethnic Folkways)
- Vol. 1 Afro-American Folk Song
- Vol. 2 Blues
- Vol. 3 New Orleans Jazz
- Vol. 4 Jazz Singers of All Periods
- Vol. 5 Chicago Jazz
- Vol. 6 Chicago Jazz
- Vol. 7 New York Jazz Before Swing
- Vol. 8 Big Bands before Swing
- Vol. 9 Jazz Piano of All Periods
- Vol. 10 Boogie-Woogie and the Riff
- Vol. 11 Small-Band Jazz from New Orleans to Bop

History of Jazz (Capitol)
- Vol. 1 New Orleans Jazz
- Vol. 2 Chicago Jazz
- Vol. 3 Swing
- Vol. 4 Jazz After Swing

The Story of Jazz (Ethnic Folkways)

Chapter 20

MUSIC OF THE UNITED STATES

When the leading European composers began to establish residence in the United States in the 1930's they found a congenial musical climate, an active concert life, and a great interest in all phases of music. With few exceptions, they were able to adjust to the conditions they found, conditions that were in large part the result of America's unusual musical history.

Virtually since the beginning of organized settlement on the American continent, music has played a large part in the life of its people, but it has always been a kind of music that was suited to the changing needs of those people. Colonists perched on the edge of a hostile wilderness or settlers moving across endless plains had little opportunity to establish comprehensive musical organizations and a system of aristocratic support like those that characterized European countries of the time. Later, when settled areas along the Atlantic Coast became secure and other settlements took root farther west, a normal musical development followed, and the foundations were laid for the kind of musical life that could prove hospitable to the world's most eminent musicians. A brief review of American musical history here will provide a better understanding of the conditions that enabled the United States to assume its world position in the art in a relatively brief time.

Musical Developments to 1920

Early eighteenth-century musical activities in New England at first centered about psalm singing. In 1640 the *Bay Psalm Book* (which included texts but not music) was published in Cambridge; it was the second book to be published on American soil. Instruction books in the art of singing and music reading began to appear in New England in the early 1700's, when a few singing schools were also established. Toward the end of the century William Billings (1746–1800) wrote a number of anthems and settings of hymns in imitative counterpoint; the latter he called "fuguing pieces," and with them he brought an air of vitality to the church music of his day.

Musical life in other regions was more diversified. Members of the Moravian religious denomination settled in Bethlehem and in other cities in Pennsylvania; in Salem (now Winston-Salem), North Carolina; and elsewhere. Wherever they settled instrumental music flourished. Chamber music was cultivated by Moravian composers, notably Johann Friedrich Peter (1746–1813); and by the end of the eighteenth century, music by contemporary European composers (Haydn, Mozart, and Johann Christian Bach among them) was performed regularly.

In the larger cities of Boston, New York, Philadelphia, and Charleston, concerts were instituted before the middle of the eighteenth century. The content of the programs was based on the European repertoire. Native-born composers began to appear also; perhaps the earliest of them was Francis Hopkinson (1737–91), one of the signers of the Declaration of Independence, who wrote many songs in the style of English composers of the time.

In the years after the American Revolution many English and French musicians settled in the United States. After 1848, and continuing through the rest of the century, immigration from Germany increased and German musicians to a large extent supplanted the earlier immigrants and the native-born musicians alike. Musical culture was predominantly in German hands; insofar as concerts were concerned, America became a province of Germany. This fact provoked a number of protests on the part of American musicians who sought to halt the German musical invasion. William Fry (1813–64), George Bristow (1825–98), and others composed operas and instrumental works in an effort to establish an indigenous repertoire. In that activity they had been preceded by Anton Heinrich (1781–1861), who had written songs and instrumental pieces in Kentucky as early as 1818. But their efforts did little to halt the flow of European musical influences.

The appearance of outstanding European virtuoso performers brought yet another foreign element to American soil. The Norwegian Ole Bull, one of the most dazzling of violinists, made his first visit to the United States in 1843. He was followed by such world-famous performers as the singer Jenny Lind, the pianist and composer Louis Moreau Gottschalk (American by birth but a musical product of France), the violinist Henri Wieniawski, the pianists Anton Rubinstein and Hans von Bülow, and many others of like stature. Eminent composers such as Tchaikovsky and Dvořák also paid visits to America in the late years of the century; Dvořák was a resident of New York from 1892 to 1895.

In the years after the Civil War a school of composers emerged in New England. The leader of this group, John Knowles Paine (1839–1906), studied in Germany and became an organist and teacher in Boston in 1862. In 1875 he was made professor of music at Harvard University, becoming the first person to hold such a position in any American institution of higher learning. Paine's compositions included two symphonies, two symphonic poems, an opera, several choral works, and many smaller pieces. In those works he demonstrated a quality of workmanship far above that of any other American composer of the time; the content of his music, however, was similar to that of contemporary German Romantic works. His work as a teacher was of great significance; many of his pupils achieved prominent places in American music after the turn of the century.

Other prominent members of the group were George Chadwick (1854–1931) and Horatio Parker (1863–1919). Both men went to Germany to complete their training as composers, and that training was reflected in their many works. Among those works, Chadwick's symphonic ballad, *Tam O'Shanter* (1915), as well as Parker's oratorio *Hora Novissima* (1893) and his opera *Mona* (1912) remained in the repertoire for many years; the oratorio is still performed on occasion. Those works were solidly and imaginatively constructed in the nineteenth-century tradition.

Perhaps the most widely known American composer at the turn of the century, however, was Edward MacDowell (1861–1908). A New Yorker by birth, MacDowell was not aligned with the New England group. After private study in his native city, he spent almost ten years in Germany as a student, teacher, and pianist. In 1887 he became a resident of Boston. His orchestral works were performed by the Boston Symphony Orchestra in the following years, and MacDowell's fame spread rapidly. In 1896 he was called to head the newly formed department of music at Columbia University, where he remained until 1904. A year later, overwork and fatigue brought on a mental collapse and MacDowell's creative career ended.

MacDowell's music is primarily lyric in character. His well-known set of piano pieces, *Woodland Sketches,* illustrates the clarity and perfection of his style, his harmonic resourcefulness, and the air of refinement that animates all his compositions. His larger compositions include two piano concertos and four piano sonatas. In those works the lyric charm is supplemented by stirring rhythms, dramatic climaxes, and fine proportions. MacDowell's music has remained in the repertoire until recently, in contrast to that of all his contemporaries. Its vigor, honesty of expression, and individuality raise it far above other American works of the time. And on the international level MacDowell is still probably the best-known representative of late nineteenth-century American music.

New Influences After 1920

The pervasive interest in Romantic expression, fostered by a generation of American composers who themselves had been trained in Germany, continued for a few years after the death of MacDowell. With the coming of the First World War (1914–18), however, the German influence on American music declined. Travel to European countries became impossible, German compositions were virtually banned from concert programs, and the long-established tradition of a German musical education lost its appeal. The music of Debussy, Ravel, and other Impressionists attracted the attention of composers and listeners alike, and for more than a decade French music played a major role in American concerts. As a consequence, many American composers went to Paris in the years after 1920 to complete their musical studies, as they had formerly gone to Leipzig, Stuttgart, or Berlin.

Then came the small but qualitatively important wave of European composers to these shores in the years beginning about 1933. American composers were now able to make direct contact with the world's leaders in musical thought without leaving their country. This inspired one group of them to find native materials to serve their musical purposes. It gave rise to a nationalistic school whose compositions were often based on legends and folk characters.

A second group of composers, often including men who were also active in the nationalistic tradition, continued to employ the principles of abstract music. The results were varied: in some compositions the expressive content was as uncompromising and objective as the European music of a generation before; and in others one heard evidence that composers had passed beyond the experiments of the previous generation and adopted a warm, lyric type of expression to which the name "neo-Romantic" has been given.

A third group, stemming indirectly from the most original American composer of the twentieth century, Charles Ives, has been made up of individualists. It is difficult, and perhaps undesirable, to label those composers as specialists in one or another type of music. Most of them have written in abstract forms and in modifications of Schoenberg's twelve-tone system when it suited their needs. They have not hesitated to adopt non-European idioms and to apply them in their compositions. Asiatic, Near Eastern, American Indian, and other exotic rhythmic and melodic types have come to expression. Some composers have employed, transformed, or transcended jazz idioms. The majority have written with traditional performance practices in mind and have relied on soloists, chamber groups, or larger ensembles for the performance of their works. Others have cultivated a spirit of improvisation and have written only sketches that are intended to be elaborated by an improvising ensemble.

Virtually all these American composers—most of them men born well within the twentieth century—have written at times without regard for the emotional comfort of their audiences and at other times with the practical needs of high-school ensembles in mind. The overwhelming impression remains that American composers of the present day can neither be classified nor can they be said to represent one particular school of musical thought. In that very characteristic they demonstrate their right to represent American culture—for the United States is too vast and too varied to have only one kind of music.

IVES

Charles Ives (1874–1954) was an unusual figure in American music: a bold experimenter who developed a personal style that was not in the least derived from the European styles of his day. Ives served as a church organist from about 1887 to 1902 in various cities near New York, and then became a successful businessman who composed as an avocation. He composed several symphonies, many descriptive

Charles Ives (1874–1954), a bold experimenter in advance of his time.

pieces, and other compositions for a variety of media, mainly before 1916; but those compositions did not come to public notice until the years after about 1930.

Ives's music taken as a whole represents a pioneering activity unique in American culture. It brought a variety of new techniques and textures to expression at a time when the musical world was just beginning to assimilate the Impressionism of Debussy. Many of the new techniques anticipated by twenty years or more the appearance of similar techniques in the works of the most advanced composers. Every kind of musical novelty and experiment found its way into Ives's music. Polytonal and polymodal writing; complex polyrhythms; tone clusters; original acoustic effects, including attempts to illustrate a band playing out of tune and a chorus whose ensemble was faulty—such stylistic elements characterize part of his music.

Experiments with the structure of music and with the very basis of metrical rhythm interested Ives also. Passages written in unmetrical prose rhythms stand opposite marchlike passages; sections in which every detail is carefully worked out are followed by sections that are left to be improvised. Gospel hymns, popular songs, wonderfully lyric melodies of his own creation, and a variety of rhythmic devices are combined in polyphonic textures ranging from the thinnest possible to the incredibly thick. The works are firmly tied to American life and culture, both through actual quotation of American tunes and through a variety of literary references.

The orchestral piece entitled *Three Places in New England* (1903–14); the work called *A Symphony: Holidays* (1904–13), with its four movements concerned with Washington's Birthday, Memorial Day, the Fourth of July, and Thanksgiving Day; the Second Piano Sonata (1909–15), with the subtitle *Concord, Mass., 1840–1860,* and with its four movements bearing the names "Emerson," "Hawthorne," "The Alcotts," and "Thoreau"—these are among the compositions that reveal Ives's close association with American life. Other works, notably the Symphony No. 3 (1901–04) and several chamber music compositions, are ostensibly representatives of abstract music. But whether descriptive or abstract, they reveal a unique mixture of indigenous materials, wide-ranging and thoughtful experiment, and a keen musical imagination of which humor is an essential ingredient.

TAYLOR

Deems Taylor (1885–1966) became known to millions of listeners during his long service as commentator for the New York Philharmonic Symphony Orchestra's broadcasts. He was an active writer on musical subjects, and his numerous and enjoyable compositions placed him high among the more conservative composers.

Taylor's orchestral suite *Through the Looking Glass* (1922), based on Lewis Carroll's fantasy, has remained a model of spontaneous, humorous, and entertaining music. His operas, *The King's Henchman* (1926) and *Peter Ibbetson* (1931), have been performed frequently and are among the most successful American operas that had been composed up to about 1930. Taylor represented, in general, the school of composers who remained faithful to post-Romantic harmonic practices. His music is full of tunes in the usual sense of that word; his harmonies are balanced between consonant and dissonant, and an element of warm expressiveness is seldom absent.

PISTON

Walter Piston (b. 1894), although born only a few years later than Deems Taylor, is in quite a different category. His music reflects a neo-Classical clarity of form, restrained and objective expression, and the finest kind of workmanship. Except in his well-known ballet, *The Incredible Flutist* (1938), he has most often avoided programmatic writing, and nationalism finds no place in his works. Writing with equal competence in many different media, he has produced a series of instrumental works that range from chamber music trios to symphonies and concertos.

Dissonance and rhythmic energy were Piston's outstanding characteristics in the 1930's. The dissonances were variously derived; they included linear counterpoint in the style of Hindemith, percussive chordal effects like those of Stravinsky, and a systematic exploitation of tonal combinations similar to those of Schoenberg. His compositions since about 1940 have revealed a somewhat warmer, more expressive tone, but they have not become any the less vital in rhythm or less rigorous in their pursuit of new harmonic combinations. Piston is fortunate in having found a style that is individual and strong. All his music is consistent with that style, and he works out his ideas under the promptings of a keen and competent musical intellect.

HANSON

Howard Hanson (b. 1896), a native of Nebraska, was the second winner of the American *Prix de Rome* and spent the three years between 1921 and 1924 in Italy. For over forty years he was director of the Eastman School of Music; in that position he worked industriously toward furthering American music. Through performances and recordings he brought music of many kinds—even the most advanced—to public notice. Yet in his own works he has maintained a conservative Romantic tone.

Two of his compositions, the "Nordic" Symphony (1922) and the "Romantic" Symphony (1930), best represent the vitality and the dramatic aspects of his style. The "Romantic" Symphony is well named, for it brings into the twentieth century something of the youthfulness and direct sentiment that distinguished many works of the 1870's. Hanson's mastery of orchestration is evident in every measure of the work: variety of instrumental colors, much orchestral detail, and sonorous climaxes are typical of his music. Other major works include an opera, *Merry Mount* (1932), a choral work, *Lament for Beowulf* (1926), and two untitled symphonies (1937 and 1943). In his later works Hanson adopted a more dissonant, compact style, but he retained the Romantic warmth and impulsive expression characteristic of his earlier works.

Hanson's influence upon a whole generation of American composers has been beneficial. The many students who came into contact with him were stimulated to work as individuals: he had no patience with imitators of his own style. In prompting younger composers to express their musical ideas in many different idioms he contributed indirectly to the variety and solid craftsmanship that are characteristic of American music today.

THOMSON

Virgil Thomson (b. 1896), a Midwesterner by birth, was educated at Harvard, and lived in Paris for several years. He is widely known as a musical journalist; his writings as music critic of the New York *Herald Tribune* between 1940 and 1954 revealed him as the possessor of a prose style that is witty, provocative, and eminently readable. As a composer, Thomson first came to public notice with his opera *Four Saints in Three Acts* (1934, with a libretto by Gertrude Stein). A variety of smaller works as well as his music for documentary films (notably *The Plough That Broke the Plains* and *Louisiana Story*) added to his reputation as a composer of entertaining, accessible works.

Thomson's style has remained direct and diatonic; his melodies are tuneful and are usually harmonized simply. The virtues of his music lie in its wide appeal and its complete absence of pretense. A sophisticated, urbane individual himself, Thomson has composed music that is simple, nostalgic, and unashamedly sentimental.

SESSIONS

Roger Sessions (b. 1896) is a native of Brooklyn. He attended both Harvard and Yale, continued his studies with Ernest Bloch, and then lived in Germany and Italy for eight years (1925–33) as the recipient of various fellowships. He has been active

Walter Piston (b. 1894), a leading American composer of the neo-Classical school.

Virgil Thomson (b. 1896), composer and music critic.

as a teacher in California and at Princeton University, and he has been an eloquent spokesman for the dignity and worth of music composed by Americans.

Of all native-born American composers, Sessions is perhaps the most meticulous in craftsmanship and the most consistent in upholding neo-Classical ideals. Like Piston, he is at his best in large, abstract instrumental works: his major compositions are three symphonies, a violin concerto, a string quartet, and two piano sonatas. Composing slowly, with a sense of self-discipline that is not typical of all twentieth-century composers, Sessions personifies the intellectual approach to music.

The most striking impression that Sessions' music makes is its impersonality. He has no interest in nationalism, in musical description, or in exotic elements; his guiding principle in composition is the rigorous handling of materials according to musical laws only. As a consequence, the forms developed in his works are models of clarity, and well-defined melodies are usually in evidence. His harmony is flexible, being composed of tonal or atonal elements as the music requires; but it is always intelligible, even when strongly dissonant. Rhythmically, too, his music shows the hand of a master craftsman; polyrhythms are not uncommon, and the textures contain a considerable amount of small rhythmic detail.

COWELL

Henry Cowell (1897–1965), born and educated in California, led an active life in Europe and the United States as concert pianist, lecturer, writer and teacher, and as a prolific composer. For many years he was an avowed experimentalist and sought to expand the expressive possibilities of music by a variety of means. Among the more spectacular of the stylistic elements exploited by Cowell was the *tone cluster:* a group of tones played on the piano by striking the keys with the closed fist, the forearm, or even with a block of wood. Tone clusters appeared in his orchestral works also, and were often set polyphonically: a series of such clusters, forming one "melody," was set opposite another. Complex rhythmic patterns and extreme dissonance were employed also; the result was music that was often irritating in its emotional effect.

About 1955, in company with many other "advanced" composers, Cowell altered his style radically in order to close the gap that had developed between composers and audiences. He wrote a number of consonant, expressive, and even sentimental works in a variety of media. Many were designed for use in high-school musical ensembles; as such they have been heard—and have probably been enjoyed—more generally than his experimental, dissonant compositions ever were. But his interest in new expressive possibilities never diminished.

GERSHWIN

George Gershwin (1898–1937) stands completely apart from the composers mentioned above. His considerable employment of jazz and the sentimental quality of much of his music find no parallels in the music of the composers we have been discussing. Jazz, as was explained in Chapter 19, is primarily a manner of performing. Certain rhythmic and harmonic practices of the jazz performer, however, are capable of being written down, and consequently can be used in other musical contexts. Many composers before Gershwin had used jazz idioms in concert music: Stravinsky, Křenek, Hindemith, and many other equally representative composers had introduced elements of jazz rhythm into their works as early as the 1920's. But none of them employed such elements as consistently as did Gershwin.

Gershwin came to the composition of large-scale, well-organized musical works with a different kind of training and a different set of musical values than most other composers. His background was that of a commercial (that is, "Tin Pan Alley") pianist and theater musician. An improvisatory, short-breathed, and "popular" style of composition was natural to him; intellectual activity, or even a balance between mind and heart, was not an essential element of that style. Poignancy, nostalgia, sentiment, and romance were the most usual moods in his music. In expressing such moods he disclosed a sensitive melodic gift, a flair for colorful, mildly chromatic harmony, and a keen sense of rhythmic variety.

Syncopation, considerable repetition of short melodic fragments, and a rhapsodic, almost Impressionistic freedom of form are striking elements of his style. Such elements are popularly associated with the jazz idiom. The universally known *Rhapsody in Blue* (1924) for piano and orchestra, his Piano Concerto in F (1925), and the orchestral suite *An American in Paris* (1928) are his principal large instrumental works. His folk opera *Porgy and Bess* (1935) has become one of the best-known representatives of American music. Those works illustrate the composite nature of his style.

Gershwin cannot be evaluated from the point of view with which we approach either the specialists in the traditional forms or the truly contemporary composers of the century. His music is a blend of sophistication and simplicity, of unashamed sentiment and sentimentality, of inspired melody and routine forms. We would do wrong to look into Gershwin's music for the detailed craftsmanship, the wide range of emotion, and the solidly constructed textures that are typical of other music. He concerned himself almost entirely with the piano and voice; his *Rhapsody in Blue,* consequently, was scored for orchestra by a professional arranger. His talent for writing tunefully and appealingly has probably not been matched by an American composer since Victor Herbert.

HARRIS

Roy Harris (b. 1898) has identified himself as the musical spokesman for America to a greater extent than any other composer. His nationalism is not entirely a matter of titles or subject matter—although the nature of some of his titles suggests a conscious striving toward nationalistic expression. Even in his abstract works a strong, rugged, and sometimes strident quality leads to their being considered representative of one aspect of American life.

In a number of orchestral and chamber music works composed between 1926 and about 1932, Harris wrote in a dissonant, harsh style, creating a texture that was often contrapuntal. Interested in self-generating forms (that is, forms that progress

Igor Stravinsky, Aaron Copland, Lukas Foss, and Roger Sessions at a rehearsal of Stravinsky's *Les Noces*.

from beginning to end without internal divisions), he developed a rhapsodic manner of writing. From the middle 1930's he often employed modal scales instead of tonal ones (see pp. 307ff); these gave his works an austere, remote quality. His Symphony No. 3 (1937), consisting of one movement divided loosely into five contrasting sections, is an excellent example of Harris' style at the time. Even in its contrapuntal passages (the fourth section of the symphony is a fugue) the music progresses in blocks of tone rather than in a true, rhythmically diverse texture; and a certain monotony of effect is unavoidable. The instrumental colors of this work are somewhat subdued, also.

Another aspect of Harris' career dates from about 1935, when folk songs and legends played some part in his creative work. Such compositions as the overture *When Johnny Comes Marching Home* (1934), the choral works *Five Songs for Democracy* and *Sons of Uncle Sam,* the ballet *What So Proudly We Hail,* and his Symphony No. 4, with its subtitle, "Folk-Song Symphony," show the direction of that interest. In comparison with purely abstract works, compositions that reflect a nationalistic point of view are almost necessarily directed toward a wider public; hence one can account for the more conservative harmonic idiom that many of these works reveal.

A scene from Copland's ballet *Appalachian Spring,* performed by the Martha Graham Dance Company.

COPLAND

Aaron Copland (b. 1900), perhaps the most prominent American composer of his generation, has been equally prominent as a teacher and as a writer on American music. Dance rhythms are more consistently utilized by Copland than by any other of the American composers discussed here except Gershwin. In the 1920's his works contained jazz idioms. His prize-winning *Dance Symphony* (1922–25), a piano concerto (1927), and other works of the time employ the syncopations, cross accents, and other jazz elements that were then fashionable.

A period in the early 1930's saw Copland abandon such idioms and write with extreme dissonance, thin textures, and sparse orchestration; his *Short Symphony* (1933) is a representative work of this period. From about 1935 his style became warmer and less dissonant. An interest in ballet resulted in such works as *Billy the Kid, Rodeo,* and *Appalachian Spring.* We are justified in speaking of a nationalistic phase in Copland's career when we consider the content of those works and others such as *A Lincoln Portrait* and *Music for Radio* ("Saga of the Prairies").

Works composed after about 1940 demonstrated Copland's mastery of extended forms; and a tighter, more detailed kind of writing was employed. But the rhythmic vitality of his earlier styles was maintained. His Symphony No. 3 (1946) well illustrates the balance, control, and excellent craftsmanship that distinguished his work for more than thirty years. A warm expressive quality is achieved without resorting to excess sentiment, and the style remains objective, sonorous, and strong.

In recent decades, however, Copland has turned to serial techniques (see p. 399). A piano quartet (1950) and a Fantasy for piano (1958) reveal various versions of the technique, with an eleven-tone row in the one and a ten-tone row in the other. With these works he has taken a place among the most advanced composers of the present time.

Music Today

It may be assumed that the composers mentioned in the foregoing pages (along with many others born before 1900) have reached their mature, definitive styles of composing. It is not likely that the works they produce from this point forward will differ radically from those they composed in the 1940's. A large number of other composers, including men who are as active as the older composers on today's musical scene, are still in the process of developing or advancing their respective styles. The works they have composed so far may not represent their ultimate contributions to the formation of an American music.

Many of these talented composers have not been as fortunate as others in achieving numerous performances for their compositions; their works, known only to a few, have not yet taken their rightful places on the concert stage. In some cases geographical isolation may be responsible; in others, the lack of an aggressive temperament. The colleges and universities of the United States are staffed by many competent, industrious composers whose works remain unheard beyond local limits.

Others of these men, perhaps because of favorable geographical location, have come to public notice in the last decade or two. They are as well represented on concert programs as were their compatriots of a generation ago. The most prominent of the group include Elliott Carter (b. 1908), Samuel Barber (b. 1910), William Schuman (b. 1910), Gian-Carlo Menotti (b. 1911), Norman Dello Joio (b. 1913), David Diamond (b. 1915), Vincent Persichetti (b. 1915), Ulysses Kay (b. 1917), Leonard Bernstein (b. 1918), Leon Kirchner (b. 1919), Peter Mennin (b. 1923), Gunther Schuller (b. 1925), and many others.

The styles of those men are as varied as their backgrounds; the individuality revealed by the men born before 1900 has been continued by those born after that date. Limitations of space prevent a discussion of even their most representative compositions; and generalizations wide enough to cover the ramifications of many styles that are, in most cases, still in the process of crystallization could only become misleading. This group of composers, however, represents only one aspect of the contemporary scene. In the light of what will be discussed later in this chapter under the heading of "experimental music," they are in a sense traditionalists.

They compose for the traditional musical media—orchestra, chorus, and all the rest—and employ the same musical materials that composers have used for centuries. And they make use of stylistic factors that relate their works to the mainstream of the world's music. Certain of those factors may be described in general terms.

A factor that is apparent in many contemporary compositions is the continued (or renewed) vitality of the tonal system. Diatonic scales have been restored to usefulness, and melodies have tended to lose some of the angular chromaticism that characterized them in the 1940's. While this music may be said to have tonal centers, it in no sense marks a return merely to the dominant-tonic relationships of the nineteenth century. The typical tonal center is neither major nor minor, but both; it serves as a unifying element around which the vertical element of the music is constructed. The concept of harmony, in its traditional meaning, has to a large extent given way to a concept of vertical "density"; music is thought of as containing tensions and relaxations rather than dissonances and consonances.

Another factor evident in many American compositions today is the use of serial techniques (see p. 399). Milton Babbitt, a mathematician, a composer, and an experimenter in music was one of the earliest Americans to employ this style, carrying it far beyond Webern in so doing. More recently Elliott Carter has served as an outstanding representative of that approach, although Carter has also brought elements from other styles into his music. Many composers are active in the expansion of serial techniques, producing advanced work in this style; but unfortunately, probably because a small gap still exists between avant garde composers and the general public, such works often come to a single performance, then slip back into obscurity.

Milton Babbitt at the controls of the RCA Synthesizer.

Elliott Carter (b. 1908), prominent American composer of the serial school.

Experimental Music

Throughout the course of music history many composers have sought to expand the limits of conventional musical materials. The gradually increasing use of instruments in the Renaissance and Baroque periods may be seen as the reflection of a need to transcend the range and dynamic limits of the human voice. The development of harmony from the early 1600's to the early 1900's represents a constant search for newer sonorities. And the Romantic preoccupation with varieties of instrumental sound was in effect an attempt to discover new tone colors.

This process of pushing back the boundaries of music has continued to the present day. Within the past few decades a number of composers have experimented with the intervals of the chromatic scale itself and developed a kind of music that employs microtones—that is, intervals smaller than half steps. Among the more prominent experimenters was Ernest Bloch (1880–1959), of Swiss birth but a resident of the United States from 1917. In 1923 Bloch composed a piano quintet in which quarter tones were employed; in this he followed the lead of a Czech composer, Alois Haba (b. 1893), who for a time worked with quarter steps, sixth steps, and twelfth steps. And in the work of the American composer Harry Partch (b. 1901) microtonality reached its most consistent development with a scale that included forty-three microtones within an octave.

Another line of experiments, conducted by obscure composers principally in New York and Chicago until about 1930, derived from the work of Ernst Toch (1887–1964), who manipulated phonograph recordings of the human voice in Berlin in the 1920s. In these experiments a number of voices speaking in a quasi-imitative texture were recorded, after which the recordings were played back at a much faster speed so that the speaking voices approached pitches even higher than those used in singing. The texts were of course unintelligible at the faster speed, but new tone qualities were produced. This work remained an isolated effort, however, was not pursued by other composers, and had little influence on later developments.

Edgar Varèse (1885–1965, born in France but active in the United States after about 1916), writing for large orchestra, composed in a style in which rhythmic and dynamic elements were exploited to the utmost. The effects he produced resembled those introduced by Stravinsky in *The Rite of Spring.* Varèse, however, worked more concentratedly in the field of rhythm, and in his well-known *Ionisation* (1931) he employed an orchestra consisting of forty-one percussion instruments (among which he included the piano) and two sirens to bring about an embodiment of the rhythmic element freed from the trammels of conventional melody and harmony.

Leon Termen (1896–1939?) invented several instruments, notably the "Theremin" (1920). On this instrument, which he demonstrated in the United States during the 1930's, an electronically produced tone could be altered in pitch and intensity by the manipulation of the player's hands. The Theremin, along with the Hammond electronic organ (which was developed quite independently of Termen), may have been among the instruments that stimulated composers a generation later to work so extensively with electronically produced sound.

Still other areas of experimentation were developed. John Cage (b. 1912 in Los Angeles) introduced the idiom of the "prepared piano" in the late 1930's. This required the use of a conventional piano on whose strings various objects (keys, coins, strips of heavy fabric, and the like) were placed in order to alter the piano's characteristic tone colors and sonorities. After attracting a considerable amount of attention with his music composed for the "prepared piano," both in the United States and Europe, Cage began to experiment with "random composition." In this kind of music (also called "aleatory" or "chance music"), random throws of dice determined how the composer was to select and organize his musical material. Under the influence of later developments in chance music, a composer writing an ensemble piece might direct one of his performers to improvise on a certain passage for a stated period of time (twenty or more seconds, for example), while other performers were directed to play as written. These and similar developments often required that a new kind of notation be devised, a notation that permitted

Edgar Varèse (1885–1965), who exploited the rhythmic element in his music.

the composer to employ symbols for various kinds of verbal directions, and also one in which traditional bar lines were eliminated in favor of marks that indicated simply the lapse of time.

Lukas Foss (b. 1922) is prominent among recent composers who have worked in the field of chance music. After study with Hindemith and a period in which the influence of Stravinsky was strong, Foss established an Improvisation Chamber Ensemble (clarinet, cello, piano, and percussion) and has written several works for it, notably *Time Cycle* (1960) and *Echoi* (1963).

ELECTRONIC MUSIC

The full development of the tape recorder in the 1940's introduced a new approach to musical experimentation, for the tape recorder made it possible to bring the resources of modern technology into the field of music. The experiments fall into three main classes: (1) those in which tones produced by the voice and by conventional instruments are recorded and subsequently altered or purposefully distorted (this class has lost ground in recent years); (2) those in which various electronic devices are used to generate new sounds; and (3) those in which nonmusical sounds (that is, noises) are suitably transformed on the same electronic devices. In all three classes of experiments the new or transformed sounds may be combined with conventional musical tones, or they may be used alone; and the three classes of sounds may be combined in any number of ways. These sounds, then, are used as materials for musical composition and result in what is generally called "electronic music." The tape recorder is the principal means for recording and "performing" the compositions that result from the experiments.

Among the techniques developed by the earliest composers in this field were some that made use of multiple recording. For example, a melody was recorded; the resulting tape was played back at two or more times the original speed, or was played in reverse direction. The new version was recorded in turn, and perhaps the process was repeated at still another speed. Finally, the two or more versions were rerecorded on yet another tape. The end result was a composition consisting of a melody accompanied by two or more modified counterparts of itself. This technique has now been virtually superseded.

Other techniques leading to quite different results were developed out of the manipulation of taped versions of single tones. A number of elementary techniques may be described briefly here in order to indicate the variety of auditory effects that became possible. (1) A series consisting of a tone and its several octaves is recorded; sections of the tape are then removed so that each tone has a duration of only a few microseconds, and the remaining short sections of tape are then spliced. The result is a "tone" that seems to double its frequency at the moment of sounding, and then to double again and again to the very top of the auditory range. (2) A series of tones is recorded, after which the section of the tape carrying the beginning of each tone is removed. The result is a series of tones none of which begin with the characteristic impact that enables the tones to be easily recognized from the standpoint of tone color. (3) The resonance that follows the generation of a tone is electronically amplified and rerecorded at an abnormal (slower or faster) speed. (4) Single tones are recorded in reverse order, so that when they are played back the moment of resonance comes before the initial impact, and the tone ends with a percussive sound.

The techniques described above were most generally applied to tones produced by the wind and string instruments in common use. A still later set of techniques has arisen out of the generation of new, electronically created sounds—"new" in the sense that their particular patterns of fundamentals and overtones (see pp. 71–72) are unlike those produced by conventional instruments, and hence have heretofore found little place in the world of music. Included here also are sounds of the type called "noises"; that is, sounds whose vibration rates are irregular, as distinct from "tones," which are characterized by regular vibration rates. Among these noises are clicks, rumbles, clatters, plops, and others of a similar nature; these are of course sounds without definite pitch. One example of the way a noise is treated may be given. The sound made by a drop of water at the moment of impact on a resonant surface is recorded, the sound is electronically extended and amplified; finally, the sound may be transposed to a higher or lower range. Thus a new bit of auditory material is made available to the composer.

In this fashion many new tones, tone qualities, and noises, however they have been produced and manipulated, have been made available to composers. The latter, in turn, have access to a number of electronic devices that allow them to manipulate the material still further in composition and recorded performance. Filters and other pieces of equipment can alter the overtone patterns and the resonance characteristics of completed works. The compositions can be played through a complex system of a dozen or more loud speakers in such a way that spatial projection can become an important ingredient of the music. Spatial projection of this kind, in which the composer may cause the work to emanate from one or another of the speakers under his control, goes far beyond the effect of stereophonic sound.

The developments briefly described here have occupied composers in many parts of the world for more than two decades. Karlheinz Stockhausen in Cologne, Pierre Schaeffer in Paris, and Pierre Boulez also in Paris were among the early leaders in this field. Vladimir Ussachevsky and Otto Luening, along with Milton Babbitt, have long been active in New York. Centers for electronic music are now found in all parts of the world.

European developments in the field took place largely under the sponsorship of radio networks that opened their facilities to experimental composers in the late 1940's. In the United States the experimental work was carried out primarily under university auspices. Probably the earliest project was the Columbia-Princeton Elec-

A page from the first published score of electronic music: Etude II, by Karlheinz Stockhausen (1956).

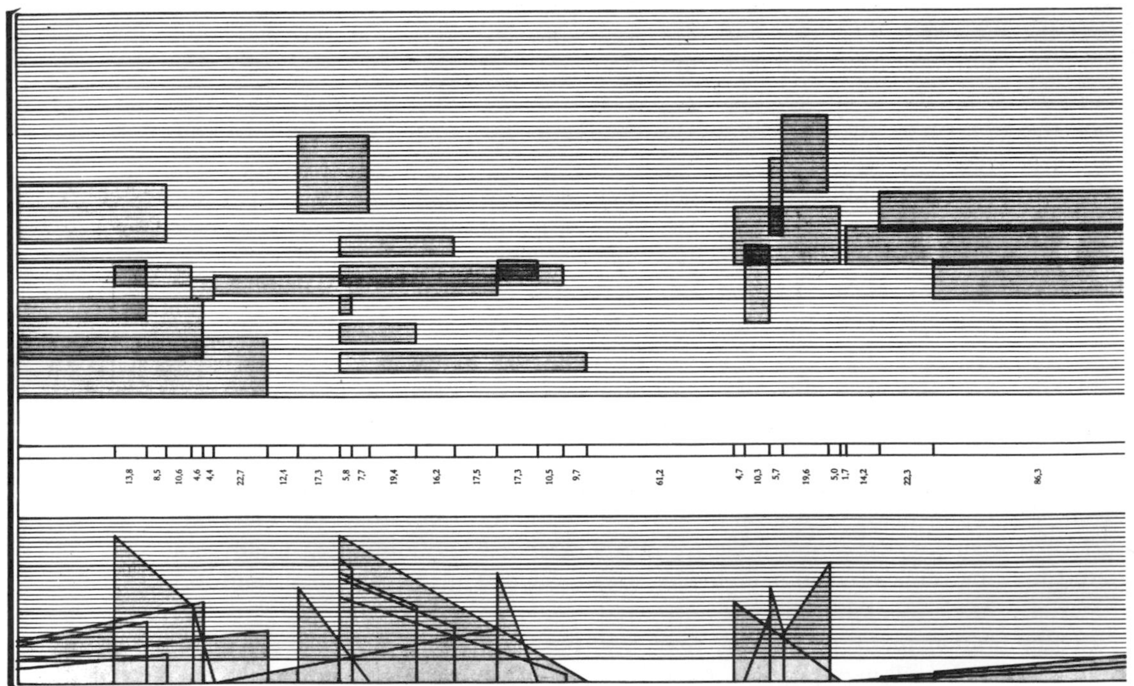

Pierre Boulez (b. 1925), eminent *avant garde* composer and conductor.

tronic Music Center in New York, operated jointly by the two universities. Early in the career of this center an elaborate electronic apparatus, the RCA Music Synthesizer, was developed. On this instrument an enormous variety of tones and sounds can be produced and manipulated. The illustration of the Synthesizer and of the composer at work at its control panel (see p. 433) indicates how far removed this work is from conventional methods of composition and musical recording. Similar, if less elaborate, pieces of equipment may now be found on university campuses across the country.

Much of the work being done at electronic centers is still tentative in nature; the limits of the field have yet to be explored and the apparatus itself is constantly undergoing improvement and elaboration. Devices that allow electronic computers to be operated in conjunction with synthesizers are now common, making yet another aspect of the field available to composers. Early works, such as *Sonic Contours* by Ussachevsky, *Poem in Cycles and Bels* by Luening (for tape recorder and orchestra), and *Poème Électronique* by Varèse, were experimental two decades or more ago. More recent composers have gone far beyond those early works, have combined conventional instruments with tape recorders in various ways, and have developed new techniques for the use of sound. Yet the majority of the more recent works may still be said to be experimental. Composers are only on the threshold of the new world of sound that has just begun to open for today's listeners to music.

It must be emphasized that these and many similar techniques are employed only to produce new varieties of sound. Raw material having thus been made available, the composer has then to utilize the new sounds in musical composition. And since the sounds so produced bear little relationship to conventional musical tones, it follows that conventional methods of composing can scarcely be employed satisfactorily here. This was the great challenge that faced composers active in this field a decade or two ago. That challenge still faces them.

COMPUTER MUSIC

Quite unrelated to the field of electronic music, which deals with tones electronically produced and manipulated, is the use of an electronic or digital computer to produce compositions for conventional instruments. The aesthetic and technical principles that underlie this work may be summarized approximately as follows: (1) A composer has available an enormous quantity of musical material in the form of pitches, tone qualities, dynamic levels, rhythmic patterns, and the like. (2) In the act of composing, the composer must make a series of choices every time he writes a note symbol; the choices concern every aspect of his material plus a complex series of relationships between one unit of material and every other unit. (3) In making his choices he is guided by his sense of order and style, and by the "laws" of musical form and theory (which is to say, by the customary practices of other composers) to which he may conform or from which he may depart. (4) These laws are in the main capable of being expressed in mathematical symbols and as mathematical operations. (5) The electronic computer is a device that can be made to select the symbols for certain tones or series of tones out of the limitless number of possible tonal combinations. (6) It does this by following certain "instructions" (that is, the musical laws themselves) given to it in advance.

As an elementary example, the following problem can be established ("programed"): the computer can be directed to produce a series of melodies using only the white notes across a two-octave range; these melodies must all begin and end with the note C; in no case may the interval of a seventh be used; and no melody may contain more than thirty-two notes. Having been programed in this way, the computer will then generate a large number of melodies in which the notes are selected at random but which follow the instructions given.

The oversimplified statement of principles given above, and the example of a possible problem, must suffice here because a more extended explanation of computer music would perforce have to be given in mathematical terms. A description of the binary system, of probability theory, of information theory, and of the computer itself would necessarily have to come into account. Such matters lie far beyond the scope of this book.

SUMMARY

Three different contemporary experimental approaches have been briefly described here: those leading to (1) tape recorder music, (2) electronically generated music, which is also recorded on tape and which is sometimes called *musique concrète,* and

(3) computer music. It must become apparent that however different the approaches may be, the composers active in the three areas have one problem in common. While they have opened a new world of sound and a new approach to composition, they are in general still at the stage of creating techniques and material. The problem concerns the aesthetically valid and artistic *use* of the techniques and materials to create a new kind of music. The new devices are novel enough to suggest that all possible varieties of auditory sensation have not yet been experienced. The musicians working in these experimental fields are competent enough to assure that worthwhile aesthetic results may eventually be expected. The results achieved so far are challenging to the imagination. One may look forward with keen interest to the work of the next few decades, confident that the musical needs of generations to come will be met in ways yet undreamed of.

One major problem remains, however. The experimental, dissonant, and unfamiliar music of the period since about 1920 caused many listeners of the time to become prejudiced against that music. The term "contemporary" often became synonymous with "unpleasant." It is possible that a portion of that prejudice has been carried over to the present generation of audiences; for today's music by American composers is often written off by some listeners without a fair hearing. Even a slight contact with representative works of the present decade can go far to assure the listener that American music is now in a new phase of its development.

Composers of that music have achieved high standards of workmanship. Their music does not limp or falter; it moves forward with directness and good proportions to the expression of worthwhile musical ideas. It is sincere music, written with full regard for the emotional needs of its listeners; it makes use of a wide variety of conventional as well as new musical resources. It gives evidence that its composers are aware of their responsibilities toward the cultural life of today. And although much of it is only of passing interest and little of it will endure beyond a few performances, it is serving an essential purpose: to lay the foundations for a truly American tradition, out of which eternal masterpieces will yet emerge.

Listening Suggestions

BARBER, SAMUEL

Adagio for Strings, Op. 11
Capricorn Concerto, Op. 21
Cello Sonata, Op. 6

COPLAND, AARON

Appalachian Spring (ballet)
Rodeo (ballet)
El Salon Mexico

GERSHWIN, GEORGE

Porgy and Bess (opera)

Rhapsody in Blue

HANSON, HOWARD

Symphony No. 2 ("Romantic")

IVES, CHARLES

Piano Sonata No. 2, *Concord, Mass.*

LUENING, OTTO

Rhapsodic Variations (for Tape Recorder and Orchestra)

MACDOWELL, EDWARD

Suite No. 2, Op. 48 ("Indian")

Woodland Sketches

MENNIN, PETER

Symphony No. 3

PERSICHETTI, VINCENT

Psalm for Orchestra

PISTON, WALTER

Piano Trio

Symphony No. 3

SCHUMAN, WILLIAM

String Quartet No. 4

Undertow (ballet)

SESSIONS, ROGER

Symphony No. 2

VARÈSE, EDGAR

Ionisation

Poème Électronique

Appendix I

NOTATION

The subject of musical notation is generally supposed to be difficult for the non-performer. While it is true that a performer must work with the details of notation for several years in order to acquire an instant, subconscious command of its resources, the principles of notation in reality are simple and capable of being understood easily. Music may, of course, be enjoyed up to a certain point without knowledge of those principles. Beyond that point, however, some familiarity with notation is necessary because many significant points about music can be made only by referring to a printed musical excerpt. The principles will therefore be set down here.

Notation includes a set of symbols called *notes,* a set of lines and spaces collectively called the *great staff,* and a set of verbal and other symbols called *expression marks.* The vertical position of the note on the staff gives a clue to its pitch; the choice of note symbol tells us about its duration; and the other symbols call attention to the desired speed, intensity, or manner of performance.

STAFFS AND CLEFS

The great staff consists of a set of eleven lines with a space between each line, the sixth or middle line being present by implication only. A note may be placed on either a line or space. A short section of the alphabet, from A to G, is applied to the staff; each line and each space carries one of those letters. The first (bottom) line of the staff is called G, after which the sequence A to G is repeated as often as necessary. Example 134 will clarify these points.

Example 134

A Few Stages in the Evolution of the Clef Signs

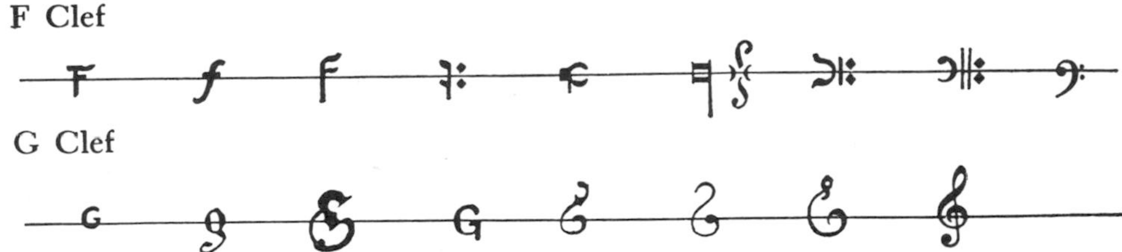

The two dots that appear at the right of the bass clef itself are reminders of the two horizontal lines that distinguish the letter F. Similarly, the spiral at the center of the treble clef recalls the letter G to which the clef owes its shape.

It often happens that a five-line portion of the great staff is employed alone; the upper five lines are so used in many examples throughout this book. Such a portion is simply called a *staff*. To make clear which portion of the great staff is being used, and to indicate which alphabet section is involved in that portion, an appropriate symbol is placed at the beginning of each staff. The letters F, C, and G were once used, but after many centuries they have been transformed into symbols that do no more than call attention to the original shapes of the respective letters. The letter F is placed on the fourth line from the bottom of the set of eleven lines, and the letter G on the fourth line from the top. When the central portion of the great staff is used alone, the middle line is drawn in solidly and the letter C is placed on that line. These letters in their altered shapes are called *clefs* (literally, *keys*—that is, keys to understanding the staff). The transformed F becomes the *bass clef* and the transformed G becomes the *treble clef;* these are the two clefs most often used.

The transformed C is called variously the *alto clef* and the *tenor clef,* depending upon whether lines 4 to 8 or lines 3 to 7 are employed. The alto and tenor clefs have played little part in this book. However, they are essential in reading orchestral music (see Appendix IV), for they are used primarily to notate music for the viola and the high ranges of cello, bassoon, and trombone. Example 135 shows the positions of the clefs on the various portions of the great staff.

Example 135

Whenever it becomes necessary to place a note beyond the limits of any staff, additional short lines, called *leger* lines, are used—as many as needed. The method employed in naming the staff lines and spaces applies also to the leger lines, as shown in Example 136.

Example 136

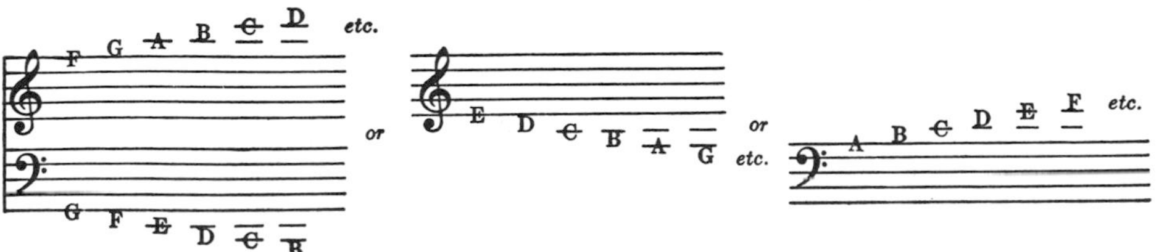

One convention of music printing often obscures these basic facts about the great staff. It is usually desirable, in piano and vocal music, to separate the two five-line portions in order to allow room for text, expression marks, or leger lines in the area between the upper and lower portions (which contain the parts played by the pianist's right and left hands, respectively). While this separation is thoroughly understood by the musician, it has the effect of placing certain notes (those surrounding the middle C) in two different positions on the great staff. Example 11*c* (p. 21) illustrates the problem. The first two notes of both the alto and bass lines, on the syllables *Can-ta,* are B and D. Yet, to the unwary, the two B's, for example, might seem to be almost an octave apart (the two D's likewise), when of course both positions of each note represent the same pitch.

NOTE VALUES

As Chapter 5 of this book explains, music is carried across measurable intervals of time, and the time is divided into units called beats. Thus we may say that a melodic fragment is a certain number of beats in length. The most usual beat is one that moves at a moderate speed, roughly 60 to 80 to the minute; its symbol is called (for a number of complex historical reasons) a *quarter note.* When a tone is to be held for the length of one such beat, a quarter note is written in the staff on the line or space that is appropriate to its pitch.

A tone may be held for two, three, or any number of beats; or it may be held for a fraction of that beat—usually for a half, a quarter, or an eighth of the beat's length. This is to say that two, four, or eight notes, respectively, may occupy the space of one beat. In each of these cases a different note symbol indicates which multiple or fraction is desired. Further, a beat, as well as its multiple or fraction, may go by in silence without a tone being sounded. This condition, too, is provided for by a series of symbols known as *rests,* which correspond to the notes in value or duration. Any combination of long or short notes and long or short rests may be utilized. Example 137*a* gives the more common notes and rests, and 137*b* a few of their possible combinations. Notice in Example 137*c* that notes that have *flags* (eighth notes and smaller) may be combined into groups by drawing the flag or flags into lines that extend across the group; the relative lengths of the notes are not changed thereby.

Example 137

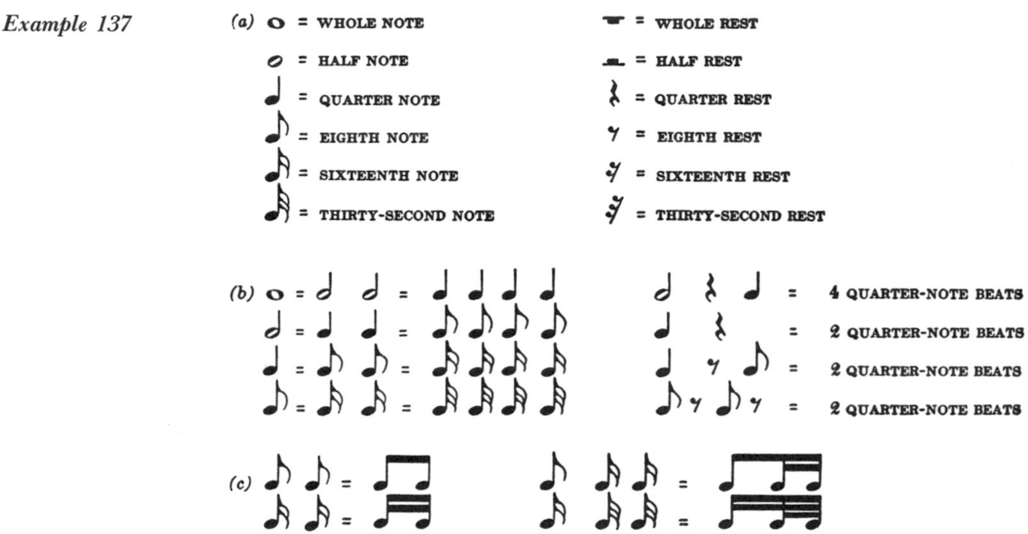

Each of the successively smaller note values in Example 137*a*, from the half note to the thirty-second, is seen to represent half the value of the note above it; for example, two eighth notes constitute a quarter, two quarter notes constitute a half, and so on. Occasionally a composer may wish to employ other values; he may wish to make three eighth notes (instead of two) equal a quarter note, for example. He may do this by including the three notes in one brace and placing a small "3" above or below the group, thus:

The group is then referred to as a group of *triplets,* and it is understood that the three are to be played in the time interval that two would require (see Example 72, p. 202, for a passage based largely on triplets). This principle may be extended to all other note values (thirty-seconds, sixteenths, quarters, and so on). It may also be extended to embrace five, six, or any number of tones in a group; the groups are then called *quintuplets, sextuplets,* and so on. Example 69*a*, p. 199, shows seven notes occupying the time of one quarter note, and in Example 69*c* a passage of twenty-eight notes extends across a measure of six eighth notes.

Any note may be made half again as long by employing a symbol called a *dot.* For example, a quarter note, which equals two eighth notes, may be dotted, thereby becoming equal to three eighth notes in length; a dotted half note is equivalent to three quarter notes, and so on. These possibilities are shown in Example 138*a*; the curved lines, known as *ties,* under the groups of three notes indicates that individual notes are not to be sounded but are to be performed as one. Symbols for rests may be dotted in exactly the same manner and with exactly the same result, as seen in Example 138*b*.

Example 138

Assume now that we have a succession of notes and wish to cast them into one of the metrical formulas discussed in Chapter 2 and elsewhere in this book. The notes themselves, as we know, indicate only pitch and relative length; a note symbol, taken alone, does not clarify the note's relationship to rhythm or meter. An additional device is needed to explain the metrical position of every note—that is, its relationship to the pattern of accents. Such a device is established by combining a number of notes into a metrical grouping called a *measure.* Measures are separated by *bars* or *bar lines,* and the note that follows immediately after the bar line carries the strongest beat of the measure. The number of beats grouped within each measure determines whether the result is duple, triple, or some other meter.

METRICAL SIGNATURES

For several centuries it has been customary to indicate at the beginning of a movement or a composition the metrical grouping that prevails in that piece. Example 139 illustrates a few melodic fragments in which the quarter note is taken as the basic metrical unit—that is, in which each quarter note receives one beat.

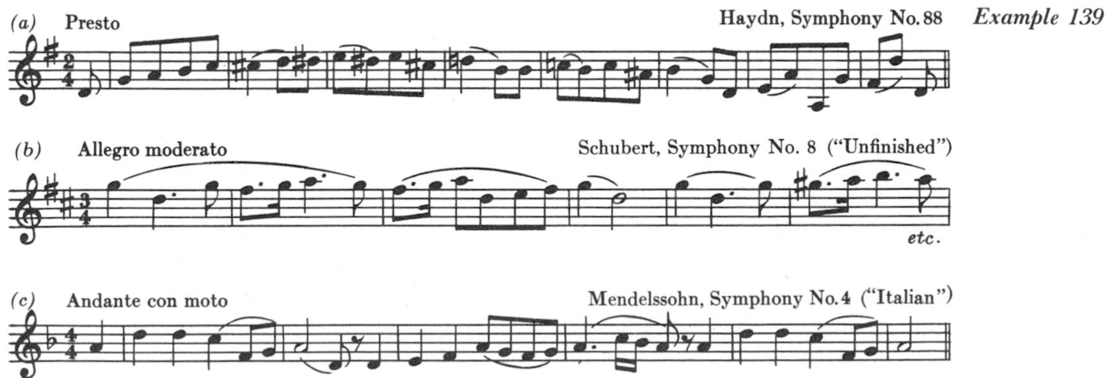

Example 139

Two quarter notes are assigned to each measure of Example 139*a*, three to each measure of Example 139*b*, and four to each in Example 139*c*.

In these compositions, as in hundreds of similar ones, the meter is identified by an arithmetical fraction that appears at the beginning of the respective movements. This fraction is called a *metrical signature,* or colloquially a *time signature.* The lower figure of the fraction indicates the value of the beat (in each of these cases, a quarter note), and the upper figure gives the number of beats in each measure. In addition to the 2/4, 3/4, and 4/4, which are very common, the signatures 5/4, 6/4, and occasionally 9/4 may appear.

Notes other than quarter notes may also serve as metrical units. Eighth notes may be used (see Example 11*b*, p. 21, and Example 38, p. 78), as well as half notes (Example 50, p. 146); very occasionally sixteenth notes or whole notes are used in this manner. The metrical signatures shown in Example 140*a* are relatively common; those in Example 140*b* are somewhat more rare.

Example 140

It sometimes happens that the relative speed of the beats makes it difficult to think of each beat separately. For example, in a passage written in 6/8 meter, each eighth note may go by at great speed; a phrase of eight such measures (forty-eight notes) may require less than five seconds of playing time. This is the case in the well-known "Italian" Symphony by Mendelssohn, as well as in many other compositions. Because it is impossible for a conductor to conduct and difficult for a player to count at the rate of approximately ten beats to the second, it is customary to think of several notes as constituting one larger metrical unit. The fast 6/8 measures, then, will be thought of, conducted, and performed as though each one contained two three-note beats, one strong, the other weak, as shown in Example 141*a*. A meter of this kind is called *compound.*

Similarly, the third movement (often called *scherzo*) of many symphonies and string quartets is usually written in triple meter and played at high speed. Here again the three beats are thought of as one beat (subdivided), and the metrical unit becomes a dotted half note, as shown in Example 141*b*. Many similar cases occur in other meters, an example of which is shown in 141*c*.

Mendelssohn, Symphony No. 4 ("Italian") *Example 141*

Beethoven, Symphony No. 3 ("Eroica")

Mozart, *Marriage of Figaro,* Overture

In the second half of the nineteenth century many composers sought to expand the means of musical expression. One result of the search was the practice of combining duple and triple meters in various ways. The simplest of the resulting compound meters is, of course, 5/4 (2/4 plus 3/4). Normally one might expect this quintuple meter to be somewhat halting or stumbling in its effect. But in the best-known example—the second movement of Tchaikovsky's "Pathétique" Symphony—the effect is charming and graceful. Example 142 shows the beginning of this movement. Another example of 5/4 meter may be found in Ravel's *Daphnis and Chloe* Suite No. 2.

Tchaikovsky, Symphony No. 6 ("Pathétique") *Example 142*

In most examples of metrical music, one metrical signature prevails throughout a large section or an entire piece. Occasionally, however, a few measures of contrasting meter are introduced, as in the third movement of Beethoven's "Eroica" Symphony. That movement as a whole is in 3/4 meter (see Example 141*b*, but near the end (not shown in the Example) four measures of 2/2 appear. This principle of contrasting meter was carried forward by other nineteenth-century composers. Tchaikovsky and Brahms employed it with particularly happy results on a few occasions, as Examples 143*a* and 143*b* reveal. In the latter case the alternation of 3/4 and 2/4 meters became a feature of the piece, and often resulted in a 7/4 meter, created by the consistent use of 3/4 plus 2/4 plus 2/4. Brahms set both signatures at the beginning of the movement, as seen in Example 143*c*. Having

Example 143

done this, he did not repeat them in the body of the piece but left it for the performer to determine by a quick scrutiny whether each measure consisted of two or three beats.

The principle of employing contrasting meters within a single piece gained greatly in strength in the last half of the nineteenth century. It becomes obvious that if this principle is carried forward consistently and if contrasts appear in considerable numbers, the chief characteristic of metrical rhythm is to some extent abolished. For in metrical rhythm one expects the distance between strong beats to be equal, and if a composer consistently employs a mixture of duple, triple, and perhaps other meters, he approaches unmetrical rhythm. His music then takes on the metrical character of prose rather than poetry.

This is actually what happened early in the twentieth century. Igor Stravinsky, in the ballet entitled *The Rite of Spring,* first performed in 1913, introduced so complex a mixture of contrasting meters that all semblance of metrical rhythm disappeared throughout long sections of the work. Passages such as the one shown in Example 144 appear. It must be said, however, that few other works (including Stravinsky's later ones) go as far as Example 144 in this direction. In most cases a short passage in unmetrical rhythm is inserted between two metrical passages. But the principle of unmetrical rhythm has musical validity (and vitality); it has become increasingly important in music of the present time.

Example 144

Appendix II

MAJOR AND MINOR SCALES

Major scales, it will be recalled, differ from minor scales in the relative positions of their large and small (whole-step and half-step) intervals. The two most common forms of minor scales—namely, melodic and harmonic—also differ from each other in this regard. The formulas of the three scale types may be reviewed here.

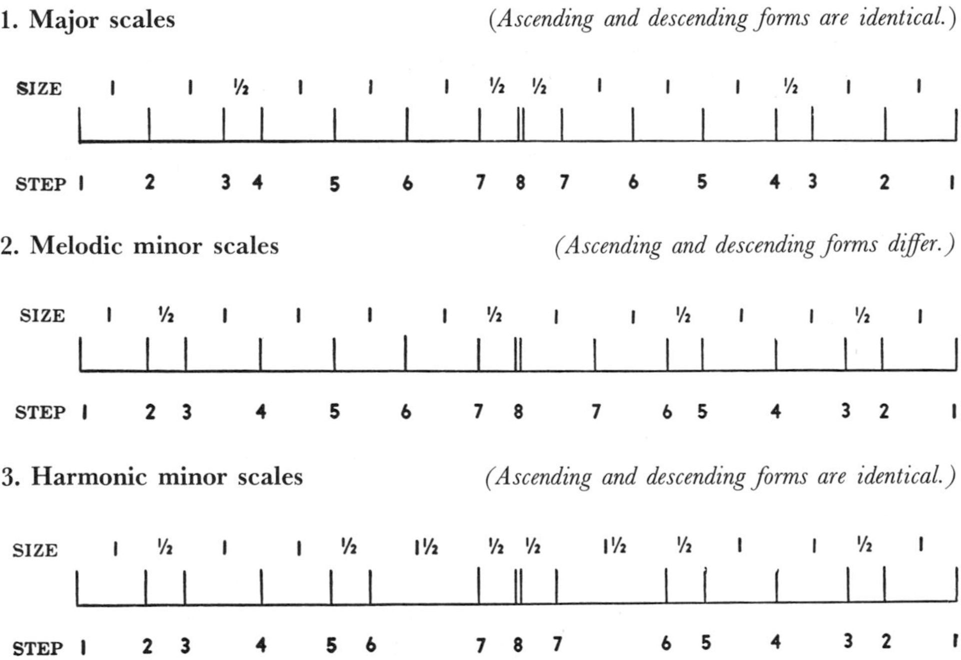

The tones of the scales are given the following names:

First *tonic*
Second *supertonic*
Third *mediant*
Fourth *subdominant*
Fifth *dominant*
Sixth *submediant*
Seventh *leading tone*
Eighth *octave*

The *circle of fifths* shows graphically the relationships between one major scale and another, as well as the relationships between a major scale and its relative minor. Proceeding around the outside of the circumference of the circle in a clockwise direction, we may see that a scale at the interval of a fifth above another scale (that is, five scale steps higher) will contain one sharp more in its signature than the previous scale. In a counterclockwise direction, the interval is reversed; each scale a fifth below the previous scale contains an additional flat in its signature.

Example 145

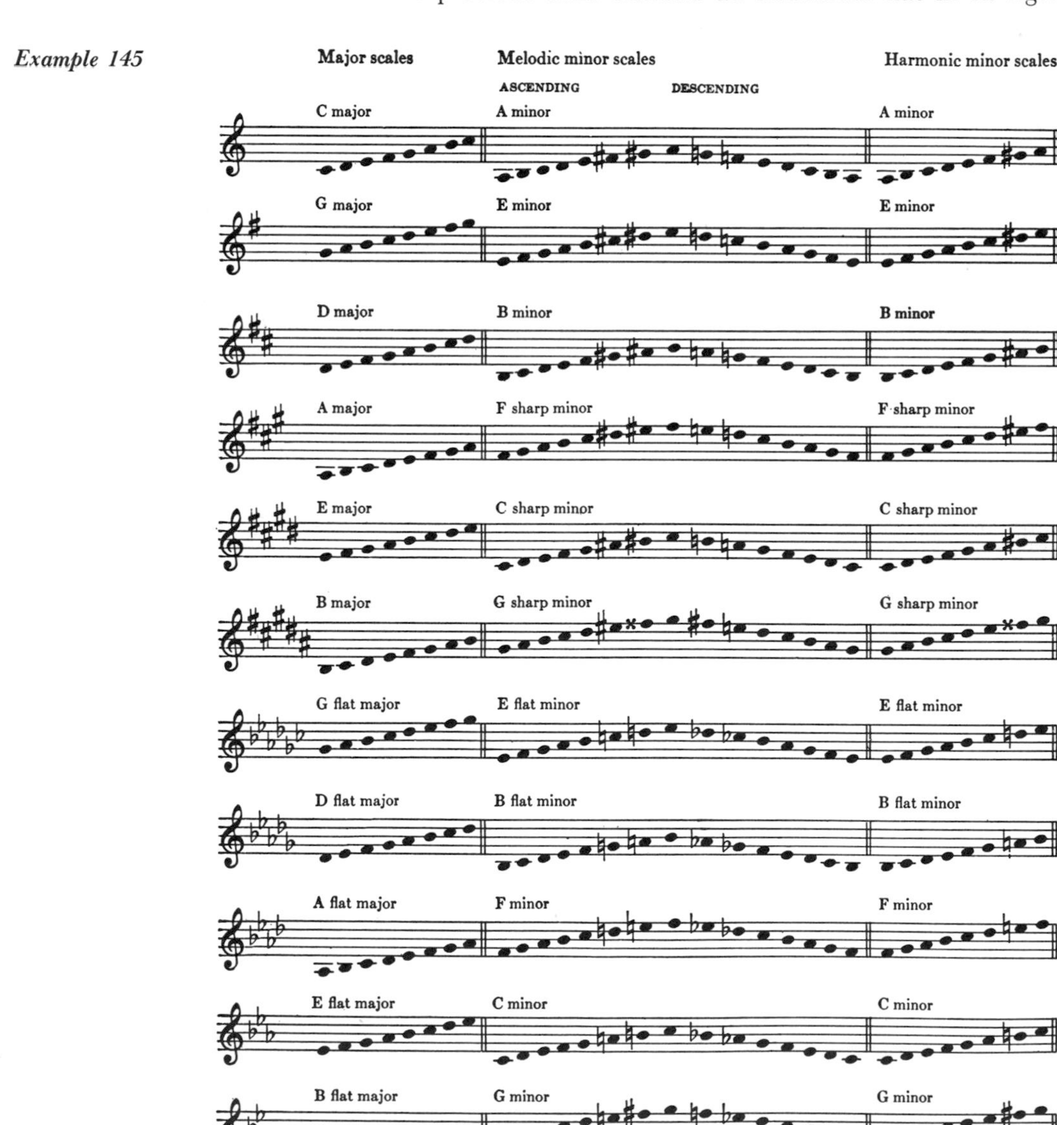

The scales at the six-o'clock position of the circle of fifths (F sharp and G flat) are called *enharmonic equivalents* of each other; in fact, on keyboard instruments they are identical in sound.

Additional enharmonic equivalents can be determined in either direction. Thus the C sharp major scale (equivalent to D flat) contains seven sharps as opposed to the five flats of the D flat major scale; the C flat scale, seven flats as opposed to the five sharps of the B major scale; and so on through all twelve possible positions on the circle.

The signatures of minor scales may be determined from the inside of the circumference. In each case, the minor signature is identical with that of the major opposite which it stands. For example, A minor requires neither sharps nor flats in its signature, for it is the *relative* of C major; E minor, like G major, requires one sharp; and so through the twelve scales.

The circle of fifths also shows in what order the sharps and flats are placed on the staff to form the various key signatures. A reference to the signatures following will show that the sharps are written from left to right on the basis of ascending fifths, thus: F sharp, C sharp, G sharp, D sharp, A sharp, and E sharp. Likewise, the flats are inserted in the order they take in the circle: B flat, E flat, A flat, D flat, G flat, and C flat.

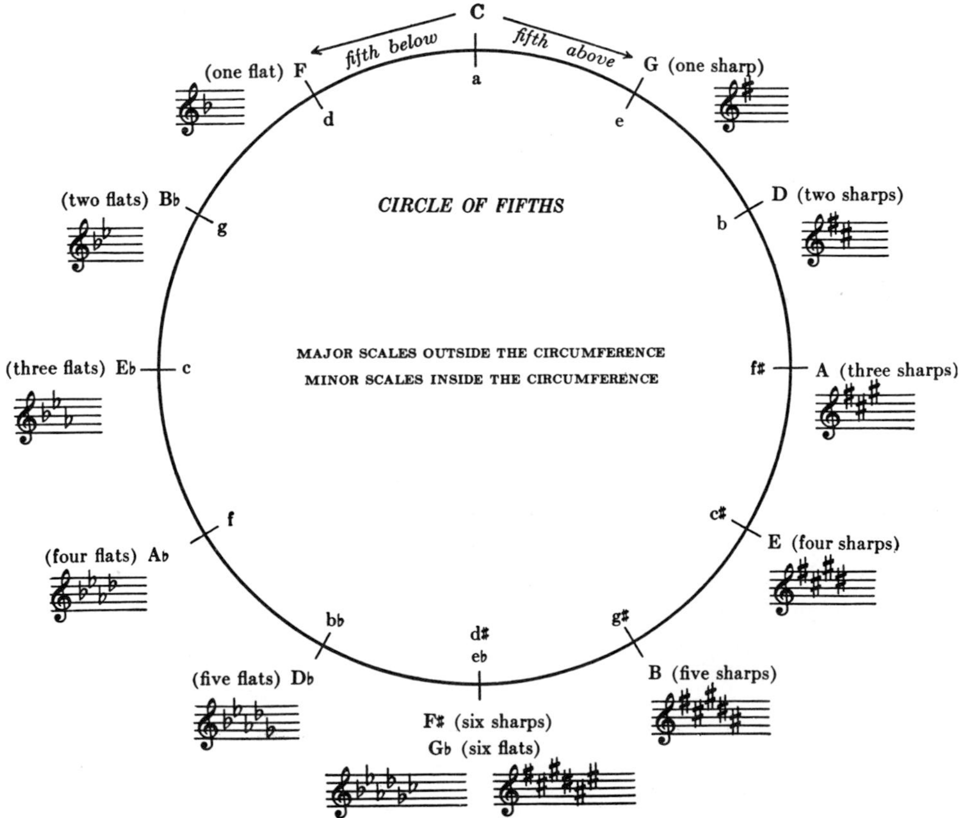

Appendix III

PRINCIPAL MUSIC TERMS

The following lists give the principal categories of musical terms, together with the definitions of the terms encountered most frequently.

1. Basic tempo indications

A musical tempo is a subjective, relative matter, even though a descriptive term attemps to define it. Each of the terms below applies rather broadly (and indefinitely) to a variety of tempos.

largo broadly, sustained; hence very slowly
larghetto less slowly than *largo*
grave slowly with solemnity
lento slowly
adagio slowly, at ease
andante walking; hence moderately
andantino, *allegretto* } modifications of *andante* and *allegro,* respectively, hence moderately fast
allegro cheerfully; hence fast
presto rapidly
prestissimo very rapidly

2. Modifications of basic tempos

The following terms may be used as modifiers of the terms in Category 1, in which cases the basic tempo is to be modified accordingly. In many cases a metronomic indication will give the exact speed desired; in other cases one of the terms from this category or from Category 7 will qualify the tempo. In the last analysis, a performer will be led by the content and texture of the music itself; by the way it "feels" in performance.

assai very
meno less

moderato moderately
molto much
mosso } movement, or motion; *meno mosso,* less motion, hence slower; *con moto,* with
moto } motion, hence somewhat faster
più more
poco somewhat
troppo too much; *non troppo,* not too much

3. Changes from one tempo to another

The following terms may be used within a composition, either at the transitions between sections or at the end of a composition or movement.

accelerando, accel. accelerating the tempo
poco a poco little by little (faster or slower)
stringendo increasing in speed and intensity
allargando becoming slower and broader
rallentando, rall. retarding the tempo
ritardando, rit. retarding the tempo
ritenuto held back, abruptly slower
calando diminishing and become slower
morendo dying away in speed and intensity

4. Returns to a previous tempo

These terms are used after a tempo change (Category 3), whenever a return to an earlier tempo is required, or when a change of notation or meter temporarily obscures the proper tempo.

a tempo returning to the original tempo
tempo primo, Tempo I in the first tempo
l'istesso tempo the same tempo

5. Basic dynamic levels

fortississimo, fff still more loudly
fortissimo, ff more loudly
forte, f loudly
mezzo forte, mf less loudly
mezzo piano, mp less softly
piano, p softly
pianissimo, pp more softly
pianississimo, ppp still more softly

6. Changes from one dynamic level to another

crescendo, cres., $<$ increasing in loudness
decrescendo, decresc., $>$ decreasing in loudness
diminuendo, dim. diminishing in loudness

forzando, fz forcing *sforzato, sf, sfz* forced *rinforzando, rf, rfz* reinforced	an accent on a single tone or chord, proportioned to the basic dynamic level

7. Stylistic directions

The following terms will most often appear within the body of a composition to indicate a desired style of performing at that point. Some of the terms may also appear in conjunction with a basic tempo indication (Category 1) and thus effect a modification of that tempo.

ad libitum at will; the performer is free to vary from a strict tempo, to perform a cadenza, etc.
affetuoso affectionately
agitato agitatedly
amabile amiably
amoroso lovingly
animato animatedly
appassionato passionately
cantabile songfully
comodo easily, comfortably
con calore with warmth
doloroso mournfully
giocoso joyfully
giusto with exactitude, evenly, in a controlled manner
grandioso grandly, in a stately manner
grazioso in a graceful manner
lamentoso in the manner of a lament
leggiero lightly
lugubre in a lugubrious manner
maestoso majestically
marziale martially
mezza voce with half voice, restrained
perdendosi becoming lost, fading away
pesante heavily
pomposo pompously
ponderoso ponderously
quieto quietly
rubato "robbed"; giving and taking from the even flow of beats
secco dry, in an unemotional manner
semplice simple, without affectation
sentimento sentiment; *con sentimento,* with feeling
sotto voce in an undertone, subdued
tempestoso tempestuously, stormily
teneramente tenderly
vigoroso vigorously
vivace, vivo in a lively manner, quickly

Appendix IV

SCORE READING

The pleasure derived from listening to a musical composition can be greatly increased by reading the music as it is being performed. A song, a choral composition, or a piano piece will offer no difficulties to one who has absorbed the principles of notation set forth in Appendix I. The rise and fall of melodic lines, the changes in texture, the phrase structures, and the formal divisions—such details can be both seen and heard; and the end result is a richer musical experience.

In going beyond piano or choral music to the pages of an orchestral or band score, one encounters a musical device called *transposition,* which has not been discussed in the foregoing chapters. A large part of score reading demands that transposition be taken into account in reading the printed or manuscript notes. Transposing, for the score reader, consists of reading notes at a pitch level different from that indicated by the notational picture itself.

Two types of transposition are in general use. One is employed by the orchestral piccolo player, who performs everything an octave higher than it is written, and by players of the bass (double bass or bass viol) and the contrabassoon, who perform the music an octave lower than it is written. This type, called *octave transposition,* provides greater ease of reading the respective parts. For were the parts not transposed into other octaves, the piccolo part would rise high above the staff and be encumbered by many leger lines; and the parts for the bass instruments would hang far below the staff (see Example 146).

The second type, called *tonal transposition,* is made necessary by the fact that in certain instrumental families two or more instruments of different sizes are in use. In the double-reed family, for example, the oboe and the English horn are essentially small and large versions of the same instrument. Because of this difference

Example 146

in size, a fingering pattern that produces the tone C on the oboe will produce an F, five tones below that C, on the English horn; the D fingering on the oboe produces G on the English horn; and so on through the entire tonal ranges of the two instruments.

To facilitate the player's shifting from one instrument to another, as he is often required to do (that is, to make it possible to play both instruments with the same set of fingerings), the tones of the English horn are given the same names and notated in the same positions as the correspondingly fingered tones of the oboe. Thus the English horn's F, G, and A are called and written C, D, and E. In effect, the composer writes each note (for the English horn) five tones *higher* than he wishes it to sound. The player reverses the process; he causes his tones to sound a fifth *below* the written notes. He plays C but produces F; he plays D but produces G, and so on (see Example 147).

Example 147

A similar transposition is employed in instruments of the clarinet family. In that family five or more sizes are in common use: clarinets in E flat, D, B flat, and A, and a bass clarinet in B flat. In the brass family, trumpets in B flat and French horns in F are the most common, but many other sizes occur. And in all these cases the composer transposes the corresponding parts as he did in the case of the English horn.

Applying the foregoing to the printed page of music, we see that the score reader must mentally read the parts of the transposing instruments differently from the way they are written. A simple calculation will aid him: he calculates the interval between middle C and the pitch of the instrument concerned, then reads the part higher or lower to correspond to that interval. For example, the part for an instrument that is pitched a whole tone *lower* than C (the B flat clarinet) must be read a whole tone *lower* than written; that for one pitched a minor third *higher* than C (the E flat clarinet) must be read a minor third *higher* than written (Example 148).

Example 148

An orchestral score is arranged in standardized fashion. Woodwind instruments occupy the top staves; brass and percussion instruments are placed below the woodwinds; and the string instruments are found at the bottom of the page (see Example 149). Any auxiliary parts the composition requires are placed between the

Example 149

Franck, Symphony in D minor

Allegro non troppo

FLUTES I II

OBOES I II (a 2)

ENGLISH HORN

CLARINETS I II IN B FLAT (a 2)

BASS CLAR. IN B FLAT

BASSOONS I II

HORNS IN F I II III IV

TRUMPETS I II IN F

CORNETS I II IN A

TROMBONES I II III AND TUBA

TYMPANI

VIOLIN I

VIOLIN II

VIOLA

CELLO

BASS

strings and the percussion. The solo part in a concerto (violin or piano or any other), the parts for harp, organ, singers, chorus—any or all of these find a place above the first violin part and below the percussion parts.

The score reader must remember to apply octave transposition to the piccolo, bass, and contrabassoon parts; to apply the proper tonal transposition to the English horn and to instruments that are listed as being in a particular key (cornet in A, for example); and occasionally to apply both octave and tonal transpositions where appropriate (bass clarinet when written in treble clef and French horn when written in bass clef). The rhythmic beat must then be felt as the performance begins and care taken to remain with that beat as the music progresses. The listener is then in a position to both see and hear the miracles the composer has wrought, and his musical pleasure will be enriched accordingly.

BIBLIOGRAPHY

A complete list of books and articles on the various aspects of music would run to many thousands of items in dozens of languages. Whole books (such as the Darrell and Gleason-Luper items listed below) do nothing more than list or describe other books. In so vast a field, completeness or even a judicious sampling is all but impossible. The following list seeks to do only this: to enumerate a few of the items that the reader of this book will find useful. In general, the books listed here serve to supplement the discussions contained in the text itself. They touch upon certain facets of music that have necessarily remained unmentioned, and they present information and points of view that may further guide the reader in his search for enjoyable musical experiences.

General Reference

Apel, Willi, ed., *Harvard Dictionary of Music,* Harvard University Press, Cambridge, 1950.

Baker, Theodore, *A Pronouncing Pocket Manual of Musical Terms,* rev. and aug. ed., Schirmer, New York, 1947.

Blom, Eric, ed., *Grove's Dictionary of Music and Musicians,* 5th ed., 9 vols., Macmillan, London, 1954. Supplementary volume by Eric Blom and Denis Stevens, 1961.

Darrell, R. D., *Schirmer's Guide to Books on Music and Musicians,* Schirmer, New York, 1951.

Feather, Leonard, *The Encyclopedia of Jazz,* Horizon Press, New York, 1955.

Gleason, Harold, and Albert T. Luper, compilers, *A Bibliography of Books on Music,* Eastman School of Music, Rochester, N.Y., 1948.

Scholes, Percy, *The Oxford Companion to Music,* 9th ed., Oxford University Press, New York, 1955.

Slonimsky, Nicholas, ed., *Baker's Biographical Dictionary of Musicians,* 5th ed., revised, Schirmer, New York, 1965.

Thompson, Oscar, ed., *The International Cyclopedia of Music and Musicians,* 9th ed. by Robert Sabin, Dodd Mead, New York, 1964.

Westrup, J. A., and F. L. Harrison, *The New College Encyclopedia of Music,* Norton, New York, 1960.

History

Bukofzer, Manfred, *Music in the Baroque Era,* Norton, New York, 1947.
Einstein, Alfred, *Music in the Romantic Era,* Norton, New York, 1947.
———, *A Short History of Music,* tr. by Eric Blom and others, 3rd Amer. ed., Knopf, New York, 1947.
Grout, Donald J., *A History of Western Music,* Norton, New York, 1960.
Kinsky, George, ed., *A History of Music in Pictures,* reprint, Dover, New York, 1951.
Lang, Paul Henry, *Music in Western Civilization,* Norton, New York, 1941.
Nef, Karl, *An Outline of the History of Music,* rev. ed., tr. by Carl F. Pfatteicher, Columbia University Press, New York, 1957.
Reese, Gustave, *Music in the Middle Ages,* Norton, New York, 1940.
———, *Music in the Renaissance Era,* Norton, New York, rev. ed., 1959.
Sachs, Curt, *Our Musical Heritage,* 2nd ed., Prentice-Hall, New York, 1955.
Strunk, Oliver, ed., *Source Readings in Music History,* Norton, New York, 1950.
Ulrich, Homer, and Paul A. Pisk, *A History of Music and Musical Style,* Harcourt, Brace & World, New York, 1963.
Westrup, J. A., ed., *The New Oxford History of Music,* 11 vols. (4 vols. pub. to date), Oxford University Press, New York, 1957.

Lives and Works

Abraham, Gerald, *Chopin's Musical Style,* Oxford University Press, New York, 1946.
———, ed., *Handel; A Symposium,* Oxford University Press, New York, 1954.
———, ed., *The Music of Schubert,* Norton, New York, 1947.
———, ed., *The Music of Sibelius,* Norton, New York, 1947.
———, ed., *The Music of Tchaikovsky,* Norton, New York, 1946.
———, ed., *Schumann; A Symposium,* Oxford University Press, New York, 1952.
Barzun, Jacques, *Berlioz and the Romantic Century,* Little, Brown, Boston, 1950.
Brown, Maurice J. E., *Schubert: A Critical Biography,* Macmillan, London, 1958.
Chissell, Joan, *Schumann,* Dent, London, 1948.
Coates, Henry, *Palestrina,* reprint, Dent, London, 1948.
Demuth, Norman, *César Franck,* Dobson, London, 1949.
———, *Ravel,* Dent, London, 1947.
Deutsch, Otto Erich, *Handel; A Documentary Biography,* Norton, New York, 1955.
———, *The Schubert Reader,* tr. by Eric Blom, Norton, New York, 1947.
Einstein, Alfred, *Mozart: His Character, His Work,* tr. by Arthur Mendel and Nathan Broder, Oxford University Press, New York, 1945.
———, *Schubert,* tr. by David Ascoli, Oxford University Press, New York, 1951.
Flower, Newman, *George Frideric Handel,* new rev. ed., Scribner's, New York, 1948.
Geiringer, Karl, *Brahms,* 2nd rev. ed., Oxford University Press, New York, 1947.
———, *Haydn,* 2nd ed., Doubleday, New York, 1963.

Jeppesen, Knud, *The Style of Palestrina and the Dissonance,* tr. by Margaret Hamerick and Annie Fausboll, 2nd rev. ed., Oxford University Press, New York, 1946.
Latham, Peter, *Brahms,* Dent, London, 1948.
Lockspeiser, Edward, *Debussy,* 2nd rev. ed., Dent, London, 1944.
Newlin, Dika, *Bruckner, Mahler, Schoenberg,* Columbia University Press, New York, 1947.
Newman, Ernest, *The Life of Richard Wagner,* 4 vols., Knopf, New York, 1933–46.
Pincherle, Marc, *Corelli: His Life and Work,* tr. by H. E. M. Russell, Norton, New York, 1956.
———, *Vivaldi: Genius of the Baroque,* tr. by Christopher Hatch, Norton, New York, 1957.
Schrade, Leo, *Monteverdi,* Norton, New York, 1950.
Schweitzer, Albert, *J. S. Bach,* tr. by Ernest Newman, 2 vols, Black, London, 1923 (1950).
Scott, Marion M., *Beethoven,* reprint, Dent, London, 1947.
Searle, Humphrey, *The Music of Liszt,* Williams and Norgate, London, 1954.
Spitta, Philipp, *Johann Sebastian Bach,* tr. by Clara Bell and J. A. Fuller-Maitland, 2 vols., reprint, Dover, New York, 1951.
Stevens, Halsey, *The Life and Music of Béla Bartók,* Oxford University Press, New York, 1953.
Tansman, Alexandre, *Igor Stravinsky,* tr. by Therese and Charles Bleefield, Putnam, New York, 1949.
Thayer, Alexander W., *The Life of Ludwig van Beethoven,* rev. ed. by Elliott Forbes, 2 vols., Princeton University Press, Princeton, 1964.
Toye, Francis, *Verdi,* Knopf, New York, 1946.
Turner, W. J., *Beethoven,* Dent, London, 1945.
Weinstock, Herbert, *Chopin,* Knopf, New York, 1949.
———, *Handel,* 2nd ed., Knopf, New York, 1959.
———, *Tchaikovsky,* Knopf, New York, 1946.

Special Fields

Apel, Willi, *Gregorian Chant,* Indiana University Press, Bloomington, 1958.
Austin, William W., *Music in the 20th Century from Debussy through Stravinski,* Norton, New York, 1966.
Bagar, Robert, and Louis Biancolli, *The Concert Companion,* Whittlesey House, New York, 1947.
Chase, Gilbert, *America's Music,* McGraw-Hill, New York, 1955.
Copland, Aaron, *Our New Music,* Whittlesey House, New York, 1948.
Einstein, Alfred, *The Italian Madrigal,* tr. by Alexander H. Krappe and others, 3 vols., Princeton University Press, Princeton, 1949.
Ewen, David, *The Complete Book of 20th Century Music,* Prentice-Hall, New York, 1952.

Fellowes, Edmund H., *The English Madrigal Composers,* 2nd rev. ed., Oxford University Press, New York, 1949.

Geiringer, Karl, *Musical Instruments,* tr. by Bernard Miall, Oxford University Press, New York, 1946.

Graf, Max, *Composer and Critic,* Norton, New York, 1946.

Greene, Theodore Meyer, *The Arts and the Art of Criticism,* rev. ed., Princeton University Press, Princeton, 1948.

Grout, Donald J., *A Short History of Opera,* 2 vols., Columbia University Press, New York, 1947.

Hansen, Peter, *An Introduction to Twentieth-Century Music,* 2nd ed., Allyn and Bacon, New York, 1967.

Hayden, Glen, *Introduction to Musicology,* Prentice-Hall, New York, 1947.

Hodeir, André, *Jazz: Its Evolution and Essence,* Grove Press, New York, 1956.

Howard, John Tasker, *Our American Music,* 3rd rev. ed., Crowell, New York, 1948.

Landon, H. C. Robbins, *The Symphonies of Haydn,* Macmillan, New York, 1956.

Lang, Paul Henry, ed., *One Hundred Years of Music in America,* Schirmer, New York, 1961.

Newman, William S., *The Sonata in the Baroque Era,* rev. ed., University of North Carolina Press, Chapel Hill, 1966.

———, *The Sonata in the Classical Era,* University of North Carolina Press, Chapel Hill, 1963.

Reis, Clare R., *Composers in America,* 4th ed., Macmillan, New York, 1947.

Sachs, Curt, *The Commonwealth of Art,* Norton, New York, 1946.

Slonimsky, Nicholas, *Music in Our Time,* 3rd rev. ed., Colman, New York, 1949.

Stearns, Marshall, *The Story of Jazz,* Oxford University Press, New York, 1956.

Ulrich, Homer, *Chamber Music,* 2nd ed., Columbia University Press, New York, 1966.

———, *Symphonic Music,* Columbia University Press, New York, 1952.

Veinus, Abraham, *The Concerto,* Cassel, London, 1948.

Theory

Bartholomew, Wilmer T., *Acoustics of Music,* Prentice-Hall, New York, 1946.

Dorian, Frederick, *The Musical Workshop,* Harper, New York, 1947.

Hindemith, Paul, *The Craft of Musical Composition,* 2 vols., Vol. I tr. by Arthur Mendel, Vol. II tr. by Otto Ortmann, Associated Music Publishers, New York, 1941–42.

———, *A Composer's World,* Harvard University Press, Cambridge, 1952.

Kennan, Kent W., *The Technique of Orchestration,* Prentice-Hall, New York, 1952.

Leichtentritt, Hugo, *Musical Form,* Harvard University Press, Cambridge, 1951.

McHose, Allen I., *The Contrapuntal Harmonic Technique of the 18th Century,* Crofts, New York, 1947.

Morris, R. O., *Contrapuntal Technique in the Sixteenth Century,* Oxford University Press, New York, 1922 (1944).
———, *The Structure of Music,* Oxford University Press, New York, 1947.
Persichetti, Vincent, *Twentieth-Century Harmony,* Norton, New York, 1961.
Piston, Walter, *Counterpoint,* Norton, New York, 1947.
———, *Harmony,* rev. ed., Norton, New York, 1948.
———, *Orchestration,* Norton, New York, 1955.
Rudolf, Max, *The Grammar of Conducting,* Schirmer, New York, 1950.
Scherchen, Hermann, *Handbook of Conducting,* tr. by M. D. Calvocoressi, Oxford University Press, New York, 1949.
Sessions, Roger, *Harmonic Practice,* Harcourt, Brace & World, New York, 1951.
Toch, Ernst, *The Shaping Forces in Music,* Criterion, New York, 1948.
Tovey, Donald F., *Essays in Musical Analysis,* 6 vols., reprint, Oxford University Press, New York, 1946–48.

INDEX

A 9
B 0
C 1
D 2
E 3
F 4
G 5
H 6
I 7
J 8

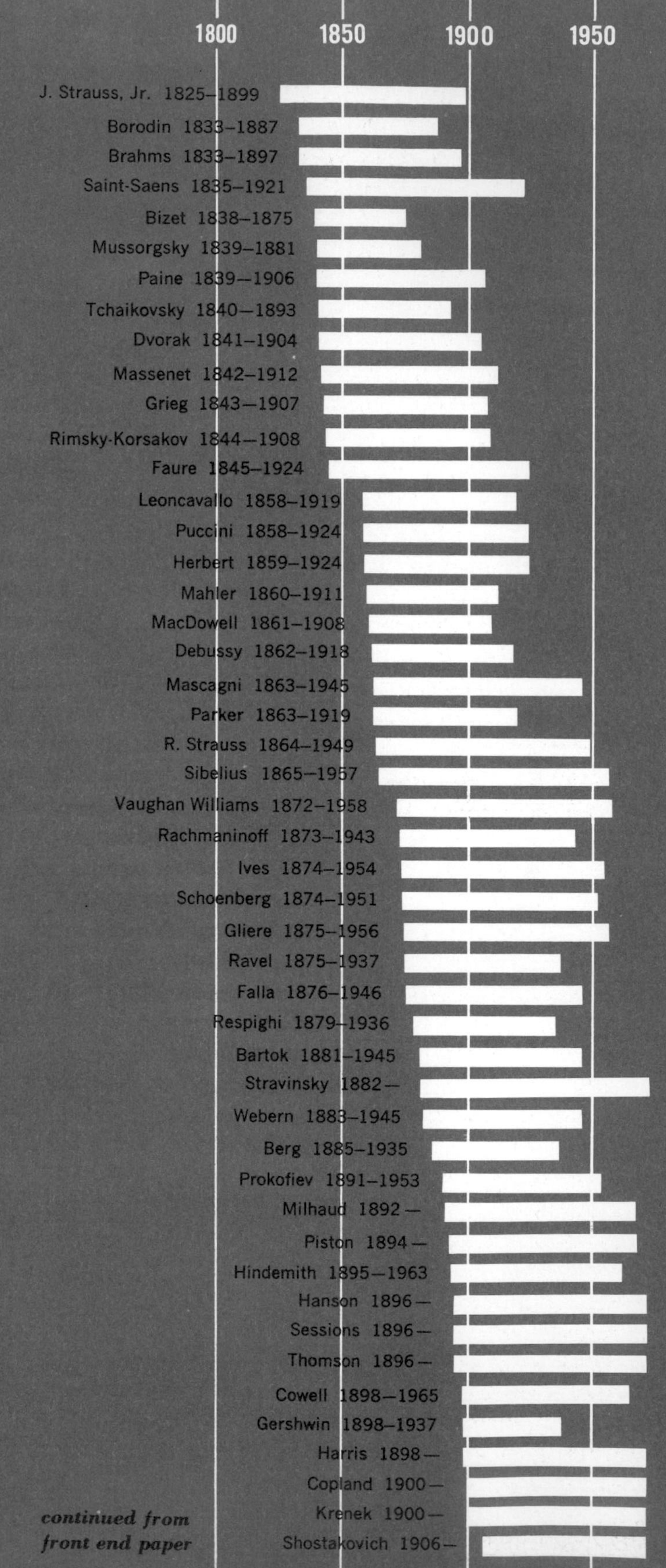

continued from front end paper